SINGER

Sewing Book

SINGER

Sewing Book

MARY BROOKS PICKEN

Published by

SINGER SEWING MACHINE COMPANY

FIRST EDITION, MAY, 1949, THROUGH MARCH, 1951, 428,000 COPIES
SECOND EDITION, SEPTEMBER, 1953, 100,000 COPIES
THIRD EDITION, JUNE, 1954, 50,000 COPIES
TOTAL PRINTINGS, JUNE, 1954, 578,000 COPIES

BRITISH EDITION
FIRST PRINTING MAY, 1954, 40,000 COPIES
EDITIONS IN DANISH, DUTCH, SWEDISH, NORWEGIAN,
FRENCH, ITALIAN, GERMAN, TURKISH, FINNISH, SPANISH,
PORTUGUESE AND OTHER LANGUAGES IN PREPARATION.

PRINTED IN THE UNITED STATES OF AMERICA

NA-3000 (REV. 754)

Dedication

This book is dedicated to women and girls—

and especially to teachers of sewing everywhere—

who enjoy the feel of fabric, the beauty of textures,

the precision of stitches, the smoothness of seams,

and who delight always in appropriate fabrics

carefully cut and made up for a happy purpose.

Introduction

The purpose of this book is to put into your hands in one complete package the means of attaining one of the happiest experiences of a woman's everyday life. Sewing, when it is done with skill and confidence, can be exactly that, for it can mean the satisfaction of family needs and wishes through the work of your own hands.

A person with a hobby is a person whose life is interesting. Psychologists say that the development of an absorbing hobby, particularly one involving the use of the hands, is one of the most important elements in leading a well-balanced and well-integrated life. When the mind and the hands are occupied with the creation of something useful and attractive, there is no room for discontent, boredom, petty worries, fears and jealousies, and there are few pleasures to equal the sense of accomplishment of holding in one's hands the skillfully finished product of one's own efforts.

Perhaps the most rewarding of all hobbies for a woman is sewing. Not only is it an outlet for her creative impulse, a way to make use of her sense of design, her deft fingers, her enjoyment of color and texture, but the things she makes can beautify her home and provide for herself and her family the kind of clothing most becoming to them at a great saving over the cost of buying such items. Best of all, sewing is a hobby that any woman with a little patience and a little practice can pursue with expertness and enjoyment.

Successful sewing does not come from wishful thinking, but from actual practical work, sitting at your sewing machine with pieces of fabric and learning to put them together beautifully. This book is designed to show you how to do so with ease and interest, to be your companion in all of your sewing endeavors, to stand at your side with suggestions, inspirations, and demonstrations that will make sewing the delight it should be. Good tools, good craftsmanship, and good ideas are all that any expert can bring to his work. It is our hope that the information in these pages will provide you with the fundamentals of all three of these requirements for your sewing.

Make this book work for you. It will bring you hours and hours of satisfaction and dollars and dollars in money saved; and it can, with your help and your sewing machine, make your family and your home the best-dressed in your neighborhood.

Acknowledgments

In our earnest desire to produce a practical, helpful sewing instruction book, we knew of no one so well equipped to prepare it as Mary Brooks Picken. Mrs. Picken, the foremost authority on home sewing, is the author of 92 books on sewing and crafts which have guided hundreds of thousands of women to successful accomplishment. For many years she was the Director of Instruction of a famous correspondence school of sewing, and since then, through her books, her magazine articles, her radio and television talks, and in her work with schools and colleges throughout the U. S. A., she has become the friend and teacher of countless thousands of women who sew. As one of the founders and leading spirits in the internationally known Fashion Group, and a trustee of the Fashion Institute of Technology, New York, she is particularly able to bring to the craft of sewing a real fashion inspiration. In this book, the latest of many excellent texts she has prepared for us, she has worked in full cooperation with our Educational Department on methods and instructions so that they are completely coordinated with the practices taught in Singer Sewing Centers.

Thanks are due to Claire F. Valentine for the format of this book and the clear and comprehensive presentation of illustrative material; to Patricia Lingane Rowe for her fashion drawings; also to Ruth Clark, Eula Hicks, Jessie Hutton and Anna Miller, of the Singer Educational Staff for aid in classroom teaching practices.

For the photographs of beautiful interiors in this book, showing a variety of decorative uses of fabric furnishings for the home, we are indebted to the following: *The American Home*, Armstrong Cork Company, *Better Homes & Gardens*, Bigelow-Sanford Carpet Company, Inc., Burlington Mills, Cavalier Corporation, Crawford Furniture Company, *Everywoman's Magazine*, *Living for Young Homemakers*, *McCall's Magazine*, F. Schumacher & Company, *Today's Woman Magazine*, and Tomlinson of High Point, N. C.

SINGER SEWING MACHINE COMPANY

Contents

Color Plates

How to Use This Book

You may have some sewing skill when this book comes into your hands. Even so, you may not be satisfied that you make pockets or bound buttonholes with enjoyable pride, that you miter a corner, cord a seam, or gather a flounce as perfectly as you would like. Whichever skill you may lack, take this book to your machine, get out some muslin or percale scraps of fabric, and practice. See how much you can improve your work by following the pictures and the text carefully for, say, a bound buttonhole, a fitted facing, a gathered edge. Concentrate for ten minutes —for twenty minutes. As you practice with this book to guide you, you will realize that there is no reason ever to apologize for your sewing or be disappointed with your results.

Just in the matter of stitching straight, a few minutes of practicing correctly can help. Use a ruled tablet sheet and an unthreaded needle on the machine, stitch precisely on the ruled lines, pivoting and turning a true corner, spacing rows of stitching evenly. Practice with any attachment you have not mastered. See how easy it is to achieve the fashion details you want with these time-saving and ingenious sewing aids. Decide what you wish to make. Choose your pattern or make your plan and find in this book the easy-to-follow directions for doing the work.

Read carefully the opening sections and the introductory material of each subject such as color, home furnishings, sewing for children, gifts, etc. before beginning any actual sewing. In these chapters you will find the general principles, standards for selection, do's and don't's, and the orientation to give you background and spare you disappointment. When you have these in mind, you are ready for the details of construction and sewing.

The essentials of good craftsmanship, the "know-how," for carrying out your ideas are assembled in text and in hundreds of diagrams for your guidance, so that you should be able to make almost anything your imagination can conceive of in the realm of fabric and thread. Even little pitfalls and precautions along the way are taken into consideration to save you time and annoyance. As for your own ideas, the book provides numerous tests by which you can gauge their rightness, becomingness, and suitability. For example, the color fans are designed to help you make the right selection of color for clothing, the color chart on home furnishings give you a wide range of choices in color schemes for rooms, the designer and decorator sketches offer a variety of styles to stimulate your imagination, and the color plates of interiors show the inventiveness and good taste of professional decorators.

Read the text, study the pictures. Then as you sew, keep this book near so you can refer to it readily. Use the Contents pages or the index to find quickly what you want and let the book help you to happier, more successful sewing.

Your Sewing Machine

WHETHER IT IS RENTED, INHERITED OR BOUGHT, EVERY woman should have a sewing machine conveniently near, whether she makes clothes or not. There are always rips and tears that need mending, and sewing-machine mending is right for seams and for sturdy items that get hard wear. Oftentimes, restitching insecure or broken seams can prolong the life of a garment.

The Portable Sewing Machine is ideal for scant quarters. It can rest on the floor of a closet in its own little case and never be in the way, yet be handy for the occasional needs or for a big job of drapery or slip-cover making, or for making dresses, coats, suits, all types of clothes, table linens—whatever one wants.

The cabinet machine of your choice is ideal as an extra table in hall, dining room, bedroom, living or sewing room; the large portable, as an accessory to a built-in sewing compartment or for use in any room in the house.

If a person is in a temporary location, a machine can be rented from the Singer Sewing Machine Company to use for a week, a month or longer. The machine, like the stove and table, is something to use every day and should be ready and always accessible for two minutes or two hours of stitching.

Never place a machine where it is hard to reach. Let it be a part of your household equipment as much as your electric iron or mixer. Use it to mend clothing before it goes into the wash, or when it comes from under the iron. For the brief stitching time while the washer washes or the cake bakes, see page 164 for instructions for bundle sewing, which will help you to make use of short periods of time to advantage in planning, cutting, machine work, handwork, and the required pressing.

Occasionally, a daughter or niece will inherit a machine. When it comes into her hands, such a machine should be checked carefully at the Singer Sewing Center. If she does not have the small instruction book right for her type of machine, she should get one at the Singer Shop and study it page by page so that she is completely familiar with all working parts of the machine. A sewing machine, like an automobile, must be oiled and the motor lubricated regularly and should be kept in the best possible running order so that it is always inviting one to use it.

To buy a machine and have it as your very own, to select for your space and your needs the machine that is right for you, is, of course, the most satisfactory way of all.

When you have a machine, whether you buy it, inherit, or rent it, do take the time to know how to thread the machine properly, to oil it, to protect it when not in use, to stitch straight, to use the essential attachments—all to save your time. Good tools are a pleasure to use. A sharp scissors that cuts, a vacuum cleaner that really cleans, an iron that glides with ease over your fabrics—such tools speed the work, help it to be interesting, improve results. A Singer Machine, in the hands of one who has taken the time to learn to use it efficiently, makes sewing pleasurable, profitable and rewarding, as it must always be if the sewing is to be successful.

Your Sewing Skills Are Like Money in the Bank

Many women want to help to earn. Experts tell us the first way to earn is to save. One dollar spent for fabric can, with intelligent planning and skillful workmanship, produce three dollars' worth of finished product. Aside from the savings made, a woman who sews well always has a trade she can use in an emergency, she can always pay her own way with sewing skills. Isn't such economy, such insurance, well worth any effort you expend in learning to sew beautifully? The more you learn about sewing, and apply what you learn, the more skillful you become.

As you sew and know the thrill of using a beautiful machine, with its perfect stitches, to make seams and gathers and bindings on material of your own choosing, you may wonder about its history and who first made such stitching possible.

History tells us that as early as the seventeenth century, men tried to devise a machine that would sew. Early in the eighteenth century, a French tailor named Barthelemy Thimmonier invented a crude wooden sewing machine but it was destroyed by a mob of angry tailors who saw in it a threat to their livelihood. Others tried and failed. Then in 1846, Elias Howe, Jr., from Cambridge, Mass., made and patented what is popularly regarded as the first sewing machine. But it wasn't truly practical. It could sew only six or seven inches at one time. Not until four years later did another American, Isaac Merritt Singer, develop the first really practical machine—one that would sew continuously or until the thread ran out, with a stitch that was the same on both the right and wrong side of the material.

Today the company which he founded is world-wide and manufactures over two thousand varieties of sewing machines. These do every kind of work from binding books to seaming hose. They make men's shirts and upholstery for automobiles. They make the shades for your windows and the carpets on your floor, hats and shoes, parachutes and pillow-cases. If there were no sewing machine, it would take a hundred times the effort and many, many times the cost to produce even a limited amount of apparel such as we enjoy today.

Mentally. Prepare yourself mentally for sewing. Think about what you are going to do. Choose a fabric and pattern right for your purpose. Practice sewing on scraps of the material until your stitch is just right and you have confidence in your ability to stitch straight. Approach the job with enthusiasm. You must want to make something lovely, to have the fun of putting pieces of fabric together, to make a garment, to handle the fabric with appreciation, to watch the beauty of the article grow as a result of your planning and effort. Never approach sewing with a sigh or lackadaisically. Good results are difficult when indifference predominates. Never try to sew with the sink full of dishes or bed unmade. When there are urgent housekeeping chores, do these first so that your mind is free to enjoy your sewing.

Physically. When you sew, make yourself as attractive as possible. Go through a beauty ritual of orderliness. Have on a clean dress. Be sure your hands are clean, finger nails smooth—a nail file and pumice will help. Always avoid hangnails. Keep a little bag full of French chalk near your sewing machine where you can pick it up and dust your fingers at intervals. This not only absorbs the moisture on your fingers, but helps to keep your work clean. Have your hair in order, powder and lipstick put on with care. Looking attractive is a very important part of sewing, because if you are making something for yourself, you will try it on at intervals in front of your mirror, and you can hope for better results when you look your best.

Again, sewing must be approached with the idea that you are going to enjoy it, and if you are constantly fearful that a visitor will drop in or your husband come home and you will not look neatly put together, you will not enjoy your sewing as you should. Therefore, "spruce up" at the beginning so that you are free to enjoy every part of any sewing you do.

Materially. Assemble all the essentials you are going to need before you begin. Have close at hand the press board and iron, a small bowl of water, preferably with a clean sponge in it, a cheesecloth and heavy muslin, press cloth, scissors, pins, chalk, small ruler, tape measure—every-thing you need to sew with—so that you will not have to jump up to get this or that, because such distractions affect your efficiency. If you are to get good results from sewing, remember that you must do it pridefully and skillfully. An uncoordinated sewing experience is not conducive either to enjoyment or best results.

Plan for Sewing Time. Make an appointment with yourself to sew, just as you would with your hairdresser, or with a neighbor to go shopping. If your intimates enjoy sewing, invite them to come and sew with you from 2 to 5 on a Wednesday, or perhaps for an evening each week. Do not spend your time planning refreshments, but insist that each bring sewing to do.

On the days when you are sewing, make the dessert in the morning; plan a quick-to-get dinner so that your afternoon can be given to the full enjoyment of sewing.

Plan what you are to make ahead of time. Keep a notebook and jot down in it what findings or trimmings you need for each thing. Work out a recipe for each garment; for example, 3½ yds. of crepe, 1 spool matching thread, seam binding, 1 matching zipper, Pattern #000. Pin a scrap of the fabric to a page in your notebook. When you buy a piece of material, take a snip of fabric to use in matching the color of threads, bindings and zipper.

Determine the construction your pattern calls for—plain seam, darts, hem, gathering, zipper closing. Look for each in the index of this book and mark each reference page. Study each detail and make a practice sample, if necessary.

If you must use the dining table or must clear the floor for a cutting surface, plan to cut several garments at one time. Roll all the pieces of each garment together, or place them in a box where you can get at them readily. Do your preliminary stitching on a garment at one time, pressing as you go. Save the basting or handwork to do when a friend drops in and you want to visit, or when you want to listen to a favorite radio or TV program.

Much happiness and benefit can be had from sewing if you plan what you will do; if you buy carefully; if you choose your patterns for smartness and appropriateness and if you cut and sew in a planned, well-organized fashion.

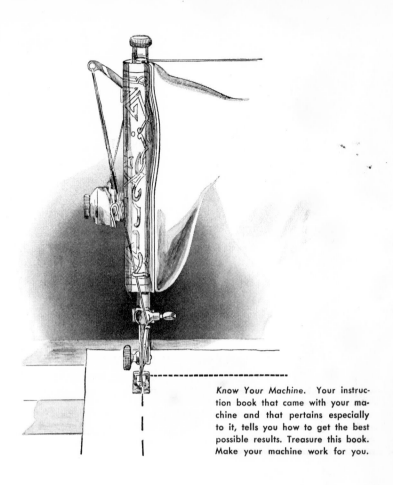

Your Attitude Toward Your Machine

THE OWNER OF AN AUTOMOBILE REALIZES THAT THIS automobile is a sensitive instrument, that he or she must take care of it—have it serviced at intervals, oil it regularly, and keep it clean. Your sewing machine needs the same care. Always cover the head of your machine when it is not in use. Never allow it to be too near an open window or a warm radiator. Heat will dry the oil in the machine, and dust may clog it, in time doing it harm. If the machine is too cold, the lubricant in the motor cup may congeal and not work as freely as it should. If you use your machine in the laundry, cover it well so steam will not affect the mechanism. Treat your machine with care. Respect it, value it, make it work for you. It can serve you for many years and do endless hours of work if you will show it even a small amount of real consideration.

Care of Your Machine. Treat your attachments (Fashion Aids) with consideration for their value and usefulness. Put them away when you are through with them. Never allow them to rattle around in a drawer or to lie loose on the machine. Have a box to keep them in and put them away where you can reach them in an instant. It takes so little time to change attachments if you have learned how, and the more attachments you use successfully, the more you can accomplish, because there is an attachment for almost every detail in sewing. Always lift the needle before you remove the sewing or an attachment. Pull the two threads back and cut them off on the thread cutter (located on the presser bar just above the presser foot) so that you never pull your needle out of line and thus blunt it. Always be sure your needle is tight in its socket. Sometimes sewing spasmodically or jerkily may cause vibrations that loosen the needle, causing it to drop from position, so check it from time to time. Take these little precautions. In other words, respect your machine,

The *Signature Stitch* is a favorite with all. Used to embroider names on handkerchiefs, scarves, pockets, blouses, collars, napkins and many other items that can be personally marked or decorated. Can also be used for scroll work and many types of motifs.

The *Etching Stitch* is ideal to use in combination with other Fashion Stitches, especially for delicate parts of a design. Also used for outlining and filling. Ideal for linens, imitation linens, all closely-woven fabrics.

The *Ornamental Stitch* looks like part of the woven fabric, especially when used as stripes, plaids and checks. Pastels on white or pastel, or black, gray or navy on white make ideal trimming for dresses or blouses.

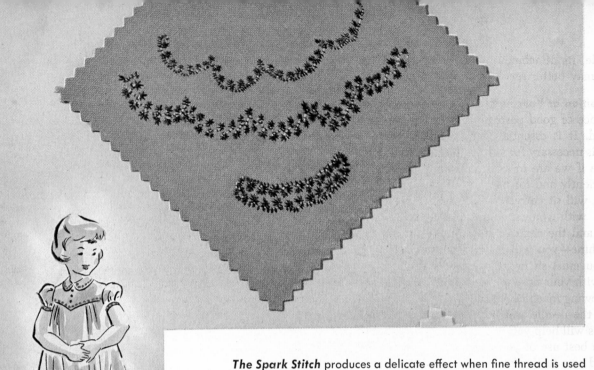

The Spark Stitch produces a delicate effect when fine thread is used in bobbin and needle—for example, mercerized sewing or silk. A circular motion of the embroidery hoop is employed. Follow a stamped or traced design and use for borders, motifs, filling stitches, or on bands between lace or embroidery. Use to connect beads or sequins in a design. Ideal on ribbons.

The Cordonnet Stitch, done with a special thread on the bobbin and a fine matching thread in the needle, gives a lacy effect, as shown below. Especially desirable for sheer organdies, closely woven gauze and net. Worked in a hoop, of course. Practice is desirable to acquire skill in crossing lines, filling centers, acquiring unbroken stems.

its needle, its attachments, its sewing speeds, so that all may better serve you.

Your Position at Your Machine. We all know the importance of good posture. It is talked of on every hand. It is essential from a health point of view; it is necessary for good appearance; and it is desirable if we are to sit at a sewing machine to sew efficiently and for hours without fatigue.

If you will sit correctly—that is, as far back as possible, with your shoulders back and tummy held in, and the chair or stool pulled up close to the machine—you will invariably have better results. You must sit in the middle of the chair or bench, with your nose in line with the needle bar on the sewing machine. In this way, your eyes can best see the needle and both sides of the presser foot. This will help you to stitch straight. You also have the best use of your hands, with one to the right and one to the left of the needle and both easy and free to serve you. If you have been sewing for a long time and have incorrect habits of sitting at your machine, using your hands, or guiding your work, correct them at once, not only for better results, but for less fatigue and a more pleasing appearance.

Master Your Machine. Take time to master your machine, to stitch straight, to pivot on the needle, turn corners and curves with skill. Learn to use the presser foot in gauging your stitching, the Narrow Hemmer, then the Adjustable Hemmer, the Gathering Foot, Cording Foot, then the Ruffler, and so on until you are expert, not only in operating your machine, but in using all the Fashion Aids, which you should think of as *skilled fingers* always at hand to help you speed your sewing work and make it look "professional."

A woman who breaks the thread short, thus unthreading her needle at the end of the stitching line, or who dreads winding a bobbin or changing from the presser foot to a Fashion Aid, or who dreads changing one Aid for another as her work requires, has not taken the time necessary really to master her machine. Don't allow such an attitude to handicap you. Take time to consult your book of instruction or, if necessary, go to your Singer Shop and have a lesson so that you can handle your machine with skill, speed and pride.

Learning to Stitch Straight. There is no reason for anyone's not making a beautiful seam, because it takes so little time to learn to stitch straight and to "power" evenly, whether by knee or foot pressure or pedal. Your pressure should be even so that

your machine starts and stops smoothly and never abruptly or by spurts. The following suggestions, practiced conscientiously, can help you master the machine.

Practice on Paper. With machine unthreaded begin with ruled tablet paper. Practice going back and forth on the lines. Then needle-stitch back and forth, keeping the edge of the wide side of the presser foot on the line; then practice using the narrow side of the presser foot as a guide. Repeat this until your eye can gauge a line and have the presser foot edge follow perfectly. A little practice works wonders in helping automatically to make a true stitching line. It is important to sew evenly, whether with a treadle or an electric machine.

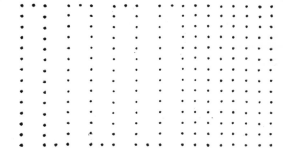

Learning to Pivot on the Needle. When you have your eye trained for distance with the wide and the narrow sides of the presser foot and for stitching directly on the line, you are ready to pivot on the needle. Do this by stitching exactly to the turn or corner, as our dotted lines show; then on the upward stroke of the needle, but before needle leaves paper or fabric, stop the machine, lift the presser foot, and turn the paper or fabric so that you get a true corner in your stitching. Put the presser foot down and stitch to the next corner; then lift and turn, lower presser foot again and stitch. If you will do this a dozen times, you will see how easy it is to lift the presser foot, pivot your work around the needle, bringing it to the point

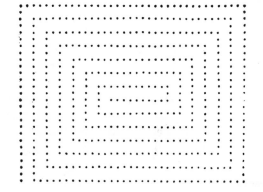

where you want to start stitching again, drop the presser foot and continue sewing. The instructions in this book frequently mention pivoting, and we want you to practice this so that you can pivot as easily as you follow a straight line.

Machine-stitching true in line and design can ornament and support fabric beautifully, so master your machine, have it do your bidding, and the beauty of your stitching will encourage your very best efforts.

Practice on Fabric. When you have finished your paper practice, take a piece of fabric—an old sheet or pillow case that is too thin for use makes excellent practice pieces. Learn to stitch on a lengthwise and crosswise thread and see how easy that is to do after you have mastered stitching on tablet lines. Draw circles with a large coin, tea cup or plate and stitch around and around in circles. See how beautifully your machine will perform with accurate guidance from you. If you are patient and

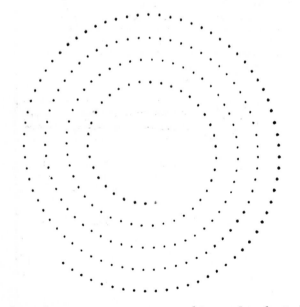

learn how to operate your machine and make it work for you, you will be continually delighted with the cooperation it will give in return.

Making Your Machine Ready. When you buy your machine, you will be shown how to thread it. You will learn to adapt your machine to all weights and textures of fabrics through the simple tension pressure and length-of-stitch adjustments. Practice threading the machine a dozen times until you are really quite skillful at it so that you will do it rapidly and automatically whenever you need to. If you dread any detail, such as threading the machine or the needle, removing the presser foot and

attaching a Fashion Aid, then do this again and again until you realize it is neither difficult nor tedious. Then you will overcome all dread or impatience.

When using another person's machine, determine whether the needle is threaded from the right or from the left, or see the instruction book. Sewing machine needles have a rounded and a grooved side. The eye is always threaded from the grooved side. Run your finger along the edge to locate it. Wrong threading will cause imperfect stitching, looping and breakage of thread. This can be prevented if you know the right way of threading in advance.

Tension. On all Singer machines, the tension is easily regulated. A well-adjusted Singer will always make a beautiful stitch. Study the Thread, Needle and Stitch Chart to see what changes are recommended in using different weights and sizes of thread and kinds of fabric. For example, when sewing with silk and synthetic thread, lighter or easier tensions should be used than for cotton thread. When you learn to use your attachments and Fashion Aids you will also learn any change that is necessary in the tension.

Adjusting the Stitch. Learn to adjust the stitch to be just the right length for the texture and thickness of the fabric you are stitching. For example, if you are stitching very fine organdie, you will want a short stitch, say approximately 20 stitches to the inch, and will use a fine thread because you want the daintiest possible work. If you are using percale, you will want a medium-short stitch, 12 to 16 to the inch. If you are sewing drill or heavy cretonne or upholstery or blanket fabric, you will want a long stitch, only 6 to 8 to an inch. First practice on a scrap of the fabric and adjust the length of the stitch so that the stitching will be uniform. A sewing-machine stitch is a beautiful thing—even, regular and exact—and you will want it so throughout your sewing. Therefore, set your machine right for the stitch length you want before you begin. A chart is given opposite that will help you to know the size of thread to use and the number of stitches per inch; and soon you will know, without even referring to the chart, the length of the stitch you want. You will learn to judge from appearance what is best for each type of fabric you are using.

When you become complete master of your machine, you should be able to make it do anything in sewing you want.

SUCCESSFUL SEWING MEANS HAVING GOOD EQUIPMENT conveniently arranged. Expert workmanship requires the best tools you can afford, kept in A-1 condition. Here is a practical list of what you need: First, your machine. That is so important that it is treated in a whole section of its own. See page 4. Your dress form is also a separate section. See page 9.

Your sewing will be more successful and more enjoyable if you learn to change the size of the needle, to use the correct thread, and to adjust the stitch gauge to the type of fabric and purpose.

THREAD, NEEDLE AND STITCH CHART
showing the relationship of
Types of Fabrics · Thread and Needle Sizes · Number of Machine Stitches to the Inch

Test the stitch on the fabric you are using. Stitches just right in length for your fabric are always admirable. Machine stitching should not be so fine as to conceal the shape of the stitch, or so long as to look like machine basting. If you are using a sheer fabric, for example, test a fine needle, say #9, with nylon thread and slightly easier tensions. Adjust stitch gauge to make 18 to 20 stitches to the inch. See for yourself the beauty of this. Remember, the thicker the fabric, the longer the stitch should be on your stitch gauge, as the fabric thickness quite naturally shortens the appearance of the stitch itself.

The finest cotton threads, size 100, are available only in black and white. Mercerized cotton, approximately size 50, comes in a wide range of colors, and is used for all finer stitching on colored cottons. Heavy-duty cotton, approximately size 30–40, is available in a variety of colors and can be used for heavier stitching on colored fabrics. Silk thread, also available in a wide color range, is used on silks and wools. Nylon thread is fine, strong, and may be used on practically all types of fabric where fine stitching is desired. Use only a moderately warm iron in pressing seams stitched with nylon thread.

For sewing-machine basting, make machine stitch as long as possible.

Types of Fabrics	Thread Sizes	Machine Needle Sizes	Machine Stitches per Inch		Hand Needle
			Inside Seams	Top Stitching	
Filmy Materials Comparable to Net—Marquisette—Chiffon — Silk — Chiffon Velvet — Ninon—Nylon Sheers	100 Cotton A Silk Nylon	9	15–20	20–30	10
Sheer Materials Comparable to Lawn—Organdie—Dimity—Batiste—Pure Silks—Paper Taffeta Silk—Synthetic Tricots—Synthetic Sheers	80 to 100 Cotton A Silk Nylon	11	12–15	15–20	9
Lightweight Materials Comparable to Gingham—Chambray Sheers—Wool Crepe—Taffeta—Synthetic Velvets—Satin—Synthetic or Wool Jersey	50 Mercerized 50 to 80 Cotton A Silk Nylon	14	12	16	8
Medium Lightweight Materials Comparable to Poplin—Pique—Percale — Cretonne — Chintz — Faille — Bengaline—Wool Flannel—Crepe—Lightweight Suitings	50 Mercerized 50 to 70 Cotton A Silk Nylon	14	12	16	7–8
Medium Heavy Materials Comparable to Cotton Velveteen—Corduroy—Gabardine—Rep—Coatings and Heavy Suitings	Heavy-Duty Mercerized 30 to 50 Cotton A Silk	16	10	12	6
Heavy Materials Comparable to Sailcloth—Denim—Ticking—Overcoatings	Heavy-Duty Mercerized 30–40 Cotton	16–18	8	10	4–5
Very Heavy Materials Comparable to Canvas—Duck	40 to 60 Linen 20–24 Cotton D Silk	18–19	6	8	3
Plastic Materials	Nylon or Mercerized Cotton	9–11	10	12	9–11

Pins. Use dressmakers' pins. They are thin and sharp and do not mar fabrics. Pins collected from the floor after sewing can be scalded with hot water and dried on paper to keep them clean.

Needles. Buy good hand-ground steel needles to be sure of perfect performance in sewing. Keep them in the package to prevent rust. Use an emery bag to polish them, if necessary. Hand sewing needles come in several kinds and sizes. Sharps and Betweens are used for general sewing in sizes #3 to #10. You can buy a packet all of one size or a mixed packet of #3 to #9 or #5 to #10. A #7 needle is preferred by many for general sewing, while a #8 is favored for whipping or fine finishing.

Sharps have a slightly larger eye than a Between, which is a very slim needle with the eye part as slender as the needle itself. Many women like a fine crewel (embroidery) needle for hand sewing, because it is easy to thread.

There are special needles for basting, for millinery, for quilting, darning, embroidery and beading. Find a size and kind of needle that you like best and buy that kind by the paper.

Use Singer machine needles in your Singer machine, for best results. Several sizes are available. The chart on the preceding page shows what size is best for each type of fabric.

Threads. Use a reliable brand of thread and choose weight and color to suit your fabric. See chart. In matching color, remember that thread when worked into fabric tends to look slightly lighter than on the spool, so buy a little darker shade than that of your fabric. Keep on hand a miscellaneous supply of colored threads most frequently used. Odds and ends of thread are excellent for machine basting.

Cutting Tools. Buy good steel scissors, treat them with care, reserve them for your machine and work basket. If you do much sewing, you'll need a pair of shears or bent trimmers 7″ or 8″ long, a pair of snipping scissors about 5″ long, a pair of embroidery scissors 3″ to 4″ long. Pinking shears are desirable for all who sew a great deal, especially for those who sew professionally.

Cutting Surface. Large flat cutting surface is essential. Use folding table or get a composition board 36″ to 40″ wide and 5′ or 6′ long so that it can be placed over a small table or on two chairs.

Thimble. Always use a thimble for hand sewing even though you have to force yourself to learn to use it. Fit it as carefully as you would a shoe or glove. It must be comfortable and should be light in weight.

Measuring Tools. You need a measuring tape, preferably one numbered on both sides, with number "1" starting from each end, a 6-inch ruler or a hem gauge for measuring short lengths and detail work, especially at the machine, and a yardstick. The Singer Skirt Marker makes it easy to mark your own skirt lengths. See page 95.

Marking Equipment. A sharp-pointed steel tracing wheel and carbon paper may be used on some fabrics for marking seam lines and notches; an awl or stiletto is convenient for punching eyelets; tailors' chalk is necessary for marking pattern perforations and fitting lines; and threads of a color different from the fabric are needed for basting and for marking tailors' tacks.

Pressing Supplies. Keep complete pressing equipment near at hand and set up to use as you sew. Press each seam before it joins another. A good lightweight iron with a dependable temperature control makes handling of fabrics simple for the less experienced as well as the expert. A cord control is a great convenience. Have a regular ironing board the correct height, a sleeve board, also a pressing mit or a tailors' cushion for shrinking fullness and pressing shaped parts of garments. A steam iron is a convenience, but if you haven't one, use clean, lintless press cloths. Keep a bowl of water at hand for dampening. A small paint brush or sponge is convenient for moistening seams. A press board of wire, or napped fabric that is specially treated, is necessary for pressing velvet and napped fabrics, as it keeps nap or pile from being flattened in pressing.

Visual Aids. A good full-length mirror for trying on and fitting is desirable and good lighting over your working surfaces is necessary. The electric light on your sewing machine is ideal for the stitching area. In addition, set up your machine to get good daylight or provide yourself good overhead light. Have good light when you sew; see what you are sewing and enjoy it the more.

Staple Findings. It saves time to have on hand a supply of the notions most commonly needed— snap fasteners, hooks and eyes, utility buttons, several weights of black and white thread, peach, navy, brown and gray, buttonhole twists, slide fasteners of lengths and colors most needed, seam bindings, tapes, edge trimmings, etc. Keep them sorted and at hand for immediate use. Labeled boxes or jars will keep all neat and in condition.

Other Supplies. A few hangers on which you can put garments as you assemble them will help keep fabric fresh for finishing touches. Beeswax is desirable for waxing thread for sewing buttons on tailored garments and for smoothing the iron's surface. French chalk, dusted on the hands, absorbs perspiration and helps keep fabric dainty as you work. An orange stick is helpful in pointing out corners after stitching, in straightening seams and in creasing tucks. Keep one on your machine. You will find many uses for it. Smoothed-out pieces of good-quality tissue paper or lightweight wrapping paper are needed for stitching lace, net, jersey and all sheers. A Singer Ripper is handy for cutting small things, such as appliqué motifs, and for ripping seams. Keep embroidery hoops for decorative handwork and for machine darning. Besides these things, have your instruction and pattern books convenient to your sewing equipment and your scrapbooks or clipping files of ideas where you can reach them whenever you need an idea or inspiration as you work.

When you are planning to make a dress, coat or suit, or to sew for your house or your children, go to your Sewing Center and see what they have there that will help you to do the work more quickly, help to make it look more professional, and give you better finish and fit than you could get without the modern aids that are there available to you. For example, fashion dictates the shape and size of shoulder pads. But some people always need some type of shoulder pad, even when fashion does not use them. The new muslin pleating tape for draperies, that you stitch on, not only saves time and gives very good results but also allows the drapery to be washed or cleaned flat—a great boon to drapery-making.

In your Sewing Centers, you can find trimmings of many kinds that help to give a pleasing result to your finished garments. See these and inquire about the Fashion Services that are available. Use them to make your work look more professional and to save time and money for you.

Your Dress Form

vvvvvvvvvvvvvvvvvvvvvvvvvvvvvvvvvvvvvvvvvvvvvvvvvvvvvvvvvvvvvvvvvvvvvvvvvvvvvvvvvvvvvvvvvvvvvv

A DRESS FORM IS A DEFINITE HELP IN SEWING FOR oneself. If your measurements require alterations in your pattern, then by all means have a form made for you so that you can adjust your pattern on your form and fit garments more readily.

A Duplicate of Your Own Figure in Plastic. Any Singer Sewing Center can tell you how a dress form, made of a thermoplastic material, is made to conform to the contours of your own body. Such a form insures a well-fitted garment, simplifies your sewing, eliminates waste and errors, saves your time, encourages individuality in design, and aids in alterations and restyling. It is especially desirable to have a dress form of the right size when sewing for someone who cannot readily be present for fittings.

Dressmaker's Dummy. There is, in addition to the thermoplastic dress form described above, a dress form sold in many department stores and some mail order houses. This usually comes in sizes 30 to 46 bust. If you must use such a form, buy one 2″ to 6″ smaller than your bust measurement, make a foundation garment of sturdy muslin or drill, fit this to yourself accurately as regards bust line, waistline, hip line, neck and shoulders. Pad the dress form with cotton batting or tissue paper to fill out this foundation. To do this correctly requires skill and time and is suggested only for those who for some reason cannot get a plastic form made to their individual proportions.

How to Use Your Dress Form. Make a bag cover for it so that it will keep completely clean when not in use. This is important especially when you use delicate or light-colored fabrics. A dress form can be stored in the corner of a hall closet, left out in a sewing room, or taken to the attic when other space is lacking. We prefer to arrange the sewing corner so that the dress form, like the iron and press board, can always be near at hand to save time and to satisfy the urge to sew even for short periods of time. See the provision made for this in "Room of Her Own," on opposite page.

Pin-Fitting the Pattern. Purchase a pattern that closely approximates your proportions. The bust measurement is the best guide for correct size. If you are under 5′ 4″ in height, half-size patterns are best for you. If you are slight of build, "Misses" sizes will suit your proportions. Pin-fitting the pattern on the Singer Form will enable you to adjust the pattern to your contour and proportions. It is at this point in creating a dress that those all-important allowances are made for the differences between your proportions and standard pattern measurements.

Pin in darts, tucks and pleats designed by the pattern. When shoulder pads or shapes are to be worn in the garment, they must be used in every step of fitting. Pin blouse front of pattern to form, starting at center. Make necessary adjustments in pattern for a correct fit.

Now pin the blouse back of the pattern to the form, starting at the center back. Make necessary adjustments in pattern. Consider seam allowances; join blouse front and back at shoulders and underarm. Allow ease across shoulders for freedom of arm movement. *Place the flat of the hand between the pattern and the form,* both front and back, to allow for freedom of movement across the bust and the back as well as for ease in the length of the blouse.

Pin front skirt sections together on seam lines, then pin skirt front to form over blouse front at waistline, starting at center front tape and working toward the side, keeping the balance line of the skirt true at the hip line. Make necessary adjustments in pattern. Proceed in the same way when fitting the skirt back pattern. Pin side seams together, allowing for full seam width and so that the side seams are positioned over the side guide tapes of the dress form.

When your pattern is adjusted to your proportions, baste in any tucks you have laid in the pattern or make tissue paper inserts where additional width or length is required, machine-basting these inserts in place so they will hold throughout the cutting of your garment. (See detailed instructions for pattern adjustments of sleeves, skirt lengths, and other measurements on pages 26 to 31.)

When your pattern is as nearly correct as you can make it, place it on your fabric and cut, following the layout charts of your pattern as regards fabric grain, seam allowances and essentials. Don't try to improve on your pattern. It almost invariably has been styled with complete regard for the right fashion silhouette and, if followed without too much interference, usually gives a satisfactory fashion effect.

Draping on a Dress Form. Many experts, especially those who demonstrate methods of draping, can take a length of cloth and drape on the form, working from the whole fabric, cutting, slashing, piecing, folding, but the less expert should use lightweight unbleached muslin, cut in waist and skirt lengths, and drape with this, experimenting until the effect desired is obtained. These draped pieces can then be used as a guide to cut from tissue, newspaper or muslin a master pattern for cutting the garment. Then notches for assembling, markings for correct seam widths and grain —all these essentials may be provided for. Many women buy muslin or use several threadbare sheets to practice draping, working to copy a fashion picture, and in this simple easy way, become quite expert in expressing their fashion ideas and in individualizing their own clothes. If you have confidence in your style, then perhaps you can drape the fabric of the garment to your satisfaction. Otherwise, do experiment with less expensive mediums until the effect desired is achieved. Even after you have draped in muslin, made a master pattern and cut your fabric, you may then want to drape this final garment, to see the finished effect.

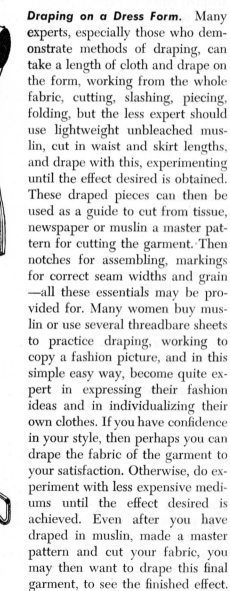

THIS ROOM (PAGE 12) WAS DESIGNED TO RENDER A maximum amount of service in a minimum amount of space. The underlying thought is that many homes have small rooms which today are serving merely as a spare guest room or as a semi-den. For these purposes the room is seldom used, even though the woman of the home today has no room which she "can call her own." The nature of these plans, however, is such that the basic elements are equally suitable in a larger room and thus can be adapted either to existing conditions or to a new home which has not gone beyond the building-plan stage.

The dimensions of the room provide a floor space of 8′ × 8′. The cabinet unit, running the full width of 8′ is 21″ deep. This depth is subject to modification as space permits. The floor is covered with linoleum, which was selected because in a sewing room where threads, lint, pins, etc., are apt to be dropped, it is easily cleaned, a point worth considering.

This room can serve the woman as her home management headquarters, as a guest room, as a room in which she can entertain a friend during an afternoon visit, and, of course, in its primary function as a sewing room.

HOME MANAGEMENT ROOM

The features in the room in connection with this phase of its usefulness consist of a built-in desk, provision for a portable typewriter, drawers in which a woman can file her correspondence, bills, etc. A convenient light is recessed over that part of the cabinet which serves as a desk and provides ideal lighting for her work at this point. Book shelves are provided for cookbooks and other references as well as her copies of the currently popular best sellers. A telephone is conveniently located for doing her daily marketing. By means of the radio she can keep in touch with the news, educational and entertainment programs. Above the desk is a built-in clock. This is a room in which she can retire and carry on the business of running a household with at least some of the efficiency aids which a man has in his office to facilitate running his business.

As a Sitting Room. If the woman has a visitor who may care to bring her knitting or her sewing, this is an ideal room in which the hostess and her guest can sit, exchange the news of the day and at the same time make progress with their hobbies. Again, the radio is available if there is an interest in a radio program, and the room is decorative and feminine enough to be pleasant for visiting as well as being properly equipped with table space for serving tea or other light refreshments.

As a Sewing Room. This room has been designed to contain in a minimum of space all of the requirements of an ideal sewing room. So often the woman is forced to lay out her pattern and cut her material either on a bed or dining-room table, to remove the knickknacks from the top of the sewing machine, and to have the dress form brought down from the attic, go elsewhere in the house to use a pressing board, etc., in order to have available the conveniences which aid so much in making sewing the real pleasure that it should be. Such difficulties she will not encounter in this room.

For laying out the pattern and cutting the material, a cutting table is provided. This table is completely concealed, when not in use, by the small doors over the desk. The cutting table is easily opened and has an ideal working surface of lightweight linoleum at a convenient height. The working surface is approximately 37″ above the floor. It is 28″ wide and at least 60″ long. These dimensions can be modified according to the space available.

Sewing. The sewing machine, with its stool, is conveniently located in front of the window where it receives the maximum of daylight (although its own illumination is furnished by the "Singerlight" and it can be used independently of other sources of light). Although many women do not realize it, pressing seams as the sewing progresses is of prime importance and for this purpose the pressing board, Singer iron and cord control are available. When not in use, they fit compactly into the closet. This board may be set up against the wall opposite the sewing machine within easy reach,

Study the convenience features of this room and see how you can make use of any or all of them in your own sewing nook. Even a minimum of space can serve you better if it is cleverly utilized.

The secret of the many features of this room is a built-in unit 21 inches deep, which entirely covers one wall, as shown above. Everything needed is provided within this partition.

Double mirrors, one mounted on the front of the center door, and one on the back of the closet door, are of great assistance in fitting a garment.

Open the center door, pull out the sliding table and you have a practical desk. A typewriter can be kept in the storage place below.

The inner doors fold back, letting down a cutting and work table for dressmaking. There's ample drawer space for sewing supplies.

This closet provides room for a dress form, iron, folding ironing board and many other articles, as may be seen below.

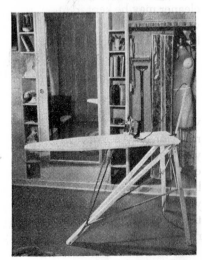

yet out of the way while the woman is sewing. The thermostatic control on the iron permits it to be left plugged-in and constantly heated to the desired temperature without danger.

The dress form is conveniently kept in the closet and may be easily taken out and replaced as needed. If it is necessary to leave the dress partially finished, there is space for it to be hung in the closet. For fitting, double mirrors are provided in the two doors so that, by standing between them when they are open, both the front and back may be clearly seen. To aid this, a light is placed over one of the mirrors.

The drawers in the left-hand end of the cabinet allow space for storing sewing materials. You will notice that these drawers are graduated in size— the top ones having divisions in which can be placed spools of different colors and types of threads as well as a variety of bobbins already threaded with the most used colors. These divisions will also be found handy for holding the small sewing-machine attachments. The other drawers are used in turn for notions, our Fashion Aids such as the pinking attachment, Hemstitcher, Singercraft Guide, Zigzagger, etc. Patterns and pattern books are conveniently stored in another of the drawers, and scraps of materials as well as partially finished smaller articles may be folded away.

When her sewing is *finished*, the woman will find it necessary to do some light cleaning in order to remove the snippings, lint and threads which have accumulated. For this purpose the Singer hand vacuum cleaner is kept in the closet. She will also find it convenient to have this cleaner upstairs when she is doing her daily household cleaning, since it is such an aid in dusting, cleaning around the edges of the rugs, etc. Her attachments for this cleaner may be kept in the closet if she desires, but we do not suggest that the closet be used as a combination broom and sewing closet.

WHEN SPACE IS LIMITED

WHETHER YOU ANTICIPATE WORKING OUT A SEWING room or only a closet or a corner in which to do your sewing or to keep your sewing materials and equipment, first consider the size of space that you have and what you need to put into it. Measure your space with a ruler or yardstick, then work these measurements out on paper, using ¼″ on the ruler to represent each foot of space available.

Plan first for your sewing machine, cutting surface and ironing board, and for a dress form if you use one. Drawers are best for patterns, fabrics, notions. If possible, provide some hanging space for a dress or coat that is in process of making, because once such a garment is basted together, time is saved if you put it on a hanger instead of folding it up and later have to repress it before beginning work on it again.

Many people take a corner in a bedroom and section it off with a screen. A bamboo-type of screen that rolls up, or a decorative screen covered with fabric or plastic, works out very well. The framework for such a screen can be made by one quite inexperienced in carpenter work. The back of the screen can have narrow shelves with spool spindles attached to hold spools. Pockets for patterns can be made, also slots for notions of all kinds. These screens can prove a real convenience, a good space saver, and a help in keeping a room looking neat when one is not sewing.

Measure any closet- or wall-space that you have back of the screen and buy two pieces of composition board to fit this. Hinge these together with wide gummed tape. This gives you a flat screen-like piece that can be placed against the wall when not in use and opened out, when needed, to use as a cutting board. A good flat cutting surface saves time and is very important to good work.

If you have a closet large enough in which you can put a chest of drawers, this can serve you well as a place for your supplies. Put all your notions in the top drawer, your patterns in the second, your materials in the third, and so on. Sometimes such a chest can be purchased second-hand and painted and made like new.

A sewing space, no matter where it is in the house, should not be inaccessible. It should be so arranged and located that your sewing is easy to get at and you can sew for either a few minutes or for hours without upsetting the entire house. Each person must work out her own individual problem in this regard, because space varies as well as the amount of time spent at sewing. If one can possibly have a room or an area near the kitchen where she can sew while food is cooking or meals are in preparation, it is a great convenience.

In any event, provide a space that makes your sewing materials and equipment handy and accessible to you, so that if you have a few minutes' time to sew you will not have to use most of it up in getting at your materials and putting them away.

Know About Fabrics

THIS CENTURY HAS BROUGHT US MANY NOVELTIES IN fabrics and many outstanding achievements in man-made fibers. The scarcity of fine silk, linen and cotton during the war years served to make us appreciate man-made fibers as never before. The need for fabrics that would function under stress and strain brought new fabrics into the picture. Several made history, and some took on qualities that few dreamed they could possess. Each year sees additional outstanding developments. Most of these fabrics are now available to the woman who sews. See page 17.

You can make bathroom and shower curtains of nylon fabric that needs only to be washed out in a bowl and hung up without ironing or stretching. Make table linens of glass cloth and lamp shades and closet accessories of cellophane or plastic, using it just as you would fabric. There seems to be a fabric for every purpose. The important thing is to know which is best for what uses and then to choose, from the wide assortment available, the fabrics that please you and that suit your purposes —from the standpoint of cost and upkeep as well as beauty and durability.

Every woman should have a knowledge of the fibers and what each will do. Man-made fibers, varying as they do from the vegetable and animal fibers, make it essential to have a real education in fibers; and that education is necessary whether one sews her own clothes or buys them ready- or custom-made.

If you have studied the subject of fibers in school, you will appreciate our cataloguing here their common characteristics in the briefest possible space. If you are unfamiliar with the fibers and how they can be handled, then these pages should open up new vistas for you—make you so eager to know more about each fiber that you will get samples of different fabrics to stitch, hem, press and decorate just for the joy of knowing how they respond to intelligent treatment.

Know Your Fibers. All fabric, except the plastic film type, and felt, is made up of fibers spun into yarns and woven together in various combinations to form yardage. The fibers are classified as vegetable (cotton and linen, for example), animal (silk and wool), and man-made or synthetic (rayon, nylon, glass, etc.). The fibers are twisted together

into long strands called yarn. The number of fibers, the tightness of the twist, the smoothness or roughness, all influence the quality of the yarns and of the fabrics woven from them.

Know your Fabric Characteristics. *Weaves.* Many types of looms are used to produce the variety of fabrics we use. Each fabric begins with yarns threaded lengthwise on the weaving loom to form the *warp.* Back and forth, over and under the warp threads, yarn is woven to make the crosswise or *woof* threads of fabric. In the simplest weave, called *plain weave,* each crosswise or woof thread alternates over and under successive lengthwise or warp threads. Muslin, percale, and gingham are fabrics of plain or even weave. Other weaves are made by varying the number of over and under crossings of the woof and warp.

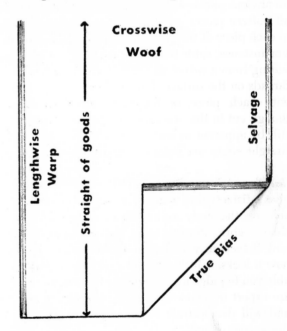

Grain. Learn to recognize the lengthwise and crosswise threads of fabrics. Learn to get a true bias line by folding back a corner at true right angles to the warp and woof and then cutting the fold. These directions of fabric threads are called grain. In making any garment, the correct placing of the grain in each section is important to the hang or drape of the garment and the whole effect.

Finishes. Some fabrics, after weaving, are "processed" to increase the weight or body of the material, or to prevent shrinkage or wrinkling, or to impart crispness or add gloss to the surface, or to make it water repellent or mothproof. These finishes affect the way the fabric handles, washes or cleans, drapes and stands wear.

Pile, Nap, Sheen. Fabrics such as velvet, velveteen and terry cloth have a surface of standing fiber ends called *pile*. *Nap* fabrics have fuzzy or hairy fibers lying in one direction on fabric surface. The nap differs in finish, depending on type of fabric. For example, wool broadcloth and doeskin have a smooth surface, while blanketing and overcoatings usually have a downy surface. *Sheen* is the effect of light reflections on a fabric surface.

Pile and napped fabrics should have all sections of a garment cut with the pile or sheen running in the same direction. Pile fabrics—velvet, velveteen, velour, corduroy, etc.—should be cut with the pile running up. Nap fabrics—broadcloth, coatings, duvetyn, etc.—are cut with the nap running down. However, many fabrics that have no obvious pile or nap need to be cut so the tops of all pattern pieces are up, so that the color sheen in each piece of the garment will appear the same. For instance, satin is a fabric with high sheen resulting from a weave which provides long lustrous threads on the surface. It should be cut with care, with each piece in the same direction. Even though cut in this way, a difference in sheen may still be apparent in certain fabrics when bias and straight edges are seamed together.

Handle. A fabric that "handles" well will usually give satisfaction in wearing, as it will be comfortable on the body and to the touch. When you choose fabric, drape it up to you—see how it falls, how it feels in your hands. Lay folds in it to see how it looks. A little practice in doing this will enable you to judge a good fabric. Many sales people are expert in demonstrating the draping of fabric and will demonstrate readily its suitability for a dress, coat or suit.

Suitability of Fabric to Pattern Design. The most frequent error that beginners in sewing make is to select a fabric and then buy a pattern completely unsuited to it, choosing a shirtwaist-style pattern for a flimsy sheer, for example. Let the pattern book or pattern salesgirl help you in choosing a pattern that, in silhouette, is appropriate to the weight and texture of your fabric. Do avoid intricate designs until you are expert in sewing.

Care of Fabric. 1. Choose fabrics that are suitable to the life they will lead when made up. For articles frequently laundered, buy fast-color, preshrunk or Sanforized fabrics. Fragile fabrics rarely survive soap and hot water and ironing or too frequent cleanings. Read the tags and labels that tell you how to handle fabrics and keep this information on file as long as the fabric is in use. Some fabrics dry-clean, but won't wash. Some wash, but need ironing with a cool iron and no sprinkling. Some need steaming rather than pressing. Some can be bleached in washing and others are spoiled by laundry bleaches. Many electric irons have different heats for wool, silk, synthetics, and cotton or linen; be sure to use the correct heat. Know before you make up fabric or press a ready-made garment exactly what you can expect from the fabric.

2. When you are working with fabric, keep it smoothed, folded or laid flat to prevent unnecessary wrinkling. Keep work surface clean and free of equipment not in use to prevent soiling or catching fabric. Hang garments on hangers as they are assembled. Put unfinished sections away in drawer or box or wrap in paper to keep clean between sessions of sewing.

3. After articles are finished, treat them with care for the character of the fabric. Brush napped fabrics to remove loose dust. Always hang garments on suitable hangers and don't put them away soiled. Remove spots or wipe soiled places such as neckline and sleeve edges with proper cleaning fluid before putting them away. Never store out-of-season clothes without cleaning. Over such a long period, soiled clothing may be permanently discolored or moth-damaged. Apply the "stitch in time" practice to frayed or torn places to prevent increasing damage. The life of fabric can be prolonged by careful and prompt attention.

Straightening. Sometimes warp and woof threads in a fabric get out of line during finishing or print-

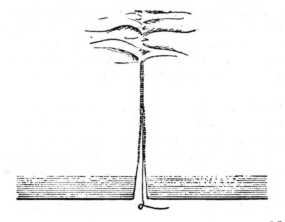

ing or rolling. Before cutting, straighten fabric so that the grain is true. Clip selvage, catch one crosswise thread and pull it gently out of fabric. Cut carefully on this line. This gives one straight end. For fabrics with even warp and woof (challis, lightweight flannels, flat crepe, percale, etc.) clip selvage and tear quickly across to straighten end.

Tearing. Grasp firmly both edges of clipped selvage; tear with force to break the threads all the way across the width. Clip selvage there. Even-weave lightweight fabrics may usually be torn lengthwise as well as across. Always test by tearing a scrap of fabric before trying long stretches. If the fabrics draw or tear with difficulty, pull a thread and cut on the pulled line. Don't try to tear ribbed or corded or very strong fabrics.

Stretching. After end is straightened to a thread, it may be necessary to stretch fabric to get it back in line. Work on a flat surface such as a cutting board or table with a straight edge. As you stretch and straighten the fabric the edge will parallel the edge of the table, as illustrated. Grasp opposite edges of the fabric at points some distance apart and stretch and see-saw diagonally. Repeat along the length. If this it not sufficient to straighten, dampen fabric and see-saw again.

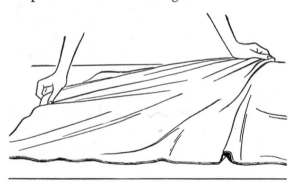

Dampening. Wet a sheet or muslin cloth and lay over fabric until enough moisture is absorbed to make straightening, by pulling and stretching, easy. Begin with the straightened end. For wool, roll with the grain straight around a board; avoid wrinkles in the fabric or the damp cloth; leave rolled until dry. For cotton or linen, sprinkle as for ironing and roll until damp all through; shake and hang lengthwise over a door or smooth out straight on flat surface to dry.

Sponging or Shrinking. Unless fabric, particularly woolen fabric, has been preshrunk so that only a tiny fraction of shrinkage may occur later,

it is a precaution to sponge it before cutting. Straighten first. Fold straightened ends in half, bringing lengthwise edges (selvages) together. Then wring out cheesecloth, unbleached muslin, or a strip from an old lintless sheet in warm water. Lay it on flat surface and place fabric carefully over this. Roll the lengths together in loose flat roll, avoiding wrinkles in either. Basting across one or both ends of woolen fabric, making sure crosswise threads are perfectly straight on both ends, helps to keep fabric from slipping when rolling in damp cloth. Leave for 8 to 12 hours, then unroll and hang over a door or lay on a flat surface to dry thoroughly before cutting. Some people prefer to make a newspaper roll, cover this with muslin, roll fabric and damp cloth on the roll and let stand for several hours, when fabric is then removed and hung over a door, straight, to dry. Top of door should be covered with paper to protect both fabric and door.

This is a good precaution and always necessary where fabric does not carry a preshrunk label.

How to Determine Right Amount of Fabric to Buy. If you can resist temptation, buy your pattern first and then your fabric because the pattern carries a fairly accurate chart telling you how much fabric in a given width you need for the size pattern.

When you do see a fabric that you lose your heart to, and have not decided exactly what pattern you will use, let these simples rules help you to determine the best lengths to buy.

Two lengths of 40″ fabric, shoulder to floor, will cut a straight sleeveless or short-sleeved dress. Allow ¾ yard more for long sleeves, three lengths if skirt is full. The average dress is approximately 1½ yards long, so 3 yards is minimum and 4 yards is maximum for sizes 20 or under. Larger sizes need one skirt length additional or 4 yards for a simple straight dress and 4¾ when long sleeves are desired. For evening dresses, the width of the skirt controls the yardage.

(When skirts are very short, measure from neck to bottom of hem and allow for depth of hem, rather than neck to floor as directed here.)

When the fabric is very expensive, as in metallics, pure silks, etc., it is most advantageous to cut a muslin garment from your pattern, fit this to your figure, then rip this and lay pieces on paper or fabric the width of the fabric you plan to use. Measure and know how much you need to buy. This practice is necessary also when using short lengths or remnants because it enables you to determine, before you cut, where you can piece or add trimming to obtain the effect you desire.

For 54″ fabric, two lengths, neck to floor, are usually enough for a straight coat with long sleeves and an overlapping front. (Remember we have advised you to cut all pieces the same way of the fabric where there is pile, nap or sheen.)

Sizes larger than 20 usually require one skirt length more than two lengths of shoulder to floor.

The above plan can guide you in jackets, skirts, blouses and slips. Take into consideration the width of your fabric, whether or not it needs to be cut all one way or whether the pattern pieces can be fitted closely together, then buy as many multiple lengths of fabric as is necessary to get the amount of fullness you desire.

For example, a blouse 24″ long with short sleeves may be cut from 1⅛ yards of 40″ wide fabric that has no up and down. A short jacket of the same length would require ⅔ yards more because of facings, deeper hems, pockets and a collar.

POINTS TO REMEMBER
IN BUYING AND USING MAN-MADE FIBERS

FIRST, BE OPEN-MINDED ABOUT THE NEW FABRICS, especially those that are a blend of natural and synthetic fibers. Man-made fibers can give lightness or firmness, warmth or coolness. In many instances they have a crease-resistant quality that is completely desirable. Natural fibers, some believe—and there is considerable proof to support this—hold color best and with them the more enduring colors are produced. Therefore, tremendous advantages are being found in blending fibers, because this produces fabrics with the color-holding qualities of the natural fibers, which is so desirable, and with the subtle color possibilities of the synthetics.

In Buying and Using Synthetic Fibers, Remember These Essentials

ACRILAN

Soft and lightweight, with full-bodied "hand" and look. Has low-stretch quality and high durability. Is wrinkle- and crease-resistant even when wet, laundering easily, drying fast, and keeping crease or pleats. Moth-proof and mildew-resistant. Acrilan fabrics or blends are used by important manufacturers for suits, dresses, sports clothes, children's wear, blankets and in yardgoods.

DACRON

Perfect for men's shirtings and washable sports apparel of all kinds, being wrinkle- and crease-resistant, quick-drying and easily spot-cleaned. Since it holds a crease and does not wrinkle, it is especially desirable for men's and women's tailored suits, and uniforms of all types. Desirable for children's clothes, dresses and blouses, requiring little or no ironing. Will probably become as versatile and adaptable as nylon, now that it has emerged into sheer fabrics, including chiffon and tricot knit, making it desirable for lingerie.

Sheer Dacron curtain materials are being made of this yarn—having, seemingly, every good quality needed in a curtain. Ease in upkeep and reasonable cost make them acceptable practically wherever glass curtains or sheer effects are used.

DYNEL

Luxurious in texture, soft, warm, durable, and wonderfully light in weight. Extensively used for pile fabrics such as fleece coatings, imitation fur cloth and velvet pile. Combines beautifully with wool, cotton, nylon, Vicara and other fibers, in challis. Used for sports apparel, women's suits and children's wear. Also used in circular-knit fabrics such as jersey, adding shape retention and softness of "hand." Moth-proof, fire-resistant, and readily laundered, it holds advantages for draperies, slip-covers, bedspreads and blankets, particularly for shipping lines, hotels, and public institutions. Requires care in pressing because it melts at a very low temperature.

ORLON

Gaining more and more favor for men's shirts, uniforms, foundation garments, underwear, tailored and soft dresses. Has good draping quality, and its bulking power gives warmth without weight, this making it highly desirable for all outer apparel. Especially resistant to sunlight, it is ideal for sports apparel and for curtains, draperies and slip-covers. Is wrinkle-resistant, washable, requires very little ironing, stays fresh-looking and is long-wearing. Has a high strength when wet and dry. Like nylon and rayon, it requires a cool iron in pressing.

VICARA

Can have a soft, luxurious feel equalled only by pure cashmere, yet is shrink-, moth- and mildew-resistant. When blended with nylon, Dynel, Orlon, Dacron, wool and cotton, adds to "hand" and drape. Easy to launder or dry-clean. Highly absorbent, it dyes well with the usual dyes, producing beautiful colors. Is used with blends in suits, dresses, sports clothes, upholstery fabrics, blankets, knit goods, knitting yarns.

USING PLASTICS IN SEWING

SCIENCE HAS GIVEN US NEW AND VALUABLE MATErials of plastic that have special advantages for accessories and home furnishings.

Handling. These synthetic fabrics need to be handled lightly. Use no pins, basting or tacks. Hang length of plastic over door and smooth out gently with hands before laying out or cutting. If any part becomes soiled, wipe off with damp cloth. Do not press or iron. Temperature affects the plastic slightly, humid atmosphere making it soft, stretchy and moist, and cold making it a little tough. Brush talcum over it to combat dampness. Touch edges gently with a drop of oil on fingertips to overcome toughness of cold.

Pattern Layout. Plastic has no grain, so that pieces may be placed in any direction if color is plain. For printed designs, lay pattern to preserve direction of motifs in all pieces. Use weights to hold pattern pieces in place. Do not pin. Draw lightly around pieces with pencil. Use paper clips or Scotch tape to hold pieces together where necessary, instead of pinning or basting. Roll pieces on paper tube in opposite order from that to be used in assembling them.

Stitching. Plastics are easily stitched on the sewing machine and the use of attachments is perfectly satisfactory. Use fine needle (size 9–11), Nylon or Mercerized Thread, light tension and light pressure, and set machine for the longest stitch suitable for the type of sewing being done. See *Walking Presser Foot*, page 127.

The following pointers may be helpful in sewing plastics with attachments.

Hemmer. Thread a hand needle with double thread. Put it through corner point of edge to be hemmed. Holding the thread, draw point of film into scroll of Hemmer and into position for stitching. Feed edge into Hemmer as usual.

Binder. No change in ordinary procedure is necessary for fabric binding on plastic. For plastic binding, cut strip of ½″ and insert it in outside slot of Binder. Edges need not be folded under as in fabric binding because plastic does not fray.

Ruffler. Run strip for ruffling through Ruffler with adjustment set at the star for a line of straight stitching to produce a gripping surface for teeth of ruffler blade. Set Ruffler for gathering or pleating. Adjust machine for a little extra pressure. If oil from the Ruffler seeps onto surface of plastic and makes it too slippery for blade to pick up, dust talcum under the blade and also along the edge. In stitching long edges of ruffling, if contact with waxy surface of plastic makes blades skip gathers, slip ½″ strip of fine emery cloth between blades to provide gripping surface for them.

Gatherer. Use talcum or emery cloth as described above if need arises. Otherwise, no special preparation is required.

Edge-Stitcher. Use to make tucks, single fold hems, French seams and overlap seams.

INTERLININGS AND INTERFACINGS

Interlinings. In choosing an interlining for a garment, consider your need of it—whether for warmth, for bulking, or to give the appearance of greater thickness to your fabric.

Sometimes unbleached muslin in a fine weave is liked, sometimes flannelette, lamb's wool, wool crepe or a "tie lining."

Tie lining or lamb's wool is often used as an interlining in coats across the shoulders and down almost to the waistline.

Milium, a metal-coated lining fabric, is an insulation and a lining combined. Nickel-metal is pressed to the back of such fabrics as taffeta and satin. Milium is particularly desirable because of its lightness and lack of bulk. An interlining is used only across the shoulders when Milium is used for lining.

Usually the pattern of the garment is used to cut an interlining. To avoid bulk in construction, lap the seams and trim the interlining close to the stitching line, then catch it to the seam edge of the garment with basting stitches. The lining of the garment is then put in separately.

Interfacings. Designers of apparel find that stiffenings or supports via interfacings are often necessary to achieve the right fashion effect. Interfacing should not be apparent from the outside. Its presence in the garment is to give form and help mold the fabric rightly to your figure. If too stiff, it will be evident; if too limp, it will not provide the needed support. Try therefore to test a piece of your fabric over the interfacing, to be sure of correct pliancy. Such materials can vary in weight and texture from sheerest net to felted padding. Your fabric and degree of crispness desired will decide your choice.

Often the pattern instructions suggest the weight of interfacing best for the silhouette of the particular pattern. One caution we give is to buy good-quality interfacing, interlining and pads. Your garment needs to be cleaned or washed, so buy preshrunk interfacing material, or shrink it yourself, so you will know that it will come through in good shape and continue to function as needed in your garment.

Lawn, nylon, nylon net and fine taffeta are desirable as interfacings for sheer wools, soft silks and fine cottons, as well as synthetics of comparable texture and weight. Some sheer and semi-sheer wools will need a fine hair canvas.

Hair canvas, sometimes known as hair cloth or mohair interfacing, comes by the yard, in varying weights and thicknesses. It has a cotton warp and a mohair-type of wool as woof. Because of its pliancy and resilance it is preferred by many tailors. Choose a weight and weave that will mold readily to the fabric of your garment.

An open linen-type-weave wool called "tie lining" is liked by many for topcoats and children's coats. It is easy to cut, especially on the bias. Still another type is a light-weight felt-like interfacing that is especially treated so that it takes cleaning, even washing, satisfactorily. This comes in a variety of weights and in shades from black through gray and white, costs about the same as other interfacings, has less "give" and must be cut to shape rather than molded through steaming and pressing.

RESTYLING

RESTYLING IS BETTER THAN MAKING OVER, AND RE-style you can, sometimes with a new pattern.

A dress or coat needs restyling when its silhouette is no longer current, when the garment is worn or damaged and needs renewing, or when weight has been gained or lost to a point where adjustments must be made.

If a garment is to be restyled, consider the length first—too short, too long? Next, the sleeves, especially the shoulder, then neckline and waistline.

Your first aim, of course, in restyling, just as in making new clothes, is to fit the new in fashion to your own type and figure. In any year, whatever the fashion, *you* come first, and you will find that there is usually a way for you to use the new.

In choosing fabrics for your restyling, buy those that will drape and hang best for *your* figure, as well as those that will harmonize with fabrics in last year's garments. If you are a little plumper than you like to admit, avoid the stiffer and shinier and bright-colored fabrics, for instance, and select a fabric in a subdued color that will drape softly, with slenderizing effect.

In choosing patterns or considering individual fashion features for your restyling, think always of what they will do for your figure. If you are short, modify the skirt widths and lengths so that you run no risk of "cutting off" your figure. Pockets need not be used if they will give too much breadth to your figure at the point where they are to be placed. Padding and fullness can be made less bulging, as your figure requires. New fashion effects can be obtained by slight modifications. Get out dresses, skirts, blouses, put them on, look in a full-length mirror, study and see how you can adapt them smartly and becomingly.

Adding New Fabric. One dress-length of fabric will provide a new panel front and back, or an entire new top, or new sleeves. Find a pattern with lines similar to the dress you want to remodel. This can guide you in cutting and help you to get the fashion effect you desire.

Using Remnants. Remnants can prove an economy or an extravagance, depending upon ingenuity in use, restraint in buying, and sense of values. Sometimes it takes more time to figure out how to style and cut from a short length than the saving on the remnant is worth. Again a remnant may have more fabric than you require and make for waste in use. Short remnants can be used advantageously, however, in sewing for children in combinations for two-tone effects. And aprons can be made, perhaps of better fabric than you would buy otherwise. One woman has a reputation for making beautiful appropriate aprons for her friends. She searches for lovely chintz, sateens and synthetics of quality, dotted swiss, organdies, printed linens and charming plastics, and styles the apron to be in keeping with the type of fabric. Such aprons are a delight to own and to wear and surely provide an excellent way to use remnants. Left-overs from dresses can be used for aprons, and drapery and upholstery lengths can usually serve for umbrella or paper-and-twine holders and book covers. Remnants left from garments are often useful in facings for hems, cutting new sleeves, inserting a new belt line.

Color and Clothes

A CHIEF DELIGHT IN MAKING ONE'S OWN CLOTHES IS being able to find a delectable color or print—an irresistible one—and using it to make a "dream dress" so becoming that every wearing brings genuine happiness.

Every woman has, at given times in her life, certain colors that are best for her. Becoming colors many prove less so as the pigmentation of skin, eyes, hair—even teeth—changes. Softer, more subdued colors become more pleasing in time than the more vivid colors once so highly flattering.

Rarely does a woman make serious mistakes in choosing her most becoming colors, but just to make sure you don't, familiarize yourself with these basic rules, the kind an artist would use in choosing colors.

The first rule is: Don't choose a color for itself alone or because it is fashion's favorite for the season. Think over the following points before you make your decision:

1. Is the color suitable for your individual characteristics? Your natural skin tone? Your eyes? Your hair color? Your figure proportions? Your personality? Your age? Position in business, community, society?

2. Is it suitable for your purposes? The occasions for which you will wear it? The season? Your mode of transportation? The type of community in which you live?

3. Is it practical?

The last question may not be a factor in all cases. If you are planning a dress for one special occasion and do not intend to wear it often, or if it is fabric that you can dye, you may not care that the color will not give service or be appropriate again. A bridesmaid's dress or a fancy-dress costume may be planned for color effect and style alone. Ordinarily, though, you have to consider whether the color is too light to keep clean under wearing conditions, or looks equally well in different lights, or goes with a variety of accessories, etc.

The second question is always important. Certain colors might be appropriate for an afternoon party in summer, but not for a business meeting in mid-winter, or acceptable for beach wear, but not for street wear in the city, or for negligee garments, but not for serviceable outer apparel.

The first question is most important of all. Complexion, hair and eye colors are so interrelated in making up the individual you that all must be taken into account in your choice of clothing color. You want to pick those tints and shades that accentuate your own coloring rather than outshine it or diminish it. For instance, there are blues so strong as to steal the blue from your eyes, while other blues will emphasize the eye color. An olive complexion may lose all its blush tones and appear only sallow when it is matched with a dress of drab or mustard brown color. The most glorious auburn hair may be made garish by juxtaposition with a red or pink that is incompatible. Study the range of color choice for each type of natural coloring considered here, for convenience, according to hair color. Not all colors within the range will be flattering to every person who comes within the type because of the individual difference in skin tones, intensity of the eye color, texture, body and light of hair.

Those having tinted hair should choose soft colors. Such people often have lines in their faces. Therefore, to avoid calling attention to the fact that the hair is tinted, they generally should use the subdued colors in the same way that those with lined faces do.

Try colors for yourself by holding up color samples against your face to be sure that skin and eyes and hair come alive in connection with the color you contemplate using. Do this with fabric in a store as you consider it. If you are in doubt, go to the ready-to-wear department and try on a dress of the color you have in mind, or buy a roll of crepe paper in the color you are considering and try this out at home in the best possible light. Do this without benefit of make-up; then when the right make-up is used, you can be even prettier in your carefully chosen color.

Experiment with new colors; make sure they are becoming before you invest in them. You know that fabric in yard goods departments keeps pace with ready-mades in the season's favored colors and textures.

Never think that any season has failed to provide for you in the choice of color. There are always some tones or tints, shades or gradations of the fashionable colors for every type. Designers and manufacturers are too well aware of the general needs to confine their output to anything that

Light and True Blonde Types

Blonde types have hair ranging from tow-head, almost white, to golden blonde, eyes that are light blue, clear blue, gray, green, hazel, or brown, and complexions varying from very fair to peach or golden tones. Colors for these types are clear and fresh looking. One precaution always when the natural color is delicate: never overpower it with too vital a color. Generally any pastel color is flattering.

LIGHT BLONDES

Colors 1 to 10, 14, 18 and 22 are generally becoming to most blondes. The brighter tints, 11 to 13 and 15 to 17, should be considered carefully. Paler types may find them overpowering. Black is good on most blondes when a touch of color gives relief.

Medium Blondes or Hazel Types

Medium blonde types have hair between blonde and brown or with an auburn tinge, eyes that are light blue, blue-gray, hazel or brown, and fair or medium complexion. Notice that the colors selected for these types are less brilliant than for the true blondes. That is because the more vivid colors would seem to detract from the more neutral natural coloring of hair, eyes, and skin.

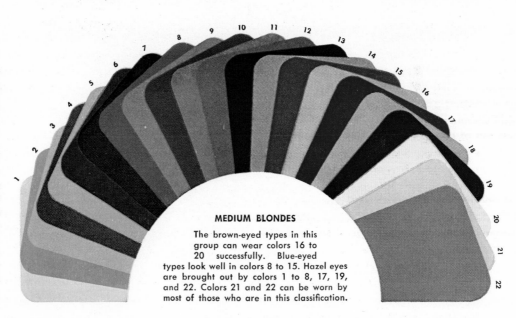

MEDIUM BLONDES

The brown-eyed types in this group can wear colors 16 to 20 successfully. Blue-eyed types look well in colors 8 to 15. Hazel eyes are brought out by colors 1 to 8, 17, 19, and 22. Colors 21 and 22 can be worn by most of those who are in this classification.

Gray-Haired Types

Gray-haired types may have skin and eye colors of any of the other groups and may vary their color choices accordingly. The selection should be suitable to the age, surroundings, and activities of the individual. Sometimes when the natural pigmentation leaves the skin and hair, the skin takes on a clear cameo quality. Soft and subtle colors and white bring out this clear loveliness without giving a washed-out look.

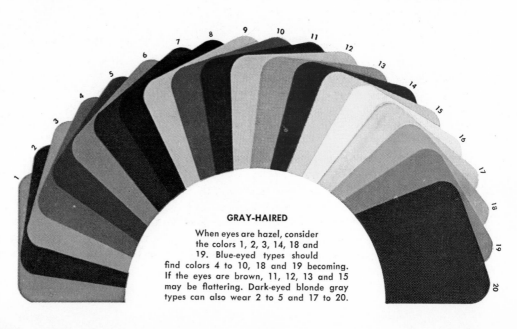

GRAY-HAIRED

When eyes are hazel, consider the colors 1, 2, 3, 14, 18 and 19. Blue-eyed types should find colors 4 to 10, 18 and 19 becoming. If the eyes are brown, 11, 12, 13 and 15 may be flattering. Dark-eyed blonde gray types can also wear 2 to 5 and 17 to 20.

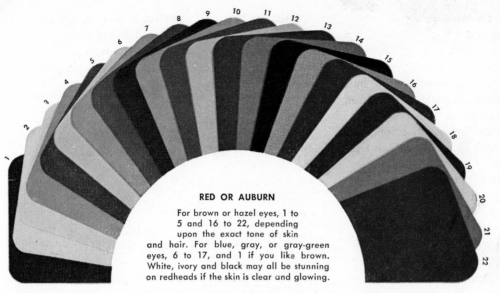

RED OR AUBURN

For brown or hazel eyes, 1 to 5 and 16 to 22, depending upon the exact tone of skin and hair. For blue, gray, or gray-green eyes, 6 to 17, and 1 if you like brown. White, ivory and black may all be stunning on redheads if the skin is clear and glowing.

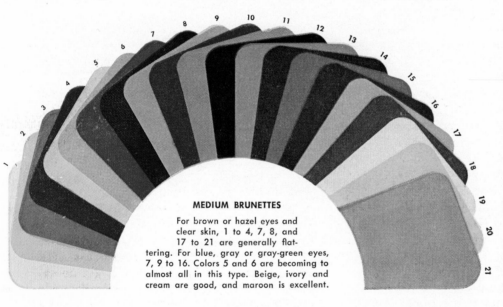

MEDIUM BRUNETTES

For brown or hazel eyes and clear skin, 1 to 4, 7, 8, and 17 to 21 are generally flattering. For blue, gray or gray-green eyes, 7, 9 to 16. Colors 5 and 6 are becoming to almost all in this type. Beige, ivory and cream are good, and maroon is excellent.

DARK BRUNETTES

Brunettes with fair skin and blue eyes can wear colors 10 to 22. Those with high coloring may choose almost any tone here, depending on eye color. Brown-eyed types can wear colors 7, 8, and 9. Black can be becoming when a high color accent is used.

Red or Auburn

Redheads range from light golden red to dark auburn, with blue, gray, hazel or dark brown eyes. Their skin tones may be from those as fair as blondes to those as dark as brunettes. When you are blessed with such distinctive coloring, play it up, emphasize it, highlight it; never tone it down. The reds, the pinks, deep purples are missing from your fan, but see the wide range of attractive browns, greens, and blues.

Medium Brunettes

Medium brunettes have chestnut or brown hair ranging from medium to dark brown, with blue, gray, gray-green, hazel, brown or black eyes, and from fair to almost olive skin. This is probably the most predominant type in America. Such types often make the mistake of wearing a drab, indifferent color, whereas a decisive color would be more becoming because it gives a real lift.

Dark Brunettes

Dark brunettes may have dark brown to black hair, eyes of blue, gray, gray-green, hazel, brown or black, and skin ranging from very fair to olive. Black-haired types whose hair is gray may also consider this color range when the natural coloring is intense. True colors in dress may be becoming. Sallow-skinned brunettes should avoid the too-yellow greens or the orange, which may intensify the yellow skin tones.

only a limited number of women can wear.

If there is some color you like particularly, but find trying to your own coloring or figure, use it sparingly as accent or in accessories.

About your figure problem—you know best what it is, but here are some general principles about the effect of color on the figure.

Black, dark tones or deeply grayed colors tend to make the figure appear smaller or slimmer than do bright or light colors. "When in doubt about color, always choose black" is a rule to remember. Black is considered by many the most chic and the most flattering. Accent for it may be had through make-up, jewels, hat, veil, or corsage.

A plain color makes the figure look slimmer than a combination of contrasting colors. A two-tone effect broken across the figure makes it seem shorter and broader. A lengthwise contrast helps to give an illusion of slenderness. Large prints or plaids may make the figure appear larger or heavier, though a dainty all-over design sometimes helps to lend daintiness to the figure.

A very small figure should not wear over-large designs in prints, plaids or stripes, and the person with a large figure will also avoid them, as well as the too-dainty or chi-chi design, preferring motifs that are moderate rather than the conspicuous or too sharply defined.

Contrast and accent should be handled carefully. A little accent, say just a touch of red on navy blue at the throat or shoulder, is smarter than a repeated accent in shoulder, belt, cuff, hat, etc. Think of this in choosing accessories of contrasting color. It is better to have the contrast only in hat and handbag, or in hat and gloves, than to have all the accessories of the second color. Not only does it make the contrast more dramatic, but it saves your figure from the trying all-over effect of spottiness. If you have a particular figure problem, such as large bust or large hips, place your color contrast or accent so that it draws the eye away from the fault and emphasizes one of your good points.

Remember always the value in the wardrobe of good basic dresses in dark color that can be made to suit occasions by the use of the right accessories and to give color pleasure through subtle accent.

Color can be a joy and satisfaction—a magic aid to creating a *you* that you are happy to present to view. Learn to use it to your best advantage and always to compliment your skin, your eyes, your hair and your figure.

STUDY THE SIX COLOR FANS

SIX COLOR FANS ARE GIVEN ON THE COLOR PAGES SO that you can study the range suited to your natural hair and complexion coloring. Each fan is designed to give a graded selection of tints and shades through the spectrum, concentrating on those most becoming to a particular type. Not every color included will be exactly right for every person who falls into the general classification, but the most trying have been eliminated from each group and the most generally becoming have been included. Make your own choice to suit your particular needs.

The density of color is the important consideration in selecting for the various types. The lower the natural pigmentation of the individual, the softer, less accented the color must be. For example, there is a blue in every chart, but some are decidedly gray, others are strong, true blues, while others have so much violet as to be, in truth, violet-blue. Brown, to compare another range, is like a milk chocolate for the blonde, while it is a deep, warm walnut for the medium blonde. A certain red under a night light might eclipse all the natural color of a pale blonde, but prove gloriously becoming to a vivid blonde. Palest yellow might bring a little sunshine color to the pale blonde and prove equally becoming to the vivid blonde. The natural coloring of a vivid blonde might be enhanced by the grayed greens, while the pale blonde might find the violet tinted blues more flattering.

Even a more difficult color may be becoming if it is used only as an accent, if its fabric texture is flattering, and if it is not too close to the face. A scarf of violet blue might be just the right accent with a navy suit, though an entire suit of violet blue might completely overshadow the individual. Consider all such possibilities before selecting or rejecting a color for your wardrobe.

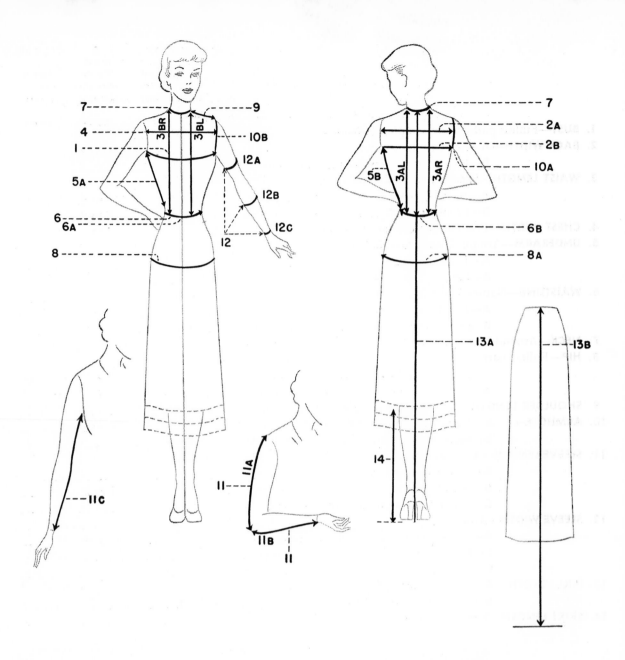

Your Measurement Chart

A MEASUREMENT CHART IS GIVEN HERE TO SHOW you what the essential measurements are. Be familiar with them so you can buy the correct pattern. Always check your pattern pieces against your measurements before laying pattern out on fabric as instructed on page 31.

For instructions on pattern alterations, see pages 26 to 31. One of the greatest advantages and economies in sewing is the perfect fit that can be achieved, plus the saving on expensive alterations.

When taking measurements, remove any bulky garments that will affect measurement, but wear whatever type of foundation garment you are likely to wear with the garment you are making. Pin a tape around waistline as starting point for other measurements. Take all measurements snugly but not tightly. Ease is allowed in pattern, but not in measurements. Bust, hips and arms should be measured at fullest part. Neck should be measured at base or collar line. Measure shoulder line from neck to top of correct armhole line. The upper arm measurement is used for short sleeves.

	1	2	3
	Your own measurement	Usual Pattern allowance for ease	Pattern measurement
	Inches	Inches	Inches
1. BUST—Fullest part—slightly higher in back	____	3 to 4	____
2. BACK WIDTH—A—Armhole to armhole	____	½ to 2	____
B—Underarm to underarm at side seam	____	____	____
3. WAIST LENGTH—Shoulder to natural waistline			
A—Back right _____ in. Left _____ in.	____	½ to 2	____
B—Front right _____ in. Left _____ in.	____	½ to 2	____
4. CHEST WIDTH—From armhole to armhole	____	½ to 1	____
5. UNDERARM—Armpit to natural waistline			
A—Right _____ in.	____	____	____
B—Left _____ in.	____	____	____
6. WAISTLINE—Natural—entire	____	____	____
A—Front _____ in.	____	____	____
B—Back _____ in.	____	____	____
7. NECK—Around base	____	____	____
8. HIP—Fullest part			
_____ inches below natural waistline	____	2	____
A—Back hip from side to side	____	1	____
9. SHOULDER LENGTH—Neck to tip of shoulder	____	____	____
10. ARMHOLE— A—Right _____ in.	____	____	____
B—Left _____ in.	____	____	____
11. SLEEVE LENGTH—Arm bent			
A—Shoulder to elbow	____	____	____
B—Elbow to wrist	____	1 to 2	____
C—Inside from underarm seam to wrist	____	____	____
12. SLEEVE WIDTH—Arm straight			
A—Upper arm	____	3 to 4	____
B—Lower arm	____	____	____
C—Wrist	____	____	____
13. FULL LENGTH—A—Back of neck to floor	____	____	____
B—Back waistline to floor	____	____	____
14. SKIRT LENGTH—Floor to hem line	____	____	____

Take all measurements on the right-hand side of your figure except where otherwise designated, unless there is a marked difference in each side. When checking size of pattern consider seam allowance.

Observe the reference numbers above and check them on chart. The heavy lines on the chart show where tape measure is placed when taking each measurement. Free measurement charts are available at your Singer Sewing Center. Keep your record of measurements up-to-date by checking them every six months.

Know Your Figure Type

SOME WOMEN THINK THEY CAN USE ONE MAKE OF pattern better than another, because its cut more nearly conforms to their body measurements. If you know your size and where you vary from the average, you can readily adjust any make of pattern to fit you so there will be a minimum of change when your garment arrives at the fitting stage. It is said that practically every pattern sold requires some change in measurements to conform to those of the individual. Often these changes are few and slight, but make them you must if your garment is to look custom-made. Save your time by knowing what changes you require and making them in your pattern before you start to cut.

Most patterns are made for a figure 5′6″ tall, with hip 2″ to 3″ larger than bust. Check your charted measurements against the individual pattern pieces and make the changes necessary so the pattern will conform with your measurements.

To help you visualize just a few of the types of figures and choose the one most nearly like yours, we show the drawings below.

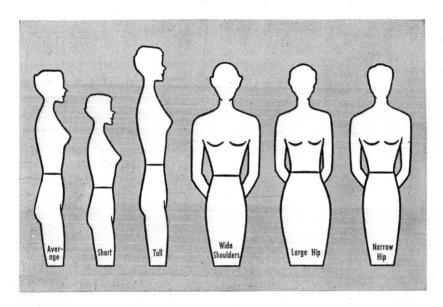

All Size 14. The figures shown at left would all be typed as the same size, in this instance size 14, yet they are decidedly different. The broad-shoulder figure would do best with a size 16 pattern, with skirt made narrower. The narrow-shoulder figure with large hip might be best with a size 12, enlarging the skirt, as illustrated on page 30. The tall figure problem is in the length, so length should be added both above and below the waistline.

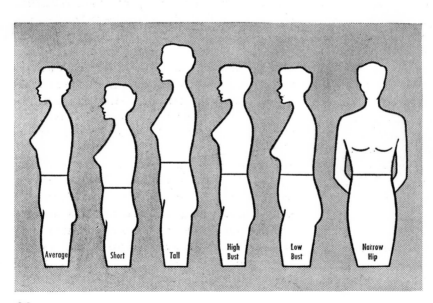

All Size 40. All figures shown are in the size 40 group. Bust and hip lines give major problems here. Average figure has no difficulty, short figure needs to shorten above and below waistline, and tall needs to lengthen above and below. High, large bust may need to add ½″ to 1″ as illustrated on page 29. Low bust, large waist should add fullness as illustrated on page 30, using a dart run in from side to give needed fullness for full low bust. Broad shoulder, narrow hip should alter skirt (see page 30).

TISSUE PAPER PATTERNS ARE A BOON TO THE WOMAN who sews, because they provide fashion rightness in sizes appropriate to the individual. They chart the way to save fabric in cutting, and many times give special instructions helpful with any distinct feature of the design. Make friends with a pattern salesperson in your Sewing Center or local department store and have her expert help when in need of advice in selecting a pattern for a new garment.

Patterns are designed in Women's, Misses', Junior and Teen-age sizes. A few companies make Larger sizes, also, and some make Half-sizes, which are for women 5'4" or less. Learn which make has styles that most appeal to you, and look at this company's patterns at intervals. You can, if you like, subscribe to a pattern magazine service that will bring the new styles to your home and allow you to select new patterns at your leisure.

Make Sure of Fashion Rightness. Be fashion-conscious. Study the fashion silhouette in magazines, in ready-to-wear advertising and in store windows. Watch the changes come—the shape of a shoulder—the fullness and length of a skirt—the cut of the neckline—the fit at the waistline—all of which are important in achieving the right fashion effect. This awareness helps you to know what to look for when you shop for patterns.

The Rule of Three. Remember this when you start to make a garment: One-third of its value lies in the cost of the fabric, one-third in the fashion-rightness of the style and its becomingness to you, and one-third in the workmanship you put into it —the cutting, fitting, stitching, finishing. For example, if your fabric costs $10, then you must add $10 worth of right style and, through your best efforts in cutting, fitting and making, produce a dress worth $30. See how easy it is to enhance the value of your fabric by good styling and workmanship. Apply this rule to all that you make and it will help you to style with greater self-confidence, hence greater ease, and will assure you of gratifying results.

Patterns to Your Purpose. Before buying either pattern or fabric, think over your needs carefully. Consider where and for what kind of occasion you will wear the garment, what accessories you already have to wear with it, how much wear and cleaning it must stand. Choose your pattern to be suitable for the fabric you have in mind, for your figure and for your purpose.

In relation to the fabric: The pattern envelopes and pattern books give you an idea of what type of fabric is best for the design. Don't disregard any information you can get about this point. More dresses are failures because of unfortunate combination of pattern and fabric than for any other reasons. A tailored garment cannot be made up satisfactorily in a very soft or flimsy fabric that won't hold a pleat or form a firm, straight edge. A softly draped silhouette is not for a crisp fabric.

In relation to yourself: Choose a pattern that will do the right thing for your figure and your own personality. Don't be misled by something that looks charming in an illustration of an eighteen-year-old if you are three times that age, or by a dashing style that flatters a Spanish beauty if you are a demure brown-head, or by a silhouette that emphasizes wrong proportions of your figure.

In relation to your purpose: If you are making summer garments, choose a pattern style that will be cool and comfortable and easily laundered. Avoid fussy little details that will be hard to keep fresh-looking or will suffer from frequent cleaning or washing and ironing. For business clothes, choose a style that will be suitable in business surroundings and can be made up in fabric not easily mussed.

Never think of a pattern by itself, but always in relation to you and your needs. If you are in doubt about any particular style, look through the ready-to-wear departments for similar styles, try them on, examine them, then buy your pattern.

Pattern Books and Counters. In your Sewing Center and in pattern departments of stores, you will find large counter books put out by pattern companies, showing their complete line of styles. New ones are issued every month, and they are usually arranged with newest designs first in each section. Look them over carefully when planning new garments. You will get the longest satisfaction from your dress if you choose the most becoming of the newer styles, because it is likely to be in fashion longer. New pattern booklets for each season are issued. Buy them to keep abreast of the new ideas. Pattern books aim to keep pace with ready-made garments in new lines and silhouettes.

Your Size of Pattern. If your figure is a true size, with all measurements proportionate—a true 12 or 14, for example—buy your pattern right for your bust and hip measurements. Do not buy larger or smaller, because patterns when made provide for ease or snugness, as fashion requires.

If your bust is large in proportion to your shoulders, then buy pattern a size smaller than your bust measure and enlarge it through the bust, hips and waist, as necessary. The fit through the shoulders and upper arms is so important in a pattern that this should be changed as little as possible, to retain the fashion effect designer has aimed for.

If shoulders and hip bones are large and you are thin, then buy a size right for your shoulders, which may well be larger than your bust size. Many women who were once a true size 14 become size 18 in bust and hip as they put on weight. For these, a size 16 pattern may be best, with enlargements made through bust and hip as measurements require.

If you are not sure of pattern size to use because of previous trouble in fitting a pattern, check the measurement scale given in the large counter books with your bust, waist and hip measurements. These books are available where you buy your patterns. Often by checking your own measurements with those given, you can make sure of a better size of pattern for you.

Combining Patterns. If your measurements vary much from the standard, it may often prove a real economy to buy two patterns. If your bust requires a size 36 pattern, for example, and your hip a size 42, then by all means invest in two patterns, one for the bust measure, one for the hip. Reconcile the measurements of these patterns at the waistline and you have less adjusting with the pattern sections themselves.

Study the Pattern. After you have bought your pattern, study the pattern envelope and decide which view you will use. Study the instruction sheet which is folded with the pattern. Do please read this in its entirety. Each make of pattern has its own way of identifying the pattern pieces. Some are perforated, others are printed. If the pattern you select is of a make unfamiliar to you, be sure to study its specific markings and instructions. A diagram shows all pattern pieces and how each is marked. Use this as a guide, separate the pattern pieces, refolding and returning to the envelope those not needed for your garment.

Pattern Adjustments

PATTERN ADJUSTMENTS SHOULD BE MADE INSIDE THE pattern rather than on the edges whenever possible. The essential style and line of a garment can be lost by shortening or lengthening only at the waistline or hem line. By cutting or darting the pattern as indicated in the following diagrams, all details in a dress should be in correct position on the figure.

To Obtain the Measurement of Your Pattern. Press the pattern pieces, lay them out and measure from seamline to seamline, using your tape. Measure half your pattern as shown here. Check such measurements against your own, as taken according to the chart on page 22. This will tell you

where changes are desirable. Remember that ease is provided on the pattern; you need not allow for it. See column 2, on page 22. If there are darts or

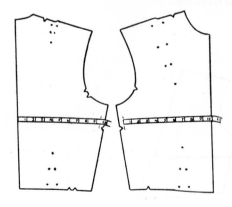

pleats in your pattern, pin them before measuring.

After you have decided on pattern alteration needs, draw a straight line either parallel or at right angles to straight-of-goods marking, as at **A**. Use this line as a guide for cutting or for making tuck to decrease. If pattern piece has to be cut completely apart, as for lengthening, then draw two short guide lines at right angles across first line as at **B**. After pattern is cut apart, the short lines are a guide in keeping pattern pieces straight.

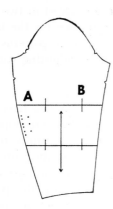

We illustrate the pattern slashed, separated for length or width and pinned to paper. Machine-baste rather than pin if the pattern is one you may use more than once. Basting will save time and insure a complete pattern. Have paper strips for piecing wide enough (4″ to 5″) so that edges can overlap and not pull away when in use. Lay all piecing strips underneath pattern pieces so that outline of pattern can always be seen. Trim away excess paper along edges of pattern before laying it on fabric for cutting.

When making folds to shorten pattern, fold pattern flat tuck-fashion, and pin.

To Shorten Surplice Front. Lay fold straight across to take up extra length and pin. Lay paper underneath edges. Make a tapered line on both sides as shown by dotted lines.

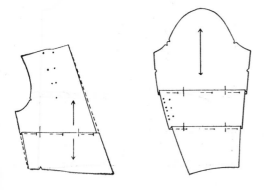

To Shorten Sleeve. Lay fold straight across to take up extra length above or below elbow, as needed, and pin. See preceding column.

To Shorten Waist. Make a fold the desired depth straight across each waist piece of pattern between underarm and waistline. Pin.

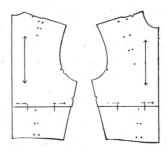

To Shorten Skirt. Lay even-width fold in all gores straight across below hip line to take up required amount. Pin.

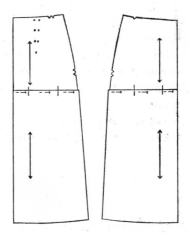

To Lengthen Sleeve. Cut straight across sleeve pattern above and below elbow for long sleeves.

Separate pattern pieces the required distance. Pin to paper strip.

To Lengthen Waist. Cut front-waist pattern straight across between bust and waistline unless bust is very high, when slash is made on the bust line. Place paper strip underneath and make required length. Pin in place. Back section may be lengthened the same way.

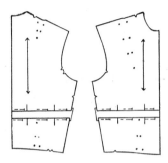

To Lengthen Skirt. Slash all gores straight across below hip line. Lay over paper strips. Pin.

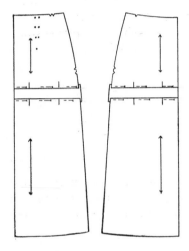

For Thin Arm (C). Draw two lengthwise lines parallel to straight-of-goods indications and about 1½" in from the notches at top of sleeve. Lay two lengthwise tucks in pattern, dividing the amount to be taken out. Pin tucks evenly.

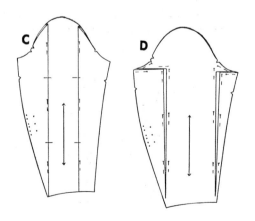

For Large Arm (D). If much width is to be added to both sides of the sleeve, draw 2 straight lines along lengthwise grain of the pattern, the back line approximately 3" from the armhole line, the front one 2". At right angles draw connecting lines to the armhole. Cut in on these lines, then down on the parallel lines almost to bottom of sleeve. Separate the pattern on each line, each section a half of the width that is needed. Place paper underneath and secure to position. Place pieces of paper along the armhole and draw in a new line to connect the sleeve seam with that of the armhole.

For a short sleeve pattern, cut the pattern apart, making cross marks first so you can place pattern on paper correctly. Separate sleeve at bottom as much as necessary for the around-the-arm measurement.

Increase armhole of front and back of waist by slashing from armhole down, as in **G**, so the sleeve can fit to place.

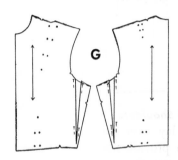

For Large Arm Muscle (E). Slash pattern from top toward but not all the way to wrist. Spread open at top to required width. Fold darts in from slash at fullest part of arm so as to bring top corners of slash together. Pin paper underneath and allow to project at top enough to restore original line.

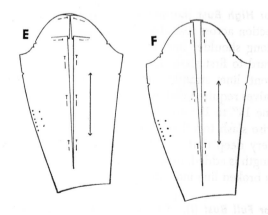

For Large Upper Arm (F). Slash pattern down center from top and separate as shown. Pin paper strip under slash, adding to width of sleeve as needed.

For Large Elbow. Slash sleeve piece from top to elbow level, then across to back edge. Lay paper underneath, spread open the required distance and pin.

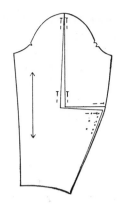

For Flat Bust. Lay fold across chest line on front waist to take up extra length in this section. Pin. Even line of armhole. Lay a fold the same width in front of sleeve so that armhole and sleeve will be correct in size for each other.

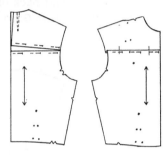

For Round Shoulders. Cut pattern across full part of back; lay over paper. Raise upper section enough to provide needed length, keeping ends of pattern together at armhole. Add enough to center-back line to keep it straight, and pin. To make neckline proper size, take up amount added at center back in small dart as indicated.

These two adjustments are shown together because in most instances, a person with round shoulders often needs the front adjustment.

For High Bust (normal waistline) (H). Cut waist section across just above underarm dart. Halfway along shoulder line, make a slash straight downward to first slash. Lay over paper. Keep center-front line straight. Separate upper and lower halves required distance. Pin. Separate at shoulder line 1¼″ to 1¾″ and bring bottom ends of lengthwise slash together, thus making a shoulder dart. Very deep darts are to be avoided. When much length is added, make an additional underarm dart as broken line indicates.

For Full Bust (I). Cut waist front from waistline up about two-thirds of length. At right angles cut toward armhole as shown. Separate slash enough to obtain bust measurement desired. Place tape as

shown in measuring. Pin to position over paper. Taper bottom edge as shown. If additional length is needed at center front, cut pattern straight in from center front as in **J.** Separate crosswise slash to gain length needed at center front. An additional dart can be used at the waistline.

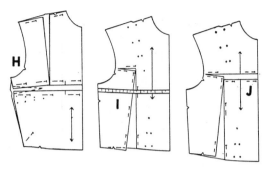

For Sloping Shoulders. On back and front pattern 1″ below end of shoulder, mark straight line across both pieces. Connect this with a line drawn down from edge of neckline at shoulder. Slash in from armhole. Overlap edges to obtain desired shoulder slope. Although armhole will be smaller, do not cut until after fitting.

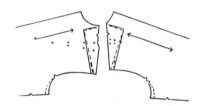

For Square Shoulders. Mark and cut as for Sloping Shoulders. Lay edges over paper and separate required amount. Pin. Raise underarm as indicated.

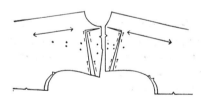

For Heavy-Above-Waist Figure. Slash waist front and back from waist up toward shoulder to gain sufficient width for easy fit.

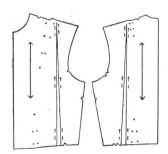

For Large Waistline. Slash pattern pieces to add width to both back and front of waist, as indicated. Divide additional amount needed into fourths and add a quarter to each side. Make same adjustment in the upper part of skirt.

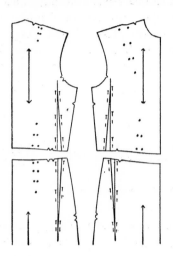

For Narrow Hips. Lay lengthwise tucks in back and front of skirt as shown.

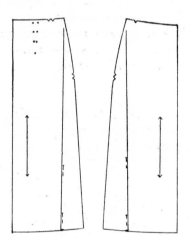

For Full Hips. Slash back and front of skirt lengthwise, from hem up to waistline at hip, as shown. Separate slash and pin to paper strip so hip is correct measurement. Remember to divide the amount needed so as to add fullness where necessary yet have it well distributed. If much width is added to the hip of a straight skirt, it may be too full at bottom. To avoid this, after spreading the slash the necessary amount, make a small dart at hipline, as at **K**, keeping slashed edges of pattern below parallel, thus retaining straight side seams. Add amount necessary to even bottom of skirt as shown. Make same adjustment on back of skirt.

See top of next column.

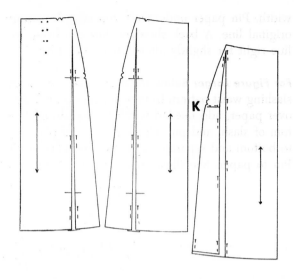

For Round, Full Back. Slash waist back lengthwise from middle of shoulder straight down to waistline. Lay over paper and separate as far as measurements require. Slash across at fullest part of back from center back to lengthwise slash. Separate this slash at center back far enough to give ease at full part. Extend center-back line to make straight edge. Pin. Cut skirt from waistline to hem line and separate the amount necessary. Pin.

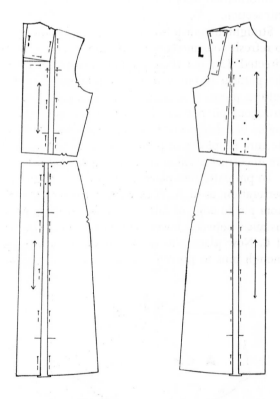

For Narrow Shoulders (L). Slash straight down from shoulder and out toward armhole about 1" above notch. Lap edges until shoulder is required width. Pin paper underneath top edge to restore original line. A back shoulder dart can bring the line right for slightly altered front shoulder.

For Figure Larger Below the Bust. Gain width by slashing waist pattern from waistline upward. Lay over paper, add needed width by separating bottom of slash, and pin. Cut skirt pattern from top to bottom and separate same distance as in waist. Pin to paper. See illustration at right, bottom of preceding page.

When you have compared all measurements and made notations of any differences, then *pin* pattern together, taking up the proper allowance for seams, and try on. Stand before your mirror and examine every line carefully. Can you close your eyes and visualize your fabric made up? When a Thermoplastic Dress Form has been molded to your figure, fittings are possible without assistance, and time is saved in assembling.

Pattern Layout—Cutting and Marking

YOU ARE NOW READY TO LAY PATTERN OUT ON YOUR fabric. Study the pattern layouts or cutting guides on the pattern instruction sheet. Three things determine which one you use:

1. Width of fabric
2. Your size
3. Up-and-down fabric

Information about matching motifs is given in this section.

Straighten your fabric (see page 15 if you want to refresh your memory on this point) and fold as directed. Lay out the pattern pieces as shown on the pattern layout you are using. Rearrange the pattern pieces if necessary, but always follow instructions on pattern and instruction sheet as to grains of fabric—lengthwise, crosswise, true bias. Be sure all pieces of pattern to be placed on fold are in correct position as regards grain of fabric.

To pin pattern in place, place a pin through one perforation, as at **A**. With ruler, measure distance from pin to edge of fabric, as at **B**. Measure same distance between lower perforation and edge, as at **C**. Now place pins around pattern edge, using enough pins to prevent fabric from slipping. You are not ready to cut until all pieces are in position and you have used plenty of sharp pointed pins so that the material is held firmly.

Always try to have plenty of room before you start to lay pattern out. If your table is not large enough, have a cutting board to lay on the bed or floor. When you have to cut on a small surface, lay out all pattern pieces before cutting any. Pin pattern in place, a few pieces at a time, and roll fabric up with pattern inside roll.

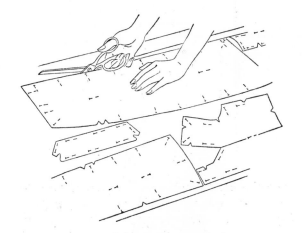

Cutting. Check each piece of pattern and its position on your fabric. Check correct grain line. Then proceed to cut, using a sharp, long, pointed shears. Cut carefully and in long smooth lines. Do not cut so that the edges of your fabric appear chopped and irregular.

Because neck measurements vary so widely, it is advisable to allow 1″ extra outside pattern edge of neckline. If neckline is too high or small, it is easy enough to cut it down when fitting, but it

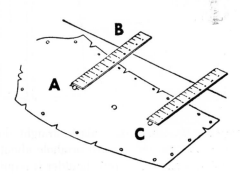

is difficult to adjust a neckline that has been cut too large, or too low, especially. Do not cut out collar until blouse or dress has been fitted and you are ready to make collar.

As each piece is cut, fold and put to one side. Do not remove pattern pieces. Do not lift fabric up from the table when cutting, but place one hand on the material, opposite shears, and keep shears on the table.

Pattern Marking. Before removing the pattern, mark perforations with chalk or tailors' tacks. See *Chart Your Way* on page 33. Also mark the center-back and center-front fold with a long basting stitch. This will be a guide to you in keeping the grain of your fabric on the straight in fitting and in placing of pockets and other details.

Remove pattern from fabric only when you are ready to work on that particular section. The perforations, notches or printed instructions on the pattern are an aid to you in assembling.

Matching Motifs. For fabrics with plaids, stripes or prints of large motifs, allow extra yardage so that the sections may be cut to match at joinings. Pattern pieces may not be placed so economically on these fabrics as for plain colors.

Plaids and Stripes. When cutting plaids, place back section on fabric so vertical bars are even on both sides of center back and with a crossbar below the shoulder line as shown. Without pinning to position, outline pattern piece with chalk, then mark position of main crossbars on edge of pattern

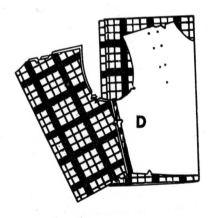

piece. Place front section on correct grain, with center front at correct vertical line. Lay back pattern along edge of front at underarm, as at **D**, adjust front so crossbars match as shown. Avoid placing boldest lines where they will accentuate the widest part of body, such as fullest part of bust

or hips. Match crossbars of sleeves to blouse, starting at bottom of armhole. It often is a time-saver in matching plaids or stripes to cut a duplicate sleeve, blouse and skirt pattern; then all pieces can be laid on at the same time and lines matched perfectly.

Cut all pieces running in same direction. In assembling, match line for line at all joinings.

To cut plaid on bias, draw diagonal line across each pattern piece and place pieces on same lines of fabric, drawn line over plaid line.

Bias-cut stripes should be planned similarly. Mark pattern pieces with line indicating slant of stripe, as at **E**. Lay pieces on so that stripes meet in waist and skirt.

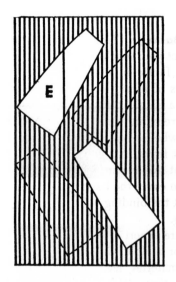

Large Prints. Motifs should be planned to fall becomingly in different sections. They should line up around skirt and meet evenly at seamlines, if possible. See **F**. Avoid buying prints that are not correctly aligned with fabric grain. They cannot be cut satisfactorily. Be sure that all pieces of dress you are cutting are cut one way of fabric, so that flowers, for instance, do not run head down in one piece and head up in another.

READ AND KNOW THE PRECEDING PAGES BECAUSE they were put into this book to provide a background and an attitude of appreciation for sewing effort—also to show you how important is the mastery of the little skills that make for success in the creative art of sewing.

To be sure of accuracy, good fit and professional workmanship in your finished products, learn these few methods of charting your steps. They are well worth the few extra minutes they take and may save you much more time by eliminating annoying mistakes.

Machine-Basting. Time is saved by machine-basting. Set your machine for the longest practical stitch for fabric in use. Then hold or pin two thicknesses of fabric together and machine-baste. Or baste a single thickness to retain shape and prevent stretching. See *Stay-Stitching* below. For example, when a bias binding is to be applied to fabric that frays, it is good to turn the edge over to the right side a scant ⅛″ and machine-baste it in place; then cover the basting with your bias binding so that the binding will not pull off in washing or wearing.

If you are expert at placing two pieces of fabric together or at following a line on the edge of a piece of material, learn to use machine-basting, for it saves time and is a real convenience. Factory workers machine-baste a great deal, but usually their fingers are very skilled in handling fabric so that there is no stretch or pulling and the pieces are blended together as one.

Machine-basting is particularly useful where the basting will be covered when the work is finished and need not be removed. For temporary basting that is soon removed, or in places where needle marks would show, you may prefer to baste by hand. Allow bobbin thread to extend at both ends of a machine-basting for ease in pulling out. To remove machine-basting, clip top thread at intervals of 5 to 8 stitches and pull bottom thread out. Never use machine-basting where one fabric is to be eased to the other.

Stay-Stitching. This is machine-stitching used to retain shape and prevent stretching, such as around neckline and armhole, along shoulder and at waistline of skirt. Make stitching close to seam-line but in seam allowance so final stitching of seam will conceal stay-stitching.

Even-Basting. Use a long, slender needle and knot your thread. See page 153 for directions on making a knot. Take long running-stitches, several at a time. Use for seams in preparation for machine-stitching or fitting. To remove, clip thread every few inches and pull out. Don't pull whole line out at once, as this may mar your fabric.

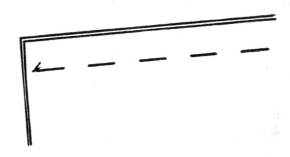

Uneven-Basting. Fastest basting-stitch. Should be generously used in holding fabrics together for stitching. Pick up several stitches on needle before pulling it through, making short stitches underneath and long on top. Some like to call this the "galloping stitch."

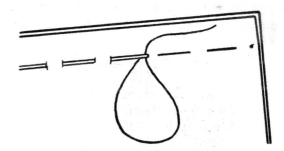

Pin-Basting. Lay the two fabric edges together and hold them so with pins. Place pins at right angles to the edge, heads to the seam edge, spacing

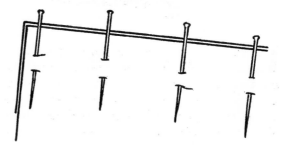

them approximately 3″ to 5″ apart. If you are expert at handling fabric, and it is firm and not slippery, pins can be spaced farther apart. Remove and put pins away as you come to them in stitching.

Diagonal-Basting. Take a short crosswise stitch through fabric, then in line with first stitch take a second short stitch in the same direction, thus forming diagonal stitch on surface. Work either toward or away from yourself, or from left to right, depending on which seems easiest for you. The under stitch may be ⅛″ to ⅜″ in length; the diagonal one from ½″ to 3″ or 6″ long, according to weight of fabric. Used to hold two layers of fabric together without slipping, especially linings and interlinings and drapery fabric. The longer stitch is most often used in home furnishings. The smaller stitch is also called *padding-stitch* and is used in tailoring.

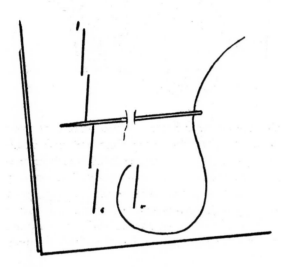

Slip-Basting. Invisible hand-basting used when working from right side of fabric, as in joining shaped sections, such as inside to outside curves, or matching stripes and plaids. Lay the two pieces of fabric right side up; turn under edge of one and lay it over other edge. Pin in position, placing pins

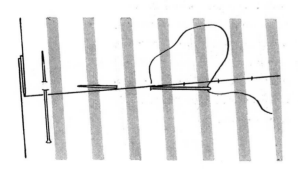

crosswise of seam. Bring needle up from wrong side in fold, close to edge. Insert needle below fold, directly opposite where needle came out. Again bring needle out through fold and close to edge. Continue doing this, thus making a series of small straight stitches crosswise of fold on right side, as shown.

How to Notch Fabrics. Patterns call for notches along the cut edges at certain points as a guide for correct matching of pieces. Barely lift edges of fabric and snip out a very shallow notch. For sheer fabrics, or those that fray easily, it is desirable to cut the notch outward, away from pattern, to avoid weakening seam line.

Marking with Chalk. After pattern pieces are cut from fabric, pin through each perforation. Use tailors' chalk to mark fabric above pin, then turn fabric over and chalk across fabric where pin shows through. This insures marking both sides alike.

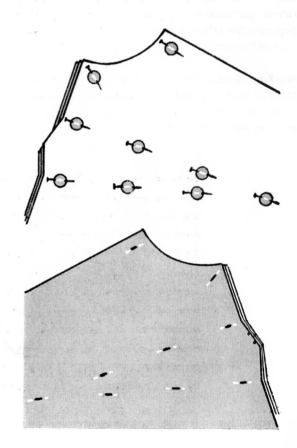

Marking with Chalked Thread. Use a double thread. Draw it through or over a piece of tailors' chalk, as shown. Then thread through perforations and fabric, leaving chalk mark on fabric. Thread will need to be rechalked frequently.

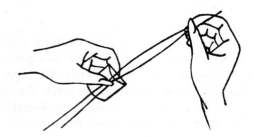

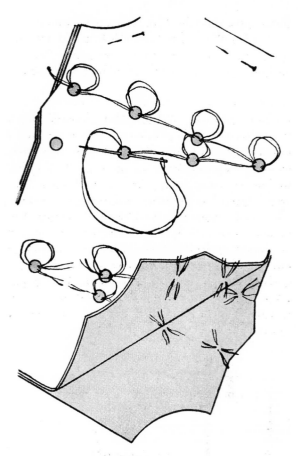

Tailors' Tacks. These are used to mark pattern perforations on your fabric. Use double thread about a yard long, contrasting in color with that of your fabric. Start by taking a stitch in first perforation through both thicknesses of fabric, allowing end of thread to extend about 1″. Take a back-stitch beside first stitch, leaving a loop the size of a finger ring. Keeping thread easy between per forations, take stitch through second perforation and then back-stitch, leaving another loop. Continue from perforation to perforation, making a loop in each, until all are marked. Clip threads between perforations in order to remove pattern. Separate the fabric. Clip the threads, thus marking each side exactly the same.

Marking Center Back and Center Front. When front or back of pattern is laid on fold of fabric, always run a line of basting along fold before removing pattern from fabric.

Left-Handed Individuals. If you work with your left hand rather than your right and find hand-sewing instructions confusing, hold the illustration to a mirror and in the mirror you will see exactly how you should hold your needle or make your stitches. A little practice will save time and enable you to read a detailed picture easily. Work from what the mirror shows, rather than from the text.

Patterns for cutting fabric have been a great boon to women who sew. Considerably more than one hundred and ten million patterns are sold each year, and it is estimated that the average pattern is used at least three times.

An itinerant tailor, Ebenezer Butterick, through the urging of his wife, Ellen, was the first to make patterns available in the United States to women who sew. He made patterns and rented them to customers, who cut from them. The first made were for men's and boys' clothing. In addition to tissue-paper patterns, there are custom-made or drafted patterns made to individual measurements. There are also plain and printed patterns. In rare instances, muslins, or toiles, made by draping fabric, are sold as patterns for cutting.

Darts and Tucks

DARTS ARE USED CHIEFLY IN FIRM FABRICS TO HELP shape the garment and provide fullness for bust, hip or elbow. Their placement, length and width are usually part of the fashion design, to provide fit and control of fullness without disrupting the design lines. Darts should be so made that they will lie smooth and end without a bulge. Tucks are narrow stitched folds used as decoration and to control fullness. They are made on the straight of the fabric, or the crosswise or bias, by hand or machine, and are often placed in groups.

Even though the position of darts is indicated on paper patterns, sometimes a change in position can make them function better and give a more becoming line. Remember, the functional purpose of bust darts is to provide fullness yet give an upward lift to the bust line; therefore fit all such darts to serve you to the best possible advantage.

Match markings of darts and pin or baste together before stitching. Always begin pinning at wide part of dart, pinning marks carefully. Stitch in same way, unless making single-thread darts, which are stitched from point down.

Place darts so that they do not detract from general lines of garment and are inconspicuous. Where there is much fullness, two or three small darts distribute it better than a single large one. Used as trimming, darts may be stitched on right side of garment, thread ends pulled to underside and tied, pressed as stitched, then pressed to one side or to form box-pleat effect. Single-thread darts can also be used as trimming and are especially neat for sheer fabrics, having no tie ends.

Shoulder Darts. Beginning at top or wide end, stitch toward point, with last few stitches parallel to fold as in **A**. Draw thread ends to wrong side and tie. Press toward center. For wools, silks and heavy linens, stitch to point; slash dart and overcast raw edges. Press flat, as in **B**. See illustration at bottom of previous column.

Underarm or Bust Darts. These are done like hip and shoulder darts but are put in horizontally or diagonally instead of lengthwise. In making bust darts, slant them upwards whenever possible, keeping the bust high for a younger line. Press such darts downward.

Body or Fitting Darts. These are wider at the center and run out to nothing at each end. **C** shows how a few stitches continue along the fabric fold at both ends of dart. Draw threads to wrong side and tie. For shallow darts in washable fabrics, stitch back on fold or reverse-stitch dart ends to secure thread. Clip dart, as indicated, to prevent drawing. Press toward center.

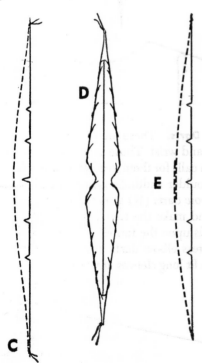

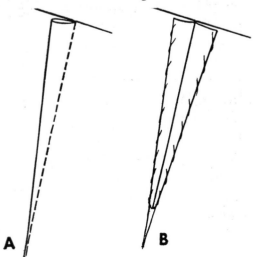

When darts are deep or in finely woven fabric, tie thread ends, then cut along crease of dart and clip edges to within ¼″ of the stitched line, as in

D. Overcast raw edges and press flat. Single-thread method can be used by stitching from both ends toward center, as in **E**.

Waistline Darts. (**F**) Used to adjust waistline fullness of bodice and skirt. Stitch to point, keeping last few stitches parallel to fold. Press toward center front or back. When stitched from right side as decoration, make single stitching or pull thread ends to wrong side and tie.

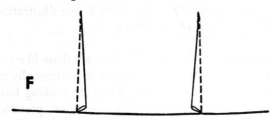

Neckline or Back Shoulder Darts. (**G**) Darts may be required at back of neck or back shoulders to give ease across back, to lift garment up on shoulders, and to assure smoother fit. In sheer fabrics, 3 to 5 darts may take up any excess fullness; in opaque fabrics, 2 or 3 are sufficient. Press shoulder darts toward center.

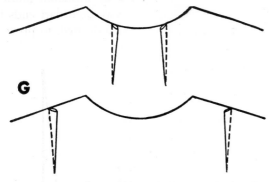

Sleeve Darts. These are of three types—shoulder, elbow and wrist. Those at *shoulder* are used when fashion calls for them to control sleeve fullness or to add shoulder width. See *Lined Short Sleeves*, page 83. *Elbow* darts (**H**) are used to give ease at the elbow and make the sleeve comfortable. Their size depends upon the fatness or thinness of the upper arm. Press elbow darts down. *Wrist* darts (**I**) are used to fit long sleeves at wrist.

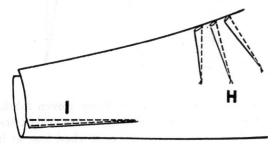

Single-Thread Darts. Make machine ready for stitching with bobbin thread drawn up, as at **J**. Unthread machine needle, then rethread needle

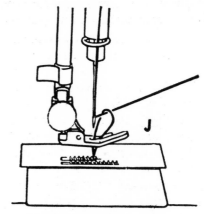

with end of bobbin thread, as in **K**, reversing the usual threading direction. Knot thread ends together as at **L**. Turn the spool to draw the bobbin thread up, winding it on the spool as in **M**. Wind

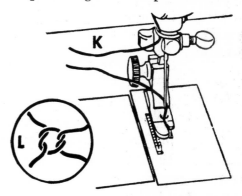

enough thread to stitch each dart. Begin stitching dart at point. The machine has to be rethreaded with bobbin thread and ends tied together for each single-thread dart.

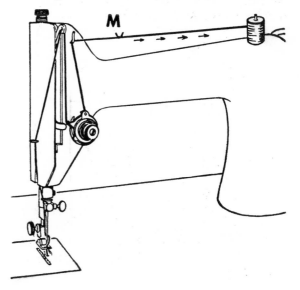

Machine Tucker. With this attachment, tucks may be made without basting, from finest pin tucks to those 1″ wide. The Tucker can be set for the size of tuck desired and also for space between tucks. While stitching one tuck, the attachment marks line for the next. Full instructions are in your attachment instruction book.

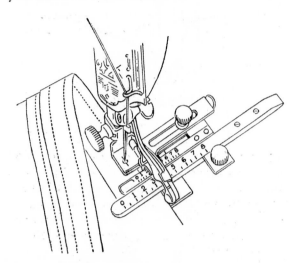

Single-Thread Tuck. Make machine ready for stitching. After basting tucks, lay fabric under machine foot. Draw bobbin thread up through fabric, as at **N**. Unthread needle and rethread with end of bobbin thread again, as in **K**. Follow instructions and illustrations given under *Single-Thread Darts* on preceding page.

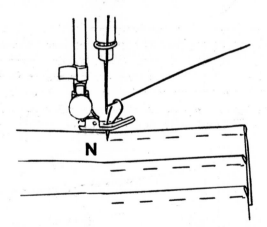

Fullness Tucks. Fashion often asks for tucks in the front of a blouse, or in front and back, or on the tops of the sleeves, or all or part way around a skirt from the waistline down. These provide decoration and control fullness. They are especially appropriate for sheer fabrics. Such tucks are easily made with the machine Tucker. Pull threads through for tying on wrong side, or back-tack for a few stitches to secure thread ends.

Cluster Tucks. May be grouped, possibly five groups across a yoke or at regular intervals around waistline or at bottom of sleeves. Fashion determines the size and length of such tucks.

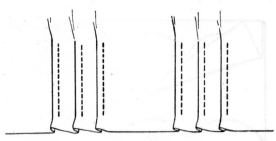

Cross Tucks. Usually very fine and used almost invariably in crisp material such as organdie, starched muslin or taffeta. When tucks cross each other, as in yokes, cuffs or trimming bands, place mats and doilies, do your crosswise tucking first with the Tucker, then do the lengthwise tucks so that each crossing will be true.

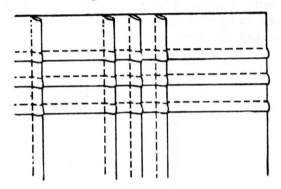

Tucked Smocking. Use Tucker or Edge-Stitcher and make as many scant ¼″ tucks as you wish. Then, using Quilting Foot as guide, stitch crosswise of tucks for effect shown. Stitch first in one direction, then back in opposite direction.

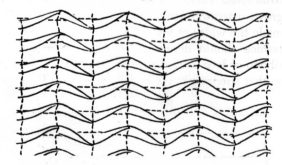

Scalloped Tucks. Measure for depth of tucks plus ⅜″. Fold right sides together, basting as at **O**, to make tuck on wrong side. Mark scallops, using basting line as guide for base of scallops. For greater ease in following outline, use your Quilting Foot for stitching. Use a small stitch and make one stitch across the base of each point as shown. After all scallops are stitched, trim off excess fabric and clip edge in at points as near to the stitching as possible, as at **P**. Remove basting. Turn scallops inside out and press. Tuck effect appears as at **Q**.

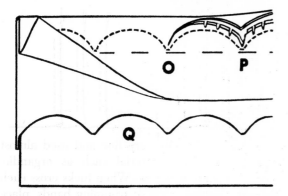

Cord Tuck with Zigzag Trim. A simple trim obtained by running a fold of material through a slot of the Zigzagger. Tuck width is controlled by width of zigzag stitch set. You can add a touch of color by stitching with a contrasting thread. See booklet that comes with attachment for details.

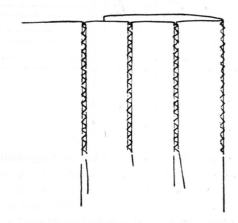

Graduated Tucks. When each succeeding tuck grows narrower, the space between is usually made the width of lower tuck. Fabric and current fashion should determine width and spacing. If ribbon or lace is used to edge tucks, stitch on first so that stitching is concealed under tuck.

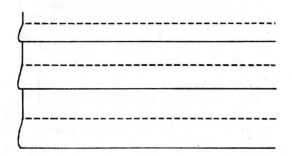

Nun Tucks. For curved edges, as in flared skirts or sleeves; often in groups of 3, 5 or 7. To have

them hang properly, evenness is especially necessary. To keep under fullness even, tuck must be put in by hand first, even if machine-stitched later.

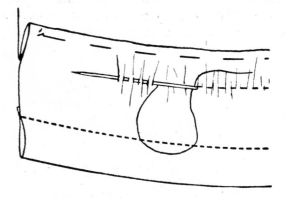

Hand-Run Tucks. To keep line true, space tucks evenly and crease on a fabric thread. Begin with back-stitch. Use long, slender needle, fine thread and tiny running-stitches to make them decorative on sheer fabrics. May be as narrow as a pin tuck or wide enough to provide fullness as in the yoke or sleeve of a baby dress.

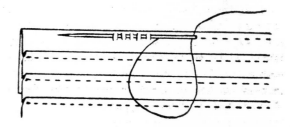

Shell Tucks. First run tucks with machine Tucker for evenness. Then with fine needle and thread, take two stitches across tuck, drawing tight to form scallop. Run needle along under side of machine-stitching to point for next stitch. Illustration for *Lingerie Hem* on page 122 shows how tuck will look when finished.

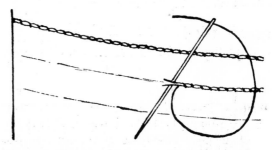

Overhand Tucks. Dainty trimming for baby things and lingerie, on a curve or above a scalloped edge. Mark first to keep spacing even, and crease. Overhand the crease. For a cross-stitch effect over tuck, use a contrasting thread, working first from the right, then returning from the left.

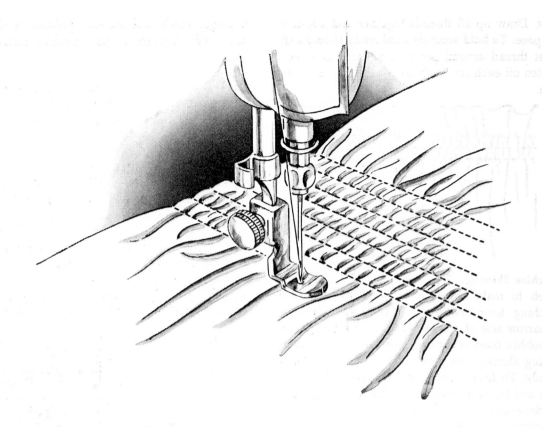

Gathering, Shirring, and Ruffling

GATHERING FABRIC MEANS DRAWING IT UP ON A thread for fullness. *Shirring* consists of three or more rows of gathers to hold fullness evenly. Only soft or sheer fabrics should be gathered or shirred. Tuck stiff or wiry fabrics. The bias of fabric gathers best, and crosswise of fabric next best; gathers on the length are least satisfactory. Gather by machine for speed, strength and evenness, using the attachment best suited to your purpose.

Spacing Gathers. Divide space for gathers into even sections, and fabric to be gathered into the

same number of sections, marking each with notches or pins. Make gathers. Pin corresponding markings together, draw up bobbin thread and adjust gathered fullness.

Stroking Gathers. This straightens the folds below the gathering line to make them hang evenly. Simply draw the needle down lightly between the folds.

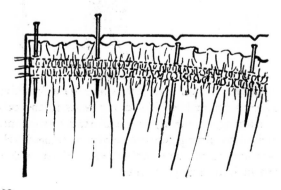

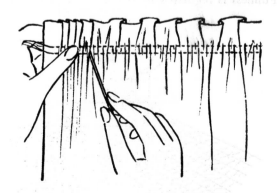

Hand-Shirring. Use fine running-stitches, spacing rows evenly. Start and finish each row with a knot. Draw up all threads together and adjust to fit space. To hold securely until ready to finish off, twist thread around pin in a figure 8 as shown. Fasten off each row with back-stitching on wrong side.

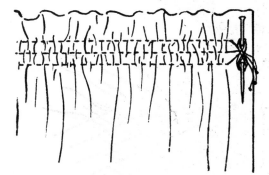

Machine Shirring. Use a strong thread and a long stitch to make three or more parallel rows of stitching. Keep lines evenly spaced by using wide or narrow side of presser foot as guide. Bring ends of bobbin threads together and pull at same time, sliding shirring along them to distribute fullness evenly. To fasten, pull each top thread to wrong side and tie to its own bobbin thread. Decorative machine-shirring is illustrated with machine smocking, page 136.

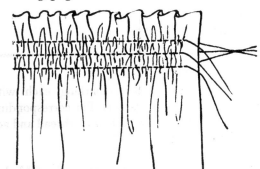

Gathering Foot. This attachment gathers fabric evenly under the needle, the stitches holding gathers securely. Use for shirring soft and sheer fabrics. Fullness is regulated by the length of stitch used.

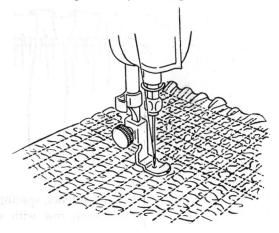

A longer stitch will increase fullness, a shorter stitch will decrease it. See machine instruction book.

Waffle Shirring. Done with the Gathering Foot. Gather fabric in one direction, then turn and stitch across gathers, as illustrated at bottom of previous column.

Machine Ruffler. This attachment is a great time-saver, especially when gathering long lengths of fabric for ruffles, etc. It both gathers and pleats. Practice on scraps of various weights of fabrics until you know the best results with each. Before starting to work on a fabric, always test adjustment for fullness on a scrap. Study directions in your machine instruction book so that you understand how to adjust Ruffler for spacing, and for amount of fullness or size of pleats you wish.

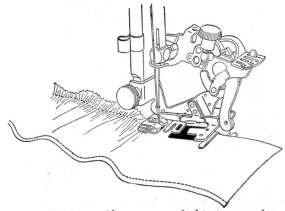

Group Shirring. Short rows of shirring used to hold in fullness at shoulders, waistline or sleeves. Keep spacing between rows even and see that all

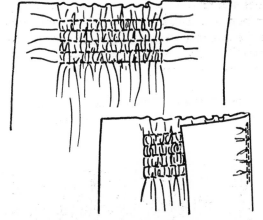

rows line up straight at both ends. Follow *Machine Shirring* for making. Tie thread ends at one end of shirring, on wrong side and finish with a fine tuck. After fitting garment, adjust to desired fullness and tie the other thread ends. Finish with a fine tuck so shirring is boxed.

Staying. When shirrings are used over large surface, a stay of bias-cut lightweight fabric can be used on wrong side to keep them in place. Cut stay the size and shape of shirred section, plus seam allowance. Turn under edge; pin, baste, then whip to place.

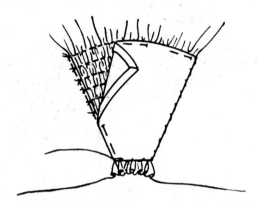

Gathering with Elastic Thread. This is practical when gathering fabric for home furnishings or children's clothes. Wind elastic thread on machine bobbin by hand without tension. Special pointers on use are given in instruction folder provided with elastic thread.

Gathers in a Slash. Follow pattern instructions for shaping garment. Reinforce before cutting slash by stitching along each side of line indicated for slash to a point just beyond end, as at **A**. Then slash between lines. Gather long edge of slash, drawing up thread until two edges are same

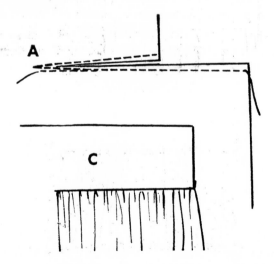

length. Fold along slash, as in **B**. Pin and baste edges together. Stitch so that gathering line is concealed in seam. Pull thread ends to wrong side and tie. Overcast edges. Press seam away from

gathers, as at **C**. If desired, top-stitching may be added close to edge above gathers.

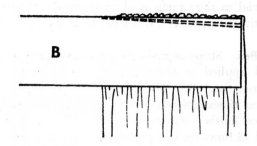

Corded Shirring. Mark line for shirring; lay cord along it, folding fabric over and stitching with Cording Foot. Stitch in as many cords as desired before drawing up cords. Push fabric along cords until shirring is even on cords and of correct length. Straighten fullness by pulling crosswise of cords. To hold cord permanently in place and to prevent cording from slipping, slip-stitch shirring to cord on wrong side. Use for maternity

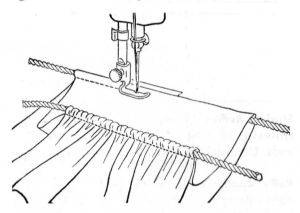

dresses by inserting medium-fine elastic cords which "give" as figure grows larger. For the neck and sleeves of a blouse, use decorative cord and finish ends with tassels or buttons so that fullness can be opened up for laundering or pressing.

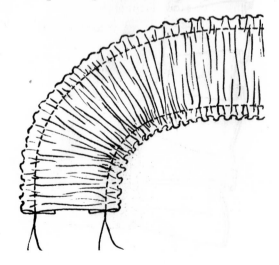

Tucked Shirrings. Make by stitching tucks in fabric with a fairly long stitch, then drawing up thread to shirr tucks to desired length. Most effective when tucks are from ⅛″ to ⅜″ wide.

Ruffles. Strips of material gathered on one edge and applied as trimming. The more sheer the fabric, the fuller the ruffle should be. Cut strip three times finished length for very full ruffle; twice finished length for a moderately full one; and 1½ times for the minimum. Bias ruffles can be made less full than straight ones.

Bias Ruffles. Cut on true bias. Seam on straight of fabric with plain seam; overcast edges and press open. Use a French seam on sheers.

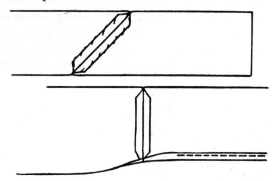

Straight Ruffles. These gather best when cut on crosswise of fabric. Clip seams diagonally on ends. Use machine Hemmer for narrow hems.

Ruffle Applied with Flat-Fell Seam. Place ruffle right side up on wrong side of fabric, with gathering line ⅜″ from edge, and stitch. Smooth fabric and ruffle out flat, right side up. Turn raw edge over ⅛″ and turn seam down over ruffle; pin. Distribute gathers evenly; then stitch flat as shown.

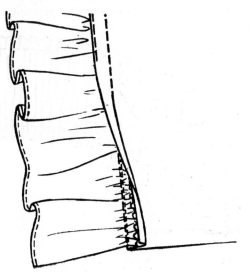

Pleated Ruffle Applied with Cording. Stitch pleated ruffle in position, wrong sides together, as at **D**. Lay cording on top of pleating along seam

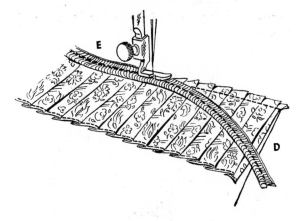

line on right side and stitch, using Cording Foot, as at **E**. Fold ruffle over so that right sides are to-

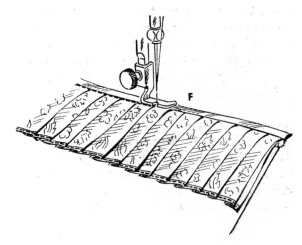

gether with cording between and stitch close to turned edge, as at **F**, using Cording Foot. Ruffle appears as in **G** on right side.

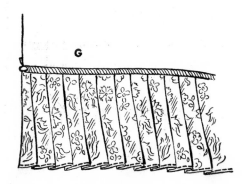

Ruffle with Heading. This type of ruffle can be applied in two different ways: The first, used often in curtains, shows ruffle hemmed top and bottom, gathered, and then stitched to hemmed edge. Picoted ruffles, gathered or pleated, are usually applied in this way. In the second, finish bot-

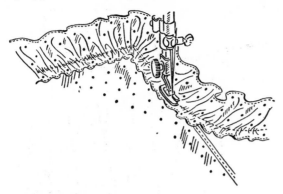

tom edge, then turn upper edge down to make heading the depth desired and baste. Gather along lower edge of heading, using machine Ruffler and a small stitch. When applying ruffle, make second stitching on top of first.

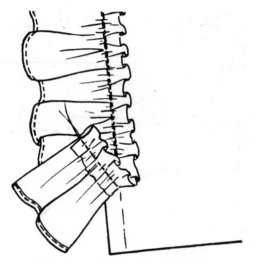

Ruffle in Seam. Baste hemmed and gathered ruffle to one edge on right side. Lay second edge

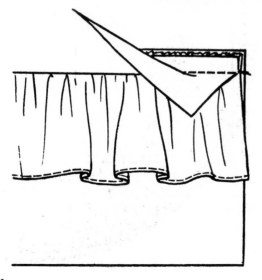

over ruffle, right side down, and stitch, concealing line of gathers. Cut these ruffles, which are usually narrow, on a true bias.

Ruffle in French Seam Turn. Gathered edge of ruffle is concealed inside a French seam turn. Place ruffle to wrong side of fabric. Pin ruffle in position.

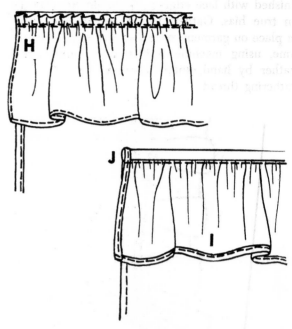

Baste and stitch ruffle in place, making a scant ⅜″ seam as in **H**. Trim seam about ⅛″ to even it. Bring fabric over to conceal edge in French seam turn. Pin, keeping ruffle on top as in **I**. Stitch along folded edge to conceal raw edges, as at **J**.

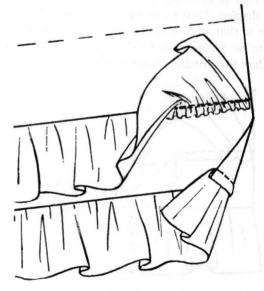

Ruffles in Tiers. Mark line for each ruffle with crease, basting or tracing wheel. Apply lowest ruffle first. Turn next ruffle away from first, spaced according to the effect desired. Baste and stitch in place. Stitch ruffles from wrong side so that when they are turned down all stitching will be concealed.

Double Ruffle. Usually made of light, crisp fabric 1″ to 3″ wide. Edges can be picoted, hemmed or finished with lace edging. Cut ruffle crosswise or on true bias. Gather through center and stitch in place on garment; or gather and stitch at same time, using machine Ruffler. For dainty work, gather by hand, stitch in place, then pull out gathering thread.

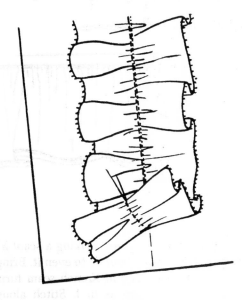

Circular Ruffle. When fashion favors circular ruffles, your pattern will provide for correct fullness and shaping. Finish lower edge of ruffle. Clip top edge so that seam will lie flat. Mark where ruffles are to be placed; pin ruffle in place. Baste, then stitch so that stitching is concealed.

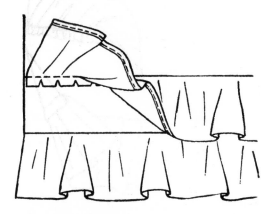

Circular Flounce. Apply to a skirt, sleeve or tunic, to a straight or curved seam. Clip seam allowance at intervals to prevent it from drawing. When

straight part of garment overlaps circular part at joining, top-stitch or seam it from wrong side.

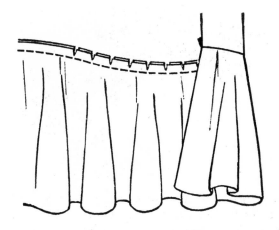

Ruffle on Square Corner. Crowd fullness to each side of the corner to prevent cupping.

Ruffle on Curve. Make ruffle twice as long as curve to prevent cupping on outside edge when ruffle is opened out.

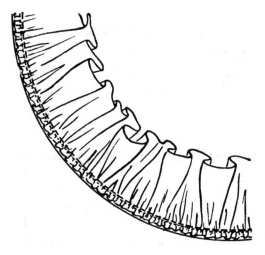

Pleats and Insets

PLEATS, GODETS, AND INSETS ARE USED TO ADD FULL-ness and give line interest and variety to clothes and fabric furnishings. Pleats may be made without a pattern simply by measuring, pinning, basting and pressing, as instructed under *Straight Pleats* below, or by following the pattern perforations, or you may have the pleating done in a shop. This is called Steam Pleating. Steamed pleats stay in very well and usually prove an economy in time.

For pleats to be straight, machine- or hand-baste them. To prevent pleats dragging or not hanging true, stitch from bottom up; for example, from hip line to waistline.

Pleating with Ruffler. The machine Ruffler makes effective shallow pleating. Can be adjusted for single pleats, or groups of pleats. For correct placing, test on a scrap of the fabric you are using before starting work. See full instructions on Ruffler in machine instruction book. Illustrated above.

Straight Pleats. Used when the top and bottom edges of the pleated piece are of equal length; any of the following types may be considered straight pleats. Stitch fabric widths together, leaving only one seam to be completed after pleating; press all seams open, and put in hem. Working on flat surface, mark position of pleats with chalk

or tailors' tacks. Then pin pleats, placing first fold on a lengthwise thread. In cotton or linen, pin and press pleats in place; measure each pleat evenly all the way. In silk, synthetics, or wool, slip-baste folds to position to prevent slipping. Press. If pleats are to be stitched part way down, turn to wrong side and stitch distance desired on folds. Then stitch across top to hold securely while finishing garment. Sometimes such pleats are used in skirt with yoke top.

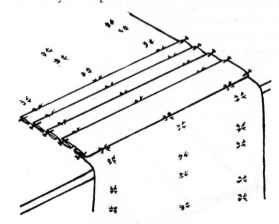

Fitted Pleated Skirt. Follow instructions for straight pleats with this difference: Mark hip line with chalk. Divide space and lay in pleats so that skirt will fit the hips. Slip-baste from hip line down to hem and from hip line up to waistline. Join the open seam, leaving space for a placket. Divide waistline into quarters; mark with pins. Cut piece of tape size of waistline; fold into quarters and mark. Match pins on skirt to those on tape. One at a time, remove top bastings and adjust pleats evenly by making under fold deeper, to take up extra width. Pin to tape. Taper to hip line, re-baste pleats that have been changed and press lightly. Top-stitch pleats along edge or stitch on the inside from 1″ below hip line up to waistline. Finish top with belt or apply to belting.

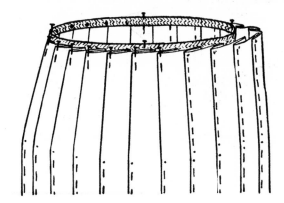

Box Pleats. Full box pleats require fabric strip three times as wide as finished piece. For example, if hip measures 38″ you need 3 widths of 39″ fabric. This allows amply for seams. Seam widths together and press open. Measure and mark position carefully as for straight pleats. Bring folded edges together, pin and baste close to edge. Press lightly. Box pleats are usually stitched part way down to hold them in position. For inside stitching, turn to wrong side and stitch along crease. Start all stitchings at same level, usually hip line. Tie all thread ends. When top-stitching pleats, be sure stitchings start at same level; pull threads through to wrong side and tie.

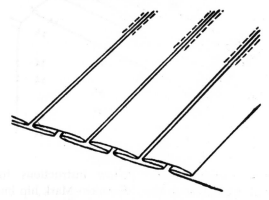

Pleats using only twice the finished length have an underlap ½ as deep as full box pleats. These are frequently preferred for home furnishings, since they take less fabric than do full box pleats.

Inverted Pleat. Just the reverse of a single box pleat. Folded edges meet on outside and fullness lies underneath. Baste fold together. To top-stitch, stitch part way down one folded edge, pivot on needle, stitch across to second fold, pivot again and stitch up other edge. Remove basting.

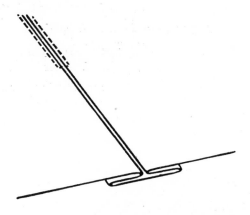

Kick Pleats. Used at side seam or edge of panel at bottom of skirt. Shaping and extra width for pleats are provided on pattern. Therefore, tailor-tack or chalk-mark perforations for guidance. When pleat is stitched, clip seam at top of hem, as at **A**, press it open inside hem and finish hem. Overcast seam edges together. Stitch carefully on right side along top line of pleat to hold it in place and prevent sagging. Pull through and tie thread ends on wrong side. Always stitch up, to avoid spreading pleat open.

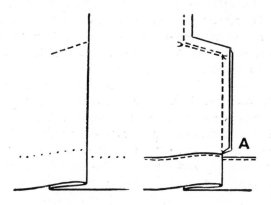

Inverted Pleat on Seam. Baste pleat. Stitch seam from top of pleat upward. Press seam and pleat fold open. Cut a piece of fabric large enough to make the facing under pleat. Baste in place, right side down. Stitch. Overcast edges together. Press. Remove basting. Put in hem, clipping seam at top of hem. See top of next page.

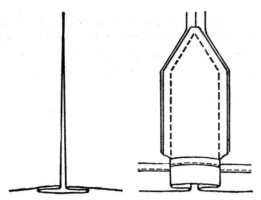

Side Pleats. Groups of pleats all turned in one direction or turning away from a center box pleat. Follow directions for straight pleats. May be stayed by top-stitching part way down or by several rows of stitching crosswise of pleat folds.

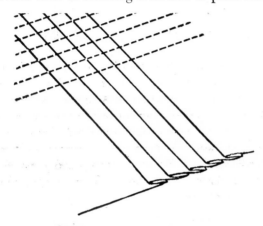

Steam Pleating (sometimes called Machine Pleating). Certain shops specialize in this type of pleating. They do accordion, sunburst, knife and box pleating, in several widths. If novelty pleating is desired, ask the shop how to prepare your material for the right effect. When you receive steam pleating back from the pleater, machine-baste across top edge, to hold pleats, before removing paper.

Ordinarily, for *knife pleating*, allow three times as much fabric as finished piece is to measure. Usually the hip measure is the guide for a skirt. For a bed flounce, pleating is required for the 2 sides and the foot, or about 6 yards of finished pleating. Seam pieces together to form a strip and put in hem before sending to be pleated. For *sunburst pleats,* the usual method is to seam fabric together lengthwise, to form a large square or circle and send to be pleated. Use plain seam, overcast, and press open. Skirt requires a square twice the finished skirt length plus 9″ to 12″. Piece through center for large enough square. Then seams will fall on sides. When square has been pleated, cut out center and adjust at waistline. Mark skirt

length and trim bottom edge. To hem, use rolled hem, or seam binding finish, repressing pleats with tip of iron after it is finished.

Pleated Ruffle or Tier. Several ruffles can be done in one pleating if picoted edge is used. Seam the widths together, measure and mark with bastings depth of each ruffle. Have these basting lines hemstitched and pleating done. Cut through center of hemstitching when finished.

Stayed Pleats. Pleats finished with stitching that holds folded edge all the way to hem. Good for any type of pleat, but especially for pleats in bias-cut skirts. Edge-stitch pleats from hemline to about 1″ below hip line, lift presser foot and pull out skirt a couple of inches. To avoid interrupting the stitching line, snip bobbin thread only and arrange upper part of garment under presser foot; turn spool back to take up slack in top thread.

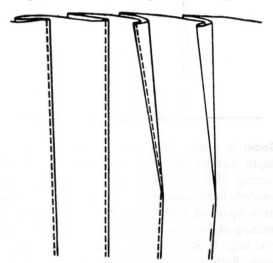

Lower presser foot and continue stitching along folded edge of pleat through all layers of fabric to top of skirt. In this way there is no break in stitching line. Turn to wrong side, thread broken bobbin thread ends into a needle and finish off.

Cartridge Pleats. Unpressed, rounded pleats used for decorative effect in garments. See also drapery headings, page 182. Mark position of pleats on garment. Using some stiffening such as grosgrain ribbon, finish strip desired width. The length should be three times measurement needed. Divide and mark strip evenly. Turn under first end and stitch. Bring up each pleat in turn, pin and stitch. Sometimes a cylindrical object, such as a pencil for small pleats, is helpful in forming pleats uniformly. Then use Cording Foot to stitch very close to the round.

48

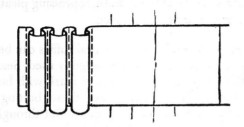

Pleated Inset. Stay-stitch seamline of opening. Clip corners of opening so edges will turn back and lie flat. Baste. Lay pleat in panel section, baste, and press. Lay opening over pleat right side up. Keep pleat straight, pin, and baste, working down from top to bottom on each side. Press, then stitch close to turned edge of opening.

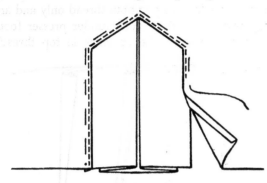

Godet in Slash. Mark cutting line on fabric to depth wanted. Stay-stitch edges of slash before cutting. Cut slash on a fabric thread to depth wanted. Baste inset piece on both sides, working from top down. Taper seam allowance from almost nothing at top to a seam's width at bottom. Ease bias edge of godet along edge of slash for smooth seam. Baste and stitch. Press seam outward. Clip off point at top of inset, as at **B**. To reinforce point in clothes, take tiny stitches at top; in home furnishings make second machine stitching, as illustrated.

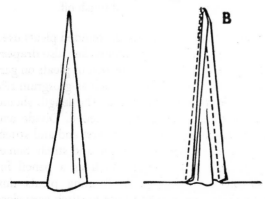

Stayed Godet. When godet is on a seam or extends well up into body of garment, stay top end

with fabric or lining to preserve shape at that point and prevent pulling out. Cut facing piece to cover top of godet on wrong side. Make narrow seam-turn in facing and whip over seams.

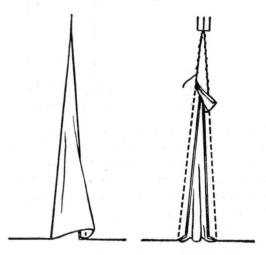

Shaped Godet. Stay-stitching on seamline helps to make smooth line. Clip seam allowance on rounded section and turn back. Baste, then press. Pin circular godet on wrong side, easing bias edge along turn-back, and slip-baste. Stitch along seamline from inside, or stitch close to turned edge for outside stitching. Remove bastings and press. Because of shaped edge, allow to hang overnight before making hem.

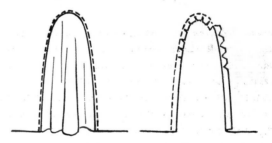

Cutting Godets. Godets are generally cut so that bottom edge measures a little less than half the length. To cut several godets at once, measure off on a strip of fabric, as shown, and mark with chalk. Center line of each godet from top to bottom should lie on lengthwise thread of fabric.

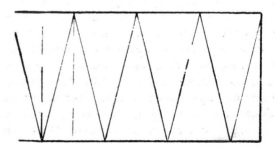

Fit Your Dress

To Assemble a Garment for Fitting. Always work on a flat surface when pinning and basting any garment together. Don't "baste in hand," because seams are easily stretched and apt to be uneven when finished. Working on a flat surface makes it easy to ease edges together. Use a #8 needle and even stitches. Make stitches about ⅜″ long.

Pin and baste darts first. Tucks and pleats are next. Use two rows of machine stitches to control any gathered fullness, making one row close to seamline, the second row ¼″ away, in seam allowance. This insures a flatter seam in the finished garment. If bodice has a yoke, pin and baste to position. When basting a gore skirt or princess-type dress, begin with center-back panel and baste side panels to it. Do the same to front. Baste side seams last, leaving opening on left side for placket.

You have cut your garment as near to your measurements as you could. Even so, when you try it on before your mirror, you may see certain refinements that you will want to make.

Look your prettiest for this try-on. A dress in its fitting stage is no doubt passing through its one ugly hour. Make any adjustments necessary to bring the garment to complete perfection for you. If you are trying on the waist part of a dress, or a blouse, lap it exactly according to the closing markings, adjust shoulders to your figure, tie a string or tape around waistline, so that you can really get the right effect. Chalk around the figure at bottom of waistline tape. This gives a line for consideration when preparing waist for basting to the skirt.

Sloping Shoulders. If one shoulder slopes a little more than another, pin along the seam, taking up the excess necessary. Baste along the pin line. Then stitch the new seam along the basted line. Sometimes a slight padding for the lower shoulder will conceal any difference and make it possible to avoid change in the shoulder seam.

A Square Shoulder. Some have one shoulder higher at the tip. This can cause wrinkles to form diagonally to the bustline. Simply clip the basting in the shoulder seam and let the seam out at the tip. If both shoulders have this tendency, lift the entire front, making the seam deeper at the neck and more shallow at the shoulder tips.

Narrow Shoulders. Sometimes slight padding at the shoulder can give a more uniform appearance to the figure and balance it better with waist and hip. Pads may be worn to advantage by those who need them, even when fashion does not demand them. Use soft pads if they improve your figure, but try to keep them from being obvious.

Short Back. If you stand very erect, your back measurement may be shorter than that of the average figure. Do not emphasize this fault in fitting pattern or garment, but make it less obvious by making the shoulder seams at the back slightly deeper than the pattern calls for. In such a case it is advisable to clip the seam allowance at the back of the neck so the garment cannot draw there.

Check Your Darts at This Time. Make sure they take up enough fullness, are correct in length and width, and give a good line. A dart is completely functional, in that it is a means of controlling fullness, yet a well-made dart can be decorative and add materially to the beauty of the garment.

Check the Skirt. Make sure the skirt is positioned correctly on the figure. The skirt may be "easier" and hang better if you stitch outside the basting lines. Or, if it seems slightly loose, stitch inside the lines. Effect is all-important. Do not fit too snug or too loose for the fabric you are using.

If the skirt seems too snug at waistline, clip the seam allowance and adjust to the figure. If it is too large, take in excess at the side seams. In a skirt, if one side at hips is larger than normal, making the skirt appear too snug, open the seam and release enough fullness to give necessary ease. If one side at hips is smaller than normal, rebaste and stitch the seam at the corrected place.

Sometimes it is necessary to lift the skirt on one side at the waistline to have the seamlines hang correctly from the waistline. This is a slight adjustment, but often essential. If skirt hikes in front, first clip the seam allowance across the front waistline. If this does not achieve perfect smoothness, lift the skirt at sides and back enough to give a smooth effect all the way around.

Be sure sleeves are basted into armhole all the way around and any shoulder padding is in place before length is checked. See *Sleeves,* page 82.

WHEN MAKING GARMENTS, YOU PRESS RATHER THAN iron the fabric. The more carefully you press, the better your garment will look when finished. When pressing, the iron has practically no motion. The amount of heat and moisture directed into the fabric and the degree to which the fabric is "dried off" is what gives desired results. A light touch is necessary so that no imprint of iron is made on the surface of the fabric. Your pressing iron should have a good dial control so as to provide right temperatures for all types of fibers—linen, cotton, wool, silk and synthetics.

Three fundamental steps of pressing seams are:

1. Press as stitched, so machine-stitching is imbedded in the fabric for perfect smoothness. Protect fabrics with press cloth and use moisture and heat suitable to fabric.

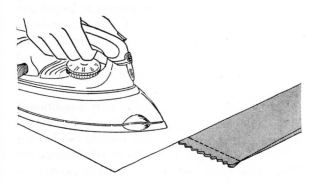

2. Open seams wih point of iron when practical. No moisture is needed at this point except on woolens or wool mixtures, where a very small moistened brush is used. A small, inexpensive paint brush is ideal for this.

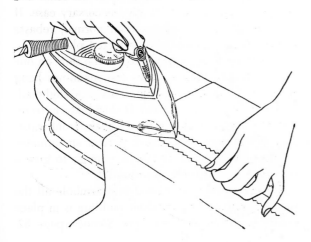

3. Steam-press seam open according to the method best suited to the fabric, which usually is a dry press cloth over fabric and a dampened cloth over the dry.

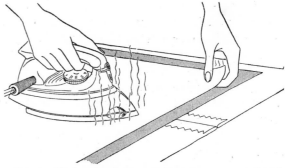

Press all seams, darts, tucks, etc., as you finish stitching. Darts should be given a directional pressing as pattern instructions indicate, over a press mit or tailor's cushion. Always press from wrong side. Set temperature control accurately.

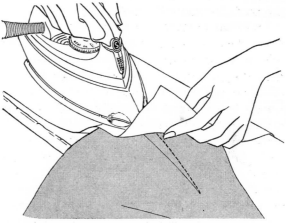

A **seam** is used to form a garment. When it is curved to fit the contour of the body, it should be clipped at intervals, as shown, so that it can be pressed completely flat.

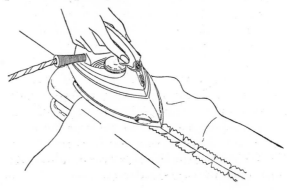

To shrink excess fullness from *sleeve cap:* Make two rows of sewing-machine stitching in the top of the sleeve, draw up bobbin threads as necessary to obtain the right size, then place top of sleeve over sleeve board or ham cushion and press as shown.

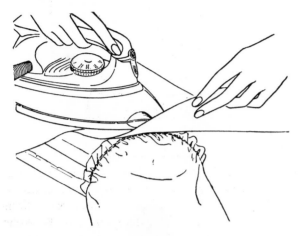

Synthetic fabrics require low heat and usually should not be dampened. This is true also of silk, especially taffeta. If these fabrics are very mussed, use a dry press cloth next to the fabric with a slightly damp cloth over this.

For **woolens,** use slightly more heat and pressure and a heavier, dampened press cloth. (Especially treated press cloths are recommended. They save time and are a protection to fabrics.) Never press entirely dry; rather, leave garment on the board until it is completely dry. A dress may be carefully removed from board and hung on a hanger until dry. If, by mistake, pressed surface becomes shiny, sponge with rough, damp cloth, or brush cautiously with fine wire brush.

If outer fabric is likely to be marked by seam, as with bound seam, lay a strip of paper under each side of the seam edge before pressing.

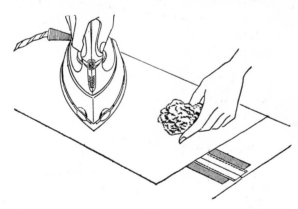

Metallic fabrics should be pressed as little as possible and then dry, with warm (not hot) iron.

Fabrics with raised design—embroidery, appliqué, trapunto work, etc.—should be pressed face down on velvet press pad or turkish (terry cloth) toweling to prevent flattening design.

Velveteen and many deep-napped or pile fabrics may be steamed, but velvets require a temperature in keeping with fiber content. Because they spot easily, moisture is best avoided on synthetic velvets and used sparingly on silk velvet. Such fabrics should be pressed on a velvet press board or on pile fabric especially treated for this purpose. Do not try to pull the fabric over such surfaces, but always lift and press, lift and press. Detailed instructions for use come with velvet pressing kits.

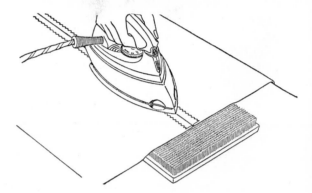

For small pressing jobs and for detail work in narrow places and corners and curves, get used to using your sleeve board. It saves time and effort by bringing detail into better vision and allows bulk of garment to rest on ironing board.

The iron illustrated has a cord control that is convenient for keeping cord out of the way.

Use a **tailor's cushion** or a press mit over end of sleeve board to press darts, to shrink fullness at top of sleeve, or to press the curve of a shoulder. To make such a cushion, cut a pattern of oval shape about 9″ x 12″. From pattern cut two ovals of unbleached muslin which has been previously freed of sizing by soaking in cold water and then pressed. Place the two pieces right sides together and stitch, leaving an opening to turn to right side, as at **A.** Turn and stuff tight and smooth with cotton batting or sifted sawdust. Turn raw edges in at opening and whip together, as at **B.**

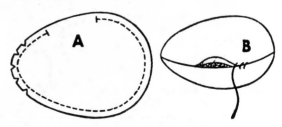

Your Sewing Machine Makes Decorating Easy

Deep-turquoise drapes, with painted walls, matching valance and wall-to-wall carpeting, help to make this room look spacious and charming. A print for couch slip-cover and a Jacquard fabric for the chair add color and variety. Velveteen pillows can be made at little cost. Follow the instructions given elsewhere in this book for making drapes, slip-cover and pillow, and your room can be as beautiful as this one.

Courtesy of *Better Homes and Gardens*

Draperies Provide Privacy for Double-Purpose Rooms

Many houses are now being built or remodeled so that a room serves more than one purpose and is adaptable for various types of entertaining. The plan above shows a large living room with a combination library and guest-room section at one end, which can be divided off and given privacy by the full-length draperies. The sturdy, opaque drapery fabric is equally attractive on both sides.

The charming, informal living room below may also double as a guest room when the traverse-rod draperies are drawn, the sofa is transformed to a bed, and one unit of the tea table nest serves as a bedside table.

Photograph by the makers of Armstrong's linoleum

A SEAM IS THE LINE OF STITCHING THAT HOLDS TWO pieces of fabric together. For strength and long wear, seams should be machine-stitched. Use matching thread. The stitches should be correct in length for the fabric texture and should run evenly in line the full length of the seam. A seam should support the garment but not restrain it. The Walking Presser Foot makes it easy to stitch plastic fabric and bias and curved seams, also to seam together fabrics having fleeced or napped surfaces.

Press seams as stitched, then press open or to one side, and finish appropriately. Give seams the professional look by using the seam finish that fashion recommends for the type of fabric.

Plain Seam. Simplest and most used of all seams. Lay the two edges together, one over the other, doing this on a flat surface. Pin or baste along seamline. Then stitch. After pins or basting are removed, press seam open. Finish seam edges according to instructions that follow, using finish best suited to fabric in hand.

Pinked Seam. Raw edges may be pinked when cut or as a finish. Use regular pinking shears. Ideal finish for firm fabrics that do not fray.

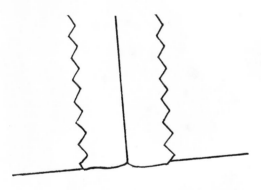

Zigzag Seam Finish. Use the Zigzagger to re-inforce raw edges of seams and thus prevent raveling. Size of stitch used depends on fabric weight. Study instruction booklet accompanying the attachment.

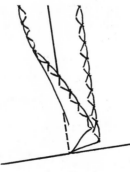

Clean-Stitched Seam (also known as *Edge-Stitched Seam*). Press open a plain seam. Turn each raw edge under a scant ⅛″ and stitch, holding away from garment. (The Edge-Stitcher makes it easy to stitch very close to edge.) This is simplest finish for lightweight fabrics, especially suited to even-weave synthetics.

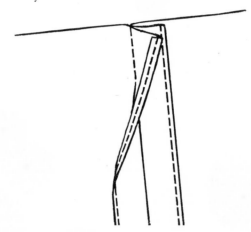

Overcast Seam. Overcast seam edges by hand, taking several stitches on needle before pulling needle out—this for speed and evenness. When fabric is loosely woven and consequently frays deeply, single stitches should be taken. Overcast edges separately when seam is pressed open. If both edges are turned to one side, as sometimes in tailoring and under a pleat, overcast together.

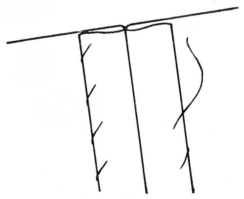

Catch-Stitched Seam. Press a plain seam open. Finish by hand. Working from left to right, with needle in position shown, catch a few threads of fabric near seamline, then into a thread outside seam allowance. Alternate in this way all along the line. Good for flannel or decorating fabrics thick enough not to show stitches through.

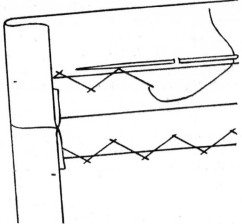

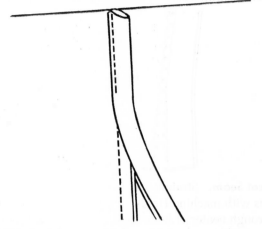

2. Used as finish on home furnishings. Machine-baste seam to right side. Trim edge to ¼". Insert edges between bias binding and pin. Stitch so that first stitching is covered. The Multi-Slotted Binder is ideal for big binding jobs of this kind.

Double-Stitched Seam. Stitch as for plain seam. Then stitch again ¼" outside first stitching line. Trim edge rather close to second stitching. If fabric frays, overcast edge, taking stitches inside second stitching line to prevent their pulling out. Good for soft or embroidered fabrics where all bulk is to be avoided.

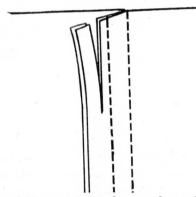

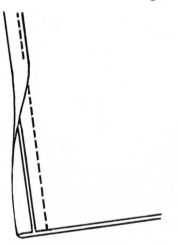

Self-Bound Seam. Make a plain seam. Trim one edge away about ⅛" from stitching line. Turn

Bound Seam. 1. Bind raw edges of plain seam with bias binding, using your machine Binder. If fabric is very heavy, apply binding with two stitchings. See Imitation French Binding, page 121. Ease binding on to prevent edges from drawing up and curling. Used in tailoring for unlined coats and suits.

under other raw edge and fold down over trimmed edge. Stitch down along first stitching line.

Machine-Hemmed Seam. Practical narrow seam made with machine Foot Hemmer. Lay top edge

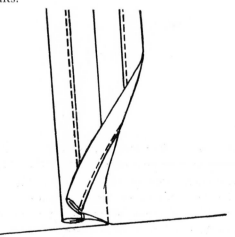

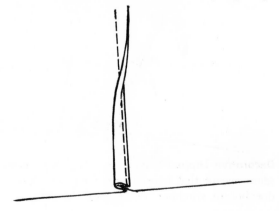

⅛″ in from under edge. Pin pieces together to prevent slipping. Place edge in scroll of Hemmer and stitch so that wide edge is rolled over to cover other edge. Good for children's clothes and firm fabrics. See your machine instruction book for further illustrations.

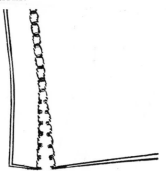

Picot Seam.   Straight-stitch seamline, then go over this with machine Hemstitcher. See page 135. Cut through center of hemstitching. Makes seam without bulk for use on flimsy fabric where no strain occurs.

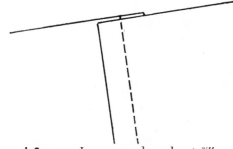

Lapped Seam.   Lay one edge about ⅜″ over the other, both right side up. Stitch down center of overlap. Good for pieced linings, paddings, etc., to avoid bulk, and for joining net or over-all lace. Often used in felt.

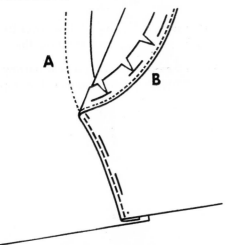

Decorative Lapped Seam.   Same as plain lapped seam except that overlapping edge is turned under before stitching. Often used in curved and shaped sections of garments. When line is curved, mark shape of overlap and underlap with stay-stitching just outside seamline, as at **A** and **B**, as guide for correct placing. Ease curved line by notching or clipping edge. Overlap edges and baste. Stitch on right side. Use slip-basting if inside stitching line is used.

French Seam.   Lay fabric edges together, right side out. Pin or baste along seamline. Stitch, taking half of seam allowance. Trim raw edges and press seam to one side. Turn to wrong side and crease on line of stitching. Stitch along seamline and so enclose first seam. Good for firm lightweight or sheer fabrics.

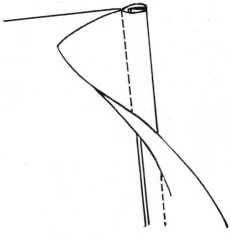

Imitation French Seam.   Stitch plain seam on wrong side. Turn raw edges in toward each other and stitch along turned-in edges.

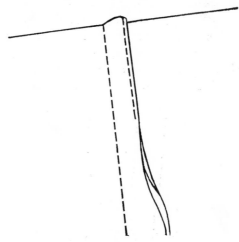

Upholsterers' Welt Seam.   Similar to French seam but made to appear on right side when finished. Make plain seam on wrong side, taking a scant half of seam allowance. Press seam open. Turn to right side and crease on stitching line. Make second stitching ⅛″ to ¼″ in from edge. The raw edges need not always be concealed within second stitching. Good seam finish for slip-covers.

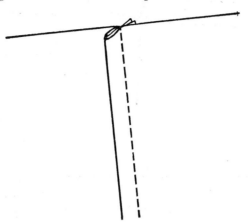

Top-Stitched Seam. Press open a plain, pinked or overcast seam. On right side, stitch evenly along both sides of seamline, using side of presser foot for guide to keep spacing uniform. Good for tailored trim.

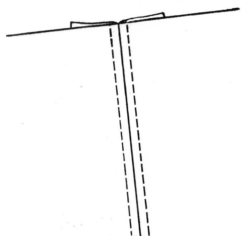

Broad-Stitched Seam. Same as top-stitched seam with an extra row of stitching at each side to catch and hold seam edges.

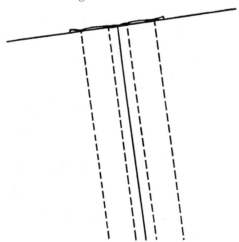

Flat Fell Seam. Pin or baste seam from right side and stitch. Trim away one edge to within ¼″ of seamline. Turn other edge under ⅛″ and pin flat so that raw edge is covered. Stitch. Good for shirts, pajamas, overalls, tailored wash garments, ruffled curtains, etc. Same seam can be made by using Foot Hemmer, but a little practice is required to do it perfectly. Lay pieces together, wrong sides facing, with under piece projecting about ¼″ beyond top piece. Stitch with Foot Hemmer, lining up outside edge of Hemmer with outside edge of seam, and just catching inside edge with stitching. Open seam and press. Then hem free edge flat to garment with Hemmer.

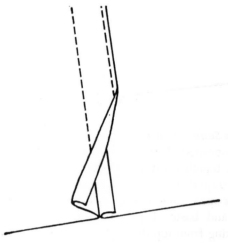

Welt Seam. Baste and stitch seam on wrong side. Trim off one edge. Press to one side so that narrow edge is covered by wide one. Baste flat. From right side, stitch an even distance from seamline so that stitching holds seam allowance flat. For tailored effect in woolens and firm fabrics, especially to panel the front and back gores of skirts. In such a case, the seam edges of the front and back gores would be trimmed away to have the seams panel these gores.

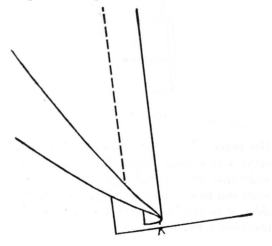

Open-Welt or Tucked Seam. Baste seam allowance on wrong side with short stitches. Do not stitch. Trim one edge ⅛″. Press seam edges to one side, covering trimmed edge. From right side, stitch parallel to seamline to form tuck, which is revealed when bastings are removed. Used for firm fabrics and especially in tailored garments.

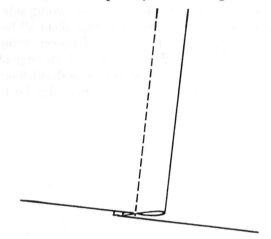

Strap Seam. Cut a true-bias strip twice as wide as strap desired. Turn in edges to center of strip and baste together, using diagonal-basting stitch. Press the strap; do not stretch it. Make a plain seam and press open. Center strap over seam on right side; pin and baste. Top-stitch both edges of strap, working from top down. For unlined coats, make seam to the right side, trim edges to ¼″ of stitching line, press seam open, cover with the strap. In upholstery, seams of this type are sometimes covered with a tape.

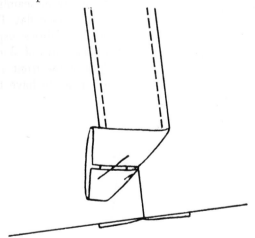

Slot Seam. Baste seam on wrong side and press open. Cut a strip, lengthwise of the fabric, 1″ wider than the two seam edges. Center strip under seam and baste. Stitch an equal distance on both sides of basted line. Remove all bastings. See illustration at top of next column.

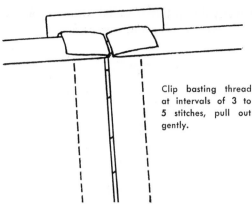

Clip basting thread at intervals of 3 to 5 stitches, pull out gently.

Piped Seam. Decorative finish with fold of bias, ribbon or braid inserted in seam. Fold bias lengthwise, one side narrower than other, and press. Baste to right side along one seam edge, folded edge inward. Lay other seam edge in correct position over this, baste and stitch. To top-stitch, turn top edge of fabric back from piping, baste and stitch alongside piping on right side. Edge-Stitcher can be used to apply piping.

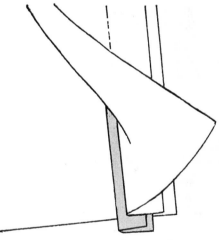

Corded Seam. Cut enough true bias to make length of cording required. See *To Make Cording*, page 124. Using the Cording Foot, machine-baste

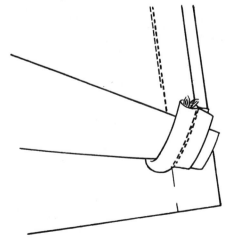

cording to right side of fabric along one seam edge, cord inward, that is, away from the seam. For final stitching, lay other seam edge right-side down in correct position and stitch. Keep foot close to cord, so as to conceal machine-basting. Used for home furnishings. Ready-made welting or cording suitable for finish on home furnishings can be bought by the yard in a variety of colors. Since the fabric to cover the cord must be cut on the bias, it is an economy to buy cording ready-made when short lengths are needed. The reverse is true when more than three yards is needed.

Welted Seam. Term for trim used on slip-covers and other home furnishings. Made with welting or cording inserted in seam. See *Corded Seam.*

Curved Seams. Shorter machine stitches allow more elasticity, so on curves always use small stitches. Curved seams such as those in raglan or drop shoulder sleeves should not be blended before clipping. Press as stitched, clip or notch to prevent puckering when seam is pressed open.

Inward Curved Seam. Baste and stitch seamline. Press as stitched. Clip raw edges, making slashes almost to stitching. Press seams open.

Outward Curved Seam. Baste and stitch seamline. Press as stitched. Notch edges. Press open.

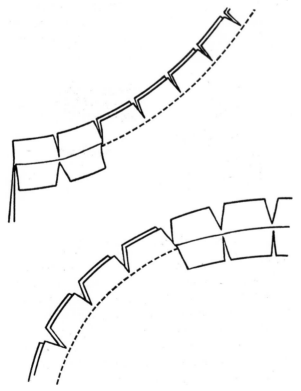

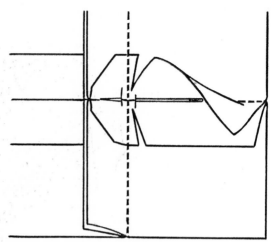

Seams That Meet. Stitch first seams. Press as stitched, then press seams open. Clip off surplus ends or corners on seam edges. Pin and stitch second seam, using a fine needle to hold seams together exactly at crossing, as shown. Clip above and below stitching line where seams cross, to prevent drawing. Press as stitched and press second seam open.

Joining Bias to Straight Edge. Lay bias edge on top of straight edge. Pin and baste in place, easing fullness as you go, so that no strain falls on bias edge. Stitch and press. If pieces are correctly cut, there should be nothing left over at end of seam. If there is, go back and full edge again to make perfect fit. If fabric is so soft as to hold back under machine needle, stitch over paper. When stitching is complete, tear paper away.

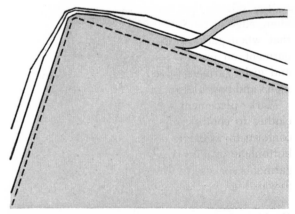

Seam Blending. This is seam thinning, and it is done to prevent bulkiness wherever seam allowances overlap, as on curved facings, pockets and yokes. Flat Fell and Welt seams are two examples of how one seam edge is trimmed away before the other edge is pressed over it and stitched. Seam thinning is important when heavy fabrics are used, as in tailoring and home furnishings.

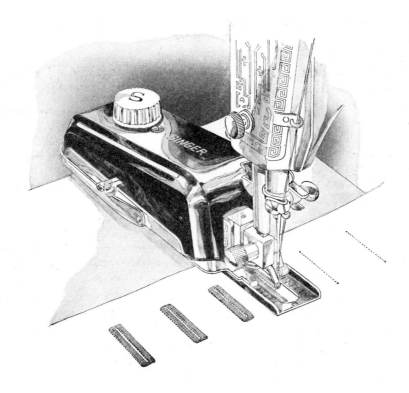

Buttonholes, Buttons, and Fastenings

Fitting a Garment with Button Closing. Make sure that the front edges of the garment are even top and bottom. Lap the buttonhole side over the button side so that there is no strain. Place pins along edge of the lap while trying on garment, so that when garment is removed you can lap the garment on exactly the same line. On women's and girls' garments the lap is right over left; on men's and boys', left over right.

Mark placement of fastenings on women's clothes to control fullest part of the bust and to conform to waistline finish. On beltless jackets a buttonhole usually comes at waistline. On belted garments spaces are divided evenly from bust line to waistline.

Machine-Made Buttonholes. Perfect buttonholes can be made with the Buttonholer shown above. Mark position and length of buttonhole on a fabric thread. Follow complete instructions given with the attachment. Cut opening after stitching is complete. The Buttonholer has five templates for making buttonholes of from 5/16″ to 1 1/16″ in length. One of these is shaped for making an eyelet-end

buttonhole for tailored garments. Additional templates are available for other sizes. You will find this attachment convenient to use, efficient and time-saving.

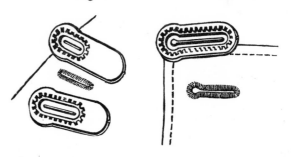

HAND-FINISHED BUTTONHOLES

Marking and Cutting. Lap two edges of garment as it will be worn and pin in place. Crease or mark down center of overlap. Using notched gauge, mark positions of buttonholes with pins. Crosswise buttonholes should start 1/8″ to 1/4″ outside center front line so when buttoned, buttons will be at exact center line. Draw with rule and chalk the exact length of buttonholes, usually 1/6″

to ⅛″ longer than diameter of buttons. Lengthwise buttonholes are cut exactly on center front line. Cut one buttonhole at a time, on a thread, with sharp pointed scissors, Ripper, or razor blade.

Staying. Reinforce buttonhole with matching thread. Take tiny back-stitch on wrong side, bring

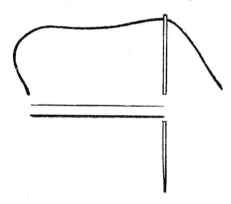

thread through and lay it along slit, ¹⁄₁₆″ from cut edge. Overcast edge and laid thread with stitches about ⅛″ apart.

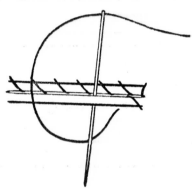

Working. With ½ yard of thread (a heavy twist is best) make tiny back-stitch on wrong side, at inside end of buttonhole. Bring needle up on right side, ¹⁄₁₆″ to ¹⁄₁₂″ from edge of buttonhole in fine fabrics, ⅛″ in heavier fabrics. Insert needle under edge of buttonhole and take stitch depth desired by bringing point through to right side. Pick up

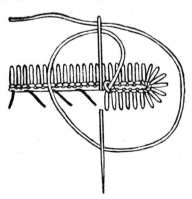

double thread near needle's eye, bring toward you and under point of needle. Pull needle through and repeat. At end, flare the stitches enough to keep purl even. Always hold work so that cut edge of buttonhole is away from you as you work.

Bars and Ends. Finish inside end of buttonhole by placing two bar threads directly across end; work blanket-stitches closely over them. Fasten with back-stitches on underside. For vertical buttonholes, both ends are squared, with buttonhole-

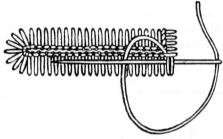

stitches worked into fabric for strength. A buttonhole used on wash garments and children's clothes is often flared at both ends and finished off with back-stitches on underside.

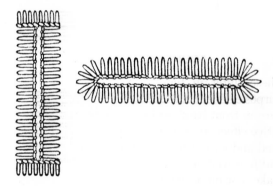

Note—Compare *blanket-stitch* on page 155 with buttonhole-stitch above. Many people confuse these two stitches.

Tailored Buttonhole. Variation of previous buttonhole. Shank of button fits into small hole at end of buttonhole and helps prevent bulging of overlap in bulky fabrics. Mark position and slash. At outer end punch a hole with stiletto or snip two diagonal slashes. Overcast. Lay a piece of heavy

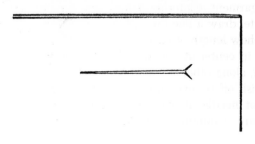

twist along edges and secure by twisting in figure eight around pin. Finish with buttonhole stitch,

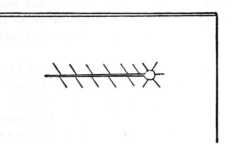

flaring around hole. Finish inner end with bar. (See *Bars and Ends,* page 60.) Used in tailored garments, men's wear especially.

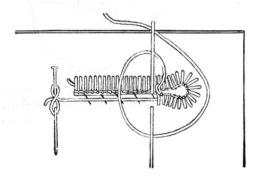

BOUND BUTTONHOLES

These differ in type according to spacing and purpose. They may be placed up and down on narrow front band, or be set on the bias for decorative effect, as on pocket. But the type most often used and easiest to make is placed crosswise. The width of welt depends on fabric. On thin material, make a scant ⅛″ welt; on heavy cloth, a ¼″ welt. A scant ¼″ is average.

Use organdie or lawn as a fabric stay for buttonholes. Cut strip on lengthwise grain and twice as wide as the length of the buttonhole. Baste to wrong side of garment.

Marking. Mark position carefully. Cut pieces of fabric eight times as wide as finished welt is to be —2″ wide for ¼″ welt—and 1″ longer than buttonhole. Lay one piece right side down, on right side of garment, centering it over line for buttonhole. Baste, draw a line through center and at each end to show length of finished buttonhole. Start stitching in center of one side. Stitch to corner, across end, along other side and end, and back to center. Finish off by overlapping stitches as shown at **A**. Pivot needle at corners to make them perfectly square. Counting end stitches on both sides of

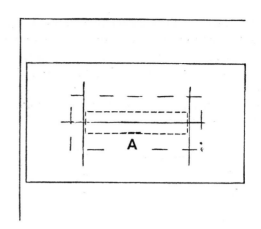

marked center line when stitching across ends is the easy way to obtain an even welt on both sides of the buttonhole.

Cutting. Cut buttonhole through both layers of fabric, from center toward each end. Clip diagonally to corners. Do *not* clip through stitching. Remove basting.

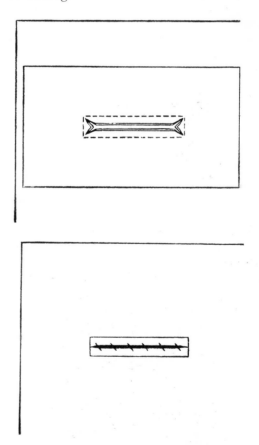

Turning Welt. Turn applied piece through slit to wrong side. Press seams outward. Bring edges of welt together in center of buttonhole and overcast edges together. On wrong side, tack together the edges of pleats formed by welts at each end. For additional strength at corners, stitch across pleats and small triangles, as at **B**.

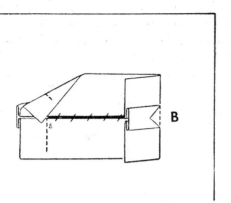

Finishing. Place facing or hem turn over buttonholes. Baste all around each buttonhole. From right side, mark length of buttonhole with pins. Slit facing on wrong side. Turn in edges and whip down. Remove bastings. Press.

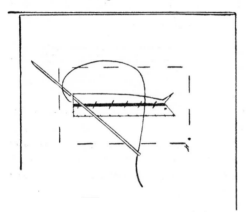

Welt or Corded Buttonhole. A fine muslin backing will help reinforce this type of buttonhole. Use individual piece for each buttonhole or one strip for a group. Make muslin the size of finished buttonhole plus ½″ all around.

Cut ½″ strip on straight or true bias. When working with heavyweight fabric, make strip a scant ¾″ wide. Each buttonhole takes two strips as long as finished buttonhole plus 1″ for making. If you have many buttonholes to make, it saves time to prepare long enough strips to serve for all buttonholes. Fold strip in half lengthwise and machine-baste, stitching near to raw edges, as in **C**. Press. For corded buttonhole, insert fine cord in fold.

Cut strip into lengths, making each piece 1″ longer than width finished buttonhole is to be.

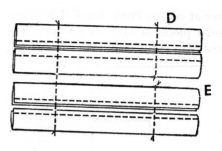

Lay two strips with raw edges together. Stitch across ends at desired length of buttonhole, as at **D**.

If more than one buttonhole is to be made, lay corresponding number of strips together and stitch across all ends at one time without breaking thread. Separate each pair of strips from group as needed, snipping stitching between folds, as at **E**.

Mark position of buttonhole on right side of garment. Pin stitched strips in position, centering slit over mark, with end of buttonhole about ½″ from edge of garment.

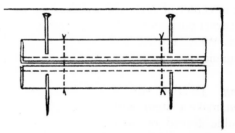

Stitch lengthwise through center of each strip, being careful not to go beyond length of buttonhole. Stitch back a few stitches at each end, as at **F**. Snip stitching across ends so strips are separate.

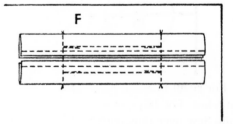

Turn to wrong side and slash buttonhole, cutting diagonally into each corner, as at **G**.

Pull strips through opening. Bring folded edges

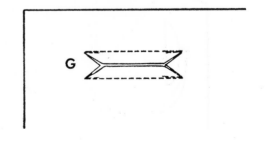

together at center. Press. Stitch three times across triangular pieces at each end of buttonhole, as at **H**. Finish wrong side as for bound buttonhole.

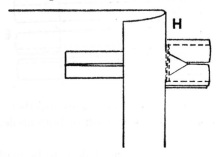

SEWING ON BUTTONS

Make sure that buttons are placed accurately, so that garment will fit smoothly when buttoned. Fasten securely so they will not come off easily.

Mark Position. Lay buttonhole edge of garment over button edge, as it will be worn. Pin in position. Mark at outer end of horizontal buttonhole. Mark in center of vertical buttonhole, placing pin at the exact position or using a lead pencil or sharp crayon. When all positions are marked, unpin the buttonhole side and prepare to sew the button on.

Sewing. To allow room for the buttonhole under button, make a "stem" with thread as you sew. Use a double thread of medium length. Start with back-stitch on under side and bring needle up through one hole and down through the second

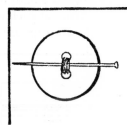

hole. For small buttons, place pins across top under stitches. For large ones, use bodkin or small hairpin. Sew over pins until button is secure. Remove pins and wind thread around threads between button and fabric.

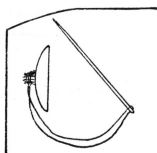

Finishing Off. Bring needle to wrong side and fasten thread with several overcast-stitches and cut off. When many buttons are to be sewed in a row, continue from one button to the next without breaking the thread. In coats and blouses, the thread can be concealed under the facing.

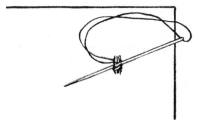

Buttons may be sewed in various ways for decorative effects, but don't use more than one way on a single garment.

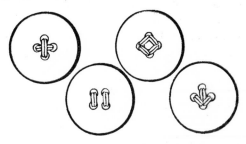

On coats, unlined or tailored garments, where inside must look as well as outside, sew a small button on wrong side. This helps to make stitches inconspicuous and gives additional strength. Take stitches through holes in both top and bottom buttons at same time.

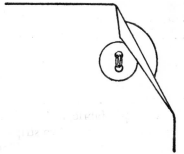

Lay pins across top button and make stem between top button and garment. Finish off with stitches in stem itself.

Large-Hole Buttons. May be attached with fabric-tubing, ribbon or tape. Bring ends through holes and whip flat to garment. To attach with leather

63

or cording, make tiny slash under button, bring ends through it, and sew flat to wrong side.

Shank Buttons. Pin in place from wrong side. Take stitches through shank. Finish on wrong side with back-stitches.

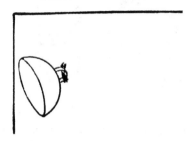

Link Buttons. To make links by joining buttons, determine length needed for connecting link and bring enough thread through the two buttons for necessary strength. Then blanket-stitch over con-

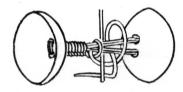

necting threads. If tubing is used to connect buttons, overcast ends of tubing and sew button to each end.

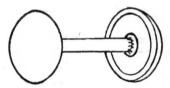

Covered Buttons. To make buttons yourself, buy molds at notion counter of the size desired, or use button-making equipment. Pad with muslin and cover with pieces of fabric. If buttons are to be hand-covered, cut muslin ⅛″ larger than mold and cut outside fabric a little more than twice the diameter of mold. Make fine running-stitch near edge of fabric and draw up thread. Whip edges together securely. Embroider or crochet motifs on fabric before putting on molds, if desired.

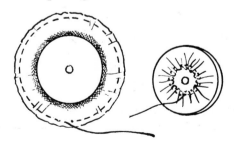

There is available a hammer kit for making fabric or leather-covered buttons on metal forms of various sizes. If you wish to use this type, follow instructions that come with the device.

Flat lead weights of different sizes may be used at bottom of coat seams or inside draperies, etc. to hold them straight. Cover like button molds, or make fabric pocket, slip weight in, and whip edges together. Apply where needed. Weighted tapes can be used inside inside hems of garments or home furnishings. Slip inside hem, tacking at seams.

Hooks and Eyes. Use small fine hooks and eyes for fine fabrics and narrow closings; coarser ones for heavier fabric or larger places. Use enough to keep opening from gaping; mark carefully so that hooks are exactly opposite eyes; sew securely. Use pins or chalk to mark position of end of hook and center of eye; notched gauge for spacing between. Overcast all around each loop with strong thread. Take several stitches through hook end to hold it flat. Take care that stitches don't go all the way

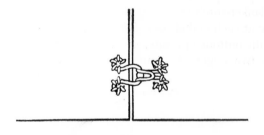

through to right side. Use round eye when edges just meet. When edges overlap, a straight eye is used. A worked eye made as at **I** can be used in place of a straight eye.

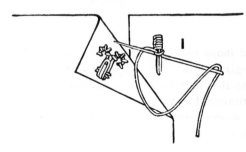

Snap Fasteners. Mark spacing and position of snaps with notched gauge. Overcast enough stitches through each hole to make it secure, taking care that stitches do not show on right side.

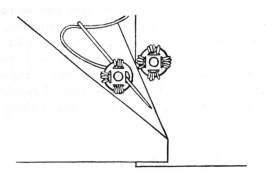

Eyelets. Punch hole with stiletto; if necessary, snip out surplus fabric with sharp scissors. Finish edge with over-and-over stitch, as in **J**, or make blanket-stitch with purl on outer edge, as in **K**.

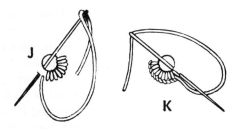

Worked Loops. With four strands of thread, shape loop large enough to slip over button easily. Blanket-stitch over loop, securing thread into fabric at each end of loop. Place loops close together, with buttons opposite, just far enough from edge so two edges of opening meet without overlap.

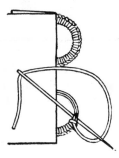

Cord loops may be made of fine cord known as "eyeglass cord." This is ideal for the purpose because it is not bulky and can be used to make continuous loops, as in **L**. It is available in black and several colors. (Illustration at top of next column.)

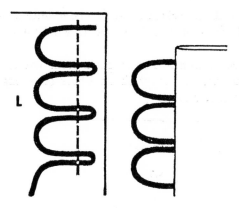

Frogs. Simple frog effect can be made with ready-made bias binding. Cut a piece about four times the length of buttonhole. Fold in half lengthwise. Pin center of length in place on right side of garment at outer end of buttonhole. Fold ends back along sides of buttonhole and cross at other end. Turn raw ends under. Pin and baste. Beginning at **M**, stitch along outside edge of binding, across end, along inside edge and back to starting point. Good for concealing worn or frayed buttonhole, especially on pajamas.

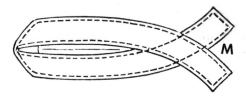

Decorative Frog of Bias Binding. Keep binding folded lengthwise. Form loops for decoration at inside end of buttonhole. Pin, baste and stitch along one edge, starting at **N**, keeping one end of tape free, as at **O**. Fold to make loop around

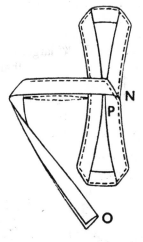

buttonhole. Slip end back under edge of bias at **P** where it is concealed and caught with stitching.

Frog of Tubing. Make of fabric tubing (see page 125) or of braid, silk cord, etc. Work piece into a series of loops that would be of correct and pleasing dimensions for garment and weight of frog.

Whip securely together on underside of looped piece to hold in shape. Sew button at inner crossing of long loop. Make another frog to match, but without the long loop. Slip-stitch both in place across opening so that button loop will fit over button. For using a fine braid or making elaborate designs, the Braiding Foot can be used. See Braiding, page 131.

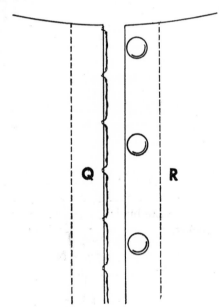

Button Loops for Sheer Fabrics. Use your Blind-Stitch Attachment to make fine loops on sheer, delicate fabrics. Make these along the edge of blouse closing, as at **Q**. Lay edge of blouse under foot so that the holding stitch catches in edge as shown and balance of stitches between form loops. Buttons should be placed so every other loop is skipped, as at **R**.

Hammer-on Fastenings. There are available a number of devices for attaching snap buttons and studs, eyelets and other types of fastenings to garments and home furnishings. Especially practical are those described below.

Snappers. These may be used conveniently on men's sports wear and work clothes, children's clothing, slip-covers, play clothes, etc. The outer finish of the snap may be a small metal or colored ring, or any one of several styles of button or stud effects. For applying them, follow directions packaged with the kit. They make sturdy, practical fastenings which can safely be laundered.

Wood Snappers. Device for snapping fabric to wooden surface, particularly useful in attaching dressing table skirts, valances, canopies, and dust-ruffles for beds. See home furnishings section for suggested uses. Half of the snap is hammered into the wooden edge of shelf, table, valance board, etc. The other half is applied to the fabric edge to be hung. Directions for setting such snaps are given with the kit. Follow them exactly for best results. Wood snappers make it easy to take off and put back such furniture skirts for laundering.

Eyelets. Metal eyelets or grommets can be obtained in various sizes for a number of uses and applied to fabric by hammering. Large sizes are convenient for shower curtains to be hung on hooks. Other sizes may be used to finish holes for drawstrings and ties on slip-covers, canvas or sail cloth beach bags, porch cushions, etc. They may also be used to provide a means of hanging up pot-lifters and other articles. Read carefully and follow directions given by manufacturer.

TOP, PATCH OR WORK POCKETS

Fashion varies the size and shape and placement of pockets; therefore let your pattern guide you in these things. Learn the basic principles of making, and all pockets are easy. The first essentials are: 1. Prepare your pocket or pockets. 2. Be sure pockets are identically placed when used in pairs. 3. Pin in place in front of mirror so that they are correctly placed for your body and reach. 4. Stay sides at top to prevent pulling off.

Work Pocket. A large pocket with slanting edge is convenient for a work garment. Turn top raw edge ¼", turn hem to wrong side and stitch. Turn raw side edges to wrong side. Place pocket on garment and pin in position.

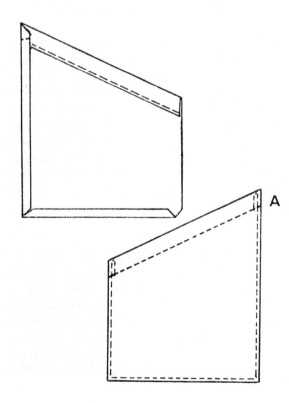

Staying. Begin at stitching line of top hem, ¼" in from edge. Stitch to top of hem, pivot and stitch to corner, as in **A**; pivot and stitch around pocket to top of opposite side, pivoting again, and stitching the depth of the hem. Pull threads to wrong side and tie. Good for aprons, overalls and play clothes.

Stitched Flap Pocket. Stitch right side of flap to wrong side of pocket. Press seam open and clip seams on both sides, as at **B**. Turn flap to right side, turn in lower edges of pocket, pin and baste to garment. Stitch. To stay, make a second stitching at top corners of pocket the depth of the flap, as at **C**.

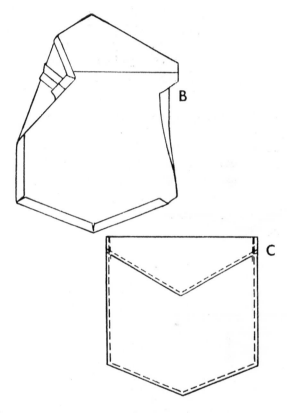

Bias-Trimmed Pocket. Shape top as desired and apply bias or fitted facing. Finish top hem by hand, as at **D**. Baste binding around sides and bottom of pocket; turn in end of bias at top corners

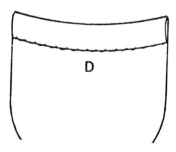

and secure with whipping-stitches. Pin in position on garment, and stitch on inside edge of binding, as in **E**. Stay pocket by stitching back a few stitches at top corners of pocket. Pull threads through to wrong side and tie.

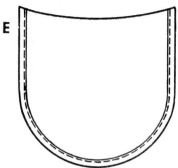

Lined Flap Pocket. Use pocket piece supplied with pattern. Cut flap and pocket from same fabric as garment, then cut pocket from lining material. Lap flap right side down on facing as in **F** and

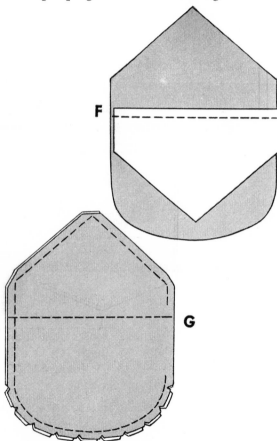

stitch, taking ¼″ seam. Turn up flap and press. Lay right side of pocket on top so flap is between layers. Baste, then stitch pocket and lining together, leaving opening as at **G**, so pocket can be turned right side out. Remove basting. Clip away corners and notch seam. Turn right side out and whip opening together. Press. This can be top-stitched ¼″ from edge, as in **H**, if desired. Turn flap down as in **I**. Pin and stitch or slip-stitch in place.

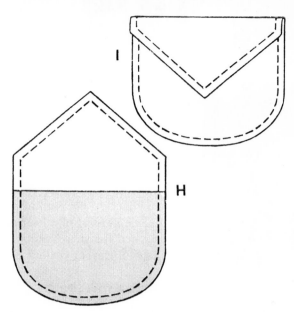

Slip-Stitched Pocket. No stitching shows on right side of this pocket. Stitch seam binding or ribbon to right side of hem edge. Turn hem allowance to right side. Stitch ¼″ from edge, beginning at **J** and stitching around pocket to other corner at **K**. Clip corners. Turn hem to wrong side and slip-stitch

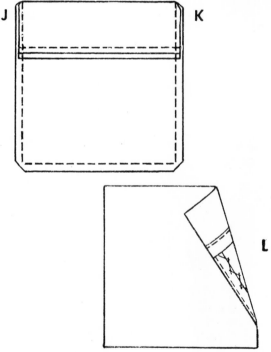

binding down. Turn lower edges to wrong side, exactly on stitching line, and catch-stitch edges down, as at **L**. Press pocket carefully. Baste pocket to garment; use matching thread and slip-stitch it in position. Secure the corners. The machine-stitching around the pocket helps it keep its shape and provides a foundation for slip-stitches.

Use Fabric to Bring Old and New into Harmony

The treatment of the windows in the four rooms here shows how fabric, color, and style of draperies can unify different periods of furniture, varying wall decorations, and color schemes. Notice the full flowered curtains, above left, marrying the rich rose and green of the rest of the room; the appropriateness of the tailored valance and deep-toned draperies, above right, to bring out the mellowness of pine panelling; the pale green print, hung full length, below left, to create a link between gray wall and deep green chair; the lime green formal drape, below right, enlivening a brown wall tone.

Courtesy of Living for Young Homemakers

Stripes and Bamboo Spell Modern

The striped denim-like fabric shown here is used in multiple ways. Such overall use makes for a striking effect. In a less spacious room you can use it similarly but more sparingly, having chair, lampshades and ottoman of plain fabric. White cording trims window seat, chairs, and ottoman.

Make the valance by stretching fabric over a board that has been fitted to the window, tacking fabric to the wrong side and using a lining over wrong side to make it as neat as the front. The fabric can be stretched over the lampshades and either sewed or glued at top and bottom. Tape is used inside to cover the raw edges.

When joining two widths in striped fabrics, be sure the stripes match. Lay fabric out and arrange seams so the stripe in the overall of the fabric itself appears unbroken.

INSERTED OR SLIT POCKETS

These are pockets that are made with extra material placed under the surface of the garment instead of on top. There are several main types:

Bias-Bound Pocket. Mark position for pocket, making it a scant ½" wide and as long as desired. Cut through center within ⅛" of each end; then clip diagonally to corner, keeping inside line, as in **M**. Cut two pouch pieces of desired depth and 1"

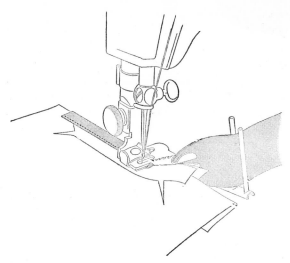

wider than slash. Cut two bias binding strips of the same length. Place one pouch piece to edge of slash on underside of garment, with pouch section extending ½" beyond slash at each end. Pin. Turn other edge of slash back out of the way. Insert bias and two edges of pocket in Binder, keeping garment right side up. Stitch binding on. Place

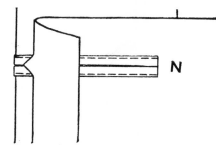

other pouch piece to opposite edge on wrong side, bind the same way. Bring bound edges together, as at **N**, and press. Turn top pouch section down

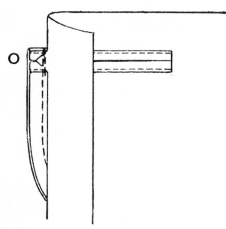

and turn triangles under, then press again. Shape pouch sections as desired and stitch around pouch, stitching twice across triangles for security, as at **O**.

Bound or Slot Pocket. Also called the *Buttonhole Pocket*, as it is made in the same way. Mark position on garment. Cut pocket material 1" wider than finished pocket and 1½" longer. Lay pocket strip on right side of garment with center of strip 1" above pocket line and baste. Mark length of pocket opening with chalk, and on each side of line mark depth of welt desired. Stitch oblong box, starting and finishing near center of lower edge, as at **P**. Pivot at corners. Remove basting.

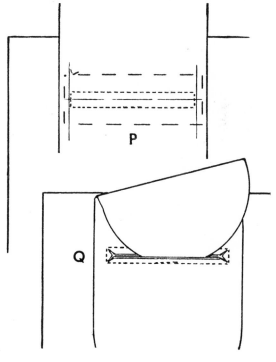

Cut through center and clip to corners, as in **Q**. Bring pouch pieces through to wrong side. Fold so that folded edges meet at center of opening and diagonal-baste as at **R**. Turn garment to right side and stitch around welts, as at **S**. On wrong

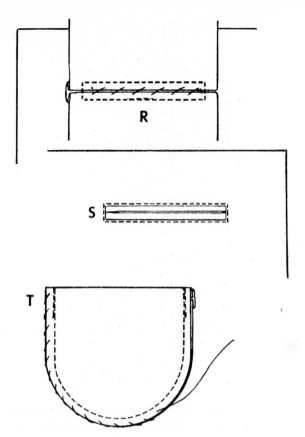

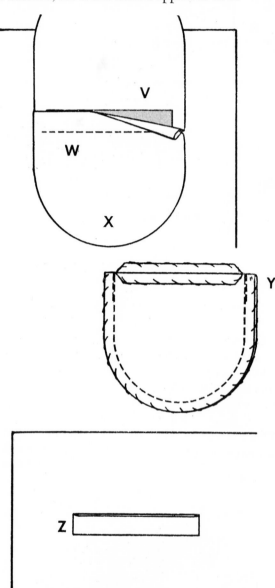

V. Fold lower pouch piece up to fill opening and form a welt. Stitch along seamline, as at **W**. Bring upper pouch piece down over **X** to form pouch. Stitch edges together, stitching twice across ends of welt, as at **Y**. Overcast all edges. When pocket is finished, the stand should appear as in **Z**.

side, bring pouch pieces together; baste and trim edges. Stitch pocket, holding pouch free, doubling back at corners, as at **T**, for strength. Overcast raw edges. Remove basting.

Standing Welt Pocket. Similar to bound pocket. Mark position on garment. For pouch, cut lengthwise strip of matching fabric 1″ wider than finished width and twice the length plus 1½″. Bring two ends together and crease on fold. Lay crease parallel to pocket line on garment and a scant ¼″ below it, right sides together. Baste and stitch, making depth of box a scant ½″, as in **U**. Cut

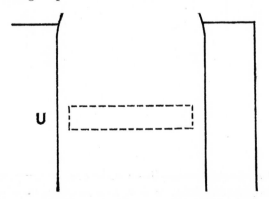

through center and clip to corners as for bound pocket. Pull pouch pieces through to wrong side. Press seams back to form an oblong opening, as in

Pockets on Seam. To make this type of pocket, in slacks and men's wear, follow instructions given with pattern.

TAILORED POCKETS

Stand Pocket. Cut firm paper pattern size finished stand is to be, slanting as desired, as in **A**. Mark center lengthwise, as at **B**. Lay pattern on fine muslin or linen with center on thread, and cut interlining same size. Lay interlining on wrong side of fabric and cut, allowing ⅜″ seam on all sides. Baste fabric and interlining together; clip seams at top corners, as at **C**; miter and whip corners. Top-stitch the stand on right side, as in **D**. Press. Cut lining same size as interlining. Turn edge of lining under ⅛″ across top and ends. Baste as in **E**. Whip to position.

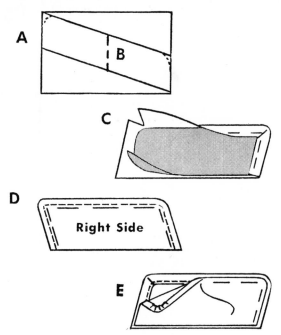

Cut stay-piece from firm, lightweight lining, 3″ deep and 2″ wider than pocket. Baste to wrong side, beneath pocket position. Basting stitches will appear on right side, as in **F**.

Lay stand along pocket-line right sides together, top of stand down. Match any checks, plaids, or stripes in fabric. Baste stand in place ⅜″ in from raw edge, as at **G**.

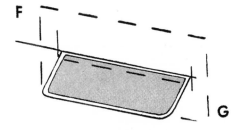

Place a pouch piece over the stand, as at **H**, and a facing piece opposite it, as at **I**. Stitch each in position making a scant ¼″ seam. Make stitching only as long as width of pocket piece and tie thread ends at each side of pocket opening. Cut pocket opening, as at **J**, taking care in slashing ends so you do not go beyond end of pocket. Pull both pieces through to wrong side and press seams open where they join the garment. Turn top of stand up, as in **K**. Baste. Stay ends of pocket under stand with fine whipping stitches. Complete

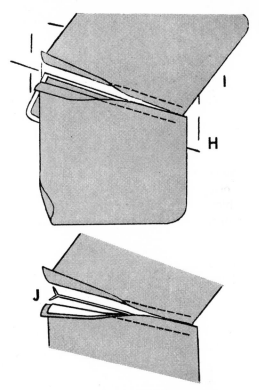

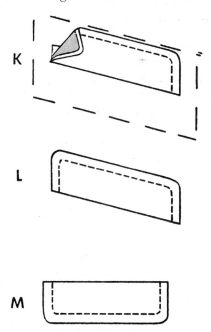

pouch by stitching raw edges together, overcast and press. Slip-stitch ends of stand invisibly from wrong side. Finished pocket will appear on right side as in **L**. For decorative effect, stands may have rows of stitching or embroidered initials.

Flap Pocket. Make like a stand pocket, but place flap to hang down, as in **M**, instead of standing up; and use facing piece to form a wide welt on lower side of pocket, so latter will have a finished look if flap is tucked into pocket.

Neck Openings and Collars

Necklines Must Fit. Give special attention to shoulder seams because upon these depends much of the success of a garment. Aim for a flat, smooth, easy line and avoid too tight facings or bindings.

Bias-Bound Neck Opening. This simple finish is most often seen on children's clothes, peasant-type blouses, pajamas and house dresses. Make slash deep enough for garment to slip over head easily.

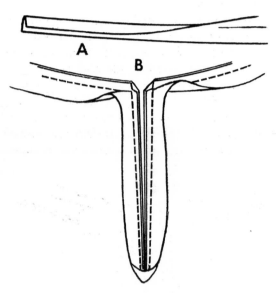

Use ready-made bias binding or binding of self or contrasting material. Cut a true-bias strip, three times the width finished binding is to be. Fold lengthwise ⅛″ off center, as in **A** and press.

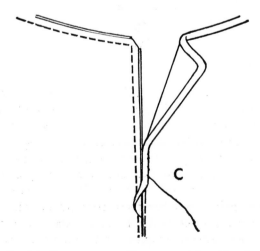

Pin binding, narrow side up, to right side of garment along neck edge. Make joining on one shoulder so that seam will be inconspicuous. Stitch, making ¼″ seam around neck edge and tapering toward bottom of slash. Take one stitch across end of slash and stretch binding slightly when rounding bottom of opening. Clip corners as at **B**. Turn under raw edge. Whip down on wrong side, as at **C**.

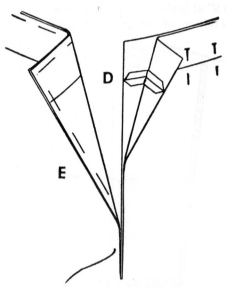

Straight-Bound Neck Opening. Apply collar to neckline of garment and facing to revers. Press seams open. Lay wrong sides together, seams matching, as at **D**, and pin. Baste around collar

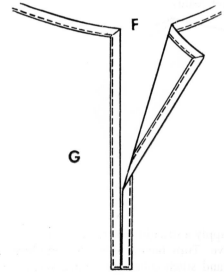

and along slash edges, as at **E**. Bind with ribbon or braid, basting carefully so both edges will be caught in one stitching. Miter corners, as at **F**, and turn under ends of ribbon at bottom of slash. Stitch close to edge of ribbon and across ends, as in **G**. (Illustrated on previous page.)

Faced Slash Opening. This is used as a back or front opening. Cut facing on same grain as garment. Seam back and front facings together at shoulder line. Turn outer edge of facing to wrong side ¼" and stitch. Place center of facing along center-front line, right sides together. Pin and baste. Stitch around neckline and down center-front line, keeping ¼" from center line, and tapering to ⅛" at bottom of opening. Take a single stitch across bottom of opening, as at **H** and continue up

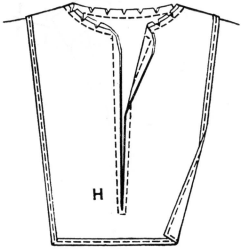

other side. Cut carefully between stitching line and trim corners away. Blend neckline seam. Clip edges and press. Turn facing to wrong side and baste close to turned edge. Press. Tack facing at shoulder seams.

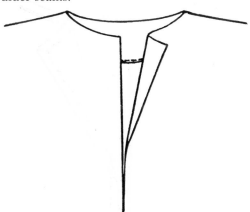

To apply a straight collar: Face slash only, as in **H** above. Turn facing to wrong side and press. Baste and stitch collar edge along wrong side of neckline. Turn under other edge of collar and hem on right side along stitching line, as at **I**. See illustration at top of next column.

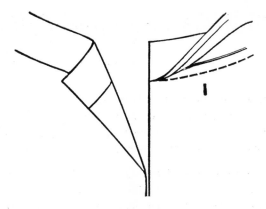

Slide-Fastener Neck Opening. This opening can be used at back, shoulder or front of neckline and in a fitted sleeve.

Stitch all seams, leaving placket opening ½" longer than fastener. If opening is on a seam, finish neckline as follows: Fold seam allowance through opening to right side and pin, as at **J**. Cut a piece of bias ¾" to 1" wide and long enough to finish neckline. Turn one edge of bias to wrong side and stitch. Lay other edge of bias around neck, right sides together. Overlap turned-back edge of placket with end of bias, as at **K**. Baste.

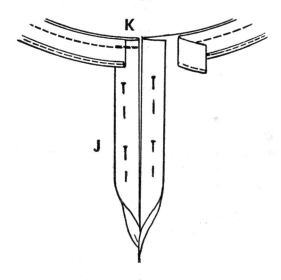

Beginning at opening, stitch around neck. Remove basting and pins. Clip corners. Turn bias and seam allowance to wrong side. Use orange stick to make true corners at top of placket. Press neck edge.

Slip-baste edges of opening together. Keep fastener closed and lay right side down along seamline with open end ¼" from edge of neckline. Allow ends of tape to extend. Then pin and diagonal-baste in place, as in **L**, at top of next page. This prevents fastener slipping while stitching. From right side, stitch around fastener with Cording Foot or Zipper Foot.

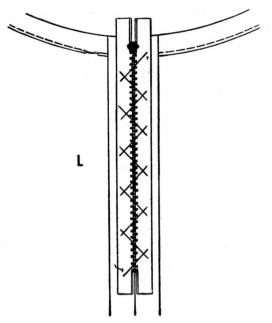

L

Stitch down one side, pivot and stitch across end, as at **M**, pivot and stitch up other side. Leave a couple of inches of thread at the beginning and end of stitching. From the wrong side, overcast seam and tape edges together or make a second stitching close to edge of tape. Thread ends into

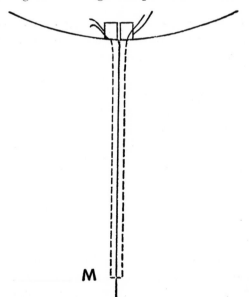

M

a needle on wrong side and fasten securely. Turn tape ends over and whip down, as at **N**. This firm, non-bulky finish can be used on neck or sleeve.

N

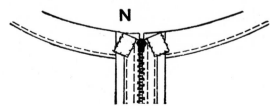

When applying a slide fastener in a slash, finish neck as in **H**, page 73. Then slip-baste edges together and center slide fastener under it. Follow instructions given above for finishing.

Slide Fastener Used as Decorative Trim. This finish can be used at neckline, shoulder, sleeve and for various types of pocket effects. Follow instructions given with this type of fastener.

Open-end slide fasteners are used in jackets, housecoats, children's buntings, etc. Follow instructions given with this type of fastener. As this slide fastener should be stitched from the bottom up on both sides, the Zipper Foot, which is adjustable, is practical to use.

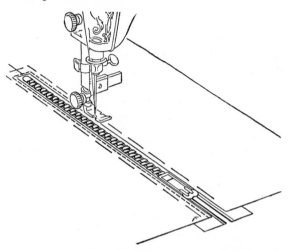

Convertible Front Opening. A neck finish which can be worn open or closed. Cut a lengthwise strip 1″ longer than the opening and 12″ wide. Match center of strip to center-front line, right sides together, and pin. Measure ½″ on each side of center

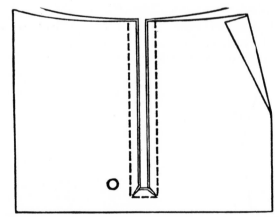

O

line and mark for opening. Stitch along marks, pivoting at bottom corners to form a square end. Cut down center, leaving a scant ¼″ seam, and clip diagonally into corners, as in **O**. Press seams open.

Turn to wrong side, folding facing to fill opening on right side, as in **P**. Lap fronts and smooth lower end of opening at corners and press. Turn back lower end of blouse and stitch placket ends

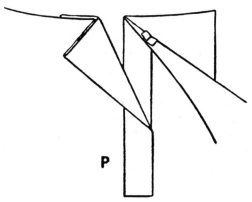

to edge of blouse at bottom of opening, as at **Q**. Make three rows of stitching here to hold the narrow seam. Use pattern to shape neckline. Apply a straight-band collar.

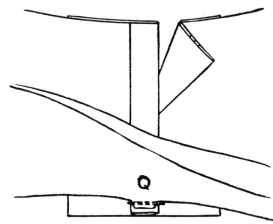

Shoulder Opening. This will vary somewhat, depending on type of neckline and way garment is finished. A concealed placket is usually made in left shoulder seam. When accented by buttons and loops, opening can be in one shoulder only, or short openings in both shoulders.

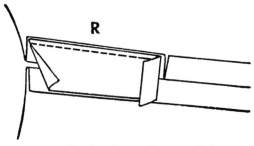

Determine depth of opening needed to admit head easily. Stitch shoulder seams, leaving opening. Clip back shoulder seam. Stitch facing to back edge as at **R**. Turn facing to underside and

stitch along fold, as at **S**. Bind front seam edge, as at **T**. Turn under raw edge of back facing in line with shoulder seam and stitch as at **U**.

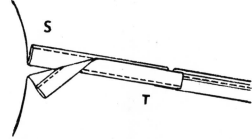

Bring back edge over opening and stitch seam edges together at end of placket, as at **V**, keeping seam free from garment. After placket is finished, pin edges together and press. Finish neckline with bias, shaped facing, or a French-fold binding. This

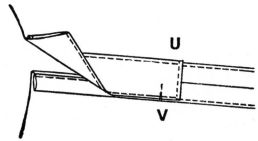

makes a flat, smooth opening, as shown below, which may be closed with buttons and loops, buttons and buttonholes, or snaps.

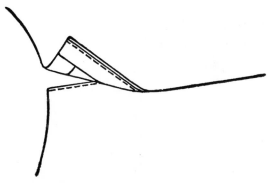

Straight Collar. Fold collar strip through center lengthwise. Stitch across ends and trim away corners, as at **W**. Turn to right side and press. Fold collar in half and mark center. Baste under part of collar across back neckline, matching center of

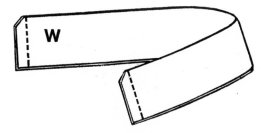

collar and neckline. Clip seam allowance of collar edge at end of facing, as at **X**. Insert collar ends between facing and garment, as at **Y**. Pin and baste. Stitch around neckline, keeping upper back

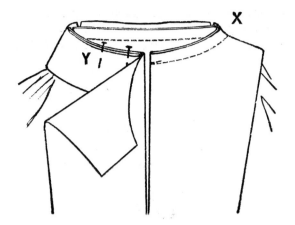

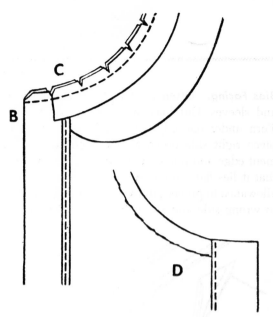

part of collar free. Trim corners and clip seam allowance. Turn facing to inside and turn back edge up into collar. Fold edge of collar under and slip-stitch across back, as at **Z**. Press.

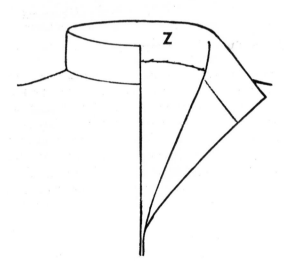

Peter Pan Collar. Use pattern to cut collar and facing. Stitch around outside edge of collar. Blend seam and notch on curve, as in **A**. Turn to right side, baste and press. Top-stitch collar ¼″ from edge, if desired.

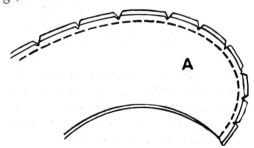

Lay collar right side up on right side of garment, matching center backs, and pin. Insert ends of collar between neckline and facing at front edges, as at **B**. Baste. Lay bias facing along neckline on right side. Stitch collar and facing in one operation, as at **C**. Trim corner and clip neckline edge. Turn facings to wrong side and hem in position, as at **D**. This collar gives a trim appearance on right side as shown below. It is often used on simple blouses, dresses and children's clothes.

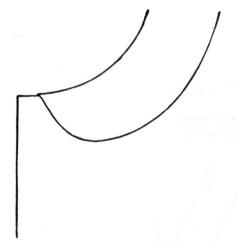

Low Necks. The finishing of a low décolleté, whether round or square, whether a collar or bertha is applied, is the same as illustrated here. First, it is important to stay-stitch so it will not stretch in handling. Use a fitted facing or a true bias, as best suits your fabric and the width of the finish you are using. In any event, it is desirable to have the facing or bias ¾″ to 1¼″ wide, so that it will not roll over. You need enough width to hold the facing to position on the wrong side.

Bias Facing. Often used to finish edges of neck and sleeves. Cut bias piece of necessary length. Turn under one edge of bias ⅛″ and stitch. Lay piece right side down against right side of garment edge and pin, easing but not stretching it, so that it lies flat. Stitch seam. On curves, clip seam allowance to prevent drawing, as at **A**. Turn facing to wrong side and slip-stitch in position, as in **B**.

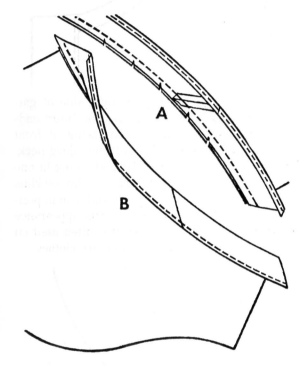

V-Neck Facing. Cut bias strip ½″ wider than required width of facing and 3″ or 4″ longer than

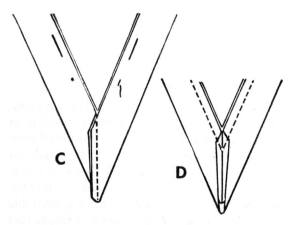

measurement of neckline. Pin center of facing at point of V, right side down. Lay edge along sides

of neck opening and pin. Baste ¼″ from edge on each side to within ½″ of V. Miter facing at point and stitch seam, beginning at the top, as in **C**. Trim

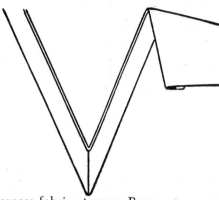

away excess fabric at seam. Press seam open and baste around corner. Stitch along sides, pivoting on needle at point of V, as in **D**. Turn facing to wrong side, turn under raw edge and stitch or slip-stitch in position.

Mitered Band or Facing. Cut facing piece on same grain as edge it will join. Lay piece right side down along edge on wrong side of garment if facing is to appear as trim on right side. Lay right sides together if facing is to be on wrong side. Pin and baste. Stitch to within 1″ of corner on each side. Miter corner, stitch, trim away excess fabric and press seam open. Finish stitching joining at corners, pivoting needle at point, as at **E**. Turn fac-

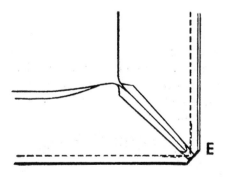

ing to other side. For right-side band facing, finish by turning edge under and top-stitching, as in **F**. (See illustration at top of next page.) If desired, piping may be used under edge. For wrong side, turn edge under and whip or slip-stitch.

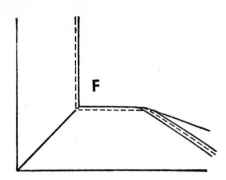

F

Facing Curve. Cut facing so that grain matches that of edge to be faced. Lay right side of facing to wrong side of garment, pin, baste and stitch. Blend seam allowance. Notch seam on curve, as at **G**. Turn raw edge of facing over, clipping curved

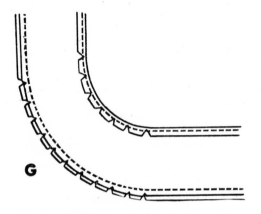

G

edge, and baste. Turn facing to right side; press, baste and top-stitch turned edge, as in **H**. If facing is used on wrong side, stitch right sides together, turn facing to wrong side and slip-stitch turned edge. When lining is used, let facing cover lining edge and slip-stitch facing to lining.

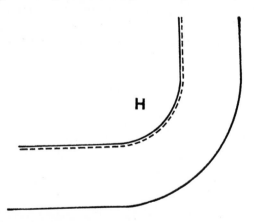

H

Shaped or Fitted Facing. Cut facing pieces so that grain matches that of section to be faced. Pin facing to garment, right sides together. Baste and stitch. Blend seam allowance. Clip seams at corners and, if curved, clip or notch so that facing will

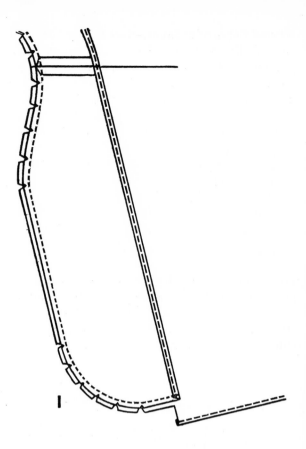

I

lie flat when turned to wrong side, as in **I**. Press seams open. Turn over raw edges of facing and stitch. Turn facing to wrong side and press. Slip-stitch in place, as in **J**.

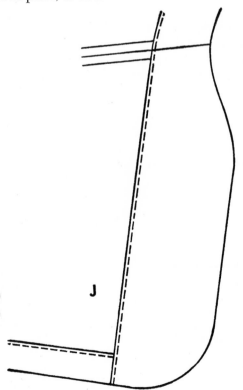

J

Mitered Concave or Square-Neck Facing. Pin and baste facing pieces to edge of neck, overlapping generously at corners so true bias miters can be made. Miter joining at corners, pin and stitch, as at **K**. Trim off corner surplus, leaving ¼" seam, and

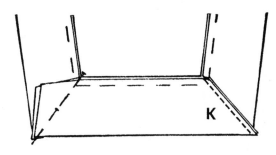

press seam open. Stitch neck seam, pivoting at corners. When used as trim, bring facing to right side, turn under raw edge and baste. Slip-stitch or top-stitch to finish, as at **L**. For facing on wrong side, stitch turned-under edge and slip-stitch in position.

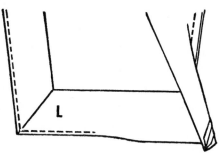

Mitered Hem or Corner. Crease hem turn on a fabric thread. Turn in raw edges ⅛" to ¼" along top of hem. Crease at corner on true diagonal, as at **M**. Open flat. Fold corner on crease and trim off

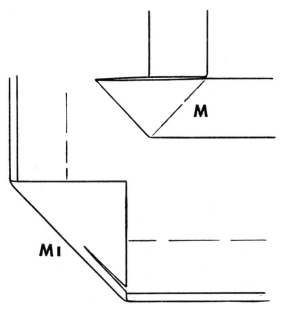

surplus fabric above crease to seam's width (**M1**). Clip off corners. Fold hem back in place, baste or pin hem close to outside edge and on each side of miter. Start with two tiny back-stitches at outside end of miter and whip edges together (**N**). To stitch joining by machine: After creasing diagonal line at corner, turn hem inside out at corner, as at **N1**, and stitch creased lines together. Trim excess. Press seam open. Turn hem back to right side.

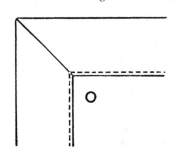

Finish hem by machine, as in **O**, or slip-stitch in place. Hems in table linens may be finished by machine or hand hemstitching.

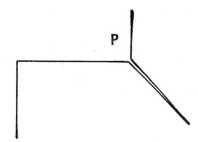

Tailored Corner. Used to reinforce and finish edge, especially where a full seam allowance is not possible, or where a hem is cut to provide a true square for a neckline or yoke. Cut corner diagonally to required depth of hem, as at **P**. Turn

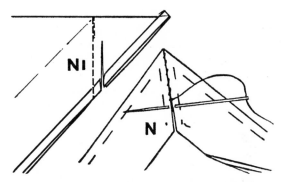

hem allowance and crease. Cut a straight piece for corner, making it twice width of hem and three times as long. Spread slash open and lay along lengthwise edge of strip, right sides together. Stitch so that seam just barely catches fabric at corner of slash. Take a few whipping-stitches over

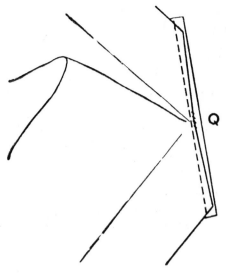

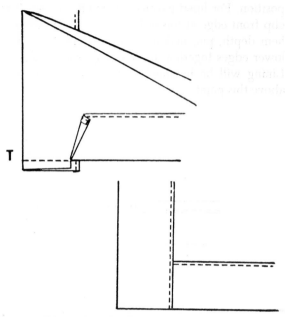

stitch, keeping free from garment. Turn facing back into position. Slip-stitch in position. For finishing a rounded overlapping corner, see *Shaped Facing* on page 78.

seam edge at narrow point of seam, as at **Q**, to add strength. Turn corner into position, press, trim off excess fabric. Turn under raw edges of hem edge and stitch, as in **R**. Slip-stitch in position.

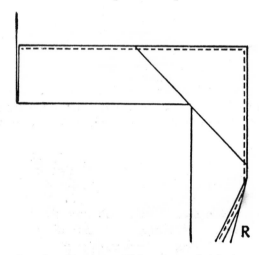

Square Overlapping Corner. This finish is used on coats and jackets where it is better not to trim excess fabric away in case garment needs to be

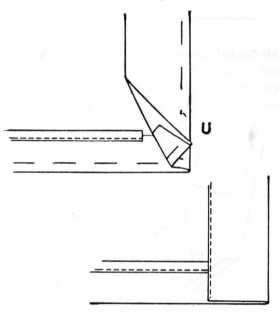

Overlapping Corner. This corner finish is used when a hem or facing overlaps another, usually narrower, hem. Bulk is avoided by cutting away some fabric thickness. Make hem turns and crease or press. Open out and cut as in **S**, so one layer is eliminated except for seam allowance. Fold wide

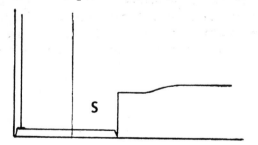

edge back so that seam can be stitched in line with other hem edge, as at **T**. Turn under raw edges and

lengthened or altered in any way. This is especially important in children's clothes. Fold hem and facing into position. Baste along lower edge of hem and outside edge of front. Turn under raw edges of hem and stitch or finish with seam binding as shown. Start binding about 1″ inside edge of front facing. Trim off corner of hem, as at **U**. Slip-stitch hem in position.

For unlined garment, turn under raw edge of front hem or facing and stitch. Fold facing in place, making true corner, and baste. Slip-stitch lower edges together and slip-stitch front edge in position. For lined garment, trim off corner. Then clip front edge at top of hem, as in **V**. Turn under hem depth, pin, making a true corner. Slip-stitch lower edges together and continue to top of hem. Lining will be hemmed or stitched to raw edge above this point.

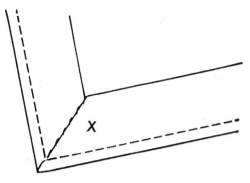

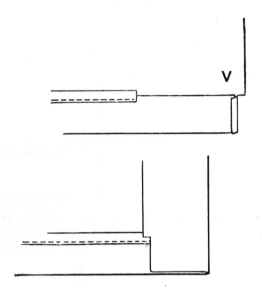

Self-Corded Corner and Edge. Mark position of hem turn all along edge. Lay cord along mark, fold hem and baste cord into fold. Baste to corner. Miter hem at corner and trim away surplus fabric,

as at **W**. Pin miter in place and continue basting along cord as before. Stitch along cord, using Cording Foot. Hem miter as at **X** and slip-stitch

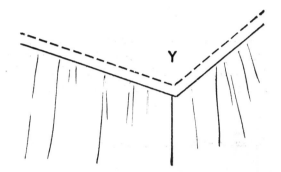

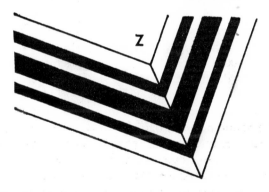

hem. When used as seam finish, insert cord and baste; then lay over seam edge and stitch along cord from right side with Cording Foot, as in **Y**.

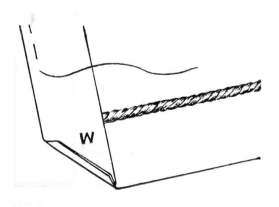

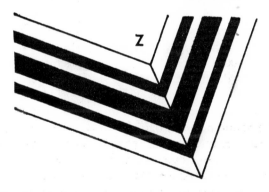

Mitering Stripes. In mitering striped or figured fabrics, use care in folding to get a true diagonal. Plan your pieces so that stripes and other designs meet exactly on the mitered line and the figure is continued precisely around the corner, as in **Z**.

Know Your Sleeves

Drop Shoulder Sleeve. This is an extended shoulder seam. Underarm seam has to be clipped near armhole to prevent puckering. Generally this sleeve is finished with a bias facing or hem, the turned edge blind-stitched to position.

Kimono Sleeve. This sleeve is formed when waist and sleeve are cut in one, with or without shoulder seam. Seams at underarms should not fit too tightly at armhole or be held too snugly at waistline. After stitching seams, clip curve of underarm seam (**A**).

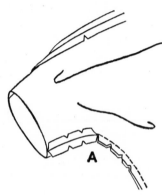

Square Gusset in Kimono Sleeve. A small square gusset set in underarm seam of kimono sleeves usually relieves strain and adds comfort in wearing, to provide such if desired, when the pattern does not. Cut carefully across underarm seam, making depth equal on both sides of seam. Trim off corners of seam allowance and machine-stitch all around opening, close to edge (**B**). Spread sleeve out, measure size of opening and cut a pattern precisely this size, plus ½" for seams. Place

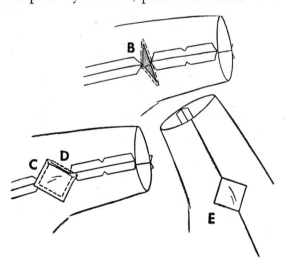

this on a lengthwise grain of fabric and cut out gusset. Pin gusset to opening on all four sides. Baste and stitch gusset in place (**C**), making a ¼" seam all around gusset but taper each edge of slash from corner to corner on all four sides, as at **D**. Right side will appear as in **E**.

There are some sleeves with gussets somewhat different in shape than the one shown. Some have the underarm line cut higher to give a free-action type of sleeve. The method of making these is usually explained with the pattern. However, when you know how to insert a gusset, none can be a problem to you.

Plain Sleeve. Follow the instruction sheet that comes with your pattern for cutting and finishing individual sleeves. Ease at elbow is controlled by gathers, darts and unstitched tucks.

Setting Sleeve in Armhole. After garment has been fitted, stitch shoulder, underarm and sleeve seams. Then adjust machine to medium-length stitch—approximately 12 stitches to the inch. Make two rows of machine stitching from notch to notch across top of sleeve, as in **F**, first row of stitching approximately $\frac{1}{16}$" outside seamline, second row $\frac{1}{8}$" outside first row.

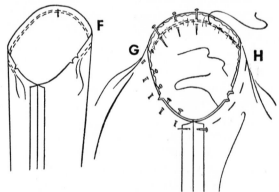

Place sleeve in armhole, centering top of sleeve at shoulder seam, notches matched and seams together at underarm. Pin at these four points. Draw up bobbin threads of both rows of stitching across top of sleeve, easing in fullness, pinning as in **G**.

With the garment right-side out, lay shoulder over hand with sleeve hanging down, as in **I**. Make sure the sleeve hangs *straight* down, that is, that the center of lengthwise thread of sleeve falls in a straight line as you hold it. If it does not, ease the fullness in top of sleeve, forward or back, to make this pendulum-like line. A basting on a crosswise thread as shown may also aid you in obtaining the correct "hang" to the sleeve. Adjust the fullness just right, then wrap the gathering threads of the top of sleeve around a pin in a figure 8. Remove the sleeve from the armhole and carefully shrink out the gathered fullness from the top of the sleeve. Use a pressing mit on the small end of the sleeve board for a shaped pressing surface. Use a slightly damp press cloth and the point of the iron. Do not press beyond the gathered line, as this will flatten the top of the sleeve too much. Again pin sleeve into the garment exactly to position. Baste as at **H**, then try on for final fit. The use of a slight shoulder pad may help a shoulder and sleeve to fit better, even when fashion does not demand them.

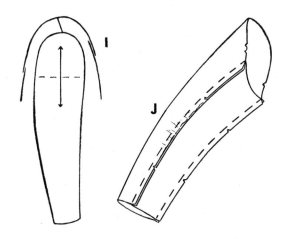

Check each sleeve carefully in fitting, as sometimes one shoulder is lower than the other or the top of the shoulder more forward, this making it necessary to place and check the sleeve of each arm individually. Sometimes occupation will in time cause a difference which must be reckoned with in fitting.

When stitching sleeve in armhole, begin at the underarm. Stitch from the sleeve side and overlap your stitching for a couple of inches at the beginning line to add strength to the seam. Even the seam edge as necessary, to make it neat. Finally, press the armhole as stitched, over small end of sleeve board. Use the point of the iron to press into the sleeve only as far as the stitching line. For a soft roll, the seam is turned into the sleeve without further pressing.

Another armhole finish is made with a second stitching ¼" from the first across the lower part of armhole from notch to notch, seam trimmed close to stitching, then raw edges overcast.

Two-Piece Sleeve (also called Tailored Sleeve). Most often used in coat or suit. Make tucks or darts if elbow ease is so controlled. Pin and baste upper and under sleeve sections together, right sides together. When ease at elbow is slight, you can control it by easing in the upper section between the notches, to make slight gathers, as in **J**. Fit sleeve. Stitch seams. When seams are pressed open, shrink out any excess ease at elbow. When inserting two-piece sleeve in armhole, center top of it at shoulder and match notches and seams.

Gathered-Top Sleeve. Using a long machine stitch, make two or three rows of gathers between notches across top of sleeve. Draw up shirring bobbin threads, winding thread ends on pins (**K**). Stitch underarm seam as in **L** and finish bottom of sleeve. Insert sleeve in armhole, matching seams and notches. Adjust fullness. Pin and baste. Stitch just inside the second row of gathers. Thread needle with thread ends and fasten off gathers.

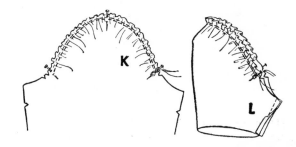

Puff Sleeve. Handled in the same way as above, only bottom of sleeve is gathered also.

Lined Short Sleeve. Use a finely woven fabric, such as taffeta or organdie, to completely line

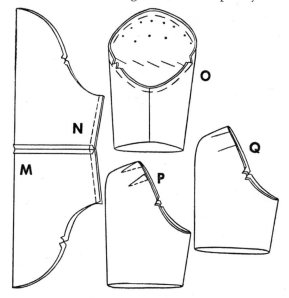

sleeve for an attractive finish. This is especially good if top of sleeve is darted or pleated. Cut lining same size as sleeve. With right sides together stitch across bottom edge and press seam open (**M**). Fold sleeve lengthwise and stitch underarm seam (**N**). Press seam open. Bring lining up inside sleeve. Baste the two thicknesses together (**O**). Baste and stitch darts or pleats in top of sleeve (**P**). Finished sleeve appears as in **Q**.

Raglan Sleeve. This type of sleeve extends from underarm to neckline, both back and front. A raglan sleeve can be either one-piece or two-piece. The one-piece has a dart in the shoulder. Stitch dart seam and press open, as at **R**. Join to back and front of garment (**S**). Clip seam allowance to prevent puckering when pressed open. Sleeve and underarm seam are stitched in one operation (**T**).

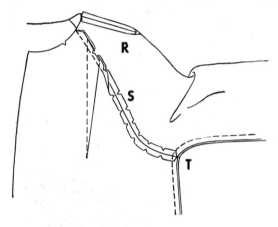

A two-piece raglan sleeve is seamed together, then inserted in armhole (**U**).

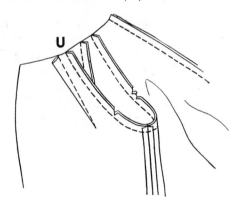

Epaulet Sleeve. This sleeve has a yoke effect extending from top of sleeve to neckline. Stay-stitch

corners as at **V**. Seam underarm. Insert in armhole, as in **W**, working from wrong side. Baste and stitch around armhole. Clip corners. Turn under back and front edges of epaulet. Lap over blouse edges. Pin as at **X**. Baste and top-stitch. If inside stitching is used, slip-baste lapped edges.

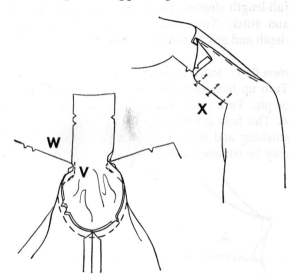

Shirtwaist Sleeve. Join sleeve to armhole of blouse with flat-fell seam before stitching underarm seams. With right sides together, stitch sleeves to armhole (**Y**). Trim away seam edge of blouse ¼″ or about two-thirds of seam's width (**Z**). Turn sleeve edge under and top-stitch flat to shirt, encasing raw edge. If shirt-sleeve opening is being used for bottom of sleeve, follow instructions on pages 94–95. The sleeve and underarm are stitched in a constinuous seam, usually a flat-fell, but a plain seam, pressed open, can be used.

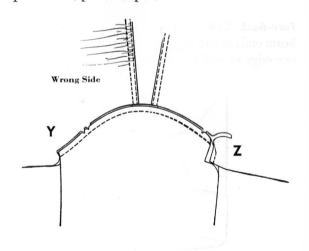

Plain Sleeve Hem. Finish for three-quarter or full-length sleeves. Turn raw edge to wrong side and stitch. Turn bottom of sleeve up required depth and pin. Slip-stitch in position.

Hem Cuff. Stitch underarm seams and press open. Turn up hem allowance to wrong side and crease or pin. Turn under raw edge ¼″ and stitch, as at **A**. This hem is turned up on right side to conceal stitching and make cuff. If desired, edge of cuff may be trimmed with lace, rick rack, etc., as in **B**.

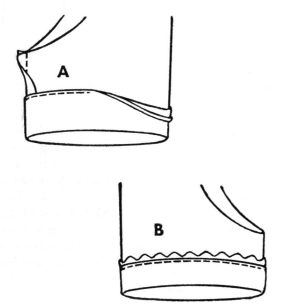

Turn-Back Cuff. Usually of contrasting color. Seam ends of cuff together. Press seam open. Baste one edge of cuff to bottom of sleeve, right side of

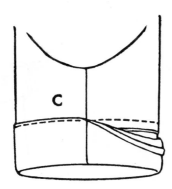

cuff to wrong side of sleeve. Bring other edge of cuff to right side, turn under raw edge and stitch to sleeve, as at **C**.

Casing at Sleeve Bottom. Turn sleeve wrong side out. Make hem turn deep enough for elastic to run through. Stitch, leaving a 1″ opening near seam, as at **D**. Cut elastic ½″ longer than size of wrist and insert into casing, using a safety pin to pull it through. Overlap ends and whip together, as at **E**. Hem opening.

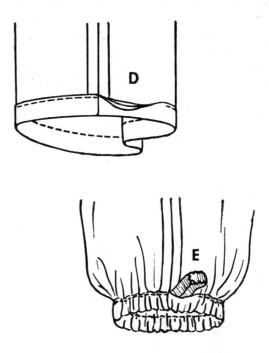

Hemmed Sleeve Opening. This is the simplest opening, but not very strong. Terminate stitching of sleeve seam at desired depth for opening. Press seam open. Turn under raw edge of one seam and hem, keeping fold in line with seamline of sleeve, as at **F**. Hem other side in same way. Gather wrist and apply cuff as for *Straight Cuff* illustrated in **J**, on next page.

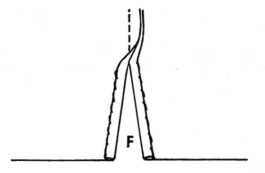

Bound Sleeve Opening. Cut bias strip ¾" wide and twice the length of opening plus about ¼". Stitch strip along edge of opening on right side, tapering seam to point at top, as in **G**. Turn other edge to wrong side; turn raw edge under and whip down, as at **H**. When the opening is on a seam, clip

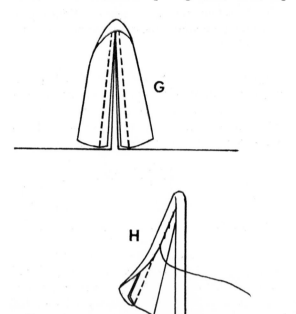

seam edges at top of opening, as at **I**. Stitch strip along seam allowance on right side. Finish as in **H** above. Follow instructions below for applying cuff.

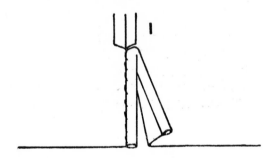

Straight or Band Cuff. Cut a straight strip, making it twice the desired depth of cuff plus seam allowance. Fold in half lengthwise and stitch across ends. Clip corners. Press as stitched. Turn right side out and press. Gather bottom of sleeve to fit cuff. Baste, then stitch one edge of cuff over gathered edge on right side. Turn other edge un-

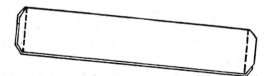

der and to wrong side and hem, as in **J**. For tailored effect, it may have button tab at end with bound buttonhole. If bound buttonhole is used, make before stitching end seams of cuff.

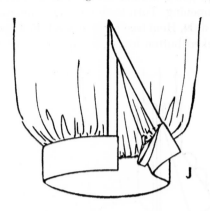

Faced Slash. Cut straight strip of fabric for facing piece. Turn one end and two sides of facing over and stitch, as at **L**. Fold through center and crease. Lay right side down on right side of sleeve over position marked for slash with crease along slash line and unfinished end at bottom of sleeve. Baste, then stitch ⅛" from slash line to point at top. Take one stitch across top, then turn and stitch down

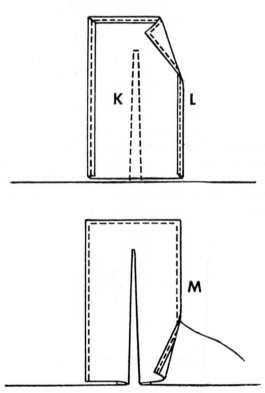

opposite side, as at **K**. Cut slash between lines of stitching. Turn facing to wrong side and press. Slip-stitch to sleeve, using short stitches, as in **M**. Gather bottom of sleeve and apply straight cuff.

Opening Faced with Seam Binding. Use binding in matching color. Stitch binding around lower part of sleeve on right side, starting at top of sleeve opening, going around lower edge and ending at top of opening. Turn to wrong side, mitering corners as at **N**. Hem free edge in position. Directions for worked button loops on page 65.

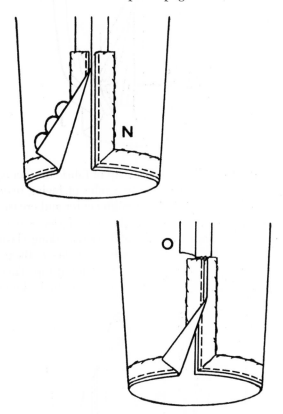

This seam opening can also be made with an underlap. Clip one seam at top of opening, as at **O**. Face in same way as above, but allow the one edge to extend over opening as shown. Whip extended end to seam on other side. Use snaps to close.

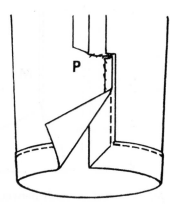

Self-Facing for Sleeves. When cutting sleeve, allow 1″ seams on each side of opening and add 1″ to sleeve lengths. Working from wrong side, turn edge over ⅛″ on three sides and stitch. Turn ⅞″ hems on sides of opening and bottom of sleeve, mitering corners. Whip miter together; cut away excess from wrong side, and slip-stitch edge in position. When underlap is desired, clip seam at top of opening, as at **P**. Make narrow hem on this side of opening and square corner. Whip top end of opening together. (Illustrated at bottom of previous column.)

Shaped Cuff. Cut cuff pieces according to pattern shape. Lay right sides together and stitch across ends and top edge. Trim seam allowance and notch curves. Turn seam edges to one side and crease down, as at **Q**. Turn cuff right side out and

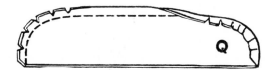

press. Lay raw edges along bottom of sleeve on right side and baste. Cut bias facing strip 1″ wide and as long as needed. Seam ends together to form circle same size as cuff. Pin along edge of cuff, wrong side up. Stitch around sleeve, as in **R**. Turn seam allowance to wrong side; turn under raw edge of bias and hem in position, as in **S**.

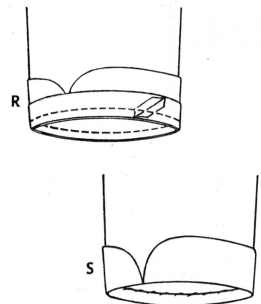

Shirt-Sleeve Opening. Finish opening before stitching sleeve seam. Slash opening. Cut pieces for overlapping and underlapping edges of slash. Bind back edge of slash with narrow strip, as at **T**. Stitch overlap piece to wrong side of other edge

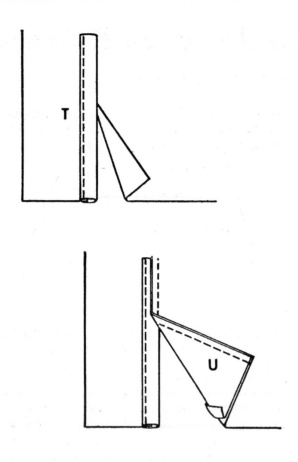

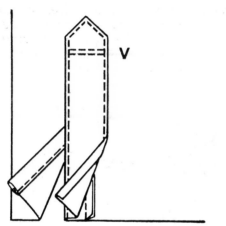

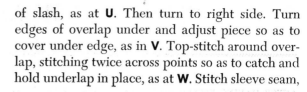

of slash, as at **U**. Then turn to right side. Turn edges of overlap under and adjust piece so as to cover under edge, as in **V**. Top-stitch around overlap, stitching twice across points so as to catch and hold underlap in place, as at **W**. Stitch sleeve seam,

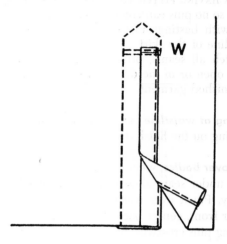

making flat fell seam. Gather wrist. Make band cuff following instructions under *Shaped Cuff*, but using muslin interfacing to give body to finished cuff. Baste and stitch underside of cuff to wrong side of sleeve and other edge to right side, enclosing gathered edges inside cuff. Top-stitch cuff as in **X**. Sew on button and work buttonhole.

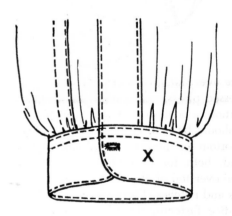

Before cutting a sleeve, always check the length in your pattern and make adjustments as shown on page 27.

Waistline Joining and Finishings

AFTER HAVING FITTED YOUR DRESS, REMOVE IT CAREfully, so no pins can come out, and mark the waistline with bastings in the blouse part and in the waistline of the skirt.

Stitch all seams, press them, then either press them open or in the direction they are to be in in the finished garment.

Joining at waistline can be done in two ways, depending on the finish desired:

Skirt over bodice, when bodice has ease or fullness. Turn under seam allowance at top of skirt. Press lightly. Pin it over waistline of bodice, matching center front, center back, side seams and notches, placing pins crosswise of seam, as at **A**. Slip-baste.

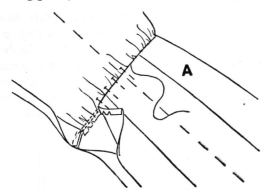

Bodice over skirt, when skirt has fullness, such as unpressed pleats, or is gathered all around. (The exception: a bouffant evening dress when the fullness should be billowy.) Turn in seam allowance on bottom of bodice. Sometimes this edge is corded, both for decoration and strength. Lap bodice over top of skirt and pin first at matching seams and notches. Then draw up skirt gathers to fit bodice, fastening thread ends around pin, as at **B**. Adjust gathers and pin. Slip-baste, as at **C**.

Inside stitching is used in one's best dresses where custom-made look is desired. Stitch after slip-basting (**C**), or pin and baste as in **D**, then stitch.

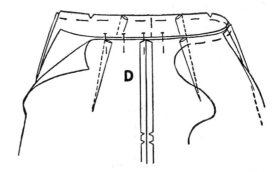

Top-stitched waistline is stitched as at **E**. This is the quickest finish and can be used when the stitching will not detract from garment's design, especially when a belt is worn.

If matching seams or darts necessitate basting from right side but an inside stitching is desired, slip-baste after pinning. See Slip-Basting, page 34.

When making simple garment where simplicity and speed are important points, you can baste front together entirely and the back also, then join the underarm seams, making a continuous seam from armhole to hem. This finish is frequently used for house dresses, aprons, children's play garments and similar informal apparel.

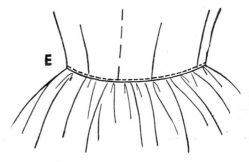

Staying a Waistline. As a finish, and to prevent stretching, stitch seam binding to the waistline seam. Narrow grosgrain ribbon, also, can be used, this being tacked at intervals to the waistline, becoming an inside belt that is hooked before the placket is closed.

Finishing skirts and waistlines when making a skirt for wear with blouses or jackets. Fit it as you would the skirt of a dress, except that you pin a ribbon or tape around the figure, pinning so its opening will coincide with the placket of the skirt. Pin the skirt to this tape and mark the waistline carefully all the way around so that when you remove the tape to seam your skirt you will continue to have a true waistline. Finish the skirt with inside belting or with a 1″ band of the fabric. A piece of seam binding, or narrow ribbon, or belting inside the waistband is a safeguard against stretching.

In using bordered material or lace yardage having a finished edge, lay in pleats or gather the fullness in to match your waistline measurement. Put the skirt on, pin your tape over the skirt, adjusting the length at the waistline to cause the bottom to be even all the way around. Take care in cutting

away any surplus that you leave enough length above the tape to allow for finishing the skirt at the waistline.

Sometimes if the lace is short and a long dress is desired, a fitted yoke can be used on the skirt to match the bodice, to give the skirt the length desired.

Many so-called square-dance skirts are gathered into a straight band, with a placket opening at the center back.

If you cut your skirt from a pattern, follow the instructions given for fitting and finishing at the waistline.

Skirt and Dress Plackets

Peasant Skirt Placket. This is the simplest and most practical placket for gathered skirts. Slash center-back section of skirt on a thread to desired depth for placket. For underside of placket, stitch

pleat at bottom, as at **C**. Stitch wide hem from right side. At end of placket, turn and stitch twice across end to stay opening as at **D**.

Placket on Skirt Seam. Used on left-hand side of gathered skirt. Cut two facing pieces 1″ longer

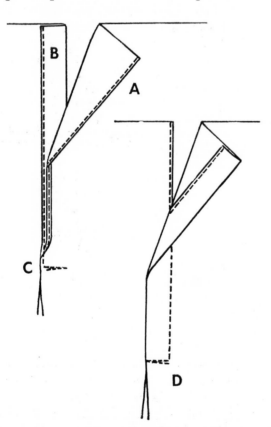

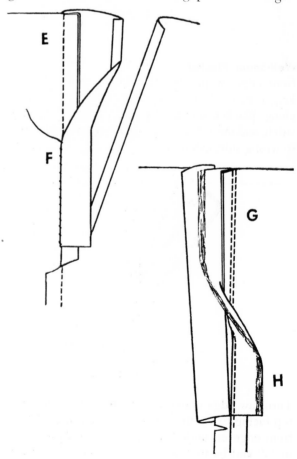

narrow hem as at **A**. Taper off at bottom. For top side of placket, make hem from ½″ to 1″ wide, as at **B**. This is lapped across underside so as to form

than placket opening. Make one strip on the sel-vage and 1⅜″ in width; the other 2¾″ in width. Fold wide strip in half, turn in both edges ⅜″ and lay over under seam allowance and stitch, as at **E**. Stitch or hem other turned edge along seamline, as at **F**. Stitch raw edge of narrow strip to overlapping edge, as at **G**. Press seam toward outer edge. Stitch through strip and seam close to first stitching as at **H**, so when front edge is turned back, stitching will be as at **I**. Overcast raw edges if necessary. Press to wrong side along seamline and press seam to one side against wide edge. Secure ends of strips at bottom by stitching or whipping. No stitching appears on right side.

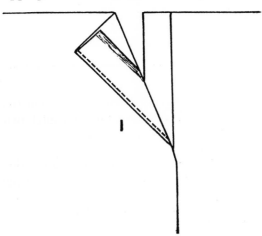

Welt-Seam Placket. Allow 1″ for welt seam on front edge of placket. Cut two facing strips 1″ longer than placket, each 1¼″ wide. Lay these along placket edges, right sides together, and stitch, making ⅛″ seam. Turn facing on under edge to wrong side, extending ¼″ beyond seam, as at **J**.

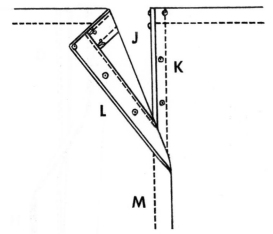

Turn raw edge under and stitch flat as at **K**. Turn top facing to wrong side so that seam lies ¹⁄₁₆″ in from edge on underside, as at **L**. Turn raw edge in ½″ and baste. Stitch on right side ¾″ in from

placket edge from top to bottom of skirt, as at **M**. At end of placket, break bobbin thread, catch seam allowance of back section under needle, and continue stitching. This forms welt. Waistline can be finished with belting and top-stitched around waistline ¾″ down from edge, as shown.

Hook-and-Eye Dress Placket. Cut two bias strips the required length of placket and 1¼″ wide. Use one to bind under edge of placket as at **N**. Lay second strip along other side of placket ⅛″ from edge and stitch ¼″ in from seam edge as at **O**.

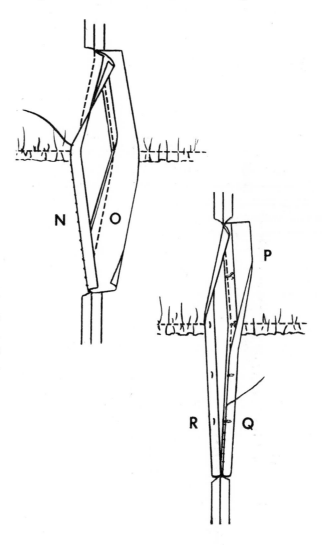

Turn seam edges to wrong side, creasing along seamline. Sew hooks along this edge as at **P**. Turn under raw edge of facing, fold edge over to cover seam edges and lower part of hooks, as at **Q**. Whip in place. Work buttonhole eyes opposite hooks, as at **R**. Clip seam at top and bottom of underside of placket and whip ends of facing pieces together at top and bottom.

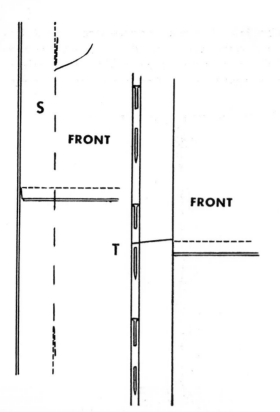

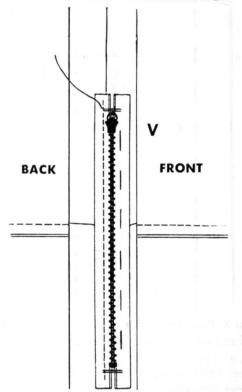

Slide Fastener Dress Placket. In cutting, allow at least ⅝″ for seam along placket. When stitching seam, leave placket opening ½″ longer than fastener. Baste along seamline, as in **S**. Press seam open. Make a fold in back seam allowance ⅛″ from basted seam as at **T**, and pin. Baste fold to left

ble. Still working from wrong side, baste front of dress to fastener, as at **V**. Turn dress to right side and stitch along this line, as at **W**. Pull threads through at top and bottom and tie. Remove bastings and press.

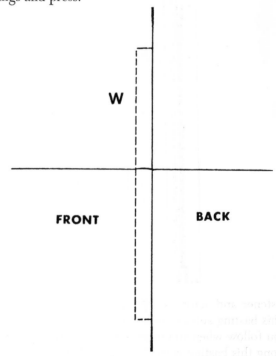

fastener tape, close to teeth, as in **U**. Stitch with Cording or Zipper Foot as close to teeth as possi-

Slide Fastener Skirt Placket. Stitch skirt seams, leaving placket opening on left side. Measure length of fastener plus ½″. Baste along seamline,

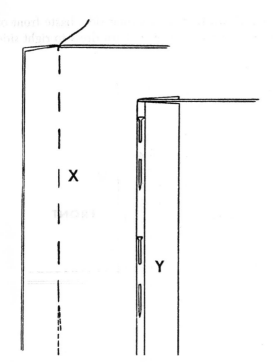

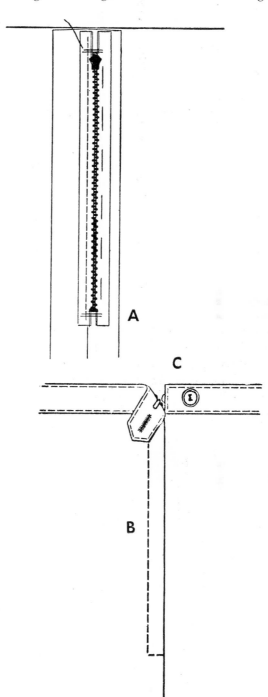

Skirt Belt. Cut belt fabric the length of waistline plus overlap and seam allowance, and twice the finished width plus seams. Fold in half lengthwise with right sides together. Stitch ends. Turn right

as at **X**. Press seam open full length of skirt. Make fold in back seam allowance ⅛″ from basted opening, and pin as in **Y**. Baste fold to left tape of fastener. Stitch along basted line with Cording or Zipper Foot close to metal line, as in **Z**. Lay seam flat, wrong side up, and baste down front side of

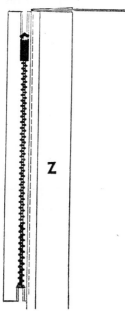

fastener and across below teeth to seam, as at **A**. This basting acts as guide line on right side which you follow when stitching fastener in place. Stitch along this basting with Cording or Zipper Foot, as at **B**. Remove basting from placket opening. Finish waistline with band or belting, catching top ends of fastener tape in seam.

side out. Stitch back of belt to wrong side of skirt waistline. Turn under seam allowance on front edge of belt and top-stitch, as at **C** above. Button and buttonholes can be used as fastening. See page 59. Use a muslin interlining when lightweight fabric is used.

Applying Belting to Waistline of Skirt. Cut belting waistline measurement plus 1½″ for seams. Make ½″ hem on each end, turning ¼″ under, as at **D**. Pin belting along top edge of skirt, extending

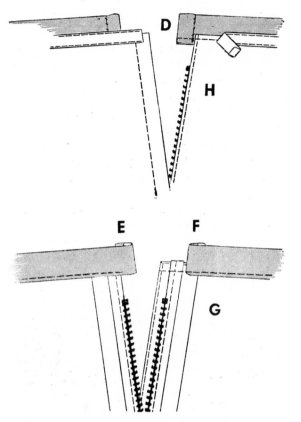

back end about ¾″, as at **E**, and allowing the other end of belting to be the same distance from the front edge, as at **F**. This eliminates the extra bulk that would result if the closing on the belting were directly under the slide of fastener. Stitch close to edge of belting, as at **G**.

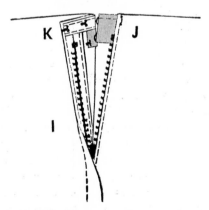

From the right side, pin and baste seam binding over raw edge of skirt top, as at **H**. Stitch along both edges of binding as shown.

When belting is turned down into place, no stitching appears on outside, as in **I**.

Sew two round eyes to back end of belting and hooks to front. Sew straight eye on back top edge, as at **J**, and hook at **K**. This hook and eye fastening helps to make placket smooth. See page 64 for detailed instruction for sewing these fastenings.

Simplified Skirt Placket. After skirt is fitted, re-baste the placket opening in the seamline, as at **L**. Stitch from end of placket down, also all other seams. Press seams open. Turn skirt right side out. Center slide fastener with its right side to basted seamline. Place top of slide ½″ below belt seamline. Pin to position, easing fabric slightly with pins crosswise, as in **M**. Baste in a straight line on both sides, keeping about ¼″ from edge of metal teeth (**N**). Always keep slide fastener closed and do not stretch fabric. Remove pins.

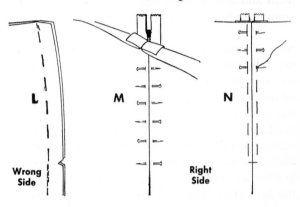

Using Zipper Foot, begin at top of opening and stitch from **O** to **P**, pivot and stitch across to **Q**, pivot again and stitch to **R**. Turn skirt to wrong side and apply facing.

From selvage edge cut a facing strip 1½″ wide and 1¼″ longer than placket. Center facing strip over fastener and pin. Baste along left-hand edge of placket, basting through seam allowance, fastener tape and facing. Stitch as at **S**. Sew across end by hand with back-stitches (**T**). Overcast edges together. Press from wrong side over a velvet press pad or thick toweling.

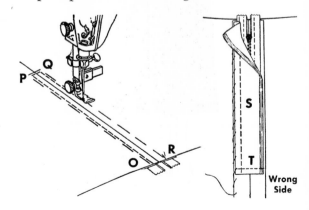

HEMS VARY IN WIDTH AND IN FINISH, DEPENDING upon the fabric and purpose.

For example, the narrowest possible hem is preferred for ruffles made of sheer fabric such as handkerchief linen, organdie, nylon and swiss. Hems of ⅛″ to ¼″ are preferred for percales, calicos, challis and such fabrics as are used for house dresses and aprons. Ginghams and table linens usually call for wider hems—the fineness and evenness of the weave making this desirable. Fashion also has much to say about the width of hems and the method of finishing. Learn all the different hems and how to make them and you will always know which is correct for the fabric and purpose.

Hem Widths. Tissue paper patterns provide the hem allowance appropriate to the type of fabric recommended for the style of pattern. Because figures vary in height, the hem allowance will be too great for a short figure and the surplus will need to be cut away after the hem is turned to provide a hem of correct width. Again tall figures, if allowance has not been made in cutting or if fabric lengths are short, may need a fitted facing to finish the hem edge. The first essential, in any event, is to get a good hem line made with chalk or pins.

Marking for Hem Lengths. There are several methods of marking hem lengths in garments. To mark skirt length: Put the garment on. 1. Use Singer Skirt Marker as illustrated, following in-

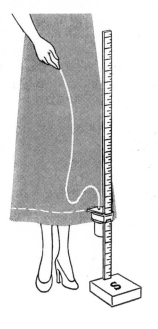

structions that come with the marker. 2. Have someone measure even distance from floor, using a yardstick, and mark the hem turn line with chalk or pins. 3. When there is no one to mark the length for you, stand before mirror, holding yardstick up to figure. Keep one end on floor, turn the body slowly and mark with pins an even distance from floor around fullest part of hips. Remove garment and measure from line down to point of desired hem length. Turn up hem and baste. Put garment on and check evenness of length before finishing hem.

To mark length of jacket or long blouse, use the second or third method above.

After removing garment, lay it flat on table, bottom edge toward you. Turn hem on marked line and pin, keeping edge in line. Baste through hem ¼″ to ½″ from the folded edge, as at **A**. Obtain a

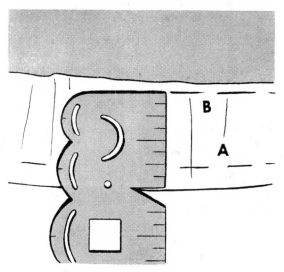

sharp crease at lower edge of hem by pressing lightly through a dampened pressing cloth. Measure depth of hem, using gauge or ruler; allow for finishing at the top. Mark with chalk, as at **B**. Trim hem evenly. Avoid laying excess fullness in pleats, which would mark the right side of the garment when pressed. A row of machine stitching with the bobbin thread drawn up acts as a control of fullness and aids in shrinking to smoothness any excess flare. Use the point of the iron and steam through a dampened pressing cloth.

Finish edge in any of the ways shown on the following pages. Do final pressing before hand-hemming or using the Blind-Stitch Attachment.

Blind-Stitched Hems. Almost-invisible hems can now be obtained on a wide variety of fabrics by using the Blind-Stitch Attachment. Easy to put in place on your machine, it will enable you to do practically invisible hemming much faster than by hand on all types of wearing apparel and household articles. Follow instruction booklet provided with your attachment. Practice, especially in preparing material for hemming, will insure your handling the Blind-Stitcher with ease and speed on all fabrics.

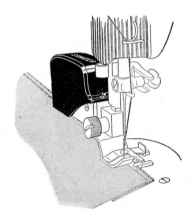

Seam-Binding Finish. The most generally used hem for dresses and skirts because of its invisibility and lack of bulk. Stitch seam binding along top of hem so that raw edge is concealed. Turn up hem; pin at seams to keep in line, and baste. Finish hem with Blind-Stitcher. Or, if you prefer a hand-finish, slip-stitch in place, taking tiny stitches in garment and longer stitches in seam binding, as shown.

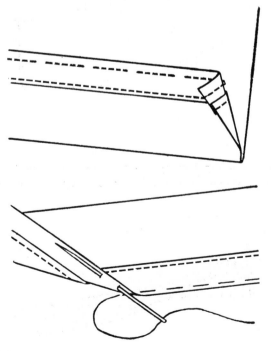

Hem with Pinked Edge. Many women who sew are intrigued with the simple hems used in ready-to-wear. These may be very easily done at home.

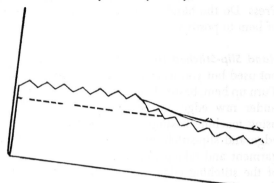

Measure depth of hem, cut raw edge with pinking shears, turn hem to place, ease and shrink any fullness, then baste ⅜″ from pinked edge. Put hem in with Blind-Stitcher; press—and you have a simple, practical, bulkless hem that imitates a hand slip-stitch. Especially good on lightweight fabrics.

Bias-Bound Hem. In fabrics that fray easily, such as open-weave woolens, sometimes it is desirable to bind the edge before hemming. Measure depth of hem. Ease and shrink any fullness. Bind raw edge, using Multi-Slotted Binder. Turn hem to position and baste close to binding, then put hem in with the Blind-Stitcher. Press.

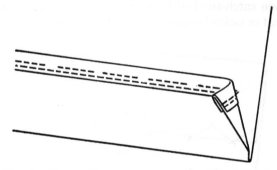

Circular Hem. Yes, you can use the Blind-Stitcher on a circular skirt. Measure depth of hem. Turn raw edge ⅜″ to wrong side and machine-baste close to fold. Turn hem to depth desired and pin

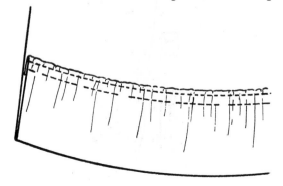

along bottom fold. Draw up machine-basting and distribute fullness evenly so entire bottom edge of hem lies smooth. Baste ¼″ below top edge of hem. Press. Do the blind-stitching, then press top edge of hem to position.

Hand Slip-Stitched Hem. When seam binding is not used but you want invisibility, make this hem. Turn up hem, baste along fold. Even the hem, turn under raw edge and stitch free from garment, using machine basting. Fold hem back along top edge and slip-stitch, picking up only a thread in garment and taking long stitch along fold in top of the stitching edge. Make stitches easy so that they will not draw or show on right side.

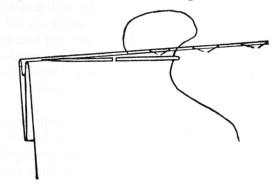

Catch-Stitched Hem. Firm, evenly woven fabric may be finished with a plain or pinked edge and then catch-stitched in place. Favored for holding coat or jacket hems in place when garment is lined.

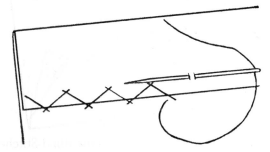

Top-Stitched Hem. Turn hem allowance and top-stitch, using 3 or 5 parallel rows. Trim top edge

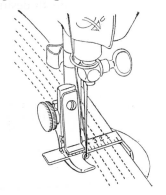

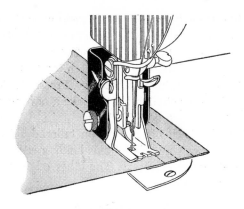

close to top row of stitching. When hem allowance is very narrow or fabric ravels, stitch seam binding to raw edge before making hem turn, then baste and top-stitch.

This is a practical finish for a slightly flared or a pleated skirt. Allow skirt to hang, mark length, make narrow hem turn, and baste. Stitch evenly and trim top edge away. Use Gauge Presser Foot (see below, left) to insure even rows.

Use the Walking Presser Foot (see above) for ease in stitching on napped or pile fabrics.

Faced Hem. Use a true bias or cut a fitted facing on same grain as circular edge. Lay facing along edge, right sides together, and stitch ¼″ from bottom. Press seam open and turn facing to wrong side. Turn edge under, clip, baste and press; then stitch top edge of facing. Slip-stitch hem in position.

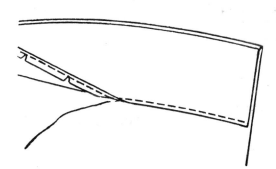

Bias Binding Finishes. Hand-baste hem close to turn. Machine-baste ¼″ from raw edge. Draw up

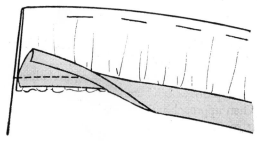

bobbin thread, easing in fullness until bobbin thread has been "easily" drawn. Lay crease of bias binding along stitching line and stitch, covering line of machine-basting. Slip-stitch top of binding in position, keeping stitches easy. Press.

On flared or circular skirts, make a narrow hem to avoid bulk.

Another finish often used on tailored skirts is shown below. One edge of bias binding is stitched to raw edge of hem turn. The other edge is slip-stitched in position.

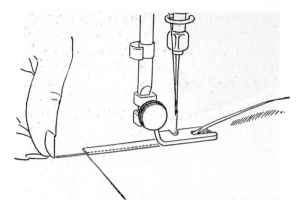

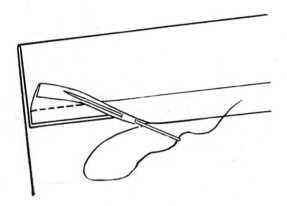

Hem Over Pleat. Clip the part of seam along pleat that would fall within hem turn. Open seam and press flat to avoid bulk inside hem. Then turn hem and finish.

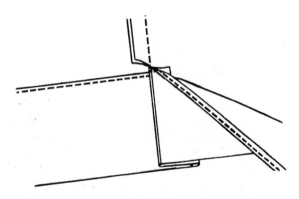

Narrow Machine-Stitched Hem. For speed and neatness, make with Foot Hemmer. Width of hem varies from ⅛″ to ¼″, depending on weight of fabric. Turn hem width for an inch or two. Crease, then slide into Hemmer and lower needle to catch end of fabric. Hold ends of both threads and pull backward as you start to stitch, keeping edge of fabric slightly to the right as it enters, so that it will turn easily, make an even hem, and allow you to sew rapidly without running off edge.

When approaching a seam, avoid bulk by clipping seam edges to a point. Before beginning a

hem on loosely woven, easily frayed fabric, stitch along edge that is to be hemmed to make it sturdier and easier to put through Hemmer. When hemming bias-cut fabrics or open-mesh and knit fabrics, it is well to slip a piece of paper underneath to insure an even line.

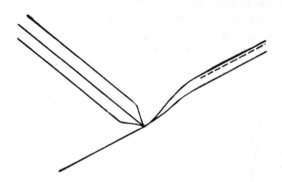

Wide Machine-Stitched Hem. For hems wider than ³⁄₁₆″, the Adjustable Hemmer is advisable. Follow machine instruction book for directions in using this attachment.

To make hem without attachment, turn under raw edge ⅛″ to ¼″, clipping turned edge at intervals so that it will lie flat. Turn up hem to desired depth, using ruler or gauge for accurate measuring. Crease or baste and stitch.

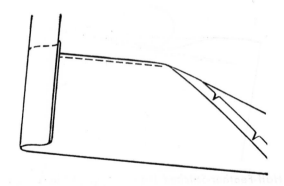

Rolled Hem. Used often as finish for delicate lightweight fabrics.

By Machine. The Flange Hemmer can be used

to make ⅛" hem on sheer fabrics. Use for long hems, as on ruffles and curtains.

By Hand. Keep fingers immaculate so that roll will stay clean and fresh during handling. To provide *body* for fabrics such as batiste, voile, sheer handkerchief linen, run row of machine-stitching close to edge, then roll edge with thumb and finger to conceal stitching and slip-stitch, using fine needle and thread. Crisp fabrics, such as organdie, hold roll without stitching.

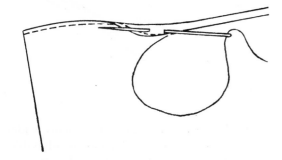

Italian Rolled Hem. May also be used on lightweight fabrics, but more often used on even weave linen for napkins and table cloths. Roll hem turn with thumb and forefinger, taking a small stitch in fabric and then one in roll until several stitches are on needle before drawing needle through.

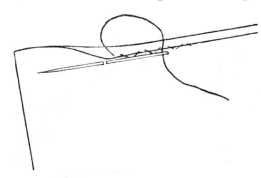

Half-Feather-Stitched Hem. A quick finish, good on fabrics with surface threads that can be caught without having needle go through to right side. Work toward yourself, catching a thread of fabric and edge of hem, bringing needle out over thread as in a wide-spaced blanket-stitch. Often used on home furnishings.

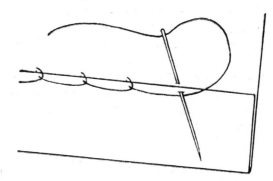

Napery Hem Turn edge on a fabric thread, crease, then turn and crease again to make hem. Fold fabric back along top edge of hem. Using strong thread, catch both creases with a small overhanding-stitch. When carefully done, this finish looks almost the same on both sides. It is chiefly used on table linens.

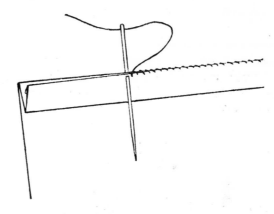

Milliner's Fold. Turn raw edge up on right side, to about double the depth of desired hem. Make second turn, bringing fold up to cover raw edge. This makes four layers of fabric. From wrong side, catch needle through three layers using an uneven basting-stitch. Finished fold may be from ⅜" to ¾" wide, according to weight of fabric. A good finish for slightly stiffened, non-washable fabrics such as net, mull, or mourning crepe.

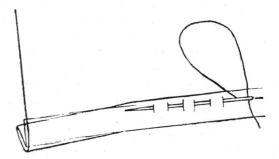

Belts and Belt Carriers

WHEN MAKING A BELT ACCORDING TO A PATTERN, follow instructions exactly as to cutting and grain of fabric. In other cases, it is generally best to make your belt on the lengthwise grain, unless there are stripes to be matched. If the belt strip must be pieced to make the required length, do this first. For a belt with a lapped fastening, allow about 4″ for finishing and lap. Try out length of a tie belt with a strip of the fabric to be sure that you leave enough length for tying and for ends of appropriate length. Belts that have a tongue buckle require a little more length than the lapped closing, say 6″ or 7″.

Turned Belt. Cut belt strip of desired length and twice the finished width plus seam allowances. Fold in half lengthwise, right side in. Stitch raw edges together on long edge of belt, making a scant ¼″ seam. Stitch across one end. Trim corners

and clip seam edges at intervals as shown above. Press seam open. With your orange stick push the closed end of the belt inside and draw rest of

length back over it to turn to right side. Press. Ends of belt may be finished in any one of several ways. Open end may be turned in and whipped across. Open end may be stitched into a seam, as at side of a dress, or turned under and attached, as to waist of apron. Stitched end may be clipped off and both ends finished alike in points or rounded tips by turning edges under and whipping. For bathrobes, fringe may be inserted in the ends, edges turned in and whipped to it. All edges of belt may be top-stitched if desired.

This belt is practical for any wash garment—house dresses and the like. It may be fastened by lapping the ends with hook and eye closing and a snap fastener to hold the point in place, or with a light buckle or slide buckle.

The method used for making it is also used for neck straps on aprons, overalls, etc., and for other types of ties, bands and straps.

Tie Belt. Soft unlined belt with tie ends, often used on lingerie and other lightweight garments. Made in much the same way as turned belt, except that opening is left in long edge to turn to right side so that ends are finished alike in the desired shape (round, pointed, etc.). Fold belt in half lengthwise. Stitch both ends and long edge, leaving an opening of 2″ or 3″, as at **A**. Press. Notch curved ends as shown. With orange stick, push

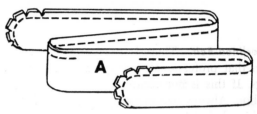

ends through and out opening. Whip edges of opening together. Press. Top-stitch edges, if desired.

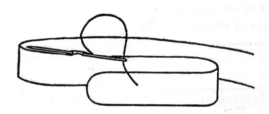

Stitched Belt. Cut a strip of firm muslin the length of the belt piece and ¼″ narrower than finished width of belt. Belt piece should be twice finished width plus seam allowance. Lay belt piece face down on table. Center muslin strip on it. Pin and baste in place. Plan the number of rows of stitching you want on belt. Stitch right side up, using

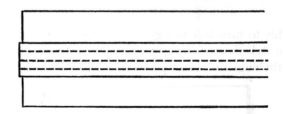

the edge of the presser foot as a guide to evenness and spacing of stitching rows. Stitch all rows from same end to avoid rippling of fabric. Lay edges of

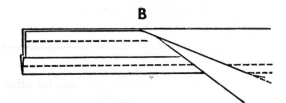

B

belt fabric together, right sides in, and stitch, as at **B**. Press seam open and turn belt to right side. Center seamline on back of belt, as at **C**, and press. Finish ends of belt in any of the ways suggested under *Turned Belt*, page 100.

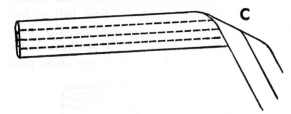

C

Interlined Belt. There is a rather stiff belting ribbon that professionals use for their belt interlinings. If this is not obtainable, use firm grosgrain ribbon. Always dampen and press ribbon before making belt to prevent puckering later. Cut belt fabric desired length and twice finished width plus ¾″ for making. Fold in half lengthwise and crease. Lay belting ribbon along crease on wrong side of belt fabric, as at **D** and stitch in place along both edges of ribbon. Turn fabric back, right sides to-

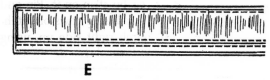

D

gether, so that raw edges meet. Make seam, keeping stitching close to edge of ribbon, as at **E**. Leave ends open. Fasten safety pin to one end and use

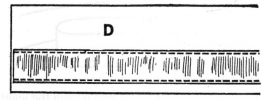

E

this to turn belt to right side. Press. Finish ends in style desired. This makes a nice belt because no stitchings show on right side.

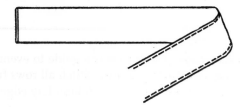

Faced Belt. Use belting ribbon or grosgrain. Cut belt piece desired length and width plus seam allowances. Turn fabric edges to wrong side, making same width as ribbon. Baste, if necessary, and press. Pin to ribbon, wrong side down, as at **F**.

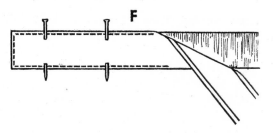

F

Shape ends as desired, turn end edges of fabric and ribbon toward each other and pin. Stitch all around belt close to edge, as shown. When very little fabric is available for a belt, this is best method to use. Make all piecings and press seams open before stitching belt to facing.

Hand-Finished Belt. This type is best for velvet, brocade, metal cloth, etc., which could not be turned without damaging the fabric. Cut belt piece and ribbon as for *Interlined Belt*. Lay edges of fabric and ribbon so that they just overlap enough to be stitched, as in **G**. Stitch fabric to top

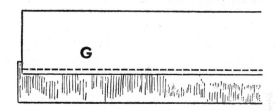

G

edge of ribbon. Fold fabric around ribbon so as to cover it. Turn raw edge of fabric in, as in **H**. Pin, inserting pins at right angles to edge. Shape ends, turn fabric edges and pin. Finish edges by hand with long whipping-stitches. Keep hand-finished edge at top when wearing belt.

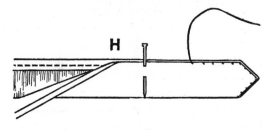

H

Plain Closing. Inconspicuous belt fastening which does not break the line of the garment with any buckle or ornament. Place round eye under edge of left-hand end of belt. Hook is sewed on wrong side of right-hand end at point where ends

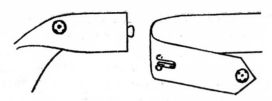

lap. Sew on snap fastener to hold the lapped end in place.

Tongue Buckle Closing. With stiletto punch two holes, a short distance apart, near one end of belt, as at **I**, leaving enough space at end to turn back over buckle and finish off. Use point of scissors and cut between holes to form an oblong opening, as at **J**. Finish edge of opening as you would a

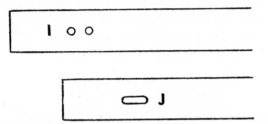

worked eyelet (see page 65). Insert buckle tongue, draw short end of belt through buckle and back over edge on wrong side. Turn edge under and either machine-stitch or whip by hand in place. Put on belt and mark correct size. Make a worked eyelet at this point and one on either side an inch away.

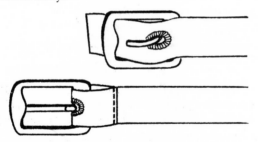

Slide Closing. Draw end of belt through and around center bar of slide. Turn end under on wrong side of belt and either stitch or whip in position, as at **K**.

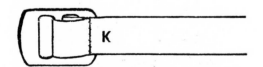

Belt Carriers. As a rule, since belt carriers should be inconspicuous, a worked carrier is used. If the carriers serve as accent on a dress or skirt, a fabric carrier can be used in matching or contrasting color. (Drawings for thread carriers and

French tack show thread magnified to about five times actual size.)

Worked Carrier. Take two or three small stitches at points just above and below belt line, making the strands of thread between them slightly longer than width of belt. Blanket-stitch over threads as at **L**. Fasten securely on wrong side.

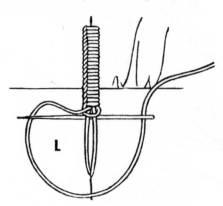

Bullion-Stitch Carrier. Mark points above and below belt line at which carrier is to be fastened. Put needle through one and out the other, leaving it in the fabric, as at **M**. Bunch up fabric on needle, as at **N**, and wind thread many times around point end of needle, as at **O**. Draw needle and

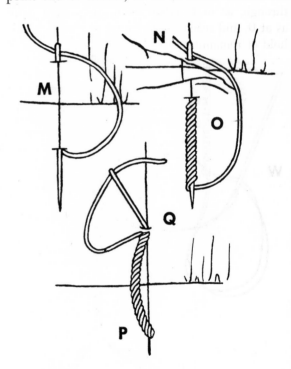

thread through winding and tighten loop down to fabric, as in **P**. Insert needle at end of carrier, as at **Q**, pull through to wrong side and secure end there.

Chain-Stitch Carrier. Mark points for position of carrier. Use double thread and knot ends together. Bring needle through from wrong side at either top or bottom point of carrier, as at **R**. Take a small

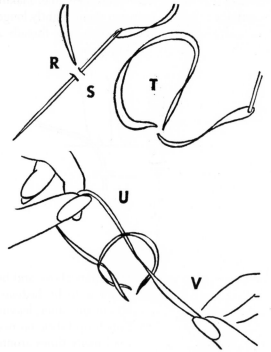

stitch, as at **S**, but draw thread only part way through, as in **T**. Hold needle with right hand, as at **U**, and reach through loop of thread to take hold of remaining thread with left hand, as at **V**.

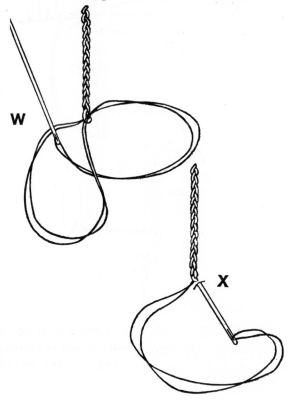

Holding needle and thread taut in right hand, pull with left hand until first loop is tightened down to fabric and a second loop is formed. Then again reach through loop just made with left hand and pull another loop through and tighten as before. Continue making loops until length of chain is sufficient to make the carrier. Bring needle through last loop to fasten, as in **W**. Put needle through to wrong side, as at **X**, and fasten with back-stitches.

Fabric Carrier. Cut strip of fabric as long as belt width plus ½″ for fastening to garment. Width of strip should be about ¾″. Fold in half lengthwise, right side in, and stitch edges together, making ⅛″ seam. Turn inside out, as in **Y**. Center the seam on back of strip and press. Turn each end back a scant ¼″ and whip in place. If desired, raw edges of strip may be turned in and carrier machine-stitched on each side before attaching.

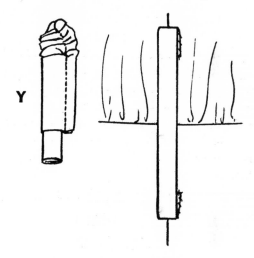

French Tack. Useful for attaching belt invisibly to garment. (Also used to hold linings in position at bottom of coats and draperies.) Taking small stitches in belt and dress, as in **Z**, or coat and lining, make several strands between them from ½″ to 1″ in length. Blanket-stitch over these threads, keeping stitches close.

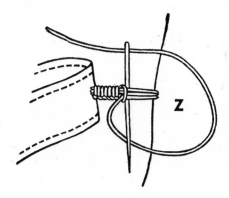

Tailoring Well Done

TAILORING IS SEWING WITH CARE, CUTTING, BAST-
ing, stitching, pressing, yes, caressing fabric to
shape to form a garment. The principles of tailoring are practically the same whether one is making a heavy or lightweight coat, a pair of slacks
or a flannel blouse. We have chosen a tailored
suit to give details of making, because in this you
will find illustrated or explained almost all the
principles necessary to know in making any kind
of garment that requires "tailoring."

Tailored suits of good design, fabric and workmanship should have a long life—five to ten years
—if care is given to the upkeep. Let the following
points guide you in selecting a suit for yourself.

In the first place, buy a fabric right for a suit—
one that will tailor nicely but that is pliant enough
to hug to your figure and not box you in like a
board. Fine worsteds, lightweight tweeds and
soft, firmly woven flannels are ideal. Choose a
color best for you—not necessarily one favored by
fashion in the season in which you are making
your suit, but one that is right for your coloring,
your activities, your own joy in ownership.

Choose a design right for your fabric and for
you. If you are short and stocky, avoid jackets that
are too long or skirts that are too full or too "cut
up." If you are tall and slender, stay away from
the extreme slim lines, and especially conspicuous
stripes. If you want to get the ultimate in wear
from your suit, then classic lines are best for you.
If a V neckline is not your best, then a Peter Pan-
type collar, or no collar, is just as classic as the V
and often less mannish and more flattering. If a
six-gore or four-gore skirt is your best, choose that,
even though fashion says pleats are good. Pleats
come and go, but a conservatively gored skirt is
good at any time.

Avoid bulk at your waistline. A slim waist is
ever to be desired. Use lightweight interfacing in
your suit and a fine, closely woven, lightweight
lining. Buttons of self-fabric are always good, but
decorative buttons can be used if you prefer. Any-
way, be as deliberate in your choice of fabric,
design and trimming of a suit as you would be in
decorating a room. Be selective, be conservative
and make a suit that will show fine workmanship
and be worth much more than the amount spent
for fabric, pattern, and findings.

When you have decided upon fabric and pattern, check pattern to see how much yardage is
required for your size. Then and then only, buy
your fabric. Notice if fabric label says it is preshrunk and ready to use. If not, sponge the fabric
as instructed on page 16. This is good precaution
and always necessary where the fabric does not
carry a pre-shrunk label.

Straighten Your Fabric. First, straighten ends of
your fabric by pulling a crosswise thread and then
cutting on the drawn threadline, selvage to selvage. Then stretch the fabric straight by pulling
diagonally until all edges come even. See illustrations on page 16. Lay fabric out on a flat cutting
surface. See the instruction sheet that comes with
your pattern and choose the pattern diagram
suited to the width of the fabric you are using. If
instructions are for cutting on a fold, as is often
the case in woolens, fold lengthwise, wrong side
up and pin selvages and ends together.

Read *all* instructions on pattern envelope and
cutting guide. Fit pattern pieces to you and make
any necessary adjustments. (See *Pattern Adjustments*, pages 26 and 31.) Place pattern pieces on
your fabric, all to run in the same direction, so
that any sheen or shading of color in the fabric
will be uniform throughout your garment. See
page 15. Make sure center of each pattern piece
is placed on the correct grain according to the
lengthwise perforations or markings. (See *Pattern
Layout—Cutting and Marking*, page 31.) Pin each
pattern piece on smoothly and place it to have
ample seam allowance. Cut out the suit, doing this
carefully with cutting shears.

Before you remove pattern from fabric mark each
piece with tailors' tacks and chalk, so that when
pattern is removed your garment will be well
charted for easy assembling. Use tailors' tacks to
mark position of darts, pleats, buttons, and buttonholes. Use a line of basting to mark center fronts
and backs of jacket and skirt.

Cut and mark lining and interfacing as the pattern indicates. Stay-stitch curved seams to prevent
stretching.

MAKING A SKIRT

Assemble Skirt. Pinning from waistline down, pin
and baste gores together, side fronts to front panel

and side backs to back panel. Begin the left-hand seam placket-length below waistline, as at **A**.

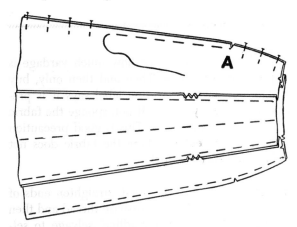

Make Belt. This is preparation for fitting: Baste and stitch straight seam binding along one edge of belt, ¼″ from edge on wrong side, as at **B**. This gives support to inside of belt and helps prevent stretching. Fold belt in half lengthwise and stitch across ends. One end can be straight or pointed, as at **C**. The inside end is straight as shown. Belt should be 1½″ longer than waist-measure to provide for overlapping as at **D**. Trim seams. Clip corners, turn right side out and press.

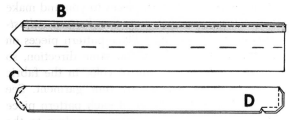

Baste Belt to Skirt. Pin and baste belt to right side of skirt, as in **E**. Fit skirt, make any necessary adjustments in fitting, then remove it. Stitch and press all seams. See *Pressing*, page 51. Overcast or pink all seam edges. Make *Slide Fastener Skirt Placket* as on page 92.

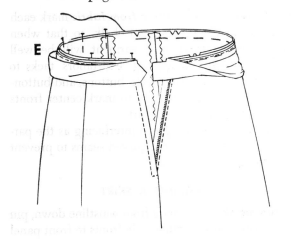

Stitch belt to skirt. Then turn skirt wrong side out. Press waistline seam up and inside the belt. Turn under free edge of belt and pin over seam edges as at **F**. Whip edge to place as shown. If desired, bulk can be eliminated by cutting the belt along a selvage edge and avoiding a bulky seam allowance. Selvage edge is whipped to position as shown in **F**. If desired, top-stitch edges of belt.

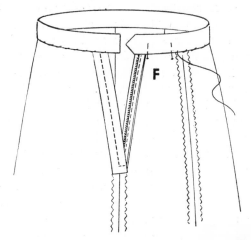

Belt Closing. Close zipper. Lap ends of belt and place pins to mark position of fasteners. For a plain finish, use two hooks and eyes in line with the zipper. Sew a snap to place if belt is pointed. Place as in **G**. See *Hooks and Eyes*, page 64. For button and buttonhole closing, see page 59. If a bound buttonhole is used, make it before belt is stitched to the skirt.

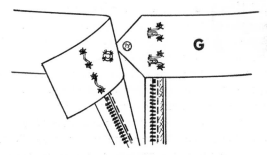

The Hem. Wearing heels of desired height, put skirt on and mark length. (See page 95.) Remove skirt. Turn up hem, pin and baste. Choose from pages 96–98 the type of hem finish best suited to your fabric. After hem is finished, do final pressing from wrong side. Avoid pressing *around* skirt bottom, rather press with the up-and-down grain of skirt to prevent stretching of hemline.

MAKING A JACKET

Assemble the Jacket. Baste any darts. Working from shoulders down, pin and baste jacket pieces together, matching notches and tailors' tacks, side fronts to front sections, side backs together or to back panel, underarm and shoulder seams (**A**).

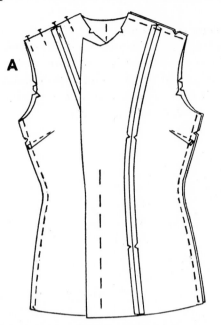

Pin, baste and stitch two undercollar pieces together (**B**); press seam open. Pin collar interfacing to wrong side of undercollar and baste along neckline edge and on roll line (**C**). Pin and baste

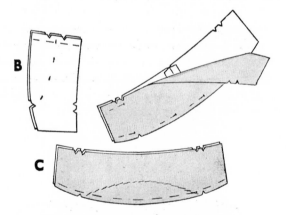

undercollar to neckline of jacket, matching notches, with right sides together (**D**). Pin and baste sleeve sections together (**E**). See also instructions on page 83. Then pin and baste both

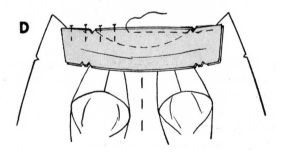

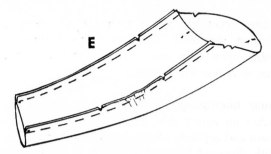

sleeves into their respective armholes. See *Setting Sleeve in Armhole,* page 82. Place shoulder pads, if used, to position, pinning them for the first fitting.

Fit Jacket. Put the finished skirt on. Fit jacket over blouse or gilet. Lap and pin fronts so center front bastings overlap each other.

Check the following when fitting: Darts. The seamlines should hang straight and smooth from shoulder to hem. Place a pin at point to indicate the correct length of shoulder and chalk this. Look at the back. If you are fitting yourself, try to have two mirrors so you can see without lifting your arms to hold a mirror. If pads are used, see if they should be thicker or thinner. (See *Fitting of Shoulders* on page 50.) If one shoulder is lower than another, correct by making one pad slightly thicker than the other or by using a pad for one shoulder and not the other.

Bustline smooth? If not, adjust seams and darts accordingly. Suit should hang straight down from fullest line of bust. If it hikes, open shoulder and drop upper front down enough. If there is a diagonal sag below bust, then lift the front at the shoulder. Sometimes the same adjustments need to be made in the back, the shoulder blades making the pivotal point as the bust does in the front.

Make sure waistline curve is in proper location, and that buttonholes are in correct position for your bust and waistline, that is, at fullest part of bust and exactly at the waistline. If you are short-waisted, then place waistline button as low as possible. If long-waisted, then it can be placed slightly higher than the exact normal.

Do armholes and sleeves feel comfortable? If necessary, clip edge of the armhole, especially at the front underarm curve. Do sleeves hang straight? Check the roll line of undercollar as to becomingness and comfort. Chalk-mark any changes necessary.

Stitch the Jacket. First remove undercollar. Chalk-mark any fitting changes and rebaste seams where necessary. Stitch darts and all seams, including shoulders. Press as stitched. Press all seams open. Clip seams above and below waistline so seams will be flat and smooth.

Front Interfacing. Pin interfacing to front of jacket on wrong side. Pin and baste to shoulder seam and armhole (**F**). Starting at neckline, baste with diagonal basting along roll line then along front edge to bottom of jacket, as at **G**. Fasten interfacing to lapels with rows of padding stitches about ½″ apart (**H**), starting close to roll line and

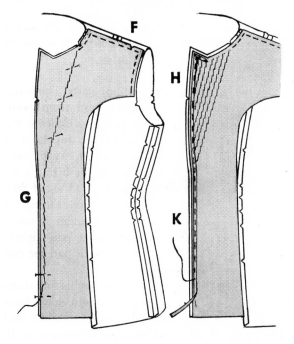

ending at seamline. Use thread to match fabric, taking up only one or two threads of fabric underneath and using long stitches on top. As you work, roll lapel over first finger with thumb, holding it firm as in **I**. Begin each line of stitches at top of lapel and work to outer edge. This will shape

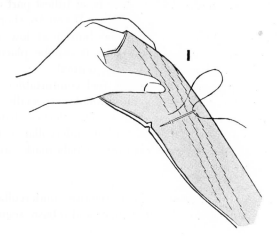

lapels as they will be worn and no stitches will pull. Trim off interfacing around lapel to blend seam edge, before applying tape.

Shrinking and Shaping Tape. Flat linen tape or seam binding can be used to tape a seam in tailoring, depending on weight of fabric. **J** shows how tape is shaped. With a small brush, dampen the tape. Use tip of iron to shrink one edge, while shaping and stretching the opposite edge.

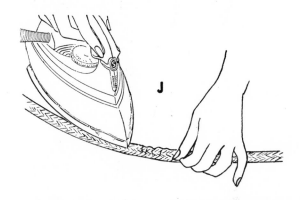

Sew the tape over interfacing along seamline of front edges of jacket. Start at end of collar line and continue to bottom of jacket (**K**).

Interfacing Undercollar. Sew interfacing to undercollar on roll line, either by padding stitches or machine, then fill in lower section with rows of stitches about ¼″ apart as at **L**. Hand padding stitches are preferable because they are invisible and collar can be worn turned up, if desired. Use

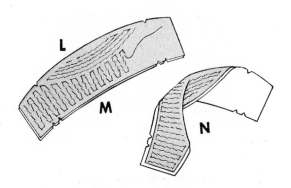

padding stitches to fasten balance of undercollar to interfacing, working up and down as in **M**. Sew only to seamline. While sewing, roll undercollar over in same way as you did lapel. See **I**. Fold collar on roll line and stretch outer edge. Press, to retain shaping, as in **N**.

Apply Undercollar to Jacket. Match center back of undercollar to center back of neckline, right sides together. When basting, work from jacket side and follow neck curve as chalk-marked in the fitting. Clip neckline of jacket wherever necessary, so curved edges do not draw. Try on, to make sure of a good fit of the undercollar. Stitch undercollar in position as in **O**. Press jacket completely, using a steam iron if possible. Trim away seam allowance of interfacing close to seamline to eliminate bulk. Clip at shoulder. Press neckline seam open on both front ends, press it up toward undercollar in back, as in **P**. Hang on a hanger to dry before doing final stitching.

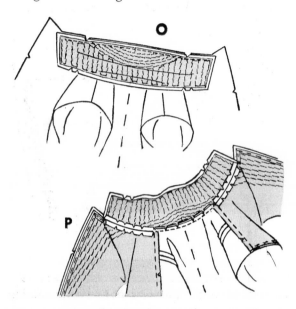

Make Buttonholes. Measure buttons and mark for width as instructed on page 59. If using bound buttonholes, make them now. (See page 61.) When using canvas or haircloth interfacing, cut away a rectangle for each buttonhole. Use a firm sheer fabric as a stay for each buttonhole. If tailored buttonholes are used, they are made after facing is stitched to position. (See page 60.) If pockets are used, put them in or on at this time. (See pages 67–71.)

Apply Facings. Pin and baste front facings to collar. Stitch. Clip seam edge of facing so front edge will be flat when seams are pressed open (**Q**). Pin collar and facings to undercollar and jacket fronts, right sides together. Baste. Starting at back, stitch around collar, as at **R**. Then, in a separate operation, stitch fronts, starting at inside edge of facing. Stitch up around lapel to ends of collar at neckline as at **S**. Overlap a few stitches for security at points where collar and lapels meet.

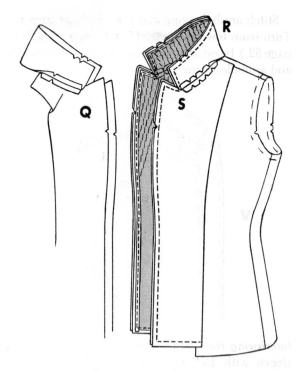

To obtain true points on lapels, take two or three stitches across point (number depending on fabric weight). See close-up of point (**T**).

Snip off all corners, then blend seams by trimming the three edges to different widths. Trim interfacing quite close to stitching line and other edges, as in **U**. Clip edges when necessary. Press as stitched.

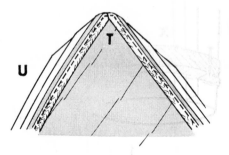

Turn facing to inside of jacket. Baste close to turned edge, around collar and down front edges (**V**), basting so seam does not show on right side. Use silk thread for this basting, as it will not mark fabric while being given first press. Then remove basting for final press.

Finish Sleeves. Stitch sleeve seams. Press open. Rebaste sleeves to position following details on page 82. Pin in shoulder pads for second fitting. Put jacket on. Check position of sleeves in armholes. Turn bottom of sleeves to desired length. After removing jacket, mark this turned edge with a basting thread.

Stitch armhole seam and trim. Press as stitched. Turn seam toward sleeve. (See *Press as You Sew,* page 52.) Insert shoulder pads, tacking to shoulder and armhole seams.

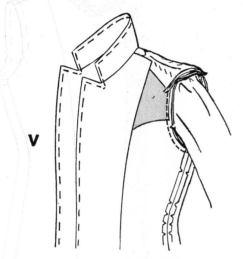

Interfacing Hem Edge. Interface bottom edge of sleeve with 1½″ wide strip of bias-cut muslin. Fold bias lengthwise, making ¼″ turn-up, as in **W**. Lay fold of bias strip above basted line around bottom of sleeve and pin to position. Tack ends of bias together and tack to seam edges (**X**). Turn

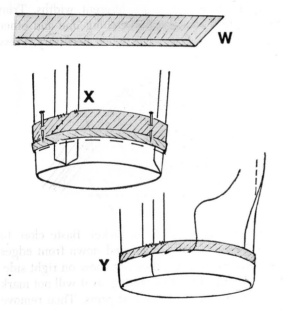

hem of sleeve up to position. Tack bottom of sleeve to the bias as in **Y**, taking care that no stitches catch through to right side.

Finish Jacket. Put on jacket. Lap and pin fronts. Check length. Turn up hem and pin. Remove jacket. Mark hem turn with basting. Press hem, steaming out any excess fullness. Insert bias muslin strip inside bottom hem as in sleeves. Tack top

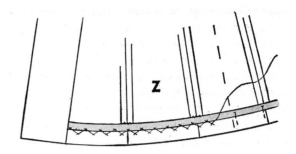

edge of jacket hem to muslin with easy catch-stitches, as in **Z**. Tack bias muslin strips to all side seams.

Pin front facings to position and fasten as in **A**, using loose tacking-stitch. Snip facing at top of

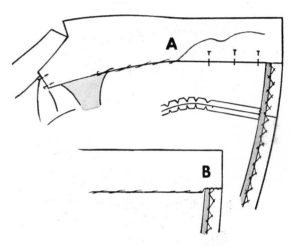

hem, turn edge under and whip to hem (**B**). Back-stitch across base of collar to secure facing at neckline and on shoulder, as in **C**.

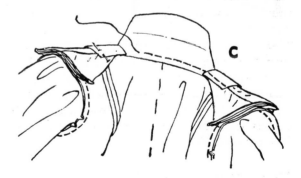

If bound buttonholes have been put in, finish these by accurately cutting facing back of each buttonhole. Hem facing against each buttonhole. Remove bastings and press. Mark for, and sew buttons to position as instructed on page 63.

Press Jacket. Press from wrong side, again using a steam iron if available. Otherwise use regular iron and a damp cloth. Do not press hard with iron. Steam fabric and leave slightly damp. If pressed dry, right side of fabric may be made shiny. After each pressing, hang jacket carefully on hanger to dry, lapping and pinning fronts as they come on figure and stuffing tissue paper under the shoulders.

PREPARE THE LINING

Stitch Lining. Make any changes in lining you made in fitting of jacket. Pin, baste and stitch all seams except shoulder. Baste and press dart tucks, as at **D**. If an ease pleat is allowed at center back, baste this in and press. Stitch sleeve linings. Press all seams open.

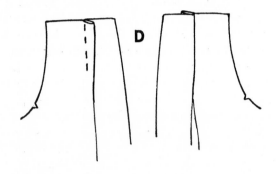

Insert Lining. Place jacket on dress form or hanger wrong side out. Place lining right side out over jacket. Match all seams and pin. Pin around armhole and along shoulder seam.

Remove jacket from dress form or hanger. Mark shoulder line and armhole line. Sew lining and jacket seams together along underarm, as at **E**, using long basting stitches. Fasten thread securely

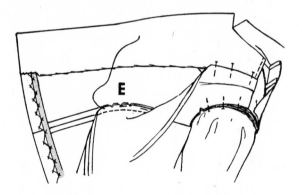

at armhole and leave bottom end of the thread free about 3″ above hem. The leeway in thread will prevent lining from drawing.

Turn in front edge of lining and pin to inside edge of facing (**F**). Slip-stitch to position. Baste front lining over shoulder seams. Turn in seam

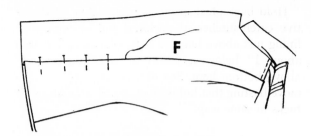

allowance on back shoulders, pin over fronts and whip (**G**). Baste around both armholes as shown.

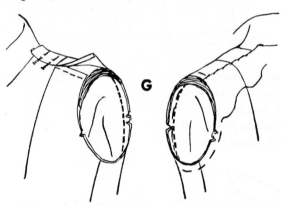

Turn neckline seam in, clipping edge for smooth finish. Pin, then whip to position, covering stitching line across base of collar (**H**).

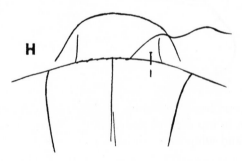

An allowance of ½″ to ¾″ is usually made for ease in lining length. Turn under hem allowance along bottom of lining and baste to jacket ½″ to ¾″ above fold as at **I**, to hold lining to position while finishing. Bottom of lining is folded back on basting line while you slip-stitch lining to jacket hem as at **J**.

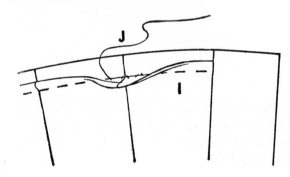

Hold back pleat in position with 3 or 4 decorative catch-stitches at neckline and at bottom of lining just above hem, as in **K**, or make a bar tack about 1″ below neckline, at waistline, and 1″ above bottom hem. See details on page 112. Remove basting that holds pleat. Finish shoulder dart tucks in same way.

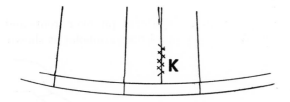

Finish Sleeve Lining. With sleeve lining wrong side out, match notches of lining underarm seam to notches of sleeve seam, and pin. Sew lining seam to jacket seam with long basting stitches as in **L**. Start basting about 3″ from top, leaving bot-

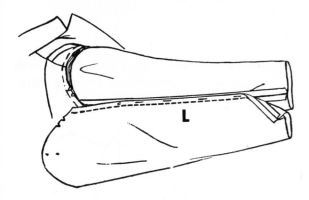

tom end free. Turn lining to right side over sleeve. Turn in top edge of sleeve lining. Easing fullness, pin and whip over armhole seams (**M**.)

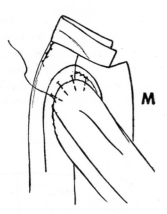

Allowance for ease in sleeve lining is about ½″. Turn up lower edge, baste to sleeve and slip-stitch to sleeve hem in same way as illustrated in **I** and **J** on page 110.

LINING A LOOSE COAT

The instructions given here are for any unfitted coat. For any fitted coat, regardless of length, the method given in lining a suit coat, on opposite page, should be followed.

Fashion varies the shape of raglan sleeves. Sometimes they are fitted in the shoulders, other times loose. The following instructions apply to all types of raglan and loose coats.

Finish hem of coat as desired. See *Hem Finishes*, page 95. Illustrated at **A**: seam binding stitched to top edge and catch-stitched to position.

Cut the lining according to pattern instructions. Allow for a tuck at the center back, which may be laid over a stitched seam that is not pressed open. Usually a lining fabric cuts to better advantage with a center back seam. If so, use it by all means. Stitch and press all seams. Pin sleeves to body of lining and stitch. See page 84. Clip the seams, then press them open. Baste the tuck as shown at **B**.

Place coat on dress form wrong side out. Lay lining right side out over coat. Pin to position as shown, matching all seams. For this, begin at neck in back (**C**) and pin along back shoulder of coat and down the underarm seam. Next, pin shoulder and underarm of sleeve seams (**D**). Starting at underarm, baste lining to coat seams, leaving thread free for 3″ above hem.

Baste seams of sleeve lining to seam of coat sleeve, removing any pins necessary. Pin the fronts to position, lapping lining over facing and turning under seam allowance, as at **E**. No extra ease is

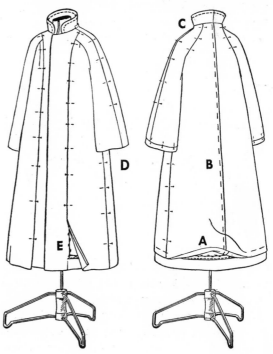

needed because fitting lining over the coat inside-out allows for this.

Finish the bottom of sleeve lining as shown in **J** on page 110. Clip seam allowance at back of neckline to prevent lining drawing at this point; turn it under and whip to position.

Turn lining hem so it overlaps top of coat hem about 1″. Measure evenly, allowing 1½″ hem plus ½″ turnunder. Press and blind-stitch or slip-stitch. French tack to side seams.

Use 3 or 4 catch-stitches at center-back pleat near neckline to hold to place. Remove basting.

TAILORED FINISHES

Arrowhead. Decorative and secure finish used at ends of pockets and pleats on tailored garments. With chalk showing position, mark a small triangle. Thread needle with fine embroidery twist. Begin with tiny stitch at **A**. Carry needle up to **B** and take a small stitch under point of triangle.

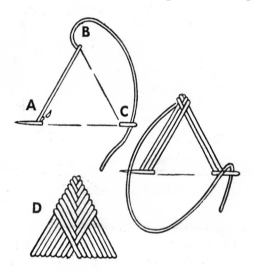

Bring needle down to **C** and put it through to **A**. Repeat this process, placing threads side by side until space is filled, as in **D**. Finish with back stitches on wrong side.

Crow's Foot. More elaborate type of end stay for pockets and pleats. Mark slightly shaped triangle

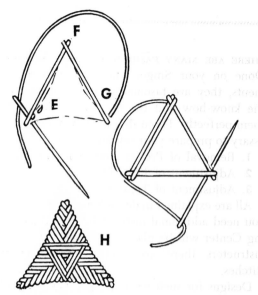

as shown. Begin at **E** with small stitches. Carry needle thread up to **F** and take small stitch under point of triangle. Turn work and take small stitch at **G**. Turn and go to **E** again, taking small stitch as before. Continue round and round until center is filled. Edges of triangle will be slightly curved as in **H** when work is finished.

Bar Tack. Secure stay used at ends of pockets, especially on tailored suits. Sew several strands of twist across end of opening. Overhand over these threads, just catching a few threads of fabric underneath, as in **I**. When bar is finished, complete ends with tiny bar tacks, as at **J**.

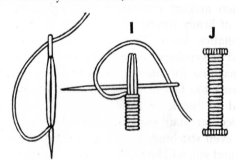

Shoulder pads or shapes are styled to the fashions. Often they are not obvious, but when used they can improve the fit of a garment or give a younger look to the shoulders. Find at your Sewing Center the size and shape of pad best for your shoulders and the garment you are making. Very thin, very soft pads, or none, are used by those having square shoulders, while figures having sloping shoulders, or one shoulder lower than the other, can be greatly improved by using a pad of the right size and shape. Often slight pads are used in the front of a suit or dress to give a rounder, fuller look. See higher-priced ready-to-wear for padding used to enhance the current silhouette.

THERE ARE MANY FASHION STITCHES, AS YOU SEE. Done on your Singer Machine without attachments, they are fascinating to do, once you get the know-how and the necessary practice to do them perfectly. Three simple adjustments are necessary to prepare your sewing machine:

1. Removal of Presser Foot when necessary;
2. Adjustment of Feed Dog;
3. Adjustment of Tension.

All are explained in detail here. If for any reason you need additional instruction, your Singer Sewing Center will be glad to help you, as all Singer instructors there are expert in making these stitches.

Designs for such work are practically limitless. Transfer designs may be used, or adaptations drawn from textiles, jewelry, wall paper or from nature. Become proficient in doing the stitches, then seek designs that best express your ideas and your needs for the fabric you are using.

Good embroidery hoops are necessary in making Fashion Stitches, as your fabric must be taut as you work. Ask at your Singer Sewing Center for a size and kind best suited to this work. Put your work in the hoops carefully. Fit and smooth it in; avoid pulling. When a sheer fabric is used and hoops do not hold it taut, try wrapping the inside hoop with a narrow bias strip of fabric, diagonally and evenly, all around.

When making Fashion Stitches, practice on a scrap of firmly woven fabric such as plain percale or imitation linen. The movement of the hoops should be synchronized with the speed of the sewing machine for smooth, even stitching. Moving the work too fast or too slowly may cause upper thread to break or result in an uneven stitch. Practice on your experimental fabric until you have even stitching, then your work will be uniform and you will be ready to apply the decoration to your fabric.

PREPARE YOUR SINGER FOR MAKING FASHION STITCHES

THE CLASS OF YOUR SEWING MACHINE CAN BE DEtermined by consulting the instruction booklet which you received with your machine. Read here what is necessary to prepare your machine for machine-darning or embroidery.

Removal of Presser Foot

To remove the presser foot on all Singer machines, raise presser bar to its highest point, unscrew, and remove foot.

Feed Dog and Bobbin Tension

To adjust the feed dog on Singer 201 Class Machines, turn the machine back on its hinges. Unscrew thumb screw **A** located in lower hole **B**. Move the feed-lifting crank **C** down so that screw **A** will enter hole **D**. Tighten **A**.

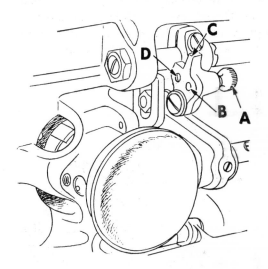

To regulate bobbin thread tension on 201–2 Class Machines, draw bed slide plate **E** to the left. Tension is regulated by screw **F**. To increase tension, turn screw toward you. To decrease tension, turn screw away from you.

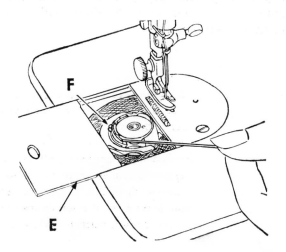

To adjust the feed dog on Singer 15–90 and 15–91 Class Machines, turn the machine back on its hinges and unscrew thumb screw **A**.

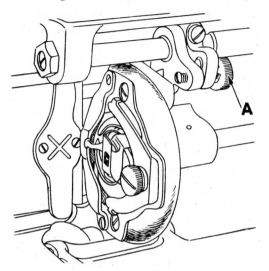

To regulate bobbin thread tension on 15–90 and 15–91 Class Machines, draw bed slide plate to left and remove bobbin case. Tension is regulated by screw **B** on the outside of the bobbin case. To increase tension, turn screw to your right. To decrease tension, turn screw to your left.

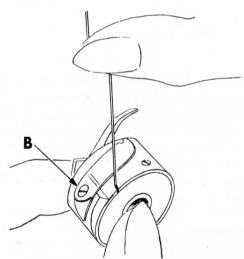

For Singer 221–1 and 66 Class Machines, a feed cover plate and screw (#121309) are provided at a slight charge. This plate easily slips on and is secured by one screw.

To regulate bobbin thread tension on 221–1 Class Machines, raise the bed extension and remove bobbin case. Tension is regulated by screw **A**. To increase tension, turn screw to the right. To decrease tension, turn screw to the left.

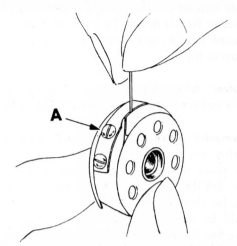

To regulate bobbin thread tension on 66–16 and 66–18 Class Machines, draw bed slide plate **B** to the left. Tension is regulated by larger screw **C**. To increase tension, turn screw toward you. To decrease tension, turn screw away from you.

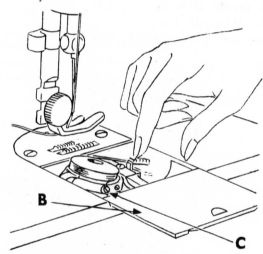

Upper Tension

The needle thread tension is regulated on your Singer by the tension control. Remember that

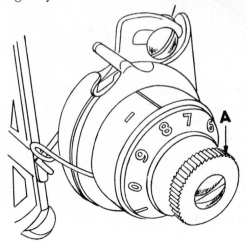

this tension can be controlled only when the presser foot is down. To increase tension, turn thumb nut (**A**) to the right; to decrease tension, turn to the left.

"Neutral" indicates position of stitch regulator as set for neither forward nor backward stitching.

Ornamental Stitch. Prepare your material by drawing one lengthwise or crosswise thread at each point where the Ornamental lines should come. Set the stitch regulator of your sewing machine for about thirty stitches to the inch. Tensions should be normal. Do not remove presser foot. Using fine thread in contrasting color for both needle and bobbin, stitch along the lines of the drawn threads, working on the right side of the fabric. This work gives the appearance of being part of the woven fabric. The best thread and needle sizes appropriate for this work are:

#50 mercerized—#14 needle; 00 mercerized—#11 needle; 0000 mercerized—#9 needle; Size A silk—#11 needle. For Ornamental Stitching, use the same size thread in the bobbin as in the needle.

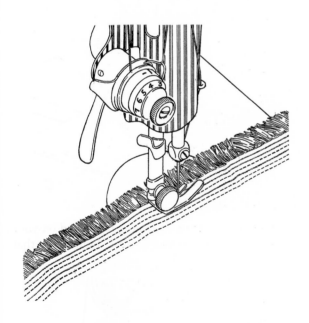

Geometric design must be employed because of the drawn threads, but it can be very effective when the lines cross. When short lines terminating at different points are chosen for your design, draw the bobbin thread up through the eye of the needle and into all points of upper threading, in reverse, as for *Single-Thread Dart* (see page 37), then stitch as described above. This will afford a locked stitch with no loose ends.

Etching Stitch. Firm fabrics, such as nainsook, Indian Head, etc., are best for this type of stitch. The Etching Stitch employs silk or mercerized thread with needle of appropriate size. Two- and three-cord embroidery thread can be used for this type of stitching with a #9 or #11 needle. A heavier thread is often used in the bobbin when a very fine thread is used in the needle. Needle and bobbin tensions should be evenly balanced as for ordinary stitching. Remove presser foot. Lower the feed dog, or cover with feed cover plate.

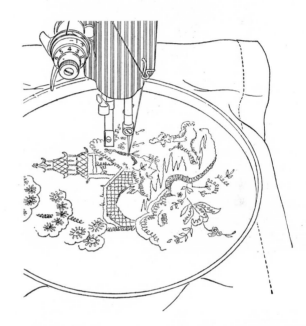

In order to maintain small, even stitches, it is well first to practice control in the direction of the hoops and the movement of the sewing machine. On a test piece of fabric, draw two parallel lines about 1½″ apart and place in the hoops so that the lines run horizontally. Place hoops under the presser bar. Lower presser bar. Draw the bobbin thread through and fasten with two or three stitches at the upper left corner inside the hoop. Then proceed with ordinary stitching, about 12 stitches to the inch, and endeavor to maintain this same length of stitch throughout the exercise. When you have reached the lower left corner, give the hoops one-fourth of a turn and take one stitch along the lower line. Then lower the needle, and again giving the hoops ¼ of a turn, stitch the second line parallel with the first. Repeat several times, then diminish the length of the stitches until the stitches are very small and the lines very close together.

You are now ready to place your fabric with a stamped design inside the hoops and follow the design with the small, even Etching Stitch. This is particularly good for figures, silhouettes or drawings of animals in outline and is well adapted to decorate children's clothes, luncheon cloths, fingertip towels, aprons and blouses.

Signature Stitch. This stitching is done with heavy-duty, mercerized, or silk thread used in both the needle and on the bobbin. The lower tension is loosened sufficiently to allow the bobbin thread to rise to the surface. The needle tension is tightened slightly. Remove presser foot and set stitch regulator at neutral. Drop feed, or cover with feed cover plate. A #11 or #14 needle is used. The design is stamped on the right side of the fabric and the work done on that side. Place material in embroidery hoops so that it is taut. Insert hoops under needle and presser bar. Lower presser bar as for regular sewing. Draw bobbin thread through to the top. The hoops are moved very slowly, the machine operated at a moderate speed so that stitches seem to pile one against another and a solid cord appears on top.

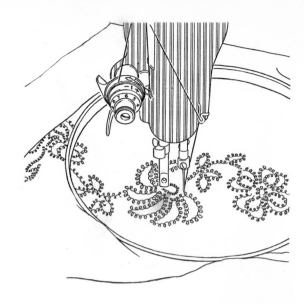

Place material in hoops, insert hoops under needle and presser bar. Lower presser bar. Hold end of top thread, lower the needle, and draw bobbin thread through to top. The work is guided in an even circular motion while following the design. The result is like tiny, radiant sparks.

Cordonnet Stitch. Use Cordonnet Thread on the bobbin and the same color in silk or synthetic thread for the needle. Loosen lower tension to accommodate the Cordonnet Thread but maintain a normal or light tension for upper threading. Remove presser foot. Drop feed, or cover with feed cover plate. Set the stitch regulator at neutral. Stamp or draw the design to be followed on the wrong side of the fabric.

Place the design in hoops, right side of fabric down. Insert hoops under presser bar. Lower

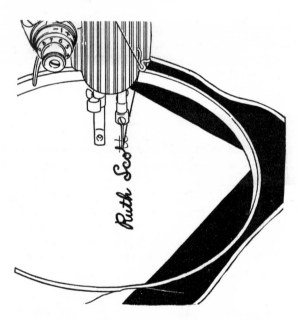

Spark Stitch. Frequently this stitch is done with a heavier thread in the needle and a finer thread of the same kind in the bobbin. The bobbin, or lower tension, is loosened slightly more than for the Signature Stitch. The upper tension is tightened. The feed of the sewing machine is dropped or a feed cover plate is used. Remove the presser foot.

The design is stamped, traced or drawn on the right side of the fabric. If following a transfer pattern, select one that you feel is suitable to your fabric and purpose.

The Metallic Stitch shown above can really provide fabric design, make the fabric more substantial-looking and, at the same time, add color and attractive decoration. One precaution is to choose good fabric to decorate so that when the work is added the article will have value.

The Bouclé Stitch, done as motif or monogram, can be used for small or large design and in contrasting or harmonizing color. Choose and place your design to be right for fashion, execute it well, and the result is sure to satisfy.

The Spiral Stitch can be used to provide design, be concentrated to carry out a motif, or used as decoration for ends of collars, corners of cuffs, or other groupings.

The Cable Stitch has many uses, such as straight lines or grouped motifs for borders, or all-over motifs as on the capelet and hat. Work out your motif, trace as many as you need, then transfer them to your fabric and do the Fashion Stitching according to the instructions given on opposite page.

Decorative stitching adds to the value of material and in skilled hands can make really distinguished-looking finished items.

presser bar. Draw bobbin thread to the top. In following the design, try to keep an unbroken line, crossing over, rather than ending off the stitch, wherever possible. When filling in a circle, begin in the center of the circle and then follow in a close spiral to the outer edge until the entire circle is covered. This stitch may be used on many types of fabric but is particularly effective on sheers, giving a frosty effect.

Spiral Stitch. This stitch is done with pearl cotton #5 or #8 wound on the bobbin and matching silk or mercerized thread in the needle. Use a #11 needle and drop the feed or use a feed covering plate. The lower, or bobbin, tension should be easy enough to accommodate pearl cotton. The upper tension is normal. Set stitch regulator at neutral. Remove presser foot.

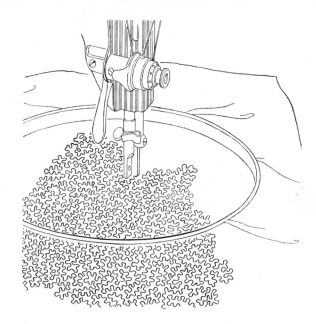

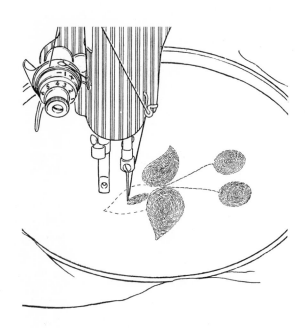

On wrong side of fabric draw circles around coins of different diameters to provide variety in the design. With work placed in embroidery hoops, right side down, insert hoops under presser bar. Lower presser bar. Draw bobbin thread to top. Begin in center of a circle, draw lower thread through and continue stitching with spiral motion until circle is filled.

The work is done from the wrong side of the fabric, the bobbin thread making the design on the right side. This is excellent for casual trim and may be applied to blouses, sleeves, skirts, scarves, or to children's clothes and household furnishings.

Metallic Stitch. Use metallic thread wound on the bobbin and silk in a matching color threaded in the needle. The lower tension is light enough to accommodate the metallic thread while the upper tension remains normal. Remove presser foot, drop feed or cover with feed cover plate, and set the stitch regulator at neutral. A #11 or #14 needle is used.

Mark a guide line for desired effect or stamp design on the wrong side of fabric and insert in embroidery hoops. Insert hoops under presser bar, right side down. Lower presser bar. Draw bobbin thread through to the top. Stitch with a medium speed, following the design. Continue stitching until desired area of fabric in hoops is finished. Pivot with needle down, remove stitched section from hoops and place another section of fabric into hoops. Continue stitching until desired area is completely stitched. Raise presser bar. Draw length of top thread through needle and cut it off 4" or 5" from fabric. Cut metallic thread about 1" from fabric. Draw metallic thread to underside. Thread hand-needle with the silk thread, turn the metallic thread end back and take 2 or 3 buttonhole stitches across it with hand-needle.

The metallic stitch is beautiful for many types of materials, from wool sweaters and finely woven woolens to taffeta, crepe, finest organdie or linen.

Cable Stitch (Controlled). This stitching may be made by winding pearl cotton #5 or #8, heavy embroidery silk, sock yarn, metallic thread or embroidery floss on the bobbin and using mercerized cotton or silk thread in the needle. The bobbin tension is loosened to accommodate the heavy thread. The stitching is then done as for plain sewing, with the right side of the material down. If desired, a thread of contrasting color may be used on top to show between the stitches. Thread the machine in the usual way and pull up the lower thread before starting to stitch. Do not remove presser foot. The stitch is usually as long as 8 to 10 per inch for straight lines and 12 to 15 for curved lines.

Cable Stitching adds a smart touch to tailored garments and accessories. Any simple design carrying a continuous line may be stamped on the wrong side.

When the design is finished, the end of the thread is threaded into a hand sewing needle and pulled through to the underside for fastening.

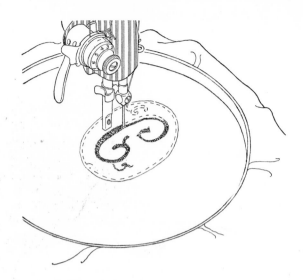

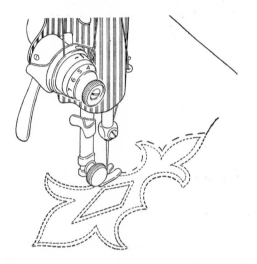

Free-Motion Cable Stitch. This stitch is done with presser foot removed and with stitch regulator at neutral. Drop the feed or use feed cover plate. Place the fabric marked with the design, wrong side up, in the hoops. Free-Motion Cable Stitching makes for greater ease in following intricate designs.

Bouclé Stitch. Use pearl cotton #5 or #8 or sock yarn on bobbin, with mercerized or silk thread in a #11 or #14 needle.

Stamp or draw design on wrong side of fabric. When applying a design to fabrics such as jersey or terry cloth, stamp the design on a piece of organdie or lawn and baste this into position on the wrong side of the fabric to be embroidered.

Prepare the machine as usual, lower feed or attach feed cover plate. Bobbin tension is released slightly more than for Cable Stitching, top tension is normal. Remove presser foot and set stitch regulator at neutral. Place stamped design in hoops. Insert hoops under presser bar. Lower presser bar. Draw bobbin thread to the top. Follow the design with a circular motion, making a series of small circles placed closely together and producing a nubby-textured, solid design. When design is complete, trim away any surplus of the organdie or lawn on which pattern was stamped.

This Bouclé Stitch is especially good for single motifs or decoration on dresses, robes and sportswear. Equally good for Turkish towels, bedspreads or college pennants.

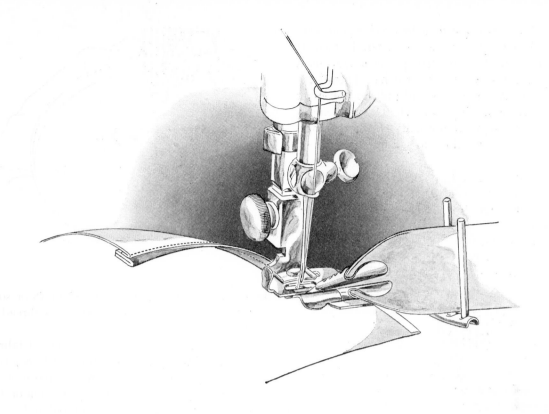

Bindings and Edge Finishes

Cutting Bias. For successful handling, bias strips must be cut so that the grain is a true diagonal of the fabric threads. To get this: Straighten one crosswise end of the fabric. Fold corner so that selvage or lengthwise edge lies evenly along a crosswise thread. Crease or press the fold. This creased line is a true diagonal or bias. Mark chalk lines parallel to the crease and as far apart as the desired width of bias strips, measuring off as many strips as necessary for length of bias. Cut on fold and on chalk lines.

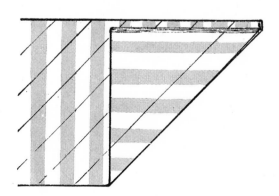

The Singer Bias Cutting Gauge can be used to cut even-width bias without measuring and marking. Simply press your first true bias and begin your cutting on this crease.

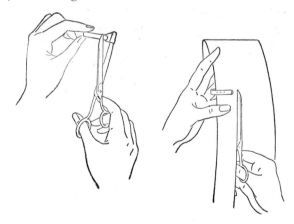

Piecing Bias. Always piece so that grain in the two pieces is matched. Lay right sides together, with ends of pieces crossing. Stitch on a thread, making $\frac{1}{8}''$ seam. See illustration at top of next page.

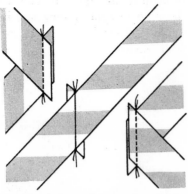

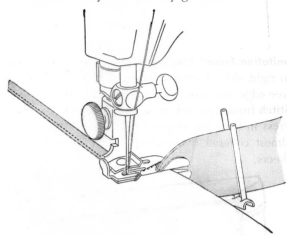

Multi-Slotted Binder. The wide variety of bindings the machine Binder will apply makes it most convenient and time-saving. It holds five sizes of ready-made binding so they can be stitched on with one stitching and without preliminary basting. Slots in the binder scroll will hold folded binding of ¼″, ⁵⁄₁₆″, ⅜″, ⁷⁄₁₆″, and ½″ in width.

A ¹⁵⁄₁₆″ unfolded bias binding can also be applied with this attachment. See machine instruction book. Good for home furnishings, children's clothes and many other dainty garments.

Bias Tube. To make a long strip of bias from a small piece of fabric, make a bias tube, starting with a piece that is roughly a bias diamond, as in **A**. If necessary to add to the fabric piece, make joining on lengthwise or crosswise grain (**B**). Mark the fabric with chalk or pencil on a true-bias line, as at **C**. Parallel to this line and as far apart as the desired width of the bias strip, mark as many other lines as piece will make. Bring straight edges together, lines matching, but with a width of bias extending beyond the joining at each end, as at **D**. Pin and stitch, forming a tube. Begin at one end, on line, and cut continuously around tube, as at **E**. When you finish cutting, you will have one long bias strip.

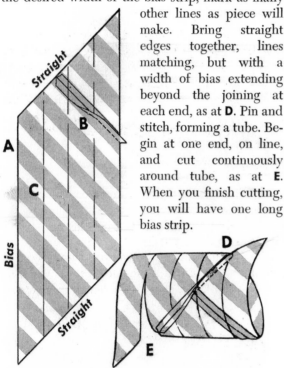

Hand-Felled Binding. Stitch one edge of binding to right side. Turn, fold under, then turn fold over edge and whip down. Bias needs to be about four times width of finished binding. Good for heavy fabrics, quilts, etc.

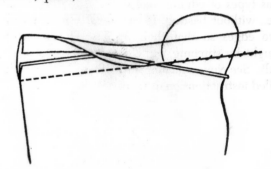

Piecing Ready-Made Bias Binding. Always join on the diagonal, never straight across binding.

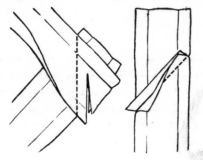

French Fold Binding. Narrow binding applied double, usually on sheer fabrics. Cut binding about six times as wide as desired finished width, which is usually ⅛″ to ¼″. Fold double, right side out, and baste to right side of fabric, raw edges together. Stitch and trim seam edge. Turn folded

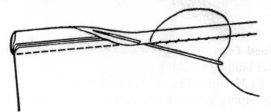

edge over and hem or slip-stitch in place with inconspicuous stitches. Good for lightweight fabrics.

Center-Stitched Binding. Stitch right side of bias to wrong side of garment. Press seam toward binding. Fold binding in to meet raw edges of seam. Crease. Then turn folded edge down over seam. Stitch through center of turn as shown.

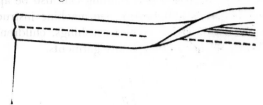

Imitation French Binding. Stitch one edge of bias to right side. Turn raw edge of bias in ¼″. Fold free edge over seam so that it covers stitching line. Stitch from right side close under edge of binding. Press in from the edge so that second stitching is almost covered by binding. Good for voiles and sheers.

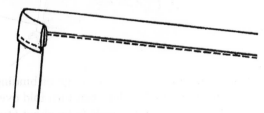

Machine Edge-Stitcher. This attachment allows you to stitch very close to an edge or to apply various types of edging, such as lace, footing, braid, etc., without basting. It has metal slots that hold two edges so that they lap just enough to be caught by stitching, but not so much as to create bulk. See your machine instruction book for detailed instructions on using it.

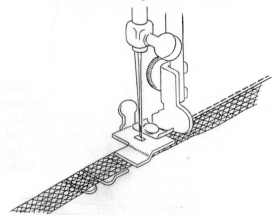

Piped Edge. Use true-bias strips or ready-made bias binding for this trim.

By Machine. Use the Multi-Slotted Binder to apply piping with a single stitching. See illustration

at head of chapter on page 119. This attachment can also be used to apply piping and binding in one operation. See machine instruction book for detailed instructions.

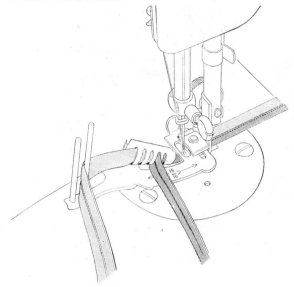

By Machine and Hand. Take a strip of bias ¾″ wide and slightly longer than the edge that is to be piped. Turn one raw edge of the piping piece over ⅛″ and stitch. Stitch other bias edge to right side of fabric. Trim close to stitching line. Turn

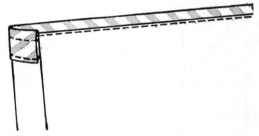

bias to wrong side, catching raw seam edges inside piping. Stitch on right side close to line joining bias and fabric. Slip-stitch free edge in place.

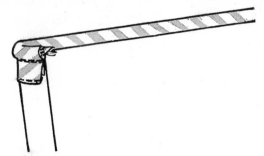

Corded Edge. Make cording as instructed on page 124. Apply in same way as for Piped Edge. If a facing is not used, as for edge of flounce, etc., turn the free edge and stitch as illustrated above. If facing is used, the free edge need not be turned and stitched.

Picot Edge. This is obtained by cutting through the center of a hemstitched line. Mark the line carefully with basting-stitches. You can do it with a machine hemstitching attachment or take it to your local Singer shop. For many yards it is wise to have it done professionally. When possible, mark fabric so that each line of hemstitching provides two picoted edges. Picot edge can be used plain or turned under ⅛″ and hemmed.

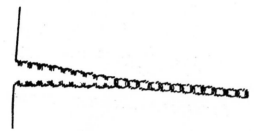

Overcast Shell Edge. Turn raw edge to wrong side about ⅛″ and stitch. Turn edge over twice to depth desired. Work from wrong side and begin with back-stitch. With double thread overcast along edge, taking several stitches at once, then drawing needle through. Tighten thread enough to give shell effect but not enough to cause edge to pucker. Good for washable lingerie edges, children's dresses, ruffles, etc.

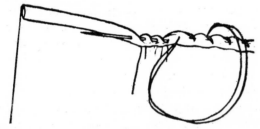

Lingerie Hem. Make rolled hem and, at intervals of ⅛″ to ⅜″, take two stitches over roll to form small puffs along edge. Between puffs conceal stitches under rolled edge.

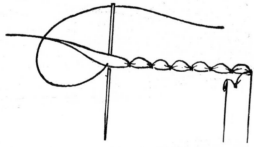

Shell Edge. Turn ¼″ hem to wrong side. Take 5 or 6 running-stitches along hem turn, then a stitch over edge, drawing hem together. Take a second stitch to fasten first, then another group of running-stitches, and continue. Good as a finish on cotton or linen. (Illustrated at top right.)

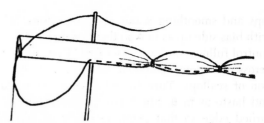

Tucked Hem. Stitch a 1⁄16″ to ⅜″ tuck on wrong side far enough in so raw edge can be folded around it. Turn edge under and fold over tuck to simulate binding. Hold in place with small, even basting-stitches or hem edge in place. Less bulky than binding for very narrow hem on crisp thin fabrics such as net or maline.

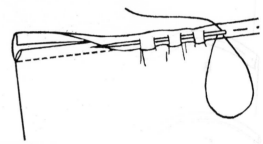

Pinked Edge. Quick effective finish without sewing; can be obtained with pinking shears, or Singer Hand Pinker. This edge is practical for firm fabrics of even weave, such as chintz or taffeta, and is used for both apparel and furnishings.

Frayed Taffeta Edge. Cut taffeta on true bias. Pull raw edge between thumb and fingers so that little puffs form evenly along fabric edge. Good for light fluffy effect on party dresses and for some types of home furnishings. Also called *Fringed Bias Edge.*

Bound Scallops. Use French fold binding for lightweight and sheer fabrics. Always use a transfer pattern or make a paper pattern for scallops, measuring with ruler and drawing curves around a coin, cup or saucer. Shallow scallops are usually easier to handle and more satisfactory in use. Deep scallops are bulkier at intersections because of overlapping of material and are apt to cup in laundering. Mark and cut scallops. Fold bias lengthwise through center. Pin and baste bias edges to right side of fabric, easing it along scallops and smoothing it out at intersections. Stitch with bias side up as in **A** so that you can watch and control fullness under presser foot. Take one stitch across each point as shown. Clip seam at intersection of scallops. Turn folded edge to wrong side and baste as in **B**. Stitch from right side close to turned edge so that stitching is almost invisible, as in **C**. If a hand finish is desired, use a narrower bias fold and hem down as in **D**.

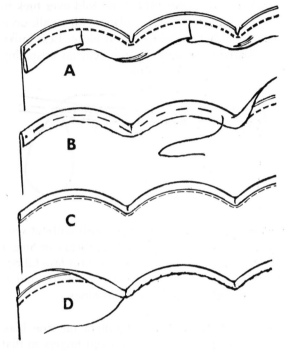

Machine-Bound Scallops. Use machine Binder as you would on straight binding. As you approach intersection of scallops, draw fabric into a fold or pleat so as to straighten out edge and allow Binder to stitch straight on between scallops. See machine instruction book. (Not illustrated.)

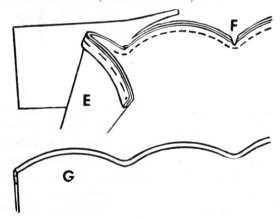

Piped Scallops. Mark and cut scallops. Fold bias through center lengthwise. Pin and baste to right side of fabric, as at **E**, easing around curve and drawing tight at corners. See illustration above.

Baste facing in position over bias. Stitch along basted line around scallops. Trim off excess facing fabric around scallops, and clip as at **F**. Turn right side out and press, as in **G**.

Faced Scallops. Trace scallops on wrong side of facing piece. Lay right sides together and baste. Stitch around scallops, taking one stitch across at each point. Trim off excess fabric, blending seam as shown. Clip and notch seam edges, as in **H**. Turn right side out, as in **I**. Slip-stitch to place.

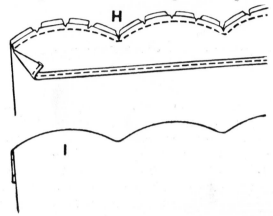

Applied Scalloped Facing. Cut band of desired depth to be applied as trim on bottom of skirt. Measure and mark scallops along top edge of band. Cut around scallops allowing ¼″ seam, as at **J**. Lay right side of band against wrong side of fabric and pin. Stitch seam along bottom edge, as at **K**. If edge is curved clip seam edges and press open. Turn to right side. Turn over top edge along marked line, clip at corner of each scallop so facing will lie flat. Baste and stitch close to turned edge, as in **L**.

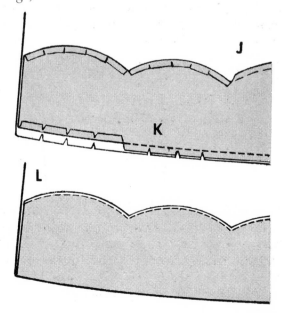

Cording, Tubing and Self-Trimming

Cording. As a finish for clothing and home furnishings, fabric-covered cording is especially practical when the Cording Foot is used to "snug" the cord in place in the seam. Cotton cable cord is available usually in seven sizes at notions counters and in drapery departments. We show small, medium and large sizes. This, when covered with a firm, closely woven fabric, makes finished cording

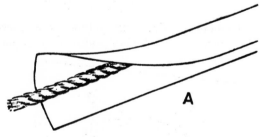

ranging in width from ⅛" to ½" and may be used as edge finish and trim, or for fagoting, button loops, or to give weight to a seamline. For very fine cording, small twine may be used. For thick cording, occasionally used on home furnishings, there is large soft cord available, and for extra heavy effects, strips of cotton batting may be cut and used to fill the fabric tubing.

To Make Cording. Cut true bias as shown on page 119, making the width of the strips fully four times the distance around the cord to be covered. Bias 1" wide is usually used to cover the smaller cords. Seam lengths together. Lay cord along bias strip on wrong side. Fold bias over cord, with top edge about ¼" in from lower edge, as at **A**, to blend

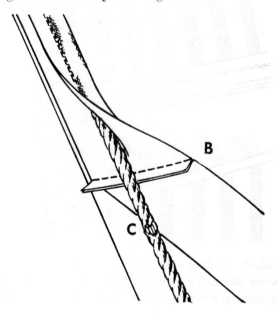

seam. Stitch, using Cording Foot, stretching the bias strip as you sew. To be sure Cording Foot hugs cord closely, hold bias and cord well in toward center of foot as you guide it under needle. See also *Corded Seam*, page 57.

When stitching a fabric of nubby yarn or one that is slippery, pin or baste close to cord before stitching.

Measuring for Cording. Try always to make sufficient cording to complete all the work. Measure all lengths to be corded and add a couple of inches for each yard of cording. This will allow cording to be eased to prevent drawing up seam or edge.

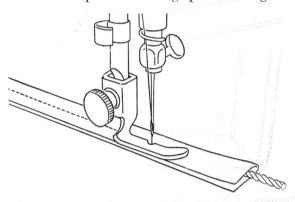

Piecing Cording. When applying cording, if cording runs short, stop stitching about 3" from end.

Rip stitching along cording for 1". Cut a bias strip of length needed and stitch to end of bias, as at **B**, making a diagonal seam. Press the seam open. Whip additional length of cord to short end, as at **C**. Fold fabric over cord and stitch. Continue stitching cording in place.

Corded Edge. When cording is used as edge trim and facing, wider edge of bias should extend enough to conceal raw edges. After cording is made, turn under raw edge and stitch. Apply cording using Cording Foot. Pivot at corner, clipping seam allowance, as at **D**. Turn facing to wrong side. Miter corner and slip-stitch facing in position, as in **E**.

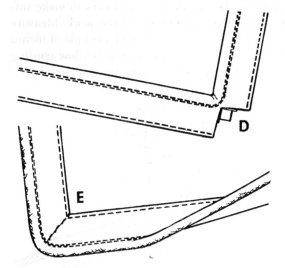

Corners. Clip the seam allowance of the cording on rounding a corner, as at **F**, so that when seam is

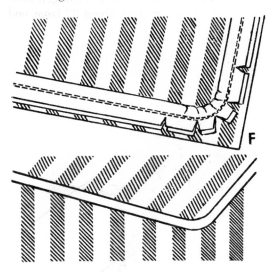

finished, cording will be smooth on corner, as shown above. To cord an inside corner, cut cording and lap it to make a true square corner, as at **G**.

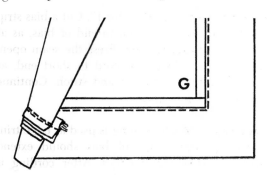

Curve. When applying to curves or scallops, clip seam allowance to prevent cupping, as in **H**.

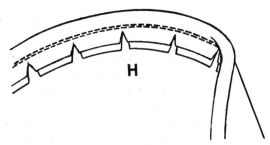

To Make Tubing. Cut a strip of bias and a piece of small cord to the length desired. Point end of bias and stitch one end of cord securely to wrong side of this bias point, as at **I**. Turn point to right side of bias and lay cord along center. Fold bias over cord with point inside. Using the Cording Foot and a fairly short stitch on the machine, start stitching by forming funnel. as at **J**. Stretch bias and crowd the cord as you stitch. Trim seam edges, depending upon fabric and size of cord used. Draw free end of cord so as to turn tube inside out and thus remove cord. Seams are pulled inside tube, as in **J₁**, and act as filling. Tubing is used for button loops and makes an effective self-trim when applied in scallops on an edge or inserted in seams to give a fagoted effect.

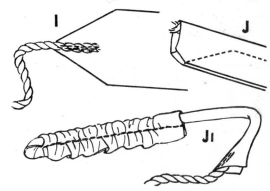

Inset Trimming. First cut tubing into even lengths, according to desired width of trimming

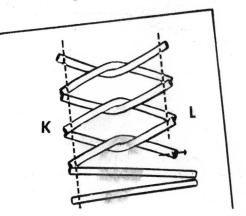

band. The lengths may be twisted or knotted. Draw guide lines on paper; then pin strips in place, spaced evenly, and stitch across ends on one side, as at **K**. Twist two lengths together; pin in place and stitch across other ends, as at **L**. The knotted lengths are spaced evenly on paper and stitched on both sides. Lay turned-under edges of fabric over stitched line and stitch close to edge,

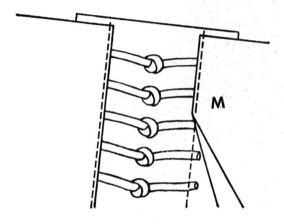

as at **M**. Pull paper away. An inside stitching can be made if you prefer that no stitching show on right side. Stitch strips or loops along one edge on right side. Lay other edge over trim and stitch.

To Make Covered Cord. When making button loops for coats, where strength is needed, cover cord with tubing. Cut bias strip double the seam allowance plus three times the width of the cord. Cut cord twice as long as finished piece needed. Fold cord in half and mark center with pin. Point one end of bias as at **N**. Stitch center of cord securely to point of bias on wrong side, as shown.

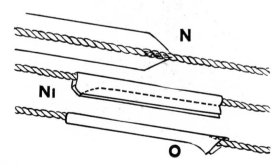

Fold point **N** to right side of fabric and fold bias strip in half over cord, as at **N1**. Stitch with left Cording Foot, starting with funnel as shown. Stretch bias strip as you stitch the full length. Trim edges to a scant ⅛″ from stitching. Pull cord through, working fabric over uncovered half of cord. Continue until tube is turned inside out over cord, as in **O**. Cut off uncovered half of cord. Apply loop to front edge of garment by pinning, spacing it to accommodate the size of the button. Stitch loop close to seamline and whip ends of covered cord to the seam, as at **P**. Apply facing by stitching from inside. Make second stitching across ends of each loop for security, as at **Q**.

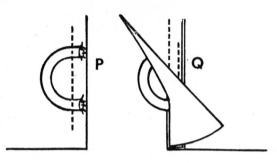

Fabric Loops. Make tubing. Measure for size of loops desired, plus seam allowance, and clip only through seamed edge of tubing at these intervals. Do not cut it in individual pieces. Measure and mark evenly with chalk or basting the seam edge where loops are to be applied. Pin tubing into loops, as at **R**. Stitch across ends slowly, lifting presser foot slightly when stitching over tubing, to prevent pressing loop out of place. Make a second stitching outside first to secure ends, as at **S**. Stitch facing or lining in position, as in **T**.

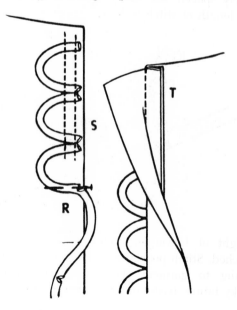

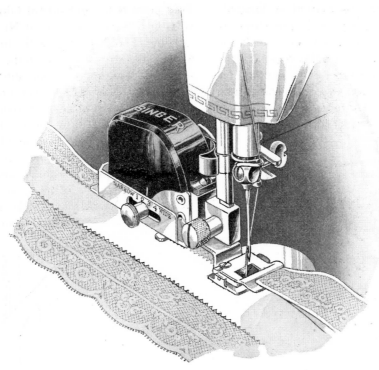

Decorative Stitching. Machine stitching can be done in a number of different ways for decorative effect.

Top-Stitching. For narrow spacing, the edge of the presser foot is guide enough for evenness.

With Seam Guide. When stitching is more widely spaced, use this attachment. Test thread and length of stitch to be sure both are right for

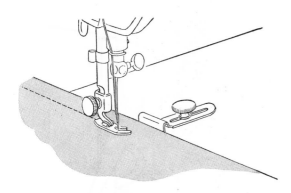

weight of fabric and number of layers to be stitched. Stitch pocket flaps, cuffs, etc., before applying to garment. For many thicknesses of bulky fabric, baste all together in position before

stitching. At end of stitching line, pull thread ends to wrong side and tie. Top-stitching may be done in parallel rows along an edge, in striped, or plaid, or checked effects throughout the fabric of the garment. Matching or contrasting threads help to vary the effects.

With Walking Presser Foot. This attachment, which consists of two presser feet, makes it possible to stitch two or more plies of fabric without slipping. Thus stitching of glossy-surfaced or pile fabrics can be done without difficulty. Follow instruction booklet given with this foot.

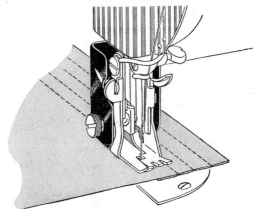

With Gauge Presser Foot. This foot has adjustable guides that insure even rows of stitching. Follow complete instructions given with attachment. Used on tailored garments when making rows of stitching for accent.

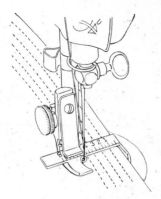

Machine Stitching with Crochet Cotton. Use No. 30 crochet cotton to thread machine, both top and bobbin, and a coarse needle—size 14 or 16. Lengthen stitch and tighten tension. Then try on scrap for practice. Use edge of presser foot as guide for edge trim. For monograms or other designs, such as in **A**, below, transfer to fabric or draw on thin paper and stitch over that. Pull paper away when complete. Pull threads to wrong side and tie. For heavier effect, stitch several rows parallel and close together, as in **B**. By using one color

A

thread on top of machine and another color in the bobbin, a variety of color combinations can be obtained.

B

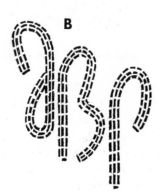

Fabric Appliqué. Trace individual motifs and cut carefully, using sharp scissors, Ripper or razor blade. For large motifs or heavy fabrics, cut paper or thin cardboard pattern. Turn back raw edges by pressing with iron over pattern edges.

By Hand. Mark position for motifs. Turn under raw edges of motifs and press. Baste when

C

necessary for accuracy. Lay on design outline. Pin and baste, as at **C**. For simple finish, whip edges down or use fine running-stitch. To accent edge add color finish with blanket-stitch. For invisible finish, slip-stitch turned edges. Stems, flower centers, etc., may be embroidered for added detail, as at **D**.

By Machine. When you use the Zigzagger, the edges are not usually turned under, as this attachment stitches back and forth over the edge, as in **E**. Turn under edges when the motifs are large or have long edges as in the monogram on page 228. If plain stitching is used, follow directions for hand appliqué and stitch close to edge.

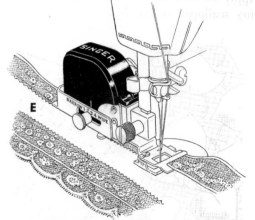

Self-Appliqué. For some dresses, suits, etc., an attractive form of self-trimming is an appliqué of the fabric itself. Cut motifs as described here, turning edges with iron over pattern, as in **F**.

Baste and stitch by machine as in **G**. Finish each motif before applying another on top.

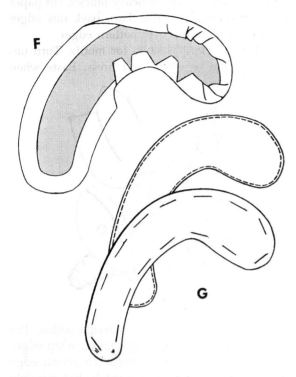

Lace Appliqué. All-over lace garments and deep lace joined to fabric should be appliquéd at joinings and seams. Pin one edge to paper. Lay overlapping edge in place, matching design as well as possible and pin a couple of inches from edge. Carefully trim around edge of motifs to gain desired line. Baste near edge of lace, following cut outline. Use Zigzagger to apply, as in **H**. See machine instruction book for adjusting this attachment.

Apply all-over lace to fabric in same way by laying scalloped or cut lace edge over material,

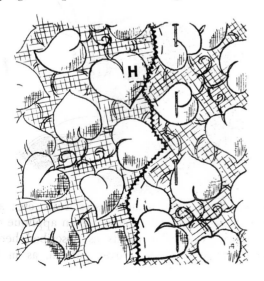

pinning, basting and finishing as described above. Remove paper when seam is finished. Trim under edge to ¼″ of seamline.

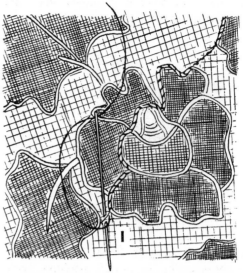

By Hand. Using thread suitable for weight of the lace, whip around cut edge, as in **I**. If lace has heavy cord around motifs, imitate this along edge by laying cord and overcasting it.

Stiffened Lace Edge. Cord may be applied to edge and stitched down with Zigzagger. Fine wire may be applied in same way. Pull paper away when stitching is complete. Trim away excess lace or fabric close to seam, as at **J**.

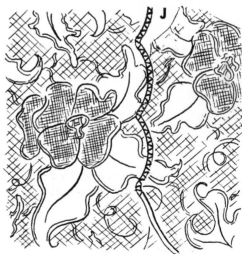

To Apply Lace Edging. Use fine needle and fine thread.

By Machine. Use the Edge-Stitcher and stitch right side of lace to right side of fabric as in **K**. Turn edge under and stitch again, close to first stitching. Trim away edge on wrong side as in **L**. See illustration at top of page 130. Foot Hemmer can also be used to apply lace trim. See machine instruction book for this method.

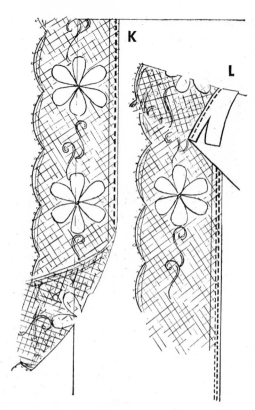

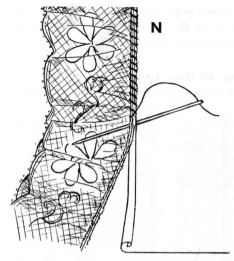

By Machine and Hand. Lay right side of lace to right side of fabric, top of lace ⅛″ from edge of fabric. Stitch. Roll edge over stitching line and overcast it, as at **M**. Press lace down over edge.

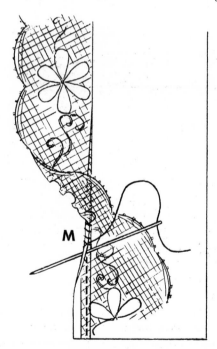

Gathered Lace on Rolled Edge. Draw up thread in top edge of lace, making lace as full as desired. Roll fabric edge with left thumb while whipping lace to it, as at **N**.

Lace Insertion. Mark position on fabric. Stitch along one edge, using Edge-Stitcher. Then stitch other edge, as in **O**. Trim fabric away under insertion, leaving ⅛″ seam. Turn edges back and stitch again, as in **P**. See illustration.

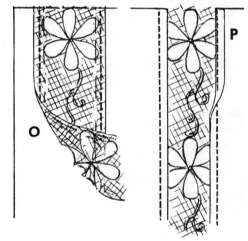

Lace on Curved Edge. Mark lines where lace is to be applied. Draw thread in upper edge of lace, adjusting lace to curve. Baste through center or

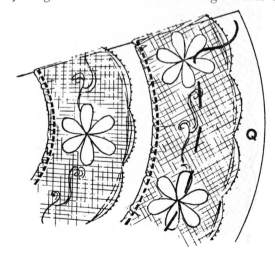

along lower edge, keeping top edge in line with marks as at **Q**. Insert gathered edge of top in Edge-Stitcher and stitch in position.

Making All-Over Lace from Insertion.
Various widths of insertion can be joined by the Edge-

Stitcher for an all-over effect as in **R**. This is sometimes necessary to make a lace yoke on panel for blouse or dress.

Lace on Corners.
For a square or mitered corner, fold lace and cut away excess at corner. Whip edges together. When lace and insertion are stitched together, a corner is often finished as shown. The insertion is mitered at corner, as at **S**, and the lace is fulled at corner and whipped or stitched to insertion, as at **T**.

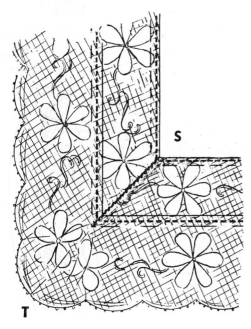

Rounded Corner. Lay tiny pleats in lace so outside edge lies flat, as at **U**. Stitch or whip in position.

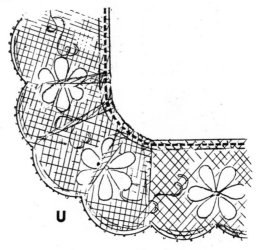

Veining.
Sometimes called *beading* or *entre deux*. A narrow open-work strip used between fabric edges through which ribbon can be run. Turn under edge of fabric and lay close to embroidered edge of veining. Stitch, using Cording Foot. Trim seams close to stitching on wrong side and finish with small overcasting-stitches, as in **V**.

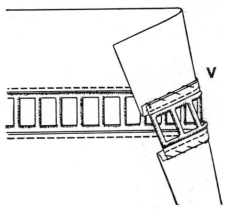

Braiding.
Braid can be applied by hand but is usually done by machine. Use a transfer pattern or make your own design. To mark pattern for braiding large area, pin several sheets of paper together with pattern on top. Then run over design with unthreaded needle in machine. Thus, all pieces are marked alike.

Soutache and pigtail braid may be applied by the machine Underbraider. Follow your machine instruction book for using this attachment. Braid is applied to right side from below, so mark design on wrong side of fabric.

The Edge-Stitcher can be used to apply flat braids, such as military braid, without basting. Mark placement of braid and stitch along line.

The Blind Stitch Braider comes in three widths, so various widths of braid can be applied to the right side of fabric. See machine instruction book for use.

The Braiding Presser Foot shown here comes in

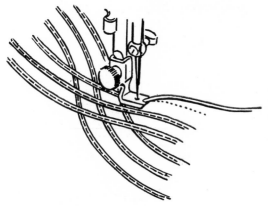

two sizes and is used to apply very narrow braid, and silk twist or wool yarn for various decorative effects as in **W**.

To finish off soutache and pigtail braid, make a small hole in fabric with a stiletto or point of the scissors, pull end to wrong side and sew securely, as at **X**.

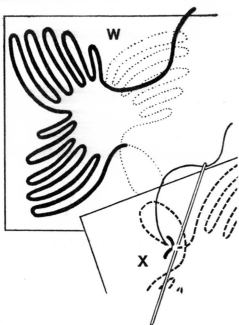

Quilting is the art of stitching two or more thicknesses together in some planned design to provide warmth, decoration or an effect of bulk. Formerly done entirely by hand, it can now be much more speedily and very effectively done by machine. Many varied effects can be produced by changing the type of stitching, the weight of padding, the fabric on which the work is done. However, the principles are few, as outlined here.

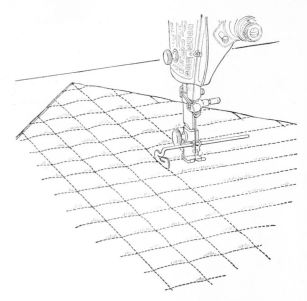

Machine Quilter. Replace the presser foot with Quilting Foot, which has short upturned toes to allow thick and padded work to flow easily under the needle. It also has a cross bar with a guide so that lines of stitching can be kept an even distance apart. This bar may be removed if the work is not such as to need this guide. Most block quilting can be done best with this attachment.

Block Quilting. Simplest type of quilting for all-over work or broad bandings. Stitching can be used to make squares, diamonds, points, rows, etc. Prepare fabric by putting in seams and pressing. Smooth out on table right side down. Lay sheet cotton or lamb's wool over this. Lay lightweight muslin or fine cheesecloth over padding and pin all three together. To prevent slipping, make rows of basting 3″ or 4″ apart, using long stitches, as in **Y**. When possible, stitch on the bias grain of fabric. If work is flat and quilting is simply rows or squares, mark on edge with chalk to indicate distance between stitchings as guide for quilter bar, as at **Z**.

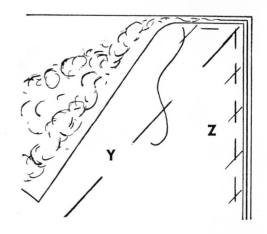

Glazed Chintz for Line, Color, and Design

As well as being highly practical for tailored slip-covers such as those shown above, glazed chintz adds the interest of contrast when its luster glows against the soft texture of the rug and the matt finish of painted walls. The flowered chintz of the draperies is placed well out on the wall beside the window, giving greater breadth and improving the line of the window.

In the room below, added texture interest is achieved by quilted valance over plain curtains, the quilted stool cushion with plain ruffle, and the quilted box spread over a plain flounce. The problem of two small windows is solved by treating them as a unit.

Photograph by the makers of Armstrong's Linoleum

Room for Comfort and Recreation

For the room that is used for fun and recreation, the recipe is gay color, sturdy fabric, and simple construction; comfort for those who use it, a minimum of work for the one who takes care of it. Sailor-blue and flag-red denim, with white duck pillows, makes the room above. The fish-net swags and the rope cording emphasize the nautical.

Below the color scheme starts with the cheerful plaid of the draperies. Its green is matched in the card-table cover, its red in the body of the slip-covers and in the inside color of shelves and cabinets. Then, to set off such gay color, the glass curtains and the woodwork are white.

Whether your hobby is sewing, reading, or any one of the many pursuits so popular with hobbyists, this type of room would be convenient and make for many pleasant hours of leisure time.

Courtesy of Burlington Mills

Working from wrong side, first stitch diagonally from corner to corner. Continue stitching, working in one direction by always beginning each stitching line from the same end.

If quilting is to fit a special shaped area or to match at seams, draw on paper, with ruler, design you want. Baste or pin design over muslin. Before stitching on design, test quilting on scrap to make sure stitch is correct and all is working correctly.

Stitch must be a little longer than for ordinary sewing to allow for thickness. Stitch carefully to keep design true. If thread breaks or runs out, begin stitching again in exactly same place. If work is large or very heavy, support it on table behind machine. Roll work as it is finished to keep it unwrinkled and avoid pressing after quilting.

Finishing Quilting. Most quilted clothes or home furnishings are finished by ordinary hems. In some instances, because quilting is rather bulky, use one of the finishes illustrated below.

Bind edges with bias binding or ribbon, as in **A**. When quilting does not come to the edges, as in **B**, the edges can be turned in toward each other and stitched close to edge, as shown.

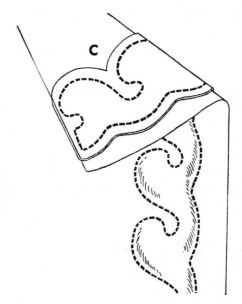

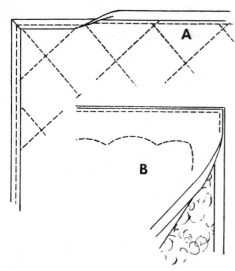

Scroll and Flower Designs in Quilting. Plan motifs carefully so they are suitably placed. Stamp or transfer design to sheet wadding. Lay wadding against wrong side of fabric, with motif up. Stitch around lines of design; then with sharp-pointed scissors trim away excess wadding outside stitching lines, as in **C**. Line or face wrong side to cover padding.

Italian or Trapunto Quilting. Stamp or transfer design to interlining of muslin, cheesecloth or flannelette. Baste or pin in place on wrong side of fabric. Stitch around lines of design with double

stitching row, taking care not to stitch across the lines at any point. This is important because padding is inserted between the two rows after the stitching is complete, to give a raised outline, as at **D**. Thread tapestry needle with heavy padding yarn and draw through openings between stitching lines until all lines are padded. To pull needle and yarn around curves, clip interlining at intervals, pull needle and yarn out; then insert again and pull through at next clip, as at **E**. Cut off yarn and tack it down with ordinary thread.

Often a few motifs in a design are fully padded instead of just outlined. Make a single stitching outline as at **F**, slash at base of motif and stuff in padding as at **G**.

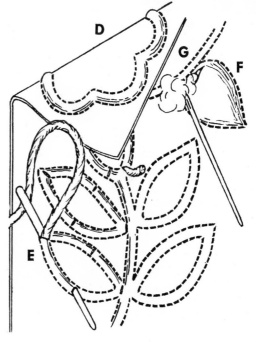

Puff Quilting. Turn back facing or hem line along edge over strip of padding. Stitch several evenly spaced parallel lines along edge as in **H**. To make

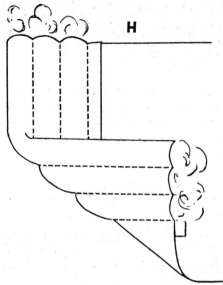

puffier, draw additional yarn through between lines under the padding, somewhat as for Italian quilting.

Fringed Edges. Easy and decorative way to finish informal table linens, scarves, etc. Cut article carefully to correct size. Make fringe in one of the following ways:

Machine-Stitched Fringed Edge. Mark desired depth of fringe along edges. Stitch with matching thread along marked line, pivoting on needle at corners. The Zigzagger may be used for this purpose with decorative effect, as in **I**. Stitching with thread of contrasting color adds interest. Ravel out fabric threads parallel to edges from close to stitching all the way to edge.

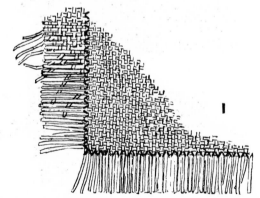

Hemstitched Fringed Edge. Mark lines for depth of fringe as above. Use Hemstitcher without the plunger. Follow instructions given with this attachment for using it. Thread machine with either matching or contrasting thread. Stitch

around marked lines. Ravel fabric threads between stitching and edges.

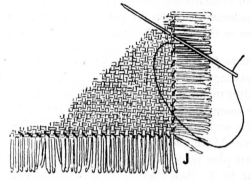

Overcast Fringed Edge. Ravel out threads parallel to edges to desired depth of fringe. Using matching thread or thread pulled out of fabric itself, overcast along edge at base of fringe to prevent further raveling, as at **J**. (See above.)

Loop Fringe. Wind crochet cotton, of weight suitable to fabric to be trimmed, around the Singercraft Guide and stitch, as in **K**. Make as much fringe as needed, following instructions given with

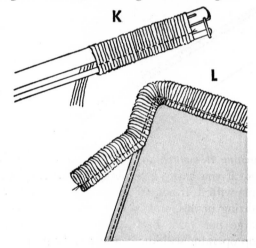

attachment. On article to be trimmed, make narrow hem turn to right side. Stitch. Lay fringe over hem and stitch fringe close to first stitching line as in **L**. Full fringe on when turning corners, as shown.

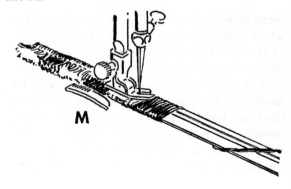

Moss fringe can also be made easily on the Singer-craft Guide. The illustration shows how a two-color combination can be obtained. **M** is the knife attachment used on the Guide to cut the loops of yarn or thread. See bottom of preceding page.

How to Prepare Fabrics for Machine Hemstitching.
If yardage in ruffling is desired, plain-seam several widths together. Avoid a bulky seam joining. Press the seams open. Mark the width desired for the ruffle with a basting thread the full length of the piece. Make the basting lines two ruffle widths apart plus seam allowance. For example, if ruffle is to be 3″, then make another row of basting 7″ away from the first. When the hemstitching is cut, your ruffle edge is finished. Place the picot edges together, pin or press to hold evenly, cut through the fold, gather the cut edge and your ruffle is finished.

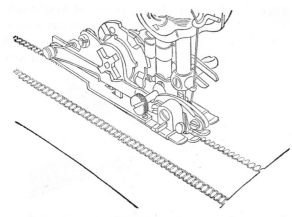

Machine Hemstitching. Use Hemstitcher attachment if you have one, following directions which come with it. If not, take your work to a shop specializing in this, and have it done at a moderate charge per yard. Baste each line accurately so shop operator will know where to begin and end hemstitching.

Picot. This is made by cutting through a line of machine hemstitching. See *Picot Seam,* page 55 and *Picot Edge,* page 122.

Hand Hemstitching. Fold in hem width and mark where hemstitching is to begin. Draw from 3 to 12 threads, depending on texture of fabric and the width of openwork desired. Baste hem so that top edge is along lower edge of drawn threads. Bring needle out at top of hem, starting at the left. From the right, insert needle under a group of threads, usually the same number of threads you have drawn, as in **N**. Pull needle through and draw thread close. Take a second stitch in top edge of

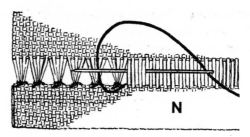

hem a little to one side of thread group just made, as in **O**. Repeat both operations until line is complete. At a corner, where hem is double, place stitches closer together to accommodate same number of threads.

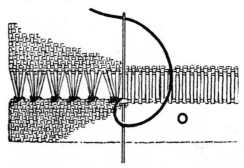

For double hemstitching, turn top edge of open line down and work along this edge in the same way, catching into fabric instead of into hem.

Inducted Thread. Fabric decoration made by drawing thread of different color or weight into space left by drawing out fabric threads. Pull out one or more threads on line desired for decoration. The number of threads depends on weight of

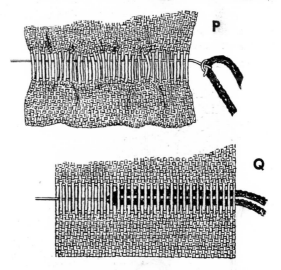

thread to be inducted. Overlap and sew or tie the decorative thread to one end of a fabric thread on the drawn line as at **P**. Then pull the other end gently and slowly until the new thread lies in its place as at **Q**.

Hand Smocking. The honeycomb stitch (see **V**, below) is one most often used in smocking. On fabrics with no dots or checks to use as guide, a transfer pattern can be used to mark even squares, or you can measure and mark dots with pencil. Illustration shows dots in pairs to indicate how stitches are taken. Be sure dots are in line with a fabric thread. Work from left to right. Knot thread and bring needle up between first dots of second row; then take small stitch through second dots, same row, and through first dots and draw both dots together, as at **R**. Insert needle to right of stitch just finished and bring out between second dots on first row so thread is underneath fold. Then take back-stitch over second and third dots first row, and draw together, as at **S**. Next, over third and fourth dots in the second row, as **T** indicates, and back to top row, bringing fourth and

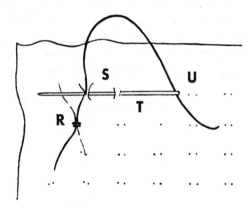

fifth together, as at **U**. Continue in this way alternating between first and second rows to end of row, making last stitches in second row. Turn work around and bring needle out in third row to right of last stitch. Work over dots in third and fourth rows, then fifth and sixth, as in **V**. Continue until completed.

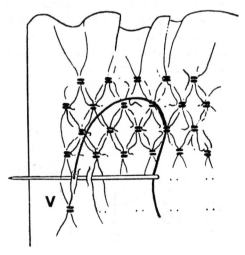

Machine Smocking. This is shirring that resembles smocking. Use #30 crochet cotton on bobbin of machine and regular mercerized thread on top. Adjust for long stitch and stitch from wrong side. Space rows evenly. Stitch twice across one end, as at **W**, to hold bobbin threads securely. Draw up bobbin threads desired amount; pull threads through to wrong side and tie. This is an easy, practical, and decorative finish for dresses of

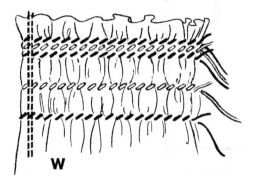

lawn, dimity, and voile. It irons and washes more easily than hand smocking.

Test length of stitch for proper fullness on a scrap of the fabric. For variety, make your rows of stitching in groups of three or more rows with space between. Using a number of colored threads will give various pleasing effects. The Gatherer can also be used for machine smocking. See machine instruction book for details.

Hand Fagoting. Lay edges to be fagoted on paper, placing desired distance apart, and baste each edge. To insure evenness of stitches, measure and mark distance between on paper near basted edges. Stitching can be done in a number of different ways, of which those illustrated here are most often used.

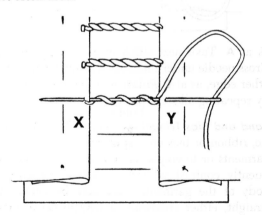

Bar Fagoting. Baste edges to paper. Bring needle out on left edge as at **X**. Insert needle directly opposite on right edge as at **Y**, twist it around thread three or more times and take stitch under left edge. When needle is pulled through, the twisted bar is formed. Take stitch downward in fold of left edge, as at **Z**, bringing needle out ready for next stitch. Repeat to end of row.

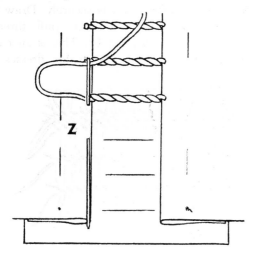

Cross-Stitch Fagoting. Baste edges to paper. Begin at top by bringing needle through to right side

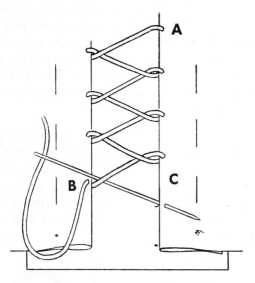

as at **A**. Take next stitch in other edge as at **B**. Cross needle under thread and insert needle under other edge, as at **C**. Pull needle through. Continue by repeating all steps until end of row.

Band and Bias Trimming. Applied bands of fabric, ribbon or bias are sometimes used to decorate garments or to emphasize lines. Fabric bands frequently contrast with the color or grain of the body of the garment. They may be cut on the straight, either crosswise or lengthwise of fabric grain, or on a true bias. When interlining a bias band, cut interlining also on the bias. Measure and cut carefully.

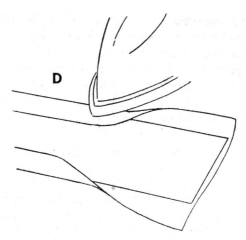

The edges on firm fabrics can be turned with the point of the iron, as in **D**. Soft or rough fabric bands should be turned, pinned, basted, and pressed before being applied. Do all stitching and pressing precisely, so that bands are even in width and smooth throughout. Always start stitching edges from the same end, as in **E**, to prevent puckering. Work on flat surface. For square corner or point in band, miter corners as on page 77.

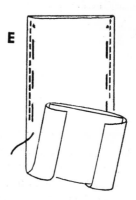

Applied Double Fold. In woolen, metallic or velvet fabrics, bands are usually made double. Cut piece twice finished width. Turn under edges so they meet at center of underside. Catch-stitch, as in **F**, or diagonal-baste edges together, as in **G**. Press. Baste in place on fabric. Stitch or slip-stitch in position. Compare *Strap Seam*, page 57.

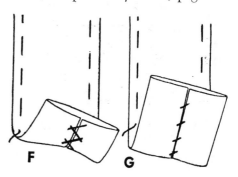

Slip-Stitched Band. Prepare band and baste in position. To slip-stitch to fabric, fold fabric back along edge of band for speed in sewing, as in **H**. For sheer fabrics and net, this is the best type of band.

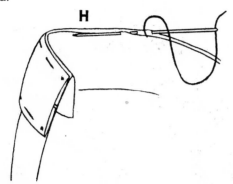

Inset Band. Prepare band by turning under edges and pressing. Cut off corners so edges do not overlap. Slip-baste carefully to garment. Turn to wrong side. Trim away fabric from under band, leaving ¼" seam. Stitch seams as at **I**, and press

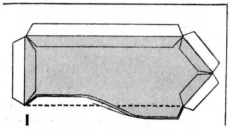

open. When finished no stitching is seen on right side, as in **J**, below. The inset type of band should not be used on sheer fabrics.

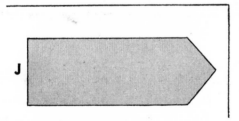

Ribbon and Bias Bands. To apply ribbon bands, mark position where stitching should come. Apply ribbon with Edge-Stitcher over marked lines, turning edges under at end, as at **K**.

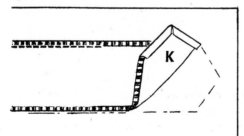

Many decorative effects can be obtained with ready-made bias folds when the Binder is used to apply them. Illustration below shows binding being applied with the Singer Binder. See your machine instruction book for detailed instructions.

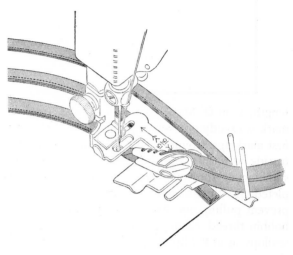

Corded Shirred Band. Cut fabric on crosswise grain, making it twice the length needed and twice the finished width. Mark the width of band in center of strip, as in **L** (below). Turn edges to wrong side on marked lines so that edges almost meet in center and crease or press. Lay cord inside fold of one edge and stitch, as at **M**,

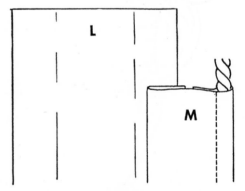

using Cording Foot. Finish other side in same way. Stitch across cords on one end as at **N** to hold in place. Shirr fabric along both cords to length desired. If fabric must be pieced, do this before cording. Shirred band can be applied invisibly by slip-stitching on both sides under corded edge.

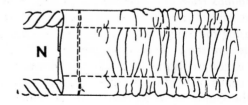

Zigzag Scallops. Use ribbon for this—the double-faced or two-toned ribbon gives a nice effect. Mark one edge at even intervals all along the

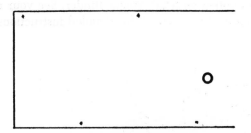

O

length, as in **O**. Mark the other edge so that each mark is exactly opposite a point halfway between first markings. Connect dots, alternating from side to side to form a zigzag line all along ribbon by stitching as shown. When stitching line is completed, tie thread ends together on one end to prevent pulling out. From opposite end, draw up bobbin thread, easing gathers along to form even scallops, as at **P**. Slip-stitch scalloped band in position.

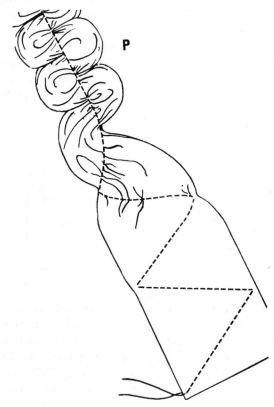

P

Trimmings from Bias Binding. A variety of decorative effects can be achieved with bias binding by using the Singercraft Guide. Two of the possibilities are shown here. In **Q**, fold bias binding so raw edges are inside, then stitch as shown. Using two colors of binding, wind in criss-cross pattern on the Guide as in **R**. Hold ends of binding in

place with a paper clip, as at **S**. Stitch together. In **T**, two colors of bias binding are laid together, raw edges inside, and stitched on both folded edges.

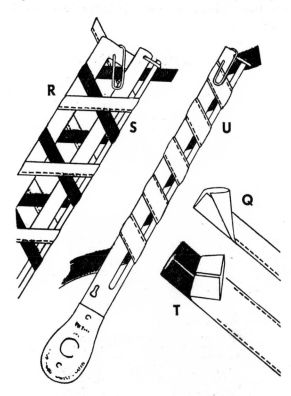

The double-faced strip is then wound around Singercraft Guide, as in **U**, and stitched through slot in Guide. Both of these trimmings are practical for cotton garments and home furnishings.

Other uses of the Singercraft Guide are shown on pages 134 and 230. Consult the instruction sheet that comes with the Guide for complete instructions on using it.

Rick Rack Applied with Singercraft Guide. Wind rick rack around Guide in same manner as binding in **U**, then stitch in position.

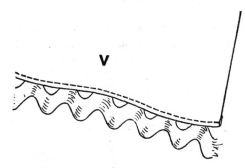

V

Rick Rack Applied to Edge. Turn fabric edge and press. Baste rick rack along underside of turned edge, catching points with the basting. Stitch as in **V**, above.

Rick Rack in Hem or Seam. Turn hem to desired depth on right side. Turn under raw edge. Lay rick rack under turned edge and stitch hem as at **W**. Rick rack can be used to trim a seamline in same way.

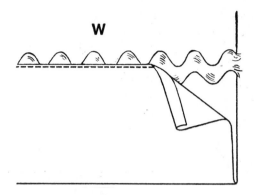

Braided Rick Rack. Use two colors of rick rack, twisting them together to form the braided effect shown. Baste braid in position; then stitch along center, as in **X**.

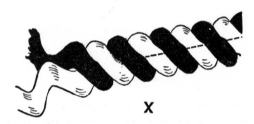

Applying Rick Rack on a Curve. Mark line on which rick rack is to be applied. Baste rick rack on this line. Bring needle up from wrong side, through the first point close to edge, as at **Y**. Put

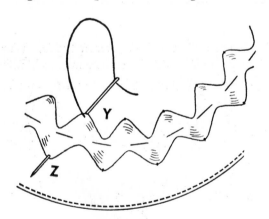

needle in just outside the point and bring it up just inside point on opposite side, as at **Z**. Repeat until all points are held in place, alternating from side to side of the rick rack. This makes almost invisible stitches on right side and long zigzag stitches on wrong side.

140

Blind-Stitcher. Although this attachment is thought of primarily as a time-saver in stitching hems, it can also be used effectively to apply a variety of decorative trims as illustrated here. Notice that the fabric, in all cases, is kept flat.

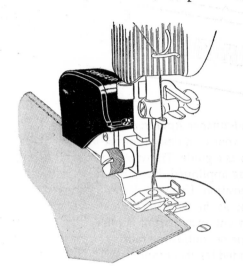

Blind-Stitcher Application of Bias Binding. Pin and baste band of bias binding flat, as at **A**, to form design or bands, as you desire. Using the Blind-Stitcher, stitch close to the edges of the binding, as at **B**. The holding stitch catches the folded edge and the stitches in between hold the bias securely to place, as shown.

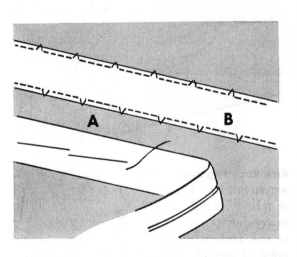

Drawn Threads. Draw one or more threads (3 to 10) along the straight edges of your fabric for open-work effect, as at **C**. Stitch over drawn thread lines as at **D**, and on each side of drawn-out group, as at **E** and **F**. Variety of thread colors can be used. Edges may be fringed and finished with the Blind-Stitcher at top of drawn thread line. See illustration at top of opposite page.

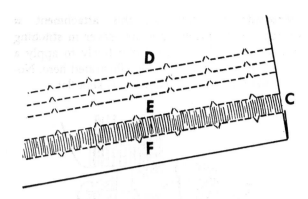

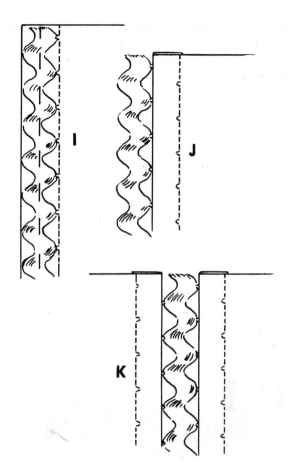

Blind-Stitcher Appliqué (Shadow Appliqué). Outline your own designs or use a simple transfer pattern as a guide. Transfer this on right side of fabric being appliquéd. Baste bands or individual motifs to position. Use your Blind-Stitcher to outline design, as in **G**. After stitching is finished, carefully cut away part of applied fabric, as at **H**. Self-fabric or contrasting fabric can be applied. Recommended for sheer fabrics.

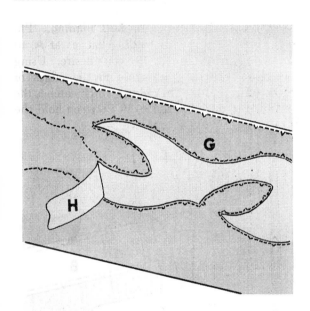

leather or a cord, simply mark for as many machine-buttonholes as you need, in the size desired. Space as in **L** to obtain the effect wanted. Make as many buttonholes as you need, open them, then draw the trimming through as shown. Trimming can be used flat, as at top of a skirt hem, or drawn up to fit wrist, neck or waistline.

Rick Rack Fagoting (best for lightweight, finely woven fabrics). Pin and baste rick rack along edge of fabric, on right side. Using Blind-Stitcher and heavy-duty thread, stitch as at **I**, along inside edge of rick rack as shown. Adjust stitch so only the point is caught. Remove basting, turn edge of fabric back and stitch flat, as at **J**. Follow same procedure on other side of rick rack, thus obtaining an open-work effect, as in **K**.

Buttonhole Slots. If you have a fabric through which you would like to draw ribbon, braid,

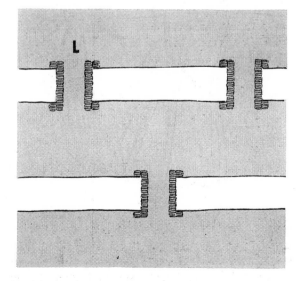

Fashion Effects with Top-Stitching. Both tailored and dress-maker styles can be given attractive accents by machine-top-stitching as shown here. See opposite for suggestions.

Designers' Sketches

THE FASHION SKETCHES HERE AND ON THE FOLLOW-
ing pages show how designers use the decorative
finishes described in the preceding chapter. Fashion is selective. One season banding or braiding is
favored, the next may bring shirrings, gatherings,
puffings, or flounces. These illustrations are given
to stir your imagination and show the variety of
possibilities in such decorations. Experienced
buyers realize that the difference in price ranges of
ready-made garments depends less on the cost of
fabric than on the good workmanship of the better
clothing. The more expensive the dress, the more
certain you are to find details such as these in its
construction.

Quilting—Top-Stitching

Quilting. Originally used to provide warmth,
quilting is now more often used for enrichment or
beautification of fabric and for purpose of design.
When fashion favors quilting for wearing apparel
and when you are master of your machine, the
Quilter, with its adjustable Quilter Bar, can help
you to make really lovely garments and accessories
(see page 132). A few designs are shown here to
inspire you to use this very practical means of
fabric decoration. Simple *block quilting,* as shown
on pockets, collars, cuffs, and belt here, can be
very effective. For evening wear, it may be given
added interest by adding sequins at the crossing of
stitching lines, as in the bolero jacket and gathered
skirt. *Italian quilting* in floral designs, as in the two
other jackets shown here, is especially dainty and
feminine. For instructions see page 133.

Top-Stitching. This is a smart and practical way
to accent the lines of a garment and to give additional firmness along edge. Stitching may be done
in matching or contrasting thread, according to
the effect desired. A single line of stitching on
heavy fabric, as in the coats at the bottom of the
opposite illustration, gives a welted effect. In
lighter weight fabrics, several parallel rows can be
used, either in all-over effect, as in cuffs, yokes,
pockets, belts and panels, or to lend importance to
a line or edge.

Corded Finishes

Cording. The illustrations here give you an idea of the many ways in which your machine Cording Foot can help you in achieving attractive and professional-looking details. Cording may be made of self-material or in contrasting color, depending on whether a color accent is desired or not. When inserted in seamlines, cording gives weight and importance to the lines of the garment. It also makes an attractive edge finish for collars, necklines, cuffs and jackets, as shown. Several additional rows of cording may be put in above the edge to give the effect shown in the flared tunic illustrated. Where a shirred section joins plain fabric, as in the blouse front at the top, cording may be inserted to give the joining a nice finish. The center dress and the bag show how corded shirring holds and distributes fullness, and the shirred bands at the top illustrate the use of cording to give a firm neat finish at the edges of the bands. Instruction for achieving these effects is given on pages 57, 124 and 138.

Feminine Frills

Ruffles. Feminine as a powder puff, ruffles are the essence of daintiness. The infinite variety of ways to use ruffles is just hinted in the illustrations opposite. With your machine Ruffler and Gathering Foot you can make these perfectly and with a minimum of effort. Center-stitched ruffles, applied on a curved line, are used in the round-necked blouse at the top and the evening dress at the bottom, tiered ruffles in the petticoat showing beneath the lifted skirt. The blouse front at top left has a ruffle inserted in a seam. The all-over ruffled effect in the jacket just below is obtained by applying center-stitched ruffles along parallel lines marked in the fabric. Study the effects here and consult pages 43, 44 and 45 for instructions for all types of ruffles.

Ruffles generally are best cut on a true bias, hemmed, picoted, or lace-trimmed, then plaited or gathered. They may, however, be made of ribbon, of lace, of a bias fold. Always press your ruffle after the edge is finished and before gathering the top. Keep ruffling in a box—do not let it get wrinkled after it has been gathered.

Ruffles for Daintiness. For lightweight, crisp and sheer fabrics, ruffles are always a favorite self-trimming. With practice, you can adapt any of the above ideas to suit your fancy. See opposite page for description.

Where the Edge-Stitcher Shines. For lace edging and insertion, ribbon and band trimmings, anywhere that a very neat narrow joining is desirable, the Edge-Stitcher is invaluable. See opposite page.

The Zigzagger for Appliqué

Appliqué. Of all the practical Fashion Aids which the sewing machine provides, none contributes more to the beauty of both design and fabric than does the Zigzagger. With it, you can appliqué the most intricate, time-taking designs, doing the work even more effectively and with far less handling than by hand. This page shows you only a few of the ways in which it can serve you. The zigzag stitching line it makes back and forth across the joining is ideal for applying the shaped edges of lace to filmy fabric, as in lingerie and evening wear. For applying fabric motifs, it also makes an excellent, secure and inconspicuous edge finish. See instructions for appliqué on page 128–129. Flower motifs, conventional designs, and monograms may all be applied in this easy way.

The particular advantage of appliqué is that it lends interest through contrast—contrast of textures, of color, and of design. The tracery of the outline against a plain surface is eye-catching. Velvet on broadcloth, taffeta on satin, satin or taffeta on organdie, taffeta on satin or net, net or lace on chiffon, plain cotton on printed, or plain silk on printed—these are only a few of the possible combinations you can use. On sheer fabrics, self-appliqué gives the shadowy contrast of a double thickness. If you are not expert with the Zigzagger, go to a Singer Shop and learn how to use it for appliqué.

Bands and Edges

Edge-Stitcher. Wherever straight smooth edges and narrow, inconspicuous joinings are required, the Edge-Stitcher proves its worth. Net, lace and filmy fabrics which are to be stitched together in bands or in all-over effects, such as the blouse at top-center opposite, are beautifully handled by the Edge-Stitcher. This attachment is also valuable for giving a crisp edge to perky ruffles, as around the neckline at bottom, and when bands of fabric, ribbon or braid are used, as in the skirt and the sleeve shown. For very fine work, use matching thread, a short stitch, and tissue paper underneath for protection. See page 129.

Fullness with Smocking

Smocking. Always a favored fabric decoration for children's clothes and young effects, machine smocking is also attractive on grown-up garments and accessories where it is desirable to hold and control fullness at shoulder, neckline, waistline, etc. "Peasant" styles can be created by using bright colored thread for the stitching. See instructions on page 136. More formal effects, as at the upper right of the illustration, require stitching with matching thread. Smocking, either by hand or with your machine Gathering Foot, should be done only in fabrics that are soft enough to look well with considerable fullness.

Many like to gather by machine, then decorate with a twisted chain or briar-stitch by hand over the machine gathering lines. This is especially attractive in plissé cotton crepe, for children's dresses, blouses and skirts.

Fullness with Shirring

Shirring. Shirring consists of two or more rows of gathers and gives soft, rich effects. When fashion approves shirrings, your machine Gathering Foot comes into its own. Use matching thread, space rows evenly and distribute fullness equally along stitching line. See page 40 for shirring instructions. The illustration here shows several ways in which fashion makes use of shirrings. Inserted shirred bands are shown in the blouse front opposite. A corded shaped band of shirring makes an interesting border treatment for the jacket at the top left. All-over shirred effects, as in the bodice and in the full coat sleeves shown, are obtained by evenly spaced rows of gathers put in before the garment sections are assembled. The generous skirt of the evening dress is not actually shirred, but is made of row after row of deep ruffling, joined with cording. Remember that shirring is always best in soft, limp fabrics, and that the allowance for making must be ample, since the gathers require 1½ to 2 times the finished measurement. Do not plan group shirrings for garments that must be washed often, since ironing is difficult.

148

Shirrings for Fashion Interest. Your machine Gathering Foot, used with skill, can provide many attractive effects of fabric decoration. See *Shirring*, opposite page.

Fabric Decoration with Braiding. When favored by fashion, braiding provides an ideal means of fabric decoration. If you are skilled at using your machine Braiding Foot and Underbraider, any of the effects above can be worked out with good result. See *Braiding* paragraph opposite.

150

Tucking and Pinking

EVERY ONE OF THE SINGER FASHION AIDS OFFERS ITS own distinctive method of enhancing garments and accessories. On this page are shown ways for using the Tucker and the Pinking Shears. The trim tailored lines of tucks in the blouse fronts at the top can be made in lengthwise, crosswise, or diagonal patterns, as shown, and evenly spaced, graduated or in groups. See instructions on pages 38 and 39. Tucking is one form of fabric decoration that is nearly always in fashion. It is attractive not only in sheer cottons and lingerie fabrics, but also in dress woolens. For tucking in children's and infants' garments, see page 161. The Pinking Shears or the Singer Hand Pinker makes the easy and attractive notched edges shown in the rosettes at the neckline (left) and in the trimming of vest, gloves, belt and bag at the bottom. Felt is excellent for pinked bandings, since it does not ravel. Taffeta, chintz, organdie, and plastic fabrics are also practical for pinking. See page 122 for instructions. The dress in the center also shows the versatility of pinking. The applied pinked bands in neck ruffle and skirt are of two different widths and so spaced as to make an interesting crosswise accent.

Trimming with Braid

Braiding. The sketches opposite show a few designs for braid trimming. Make your own motifs, choose a transfer pattern, or take a rubbing from a pattern and transfer this to your fabric for the braiding lines. Learn to use both the Braiding Foot and the Underbraider expertly before beginning such work. (See page 131 and 132.) Braiding can give you a decorative touch at neckline or pocket. It can accent the lines of a long-torso dress or a short bolero. Braid can add distinction to a simply cut evening wrap and give a note of interest to a plain bodice or the lapels or peplum of a dressmaker suit.

Fagoting and Hemstitching

FABRIC DECORATION WITH OPEN-WORK DESIGNS AND with self-trimming can provide attractive fashion details. Open-work is particularly appropriate for summer clothing and lightweight fabrics, while the tubing is suitable for somewhat heavier fabrics.

Both the Singercraft Guide and the Hemstitcher can be used for open-work lines. The choice depends on the effect desired. The Hemstitcher gives a narrow line of open-work and does this in stitching directly on the fabric. The collar and bodice front at the top right show how hemstitched designs appear. The Singercraft Guide makes an open-work insertion which is applied in seams or in slashes placed to contribute to the dress design. The lines in the deep armhole and shoulder at top left, the deep ruffled cuff at the left and the ruffled yoke at center are done with the Guide. Use yarn, braid, tubing, crochet cotton or embroidery floss to make your insertion, depending on the fabric used in the garment.

The Hemstitcher has another very practical and effective use. It provides the dainty edge finish of the picoted ruffles in the sheer dress at center right and the yoke beside it. This is produced when hemstitched lines are cut in half. See page 122. Other uses of picoted ruffles are illustrated on page 145.

Tubing

SELF-TRIMMING WITH TUBING CAN BE USED IN A VARIety of ways. It, too, can provide open-seam insets, as in the diagonal lines of the blouse and the neckline shown here. The tubing, made with the Cording Foot as on page 125, is cut and stitched in parallel lines to give the ladder pattern of the blouse and inserted as described on page 126. A contrasting color used here accents this line. This arrangement may be varied by knotting each cross bar, as shown in the design at the left.

As an edge finish, tubing is also attractive when arranged in the looped or scalloped line shown on the off-the-shoulder neckline and the cape coat at right. See page 126.

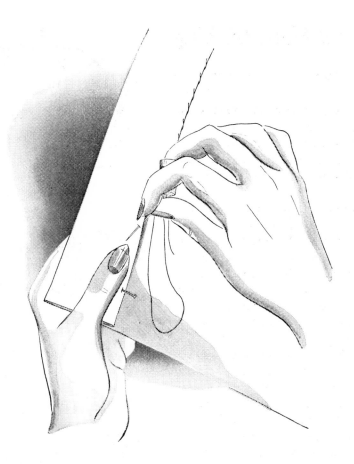

Hand Sewing—Stitches

Preparation. You use both hands when you sew —one to smooth the material in front of the needle, and the other to guide the needle. So it is essential that your hands be immaculately clean. Cover perspiring fingers and palms with French chalk to protect the material and to allow it to slip easily through your hands.

Choose the right needle for each job—a fine one for thin fabrics, a larger one for thicker materials, and suit the thread to the needle's eye. See the *Thread, Needle and Stitch Chart* on page 7. Choose a lightweight thimble and fit it as carefully as you would a shoe—never snug, yet not too loose.

A work table, even a collapsible one, is desirable. It allows you to spread out your work, see what you are doing and readily assemble a dress or skirt for basting. Keep tape, ruler, needles, thread, scissors, pins, chalk and other constantly needed supplies near at hand.

To Make Knot. Wind thread end in a loop around your forefinger. With the thumb, roll the end away from you around and under the loop. Continue rolling with thumb until thread rolls off tip of finger. Then hold the knot with the thumb, pulling thread from needle end to tighten. As a rule, a small knot is made on the end of threads to be used for basting, gathering or shirring. When removing hand bastings, clip the knots off before removing the stitches. Begin and end all other hand-sewing stitches with tiny back-stitches in the line of sewing.

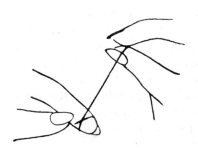

Running-Stitch. Use a long, slim needle, size 7 or 8. Weave point of needle in and out of fabric several times before pulling thread through. Working quickly helps keep stitches uniform. Work for evenness first, then speed. Use for seaming, gathering, tucking, mending, quilting and many kinds of delicate work.

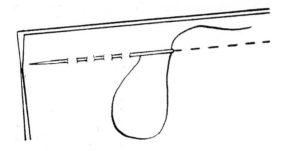

Back-Stitch. Use a short needle. Take a stitch through fabric; then put needle in halfway back through first stitch and take another stitch underneath. This makes a long forward stitch on underside and a short backward stitch on surface. Continue all along the sewing line.

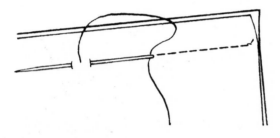

Combination-Stitch. Take three or four running-stitches, then one back-stitch to stay the seam and prevent thread from pulling. More secure than running-stitch and quicker than back-stitch.

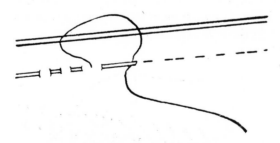

Overcasting. Finish for raw-edge seams, especially in bulky fabrics or ones that fray easily. On heavy fabrics, take one stitch at a time over the edge; on lightweight ones, take several stitches on

the needle before pulling it through—this for speed. Keep your thread easy; never draw it tight enough to pucker the edge.

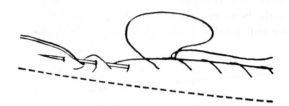

Overhanding. Make short, but not tight, over-and-over stitches along the very edge of the seam. Baste edges together to prevent slipping. Use a short, fine needle and strong thread. Good where an almost invisible seam is desired and for joining selvage edges, lace, insertion and grosgrain ribbon. Turn raw edges down ¼" when overhanding together.

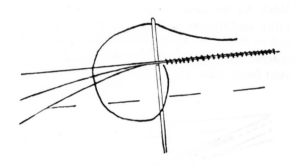

Hemming or Whipping. Bring needle out at edge of fold in position for first stitch. Inserting needle diagonally, catch one or two threads in fabric and then bring needle through folded edge of hem. Pull thread through and make another stitch below in same manner. Continue working toward yourself. Take almost invisible stitches through to right side, and slanting stitches of even length on wrong side. Never draw thread tight.

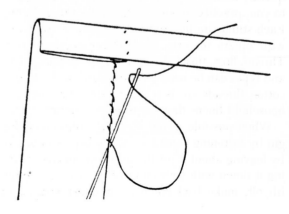

Running-Hem or Vertical Hemming. Slip knot inside hem and bring needle out at edge of fold. Just outside the hem, directly opposite point where needle came out, take up one or two threads of fabric and bring needle out a stitch-length ahead in the hem, as close to turned edge as possible. Use for stiff fabrics, linens, ribbons, brocades, etc.

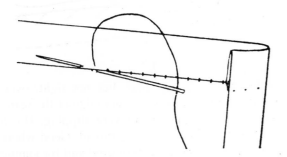

Slip-Stitch. For invisibility rather than strength, as in hems, folds or facings. Turn hem and baste near turned edge; then turn under raw edge and stitch for firmness. Catch needle in a thread of fabric and then in hem turn, keeping stitches easy unless fabric is heavy. Where no strain occurs, stitches may be ½″ apart. In heavy fabrics or in skirt hems, place close together.

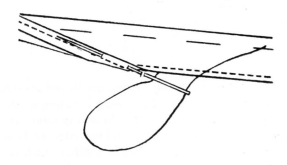

DECORATIVE HAND-STITCHES

BASIC HAND-EMBROIDERY STITCHES MOST FREquently used are shown here. If any are unfamiliar to you, practice making them on a scrap of fabric. Each stitch can be used individually or combined with others to form more elaborate decoration. Thread, floss, tinsel, and yarn of all weights, colors and types can be used for these stitches. Fast-color cotton threads are best for children's clothes and household linens that are to be laundered.

When possible, avoid knots in embroidery. Begin by fastening thread with tiny back-stitches, or by leaving about 2″ of thread on underside, catching it down with your embroidery stitches. To finish off, make back-stitch in or under stitches or whip thread down on wrong side with tiny stitches of fine cotton thread.

Blanket-Stitch. Turn hem slightly narrower than blanket-stitch is to be. Baste it in place. Work from left to right. Insert needle just above hem turn; bring out at edge of hem over thread so that it forms blanket-stitch when pulled through. Space stitches evenly or group three or five together with a longer stitch or space between groups.

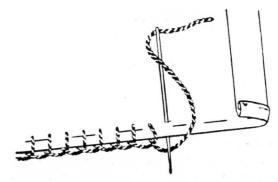

Feather- or Brier-Stitch. A variation of blanket-stitch, done alternately on each side of a line marked by basting, creasing or transferring a pattern to fabric. Vary by placing 2 or 3 stitches on each side of line.

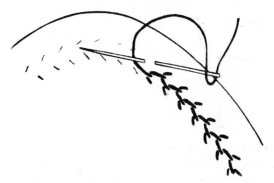

Cross-Stitch. One of the oldest decorative stitches. Work along a row, taking flat overcasting-stitches; then turn and work back parallel over first row of stitches to form a cross. As evenness is important, cross-stitching is often done over canvas.

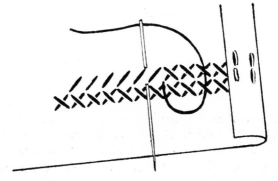

Chain-Stitch. Bring needle out on right side of fabric; hold thread on fabric surface with end of thumb while you take a stitch, so that needle crosses over thread to form a loop. A succession of stitches forms a "chain." Use firmly twisted thread; keep stitches even, easy, medium in size.

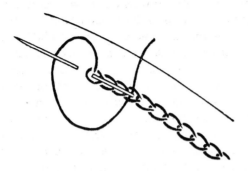

Lazy-Daisy. Simply a longer chain-stitch arranged in flower form. After catching each loop with a stitch at petal-end, bring needle down behind the point of the loop and back and out at the center, ready to make next petal. To make leaves, make single loops along stem.

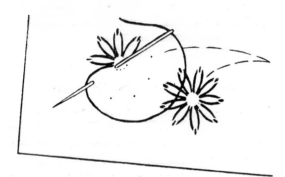

French Knot. Pull needle through from wrong side. Hold thread close to fabric with thumb and finger, twist needle around it 3 to 5 times, the number of times depending upon the size of thread and knot desired. Put needle into fabric near where it came up; pull thread to wrong side, bringing knot snugly against fabric. Repeat, spacing knots to form design. French knots may be used as centers of flowers or wherever a dot is desired for accent.

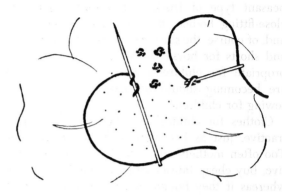

Long-and-Short Stitch. Over-and-over type of stitch, alternating long and short. Is used for appliqué, for filling and for edging designs such as fruit and leaves. Use fairly heavy thread or yarn, making stitches as deep as size of motif requires.

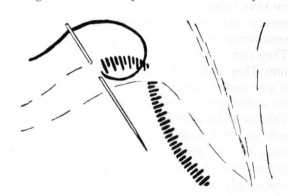

Hand needlework, first done with crude fish-bone needles, was greatly prized by the Babylonians and Egyptians. In fact, in the early ages, needlework was an art with all Mediterranean civilizations. Needlework stitches are much the same the world over, Oriental stitches being the finest. The Chinese were the first to use the steel needle. Steel needles were manufactured for sale in Nuremberg, Germany, in 1370. The peasantry in Europe are especially adept at bold, colorful embroidery. Much hand-embroidery is copied beautifully on the sewing machine. See Learn to Do Fashion Stitches on page 113. The first embroidery attachment made for the sewing machine was invented by I. M. Singer in 1855.

FASHION IS JUST AS IMPORTANT IN CHILDREN'S clothes as in adults'. There are always classic styles, such as smocked dresses, pinafores, the peasant type of frock with gathered skirt and close-fitting bodice, that are nice for little girls and, of course, the shirt and overalls or shirt blouse and shorts for boys. The selection of fabrics appropriate for children's clothes and colors that are becoming should be taken into account in sewing for children.

Clothes for children can be made just as attractive, just as becoming as those ready-made. Too often mothers, impelled by an economy motive, buy cheap fabrics when sewing for children, whereas if they bought really the best available appropriate fabric, styled and made the clothes with an eye to becomingness, fit and fashion, they could very easily duplicate at a fraction of the cost the "just right" garments shown often in the most exclusive shops. Top designers never skimp on skirt fullness. They use two full widths to insure a perky skirt. They make deep hems. They concentrate on daintiness when it is the essential. They size clothes to fit, not for children to grow into. They make collars appropriately narrow, and if wee pockets and tiny puffed sleeves are needed for a chic appearance, then that is what they have. Talk to a designer of children's clothes and she will say that mothers too often lose their style sense in their desire to be practical. Don't compromise with becomingness. Children should look charmingly adorable when dressed up. A grain of practicality, yes, but don't, please, salt down the style.

Children whose mothers can sew with skill and with a flair for fashion rightness are fortunate. More clothes are possible and, best of all, clothes that are individually becoming. Children begin at an early age to develop a sense of good taste and desire for good grooming, which, if aided by a mother's good taste and guidance, can be of value to them all their lives.

Mothers who can sew are doubly fortunate. The actual savings accomplished can, of course, be a matter of importance in any budget. And the satisfaction of having clothes for your children that are becoming, individual, and constructed for happy wear and ease in washing is rewarding.

Sewing for babies, whether it is preparing a layette for an expected arrival or making infants' clothes for gifts, involves only the most simple procedures, and is an ideal opportunity to start at the beginning and work up as the child grows. Baby clothes should be simply made of soft materials with few fastenings, of fabrics that can be washed often and bleached occasionally, and that require a minimum of time in ironing.

Sewing for little boys, until they get to the age of tailor-made, long-trouser suits, is a dressmaker job involving tailored touches. Rompers, overalls, coveralls, shirts, shorts, pajamas and other little-boy clothes are fun to make.

Sewing for little girls is a pleasure that can develop into a creative hobby. The feminine instinct and feeling for clothes is one that begins almost with the first step. A mother who sews for her daughter and works with a child to create attractive clothes can, quite early, instill an appreciation of quality and workmanship that is not easily acquired by other means.

MEASUREMENTS FOR CHILDREN

Chest, waist and length measurements are important in cutting clothes to fit children. Rarely are two children of the same age exactly the same size. Patterns give chest measurements and one can buy the pattern correct for chest, then lengthen or shorten the pieces as the individual length requires, doing this in accordance with the method given for adults. (See page 26.)

FABRICS AND FASTENINGS FOR CHILDREN

There are certain fabrics that are traditionally favored for children. Some of these come in new designs and in new colors each season, but their weave and construction seems to make them always preferable to novelties. In the main, the favored fabrics have sufficiently smooth surfaces to mean ease in ironing and to avoid picking up dirt. Sunfast colors are an essential in children's clothes. The Department of Agriculture, Washington, D. C., has published some interesting studies in this regard which are worth sending for. Any fabrics used should be firm enough to hold buttons and buttonholes or hammer-on snaps to make it easy for children to put on and take off their own clothes and to button themselves up. This is important in teaching children self-sufficiency and is well worth a mother's special efforts in designing and planning. If you are in need of a gift for a baby, make something from this list. The mother will welcome it and you will know the satisfaction of giving something practical and usable.

A PARTIAL LIST OF FABRICS SUITABLE FOR CHILDREN'S CLOTHES

Play Clothes

Corduroy
Denim
Seersucker
Cotton gabardine
Broadcloth
Gingham
Poplin
Percale
Calico
Appropriate
  synthetics

Underwear and Nightwear

Nainsook	Poplin
Cotton crepe	Fine percale
Cambric	Jersey
Cotton flannel	Softest synthetics
Seersucker	

Dress Clothes

Linen
Chambray
Eyelet embroidery
Velveteen
Sheer cottons
Organdie
Dotted swiss
Piqué
Fine lawns and
  muslins
Appropriate
  synthetics

Baby Clothes

White lawn
Fine soft cottons
Cotton flannel and
  jersey
Terry cloth
Handkerchief linen
Soft fine silk
Softer synthetics

Robes

Terry cloth
Cotton crepe
Quilted cotton
Corduroy
Flannel
Broadcloth
Velveteen
Vicara types

LAYETTE

First Clothing Needs	Minimum		Bath Needs	Minimum
Diapers	4 doz.		Towels	4
Shirts	4		Wash cloths	3
Wrappers (kimonos)	6			
Sleepers	6			
* Bands	3		**First Crib Needs**	**Minimum**
			Sheets	4
First Comfort Needs	**Minimum**		Crib blankets	2
Cotton wrapping blankets	4		Spread	1
Wool or part-wool			Mattress protector	1
wrapping blankets	1		Pillows	2
Pads	4		Pillow cases	4
Rubber sheet	1			
Diaper covers	2			
Plastic panties	12		**Out-door Needs**	**Minimum**
Rubber panties	2		Hoods or bonnets	2
Wool soakers	2		Bootees	2
			Coat or bunting	1
Second Clothing Needs	**Minimum**		Carriage robe	1
Dresses or rompers	2		Carriage pillow	1
Slips	2			
Bibs	4			
Sweater	1			

* Used if recommended by doctor. Required only if baby is born at home. Generally used for two weeks only.

THE IMPORTANT THING IN STARTING TO SEW DAINTY things is to equip the sewing basket at the outset with fine cotton sewing thread. There should be fine needles, and dainty edgings, fine bindings and tapes—all dainty enough to belong to Baby and delicate enough to be appropriate to the garments that you make. When you are shopping, buy the essentials in notions so that they will be at hand when you are ready to sew.

The texture of materials for baby things is most important. The yardage is usually so small that a satisfactory quality is not expensive. Woolens must be very fine to be soft enough. Batiste and nainsook are favored for the best dresses; nainsook and long cloth for dresses, slips and night dresses; fine flannel, cashmere or sheer synthetics for sacques, kimonos or wrappers.

Machine Work. Many women exclaim regretfully when they see machine stitching on a baby's garment. But there are no regrets if one takes the precaution to buy fine sewing thread and uses a fine needle and short sewing stitch. It is a fault only when one forgets to change the needle and the thread and uses thread and needle that are in keeping with regular household articles or garments.

Many of the finest baby dresses that are French-seamed have the first seams stitched on the machine and the second seams done by hand. This is an ideal way because the machine stitching gives strength to the seam and allows it to hold

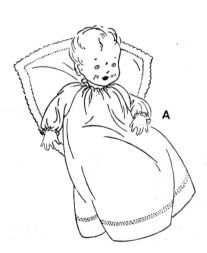

better in laundering, and to all appearances, the dress is entirely handmade. Any French seam, however, can be done beautifully by machine. Fine tucks can be put in by machine and then the tucks pulled crosswise gently to give a hemstitched effect.

Bishop Dresses. The most practical and popular baby dress is the Bishop or raglan-sleeve dress, as in **A**. This provides a roomy armhole and is slightly easier to make than a dress with a set-in sleeve. See illustration in previous column.

Before stitching underarm seams in sleeve and body of garment, seam the armholes, as at **B** and **C**, using a French seam. Hem the neck and sleeve

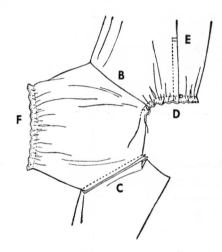

edges with the Foot Hemmer, as at **D**, or, using the Edge-Stitcher, turn edge back about ⅛" and stitch on very edge. Trim close to row of stitching; then roll stitched edge under and stitch again. Make a hemmed placket for the back closing, as at **E**. See **A**, page 90 for instructions.

Gather edges of neckline and bottom of both sleeves about ¾" in from edge as in **F**. Stitch a narrow tape to underside of gathers to hold fullness in place. Stitch underarm seams. Use a worked loop and small flat button at top of placket.

Another way of gathering the neckline and sleeves is to make a narrow tuck on wrong side ¾" from edge. Run a narrow tape through these casings. The tapes can be drawn up and bows tied for wearing. They can be opened out for ease in laundering.

159

A ruffle may be added to the lower edge rather than a hem.

Several rows of tucks may be used to decorate either a plain or ruffled edge.

Round Yoke Dresses. A favored baby dress, one especially preferred in handmade dresses, is the round yoke dress, as in **G**.

Round yoke dresses are also used for little girls two and three years old. In such cases the fullness is usually held in with smocking. Outline stitches are sometimes used over machine shirrings to give a smocked effect.

Adjust the fullness evenly to desired width, as in **H**. If the material stretches easily, run a stitching line all around one-eighth inch in from the edge, to hold it to shape preparatory to joining the yoke.

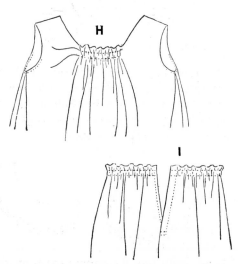

Make hemmed placket in back, as at **I**. Placket opening plus yoke should measure at least 8 inches

to allow the dress to be slipped on and off easily.

As the center front of yoke is cut on a lengthwise fold, the hems in the center back are slightly bias, as in **J**. Stitch a lengthwise piece of the material or a piece of tape inside the hem, to serve as a stay for buttons and buttonholes.

Hem neckline, using your machine Hemmer. Whip narrow edging around neckline, as at **K**.

Entre deux, or veining, can be used around yoke, as at **L**, the body of the dress being joined to other edge of entre deux.

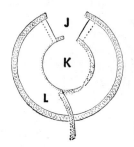

Turn raw edges of yoke and dress under and lay turned edges close to embroidered edge of entre deux and baste. See **V** on page 131 for stitching instruction.

Wrist edge of sleeves can be finished in either of two ways:

For the first, apply lace to narrow or rolled hem. See **M** on page 130. Run row of gathering ½″ above lower edge, as at **M**. Adjust gathers to fit and apply narrow insertion over gathers as shown.

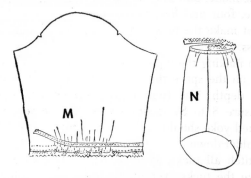

For the second, gather lower edge of sleeve and finish with a narrow facing. See **A** on page 77. Then whip lace edging to edge, as in **N**.

In place of a plain hem, a decorative hem, as in **O**, can be used. The bottom edge of the dress is scalloped and turned to the right side, as shown.

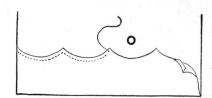

The side seam at the hem, therefore, must be clipped and edges turned to the right side before hem is finished.

Clip the curves of the scallops ⅛″ and turn the edge so that the shape of the scallop will be retained. Lift the presser foot and pivot the needle at each point of the scallops so that an exact turn will be made. The top of scallops may also be finished with French knots, feather-stitching or lace. See *Decorative Hand-Stitches* on page 155.

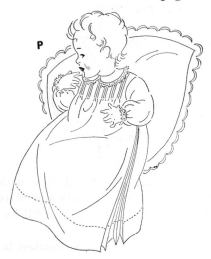

Tucked Yoke Dresses. Baby dresses should have some fullness provided, either by means of gathers, tucks or yoke fullness.

Tucking is very practical, especially when machine-made, and may be put in in groups of two, three, four and five, as many as desired. In any event make the tucks tiny enough to insure daintiness.

In making the type of dress shown in **P**, decide first on the space the tucks will occupy in width and depth. The front of the infant's dress will measure 8 to 8½ inches across. The depth of a tucked yoke should not exceed 3½ inches from the shoulder down.

Stitch all tucks, as at **Q**, before cutting dress. Make the tucks even at the lower edge, using a pin to pull the stitching back. Pull the threads to the wrong side and tie the two threads at the

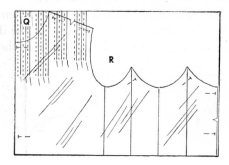

end of each tuck. Take care to avoid tightening.

Fold fabric lengthwise on center front and pin on front of pattern, as in **R**. Many patterns allow an inverted pleat at underarm as is shown opened out.

Finish the end of the tucks in back, lap the placket and pin it in correct position, as in **S**. Place the pattern on, center-back of pattern to center-back lengthwise fold of dress.

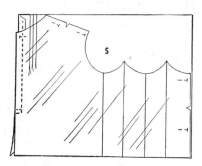

French-seam the shoulders and underarm seams. Put in a 3″ to 5″ hem. Then lay in pleat at underarm and stitch around armhole to hold in place while inserting sleeve.

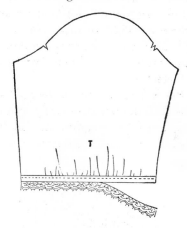

The wrist edge can be gathered and ⅜″ finished band stitched over gathers, as in **T**. When practical, finish the wrist edge before stitching the underarm seam. A narrow lace edging can be sewed to lower edge, if desired.

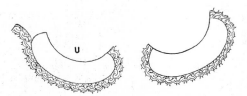

Avoid stretching the curved edges of the collar sections. Allow the lace to ease in on the curve so that it will lie flat, as in **U**. Edge can be rolled and lace whipped on. See page 130.

Smartness Essential in Children's Clothes

SMARTNESS IN CHILDREN'S CLOTHES BEGINS WITH *fit*. This is why many persons feel that dresses that can be "tried on" are smarter, prettier and more becoming than clothes made at home. Patterns have charts giving the measurements of waist, chest, and length of the dress that can be made with the enclosed patterns. Before buying a pattern, measure the child accurately and buy a pattern according to measurement, not to size, as given on the pattern envelope. A six-year-old child may wear a dress made from a size four pattern, and a four-year-old wear a dress made from a size five pattern.

Many people make the mistake of making children's clothes that are too large and are worn out before they are grown into. It is far better to have a few clothes that fit correctly than it is to have a half dozen that fit badly and add nothing to a child's attractiveness. Coats and outer wear can be made so that hems in sleeves and skirt can be let down to allow for growth, but the little dresses, shorts, overalls and everyday clothes should be made to fit without too much allowance for growth alterations.

Fit. Shoulders should be at the shoulder line, not drooping over the shoulder bone. Waistlines should be midway between the hip bone and the end of the ribs to balance the finished garment properly.

Short sleeves usually come only half way between the elbow and shoulder, and, if puffed, even shorter than that. Long sleeves should come just to the wrist bone. The right sleeve length has a definite relation to the fashion rightness.

Skirts for small girls, to be smart, should be made of 2 widths of 36″ fabric and they should be short—midway between the knee and hip. As the child grows older, the skirt length gets longer and is knee length at approximately ten years. Shorts for boys also follow this rule.

Becomingness. Color and line are factors that contribute to becomingness. The trimmings that are used add interest. When sewing for children, study color in relation to their skin color, eyes and hair. Hold pieces of material in front of them before a mirror and choose those that add to the total flattering picture. When buying material and patterns, study the fashion magazines and children's catalogues for ideas for trimming. Pattern books give many good ideas. The advertising of papers can supply ideas for new and interesting details.

Before Adding the Finishing Touches to Children's Clothes. Be certain that you have made collar as in pattern. When ruffled trimming is used, make the body of the collar smaller so that the finished collar with the ruffling will be no larger than the pattern. Notice the exact amount of seam allowance in the pattern, and be sure that you use all the allowance. The depth of a collar is important to the style effect of a garment. On tiny clothes even a half inch makes a difference.

Plan children's clothes with thought. When buying material, buy all notions and trimmings so that you can match or contrast with the best results. Put as much thought into the fashion rightness of a child's dress as you would into one for yourself.

If you feel that you cannot make as "cute" clothes for your children as you can buy ready-made, then take your little one to a quality shop, buy a dress or suit that you know is really becoming to use as a model, even if you have to pay extra for the style and the material. There is a right style for every youngster if you just take time to find it. When you have the garment home, carefully make a pattern, possibly recutting an old tissue-paper pattern or making a new one. Measure the fullness of sleeves, the size of collar, the sleeve and shoulder lines and make as exact

Children's Room

Authorities say that we can not begin too early to develop in children an appreciation of attractive surroundings. In the nursery shown opposite, with its canopied crib and more grown-up bed, decorations are gay and playful enough to please a toddler yet not so babyish as to embarrass an older child. Both the glazed chintz fabric and the painted wood of the furniture are easy to keep clean. The flowered pattern of bedspread and valance provides a center motif for the chair cushion and the striped fabric of the slip-covers repeats the solid color of the draperies and the wall-to-wall rug of shaggy cotton pile.

a pattern as you can. Buy material as nearly like that in the garment as you can. Then copy to the last detail the "store" dress. Make several garments in different becoming colors from the same design. You can, in this way, save money, have the satisfaction of making clothes for your child, and yet be assured of becomingness and good style. Such a plan can pay real dividends, especially if you feel unsure of your ability to produce the new fashions without a definite guide. If in doubt as to your own ability to style for smartness, then follow the above procedure in making clothes for yourself as well as for your children.

AMOUNTS OF FABRIC REQUIRED

Two lengths of fabric, shoulder-to-toe, plus hem allowance, will usually make a dress for sizes from infant to three-year-old. Children from three to twelve require usually three lengths. After that, fashion dictates the skirt fullness and whether there are sleeves or not, so that the required amount of material varies after twelve according to the prevailing style.

Boys require only slightly less fabric than girls. Facings, straps, cuffs, pockets, reinforcements and other essentials of their apparel make necessary additional fabric.

Fabric requirements for the style in each size are provided on pattern envelopes.

ADJUSTING TO GROWTH

For garments for little girls, you may lay a tuck on the inside just above the waistline for additional waist length and another tuck in the hem of the skirt part. These tucks may then be let down as the child requires additional length. If fabric has faded, these strips may be covered with strips of bias binding, embroidery insertion, or contrasting bands of fabric.

The shoulder seams of slips can be opened and two straps put on each shoulder to drop the slip to the desired length. Long-sleeved shirts, blouses and dresses may have an additional inch tucked into the length of sleeves to be let out as the arms grow longer. Usually such tucks can be put in with a long machine-basting stitch so that it is easy to remove the stitches.

Buttons on blouses for little boys may be lowered or straps lengthened on overalls and shorts to allow for growth.

When making straps for overalls or shorts, allow several inches for growth. The buttons can be moved to make the straps longer.

How to Bundle Your Sewing

IF WOMEN ARE TO ENJOY THE LUXURY OF TIME, they must learn to save their time in their home-making tasks, especially if they are to make space for sewing. There was a period when the housewife spent the entire morning washing the dishes and making the beds. We are now less indulgent with our chores. We pick up as we go and aim to get the housekeeping tasks done in the minimum of time, even though this requires concentrated effort.

One way to save time in sewing is to cut several garments at once, cutting all the essential pieces for each garment, writing little notes to yourself if there is piecing to be done or anything special to remember when you are at the machine

sewing. Roll or box the pieces for each garment so that you can do all the machine work at one time. The essential handwork can be done in leisure moments and thus more can be accomplished than if you cut as you sew and sew only when the spirit moves you. A little practice with bundle sewing to get the idea, then the habit, will quickly show you how such a plan helps you to visit with a neighbor or the family, enjoy a TV or radio program, or take your work as you go visiting and all the while make progress with your sewing projects. Once the habit of bundle sewing is yours, you will want to have ready half a dozen bundles or boxes so that just the right sewing can be done while you enjoy something else in your day or evening.

Make Your Bedrooms Gay with Color

The quilted spread and shams are made of a fast-color gingham alike on both sides, easy to quilt, and with a lifetime of wear. Acetate faille, flowered as used here, is not expensive, so you can use it generously in decorating a room. Make your draw curtains long or short, as desired. The center photo below shows how padded headboard is fastened to baseboard. See instructions for making on page 215.

Match your patterns in the flouncing. Machine-gather the flouncing, then stitch a band of plain cotton or muslin to the top, concealing gathered edge. Pin flounce around edge of box spring so hem clears floor. Baste band to box spring, using long diagonal stitches to hold it securely. Shown in photo below, left.

Make double ruffles for the under-sham and attach to fabric which is two inches smaller on all four sides than the quilted sham. See page 211 for making. Note difference in size in photo below.

Café Drapes and Canopy Make an Ideal Twosome

The horizontal lines of the valance and café drapes unify two windows, giving a bay-window effect as background for an intimate furniture grouping. The amount of drapery and the depth of the valance used depend upon the size of the windows and the amount of light or privacy desired. See page 176 for detailed instructions. The plain Everglaze-finished cotton of canopy and café drapes gives a sheen which contrasts well with the printed cotton bedspread, drapery, valance and couch cover. White lamps and milk-glass ornaments repeat the white of the chair covers to add sparkle to the room. White presents no problem when the new synthetic fabrics are used, since they clean so easily and give long wear.

Planning Clothes for Children

THE PSYCHIATRISTS SAY THAT UGLY DRESSES HAVE caused more complexes than have "prettier sisters" or "scolding mothers." Every child has the right to becoming, yes, pretty, clothes. Well-fitted clothes in good taste and of a becoming color are musts for children. The person who has the privilege of dressing a child should take all these things into consideration and plan and make clothes that meet all requirements—aesthetically and practically.

Even made-over clothes can be fashioned smartly by complete recutting, restyling, dyeing if necessary. Good fabrics are always worth one's time and effort. Many times it is practical to make over clothes for children, but they should not be cut down to fit. They should really be restyled— completely remade from the fabric to look as though they were entirely new garments originally intended for the child.

Always in sewing for children the essential of cleanliness must be kept in mind. Clothes that must go to the tub frequently should never be elaborate. Have an eye on the laundry problems, especially ironing, when you make school garments for a child. Try to make collars, sleeves, pockets all so that they will go quickly under the iron and not slow you up, because a fresh outfit every day is almost a necessity for children. In grandmother's day, little girls wore a dark dress the whole week through, but when they came home, they put on aprons to cover their dresses and protect them from soil. Today with our laundry facilities, we think nothing of a clean dress or blouse or overalls every day, but we must give regard to the time consumed in ironing, and the place to do that is at the sewing machine, where we can make sure that there are not too many ruffles, too many decorative details.

Sew sturdily, use size 30 thread and buy fast-color fabrics that will take hard wear and many washings. Synthetics are worth your attention, as they are becoming increasingly important. Denims, corduroys, percale and broadcloth are all good in cotton, as every mother knows. Allow ample hems for growth and shrinkage. Avoid tight armholes and sleeves that are so full that they are difficult to iron.

School clothes should be considered as being play clothes as far as style and construction are concerned. They should be simple, well made, and easy to keep clean. Just as in the business world fussy clothes are out of place, so school is no place for elaborate clothes. Good grooming and cleanliness are important for school children. Many advanced schools have standard uniforms for school wear. It was found that studies improved and the attention of children held more readily when clothing was restricted to plain simple things. Let us say again that having the proper clothes for the occasion can instill in children a sense of style and fashion that will guide them all their lives.

Simple cottons, skirts, blouses, sweaters and suits are almost standard school wear for girls. Silks, velvets, and sheer fabrics have no place in the child's school wardrobe.

School boys who have not graduated to the long pants and coat age are easily kept clean and neat in denims and corduroys.

Children love pockets. If you use them, stitch them twice on each side so they cannot tear out. A 1½" square of press-on tape ironed directly over the stitching at top sides of each pocket on wrong side will help to prevent pockets tearing out.

Night Clothes. Pajamas or night dresses are made on the same principle as daytime clothes. They should have sturdy fastenings, be easy to launder, easy to get into and out of. They should be made in fabrics that will wear well. Many mothers like to use double fabric for the back across the shoulders and for the elbows for extra wear, stitching a piece in when the garment is made to save mending later on. Fashion is almost as important in night clothes as in day clothes and children can look adorable, "like pictures of angels," in their night things if the fabrics are attractive and well chosen and the styles becoming.

Cotton crepe pajamas for summer wear and cotton flannel and jersey for winter, and synthetics throughout the year, are ideal fabrics for night clothes. They need very little ironing and are easily washed.

Blouse-style pajamas for boys are practical and have the advantage of not having buttons to come off or buttonholes to fray out.

Use zippers in places where children can zip themselves into their clothes. To make zippers last longer, close them before garments go to the tub.

The garment is then easier to iron and holds its shape better.

Avoid tiny buttons. Medium-sized ones are easier for little fingers when buttoning their own clothes. Space buttons just far enough apart so you can get the point of the iron between them when ironing. Be sure to buy buttons that wash. New synthetic buttons are ideal for children's clothes —colorful, inexpensive, and wash and wear well.

For buttonholes that won't tear out, use sewing-machine buttonhole-maker or machine-stitch twice around edge of the buttonhole, as close as possible, using a short stitch, before working it by hand.

Party clothes should be made for the occasion. The style effect, the color, the fabric are the chief essentials. The sewing in most instances should be kept at a minimum because such garments are usually not worn enough to warrant the care that you would put into even a little tailored blouse or school dress. The pattern books give good designs for party clothes and should guide you in selecting a dress for a flower girl, a school play, or dancing class party. Try not to oversew on such clothes, but work for the general effect and becomingness.

Play clothes should be simple and sturdy. For satisfactory service, it is better to have two simply styled sun suits than one detailed dress or suit. Play clothes should be designed so that the child can get into and out of them without help and so that if there are two or three changes of suits in a day, the washing problem will not be too great. White, yellow and blue always seem popular for children's clothes, but lavender, pale green and pink have all become favorites with many mothers in recent years. Pinky lavenders seem good for both brunettes and blondes and make a change from the ever-favored yellow and blue. Perhaps one reason why they were not so favored in the past is that they were not fast-color, but today all colors are fast when so indicated in the label.

Teaching Children to Sew

THERE IS REAL ADVANTAGE IN TEACHING CHILDREN TO sew—boys and girls. No matter what they do with their hands later, whether they become artists or sculptors or electricians or radio or television repairmen—technicians of any kind—if the muscles of the fingers and the hands are trained to sew, this training can be beneficial.

The blunt needle with yarn for canvas stitchery is the best beginning work for small hands. Teach a child first to make an X and then little designs on the canvas. Later, as the child learns to handle the needle, a coarse needle should replace the blunt one—a size 3, which has an eye large enough for a child to thread, is good. When the child is old enough to sit at the machine, teach first how to stitch straight on a piece of tablet paper with the needle unthreaded, how to lift the presser foot, guide the paper through, keep fingers away from the needle and wheel spokes. A child is usually fascinated by the sewing machine and likes to operate it. If care is taken first to teach the essentials —how to protect the needle by never pulling it out of line, by lifting the presser foot and lowering it carefully, by stitching evenly and not with too quick starts or speeding—the child will soon learn to respect the machine and to use it correctly.

Children should not be told that they cannot touch the sewing machine, but rather they should have helpful guidance and real instruction in the use of it so that it will be a pleasure. Then when they do begin to sew, they should have simple articles first, then garments planned for them to make—perhaps doll clothes first, then little straight aprons for mother, dish towels to hem, things that they can make quickly and without complications. There is nothing so discouraging to a child as to undertake something with the thrill of anticipation and then come up against details beyond his skill. If children are taught details gradually and intelligently, they will like working them out and will have the patience to do it because they will see achievement. They should not undertake pockets, bound buttonholes, detailed shapes and forms until they are ready for them. The practice of making a sampler of bound buttonholes or pockets is good; a child who understands the advisability of this is usually very happy to experiment and thus gain the know-how as well as practice and will proudly consider such a project an accomplishment, rather than a chore.

CHOOSING FABRICS FOR HOME DECORATION CAN BE A great deal of pleasure and fun. To be sure the pleasure lasts throughout the life of the fabric, however, there are a number of considerations that should enter into the choice. Your fabric must be appropriate in color and texture to the room in which it is to be used. Window curtains may be chosen either to give greater privacy to a room, or to let in as much light as possible. You must select to please the people who will use the room. Fabrics that might be dainty and charming in a young girl's bedroom might be completely impractical and inappropriate for a growing boy. The length of time you must keep the articles you make and the amount of wear and cleaning or laundering they will have to stand are also points to think over. Porch slip-covers are expected to withstand more weather, and harder use than indoor slip-covers. Articles to be used in children's rooms are likely to need more frequent laundering or dry cleaning than those in adults' rooms. Failure to plan with such considerations in mind may mean that the things you work with pleasure to make will be troublesome or unsatisfactory in a very short time.

Most drapery fabric comes 50" wide, and the synthetics are so reasonably priced and now are so good-looking that you can afford to have beautiful draperies at the price you want to pay. Drapery fabrics come also in blends of the natural fibers with the synthetics. Your job is to seek and find, in texture, in weight, design and color, especially color-fastness, what is most nearly right for your room.

Special Precautions. Buy your fabric for home decorations in the drapery rather than the yard goods department, unless you are definitely sure that you want something available only in dress fabrics. The drapery fabrics are planned for home furnishings and are more satisfactory in width and texture for the purpose. Also, in the drapery departments or local sewing-machine shop, you will find the matching bindings, tapes and fringes.

Measure for your needs carefully so that you do not run short before completing the project.

Take samples of the fabrics you are considering when you go from one store to another so that you can be sure of matching colors or blending tones. Carrying color by eye can be very deceptive. Take swatches home and try them where you intend to use them to be sure that you have chosen well.

Consider the colors in adjoining rooms, so that you don't have a shocking clash when doors are open between rooms.

Planning a Color Scheme. The safest way to plan a color scheme is to start from something permanent in the room. If you already have a rug, use its basic colors in curtains, slip-covers, cushions, etc., so that your whole effect will be harmonious. Don't think that this limits you to any one color scheme. A great variety of different plans could be worked out from any starting point. Contrasts of tints and shades of the basic colors, variations with floral designs, geometric patterns and plain colors, and changes in texture can make an endless chain of decorative possibilities. Perhaps you start from a picture rather than a rug, or from a beautiful pottery lamp or a vase. It doesn't matter, so long as you like it and intend to make it a feature of your room. Perhaps you start merely from the personality or interests of the family or of the person who will use the room most. Select your fabric colors to be becoming to the person or to make a good background for his activities and hobbies. To avoid an overactive, busy feeling in your room, restrict your colors generally to three—a main color, a secondary color that blends or contrasts pleasantly, and a third that you use in smaller quantity for accent. Avoid the restlessness of too many patterned or figured fabrics in one room. It is often effective to combine a plain color with one flowered fabric and one severe striped fabric, but a room with a flowered rug, flowered wallpaper, and different flowered fabrics for curtains and slip-covers is likely to make the beholder a little dizzy. If you must live with your decorations a long time, remember that plain colors are less tiring than figured, and that more conservative schemes are less wearing to the eye than bolder treatments. A beautiful print of some favorite picture, a motif cut from a piece of chintz or cretonne, can help you to assemble colors harmoniously.

Color Charts. A number of suggested color schemes are worked out in the next two pages, taking their cue each time from the more permanent items of decoration, such as walls, floor coverings, upholstery and draperies. Two or more colors for upholstery are suggested in each scheme.

With floor covering of	Use walls of	Use draperies of	Use upholstery of	Use accents of
Figured—Brown, tan, green	Light blue-green	Dark blue-green	Brown / Copper	White
	Brown	Gold	Gold / Medium green	Bright green
Mulberry	Light gray with pink cast	Wine and gray stripe	Green-blue / Deep rose	White
	Floral wallpaper, rose and green	White or rose	Pale green / Rose	Gold
Dark Blue	Yellow	Print—yellow, blue and green	Light green / Medium blue	Red
	Striped wallpaper—blue, white, yellow	Yellow	Yellow / Blue	White
Light Gray	Rose	Light Burgundy	Blue / Wine and rose	Silver
	Blue	Blue with dark red trim	Deep red / Gray	Silver

With walls of	Use floor covering of	Use draperies of	Use upholstery of	Use accents of
Scenic wallpaper, browns and greens	Green	White or lime	White and gold / Green	Red
	Beige	Brown	Dark green / Brown	Orange or lime
Natural wood, light finish	Light tan	Yellow	Medium green / Print—green and brown	Dark brown
	Blue-green	Light blue-green	Soft red / Gold and green stripe	Black
Gray blue	Delft blue	Yellow and light blue stripe	Warm yellow / Same stripe as draperies	Wine
	Floral—blue and rose shades	Rose	Rose / Wine	Blue
Rose	Beige	Ivory	Ivory / Rose	Soft blue or red
	Deep aqua	Print—aqua and Burgundy	Print—same as draperies / Aqua	Gold

With upholstery of	Use walls of	Use draperies of	Use floor covering of	Use accents of
Dark Red (plain or figured)	Dark green	Print—Yellow, green, red	Gray beige	Gold
	Cedar	Print—Brown and white	Brown	Green
Rose Beige **Blue**	Light rose	Deep rose	Medium blue	White
	Light cool gray	Rose and blue	Cool gray	Wine
Brown **Gold**	Beige	Light clear blue	Dark brown	Bright blue
	Light green	Print—green and white	Beige	Orange
Light green **Bright red**	Green	Ivory	Dark gray-green	Gold
	Warm gray	White	Warm gray	Green or white

With draperies of	Use walls of	Use floor covering of	Use upholstery of	Use accents of
Print—Bright red white and black	White (match white in print)	Gray	White with red trimming Gray	Green
	Gray	Black	Gray Light green	White
Natural with gold thread	Green-blue	Dark Green-blue	Beige Coral	Lime
	Medium brown	Beige	Blue-green stripe Brown and white	Coral
Print—Floral, Multi-colored Wine background	Grayed blue	Wine	Blue Blue and wine stripe	Lemon yellow
	Soft yellow	Deep gold	Gold Wine	Blue
Rose and green	Pale green	Cool red	Print—Multi-color Light green	White
	Soft rose	Grayed green	Light blue Medium green	Cool red

HOW TO ESTIMATE YARDAGE REQUIREMENTS

Slip-Covers for Overstuffed Chairs. In general, an all-over slip-cover for an overstuffed chair takes five times the length of the back from top to floor, plus a yard for cutting and seams. If you are planning a pleated flounce, add at least an extra yard, and if the fabric has a large flowered pattern or other design that must be matched, add two yards.

Chairs without arms or slip-covers that do not extend to the floor take proportionately less. The following tables give approximate requirements for various types of slip-covers and bedspreads.

Remnants. When you use remnants or combine two different fabrics in a chair, you need about ¼ yard more of each than for a one-fabric slip-cover.

Never be scanty with your estimate. It is better to have too much than not enough. Extra material can be used in cushions or other small articles, but it may be difficult to get more of the same fabric if you run short.

Bedspreads are easier to measure for than a chair. You need to consider only length and width of the box spring, the side and end overhang, and any allowance for sham covering at the top. Simply add these in total inches, and divide the inches by 36 to determine the yardage necessary. Oversize beds, those made to order, should be measured both for width and length and yardage estimated accordingly.

The tables given here are generous in amounts required. If you are careful in measuring and cutting, you may easily save one half to one yard on the majority of these estimates.

DRAPERY FABRICS AND LININGS

DRAW DRAPES ARE FAVORED BY MANY FOR PICTURE windows. They allow full view in the daytime, yet provide privacy at night. Draw draperies are usually lined and if warmth is a problem, an interlining such as Canton flannel is used. Some like to use Milium, the metal-backed lining material, such as is used in coats. This can be used as a lining alone or handled as an interlining. The reason for finishing lining and interlining separately is that the sun burns lining, often making replacement necessary, especially in draperies made of good fabric. In the West and South where many houses are painted a color such as pink,

BEDSPREADS

	36-inch Yards	50-inch Yards
Full Size Bed—4' 6" × 6' 3"		
Three-Quarter Size Bed—4' × 6' 3"		
Plain sides	7½	6
Shirred sides	9	7½
Pleated sides	11	9
Twin or Single Bed—3' 3" × 6' 3"		
Plain sides	5½	5½
Shirred sides	6½	6
Pleated sides	8½	7½

Hollywood Bed (usually without a foot board) Sizes vary. Measure width, length, and from top of mattress to floor.

SLIP-COVERS

	MATERIAL PLAIN OR STRIPED		MATERIAL WITH A DESIGN	
	36-inch Yards	50-inch Yards	36-inch Yards	50-inch Yards
Wing Chair—Cushion	9½	7	11	8
Sofa—3 Cushions	20	12	22	14
Armchair—Cushion	8½	6	10	7
Cogswell Chair—Cushion	8½	6	10	7
Love Seat—2 Cushions	12	8½	15	10
Chaise Longue { No Cushion	8	6½	10	8
Chaise Longue { One Cushion	11	8¼	13	9½
Slipper Chair	3	2½	4	3¼
Pillow Back Chair—One Cushion	8½	7¼	10½	8
Studio Couch—Three Pillows	14	9	16	10

gray or light yellow, the lining of drapes is made of colored sheeting to match the color of the house. In some instances the lining matches the trim of the house, but more often the paint color. Colored sheeting can be bought by the yard. It wears well, holds its color and is completely satisfactory as lining. Always remember that your windows should look as nice from the outside as from the inside. The way you dress them can add much to the beauty of the exterior.

Most drapery departments carry white, cream and ecru sateen linings in several price ranges. If you want to use lining, buy a good quality that will wear well and wash or clean with your drapery fabric. Take care that it looks well from the outside when draperies are closed.

When stitching a textured drapery to a lining, the Walking Presser Foot attachment is a safeguard, as this insures against the drapery fabric slipping or the lining tightening in the seam.

ESSENTIAL EQUIPMENT

IN ADDITION TO THE EQUIPMENT AND THE DEPENDABLE machine you need for any kind of sewing (see page 7), fabric furnishings require a few more tools. *An idea scrapbook* is an aid and inspiration. Any large blank book will do, so long as it is convenient for filing away pictures, samples, lists and notes on things you see or would like to have for your home. Some have found it convenient to paste envelopes in such books to hold small pictures, samples, etc., for any contemplated project.

Heavy-duty thread is useful for work on slipcovers and draperies, and the *large-sized spools of thread* often obtainable are convenient. Draperies and slip-covers use quantities of thread in their long seams, so fill several bobbins when you start work, thus saving your time later.

It is almost impossible to finish a job of home decorating without a *regular hammer*, a *small tack hammer with a claw*, an *awl*, *screwdriver*, *pliers*, *picture wire*, various sizes of *tacks*, *nails*, *hooks* and *screws*, and some *household glue* or *cement*.

CARE OF FABRIC FURNISHINGS

SINCE YOU EXPECT FABRIC FURNISHINGS TO LAST FOR several seasons, some consideration must be given at the time of making to the method of cleaning to be used and to the durability of the material you use in them. Don't dream up any scheme for pleating or hanging that will be too difficult to manage when the time comes for taking them down and having them cleaned. Buy modern pleating aids that will last through the life of the fabric. Use

strong substantial fixtures that will not give under the weight of draperies nor bend and break as you put them up and take them down.

In this regard it is a good idea to visit a museum, Mount Vernon, General Lee's home, Williamsburg, to see how long some draperies have lasted. This should inspire you to choose lovely fabric, put your best sewing skill into the making, then to have your draperies hung in a professional manner so that they will please you over a long period of time.

Protect fabric furnishings against excessive soiling by brushing them or using the hand vacuum cleaner as you do your regular housecleaning. Surface dust is removed and the greasy layer of airborne dirt usually does not settle long enough to stain. This simple cleaning preserves the fabric by eliminating the frequent need of more drastic cleaning.

For washing or dry cleaning where modern pleating aids have been used, remove rings and pins and straighten out pleats of draperies. For dry cleaning, sewn pleats may be left in but hardware is usually removed. It is best to discuss this with the shop doing your cleaning.

If you have left a shrinkage allowance in making, let it out before washing. If, after washing, lining has shrunk less than fabric, take a tuck in the lining. Begin your washing by dousing curtains in clear water to remove surface dust. Sometimes several such rinsings are desirable to keep the soil from "killing" your suds. Then wash several times in suds. Then rinse to remove all soap.

After washing draperies or curtains, squeeze or press out water rather than wring. Hang them straight on the line, pulling hems straight so that when they are dry, they are not badly wrinkled or twisted. Cotton net and lace curtains need to be dried on curtain stretchers. Synthetics can be hung wet and will dry. Only their hems need to be ironed, if they are a kind that you can iron. Stretch all other types of curtains evenly, usually on stretchers. Iron them lengthwise, not from side to side. Do not fold them unless you must put them away for the season. Iron them straight, hang them over a door or lay them on a bed until ready to hang, and do hang them as soon as possible.

For ruffles that need stiffening to look fresh and crisp, use cooked starch or gum arabic. Many organdie and synthetic curtains now carry a permanent finish guarantee.

Slip-covers may be cleaned at home. If you do them, wash or clean as you would draperies of the same fabric. Then press them, using the sleeve board and tailor's cushion to help you smooth out the corners and curves.

Cover put-away draperies and other fabric furnishings with dark paper or fabric to prevent yellowing or soiling, especially on the folds.

Windows and How to Drape Them

THE TYPE AND NUMBER OF WINDOWS, THE AMOUNT of light and ventilation desired, the wall space and its decorations, the use of drapery or blinds to provide night privacy—all these points must be considered in planning curtains or draperies. The style of architecture also has much to say about the way you dress your windows. If you live in a private house, the effect from the outside must be reckoned with, as sometimes it is desirable to have all the windows on one floor or one side dressed alike.

Double Sash Window. A. Ordinary window with upper and lower sections that may be raised or lowered. Almost any type of curtain or drapery may be used with these, your choice depending upon the effect you want.

Bay Window. B. Group of two or more windows usually forming a little alcove. The most satisfactory way to treat these is to make them a unit. One way is to hang draperies just at the outside edges of the end windows and draw the group together with a single valance. Glass curtains may be hung straight as a group, or ruffled organdie curtains may be crisscrossed and tied back at the sides. Usually the cheerful effect of this light-giving alcove is better preserved by using sheer curtains with a minimum of heavy drapery.

Dormer Windows. C. Small gabled window on sloping roof. Draperies are not usually appropriate for these. An informal glass or tie-back type of curtain proves best.

French Window or Door. D. Floor-length window resembling two glass-paneled doors, either leading to a porch or terrace or between rooms. Generally best handled by using a glass curtain with rod and heading at both top and bottom. If draperies are used, they usually are at the sides and are held in place on rods at both top and bottom, like the glass curtains.

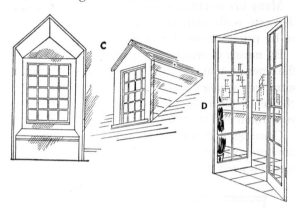

Casement Windows. E. Double or single hinged sashes which swing either in or out, like doors. Those which swing in may have either a glass curtain with double rod and casing or the kind of rod that swings like a crane to allow movement of the sash. Those which swing out usually have curtains placed at the side or a crane rod, so as not to interfere with the opening and closing, or draw curtains fastened above the sash. The point is not to have the curtains swing out with the window.

Louver Windows. (Not illustrated.) The slot type that open out may be dressed as any double sash window, the curtains and draperies being hung from the top of the window to the sill or floor,

OFTEN IN OLD OR REMODELED HOUSES, WINDOWS seem small for present-day draperies, especially where modern furniture is used. It, therefore, is quite in order to change the shape of the windows to get a more spacious or less high or more unified effect.

Many like to eliminate pictures in bedrooms and decorate walls with fabric by extended windows, or by using mirrors for panels.

By means of window draperies, you can soften the lines of a room, provide color, amplify space, introduce a more luxurious feeling through your choice of the right fabrics, colors and styles for your room and its other furnishings.

Consider first the possibility of changing window proportions inside the room to achieve the effect you want. For example:

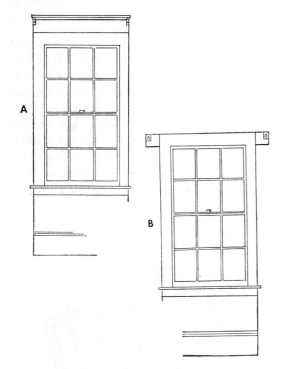

To Add Height. Add a wooden extension of desired height above window. Place fixtures on this extension as you would on window frame. See **A**.

To Add Width. Extend top of window frame at sides with two wooden blocks fastened to wall. Blocks may extend enough on each side to hold the entire drapery, thus practically doubling the size of the window. This is especially desirable when you want outside light. Place fixtures at top outside corners of blocks so that draperies will hide the carpenter work. See **B**.

To Add Both Height and Width. Decide the overall width you want for your draperies. Cut a 4″ by ½″ wooden board the length you want. Place this above window at desired height, as in **C**. Attach fixtures to this board. The drapery will conceal board and fixtures.

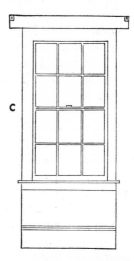

Valance Board. A board attached horizontally at top of window frame, as in **D**, to provide a means of hanging fabric valance. The board is as long as width of window frame, usually about ½″ thick.

For circular valance and some draped valances, use a valance board with a short strip of wood extending down on both sides, as in **E**.

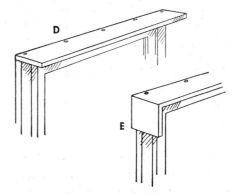

One other way of treating windows helps to change the apparent proportions—combining two or more windows as a unit and making the draperies as if for one large window.

Fixtures

NO MATTER HOW WELL-CHOSEN YOUR FABRIC OR how beautifully made your curtains and draperies, they cannot look their best unless the fixtures on which they are hung are correct for the type of window and drapery and sturdy enough to bear the weight and function as they are intended to. It is worth a little extra expense to get exactly the right fixtures. Look over the displays in a good curtain department and decide which type will best suit your purpose. Illustrated here are several of the most popular and useful types.

The adjustable flat rods shown below are available in single, double, and triple arrangements, for hanging one set of curtains, a combination of glass curtains and draperies or crisscross curtains, or glass curtains, draperies and valance.

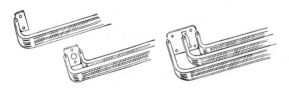

For casement windows or French doors or transoms, the round rod cut to fit the space is conven-

ient, because it holds the curtain close to the glass and allows free movement.

The swinging crane may be desirable for casement windows that open inward or where it is convenient to be able to swing the curtain aside at times.

If draw curtains are desired, the traverse rod can be used. It has a pulley system for opening and closing the curtains. The use of such rods and curtains can give your rooms great adaptability. See, for example, Color Plate facing page 69.

For arched doorways or windows, there is available a curved metal type with eyes to hold the hooks on your curtain or drapery.

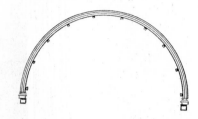

For both windows and doorways, the pole with rings is often used. It allows draperies to be drawn together if desired.

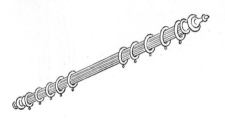

There are many types of pin-on and sew-on hooks which serve to attach the drapery to the rings or rods. For light curtains, the pin-on type, as in **A**, are satisfactory. For heavier fabrics, the sew-on hooks, as in **B**, give more support. **C** shows another type of pin-on and sew-on hook.

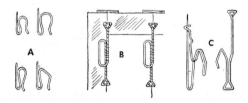

Place your fixtures before measuring for draperies. Usually screws are more satisfactory than nails for securing fixtures unless the fixture and the curtain are light.

Pulley Cord for Draw Curtains. Cord and rod must be strong enough to stand weight and pulling. Rings must be large enough to accommodate cord easily with room to pass through. Bring cord through ring **D** and through all successive rings to ring **E**. Knot cord around this ring and then insert it through rest of rings to other end of drapery, where it passes through fixture **F** at side. Then bring back through rings to ring **G** and knot, continue back through all other rings to beginning. Weights on ends of cords, as at **H** keep cords taut.

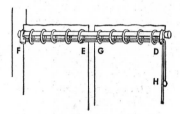

Anchoring Curtains. The outside edge of curtain and valance should hang in a straight line and against the wall as though it had grown out of the wall. As an aid to keeping the line, sew a ring to hems of curtains, top and bottom, also to valance, if used. Rings are placed in line with the rods, as at **I**. Cup hooks are screwed into wall or base board in proper position as in **J**. Rings are caught over hooks. The edge of curtain must be held taut.

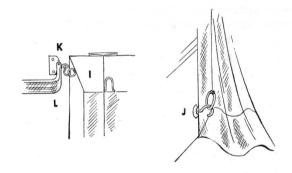

Return. This is the term applied to the distance between the turn or corner of rod to wall where fixture is fastened, as from **K** to **L**.

For modern houses with large glass windows, traverse rod pull curtains are most satisfactory as window coverings. In many instances, such curtains—especially in bedrooms—are interlined with an opaque black such as sateen, cotton flannel or percale, so that no light shows through. This interlining is simply sewed in with the lining and completely covered.

Dressing Your Windows

MEASURING FOR CURTAINS AND DRAPERIES

START WITH EXACT MEASUREMENTS OF THE WINDOW itself, and measure each window individually. Often windows in the same room are not identical, even though they appear to be the same size. Place tapes for measuring as shown below. Curtains may be made just to cover the sash, leaving the woodwork in view, or may cover the woodwork to the bottom of the apron, or may cover the entire window structure and fall to the floor. Place your curtain fixtures before measuring and figure the length from top of fixture down.

For Glass Curtains, add to length measurement
3″ for 2¾″ hem, thus allowing for ¼″ turn
5¾″ for 1½″ casing, having ¼″ turn and 1¼″ heading
1″ or 2″ per yard for shrinkage. This is important even for draperies that are dry cleaned.

For Draperies, the heading is usually deeper than for glass curtains. Add, therefore, as many inches more than the allowance for glass curtains as your drapery heading requires. Hems at top and bottom are usually 3″ deep.

Shrinkage allowance may be taken care of in drapery lengths by basting a tuck in the hem to be let out before dry cleaning.

Fullness is determined by the weight of fabric. Very fine sheer fabric should be quite full, usually twice, often three to four times width of window. Heavier fabrics often 1½ times to twice the width. Drapery width is determined by type of pleating used at the top and by width of window, especially if drapery is drawn at night. Usually one to two full 50″ widths of drapery fabric are used at each side of a window.

WIDTH

(jamb to jamb) _____ inches

LENGTH

(fixtures to sill) _____ inches

(fixture to bottom of apron) _____ inches

(fixture to floor) _____ inches

If you measure all your windows and keep a record such as this, you will always know how much fabric to buy whenever you want to make new curtains.

CURTAINS AND DRAPERIES

BEFORE MEASURING OR CUTTING LENGTHS FOR WINDOWS, straighten fabric as directed on page 15. This is important to insure curtains and draperies hanging straight. Fabrics are frequently twisted in winding on rolls or boards in final finishing and may be far from true grain.

Pull a thread or tear to get a straight end before cutting. Work on a firm flat surface, a large table if possible, or if necessary on the floor, so that cutting and measuring are perfectly true.

Decide how much shrinkage allowance in length is necessary before cutting. Allow on an average of 1″ to 2″ per yard. Loosely woven fabrics shrink more than do the firmer fabrics. Remove selvages on most fabrics before making side hems; otherwise they may cause the edges to draw or pucker.

Hems for Glass Curtains. Finish side hems before finishing at top and bottom. For narrow hem, use Hemmer as instructed on page 97. Such a hem may be used on outer edge of curtains, but hems coming together at center of window are usually 1″ or more wide.

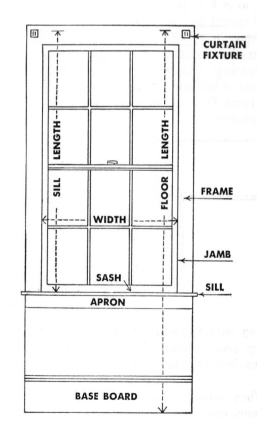

For wider hems, turn raw edge ¼″ and crease, as in **A**. Turn hem to desired depth and crease on

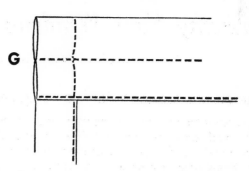

thread. Measure every few inches to insure evenness. Pin as in **B**. Baste and stitch. In most cottons

in **H**. Keep crosswise grain of ruffle in line with crosswise grain of curtain.

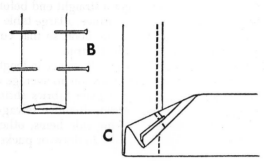

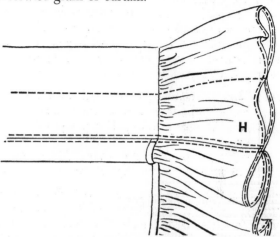

and some synthetics, hem can be pinned, pressed, then stitched without basting. When turning bottom hem over side hems, cut off corner, as at **C**.

Plain Casing. Make plain hem, leaving ends open for inserting rod, as in **D**. Stitch back at ends of hem, as at **E**, to prevent pulling out. Make casing deep enough for rod to slip in easily. If shrinkage allowance is a couple of inches, put in a tuck just under the casing on the wrong side, as at **F**. If shrinkage allowance is several inches, divide amount in half and put tucks at both top and bottom hems. Put tucks in by hand, using short basting-stitches.

Stiffened Heading. When heading is wide or material is too soft to stand properly in position, use lightweight crinoline or heavy organdie to stiffen the top. Cut stiffening on a thread, the finished width of curtain. Lay along top edge of curtain with ends in from both sides the depth of side

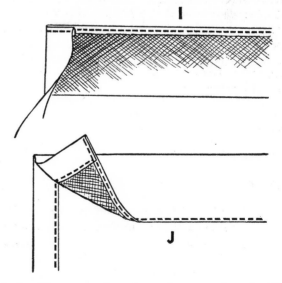

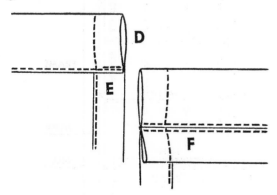

Casing with Heading. Make hem the depth of casing plus heading. Then stitch across parallel to hem line, as at **G**, to separate casing from heading.

When making heading and casing in ruffled curtains, carry stitching out through the ruffle, as

hems. Turn top edge of curtain over edge of stiffening and stitch, as in **I**. Make side hems, then turn top hem in position as in **J**, and stitch casing and heading.

Faced Heading and Casing. When material must be conserved or when curtains must be lengthened, facing may be applied to finish top. Cut a crosswise strip of desired depth, adding ¾″ to 1″ for seams. Stitch facing to right side top edge, as in **K**. Bring to wrong side, turn under raw edge, and stitch, as in **L**. Band of fabric in suitable color and texture may be used to lengthen draperies that are too short, a situation that can occur when one moves from one residence to another.

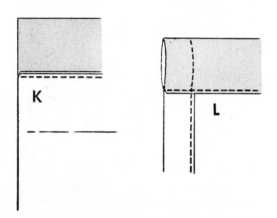

Double Casing and Heading. For casement windows or French doors, as illustrated on page 172, glass curtains may be finished at top and bottom with a casing and a heading. Make the two ends identical (see preceding page). Allow perhaps ½″ for shrinkage in short curtains, making curtains slightly loose until after first washing. For long ones, conceal shrinkage allowance behind top hem. Such curtains are usually put on the rod while wet and dried in position. Care in doing this is necessary, especially with some types of rayon.

Weights are sometimes necessary in the hems of glass curtains. Use the round string weights for this purpose. Lay weights along fold of bottom hem. Catch ends in side hems.

Hems for Draperies. Make bottom hems 2″ to 3″, using the wider hem for heavier fabric to give weight to bottom of drapery and possibly to conceal metal weights. Illustrated here are three types of draperies, unlined, lined and interlined. The unlined and interlined show the use of uneven side hems, such as used in custom-made draperies. The lined drapery, most generally used, is made with even side hems. See diagram **X** on opposite page.

Side hems can be even, as shown in lined draperies, or a wider hem on center edges and narrower on outside, as shown in unlined and interlined drapes. The uneven hems may be neces-

sary in order to have fabric motifs placed properly. Clip side selvages at intervals or cut selvage away completely to prevent tightening of the edges. Center hems are 1½″ to 2″ wide and side hems from ½″ to 1″ wide.

The top hem is usually 3″ but can be as much as 6″, depending on finish being used and overall length of drapery. When pleating heading is used, as shown on page 183, only ½″ to 1″ turn is needed.

Stiffening for Top Hem. Cut crinoline or lightweight buckram in crosswise strips of desired width. Lay along top edge. Turn over raw edge and baste or stitch, catching edge of stiffening. The end of stiffening should be in from edge to depth of side hems, as at **M**.

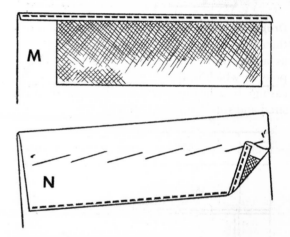

Unlined Draperies. Turn top hem and diagonal-baste, as in **N**. Put in bottom hem, as at **O** (below). Before making center hem, cut away corners, as at **P** and **Q**. Turn raw edge and stitch, as at **R**. Pin and slip-stitch hem, then whip corners

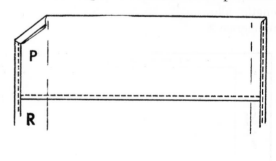

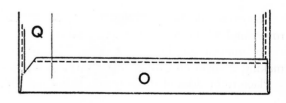

down, as at **S** and **T**. Make narrow side hem. Machine-stitch or slip-stitch in position and finish corners, as at **U** and **V**.

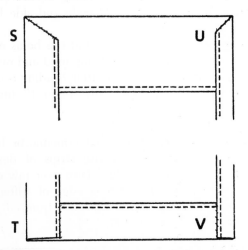

Draperies with Casing. First put in bottom hems, then side hems. Turn down top hem and stitch, as at **W**. Allow 2½ times the diameter of rod or pole on which drapery is to be hung for depth of casing. If a heading is wanted, allow depth desired and stitch as shown.

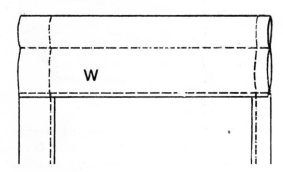

Lined Draperies. Buy lining fabric of same width as drapery fabric. Remove selvage from both. Cut lengths, allowing for hems and finishing as shown in diagram **X**.

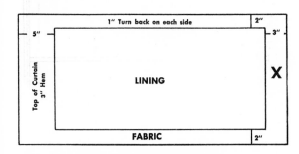

For even side hems, linings should be 4" narrower and 8" shorter than drapery fabric.

For uneven side hems, cut lining 6" narrower, making 2" hem on center edges and 1" on sides.

Place right sides of drapery and lining together with top of lining 5" below top of drapery, as at **Y**. Pin lengthwise edges together, placing pins across seam, as at **Z**. Stitch, making ½" seam, as at **A**. Always stitch both sides from top down. Clip seam every 4" or 5" to prevent drawing, as shown. Press seam open. Turn right side out and press.

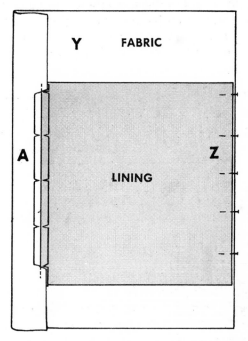

Pin crinoline strip across top of drapery on wrong side, keeping ends even with hem folds on both edges, as at **B**. Stitch along bottom edge of

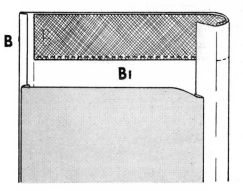

stiffening, as at **B1**. Fold heading down and pin. Trim away surplus at corners as at **C**. Make ¼" turn on bottom edges of drapery fabric and lining.

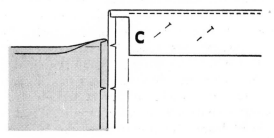

Stitch on fold. Then turn drapery hem to position and pin. Turn up lining hem so it will hang about 1″ below top edge of drapery hem, as at **D**. Pin. Heavy drapery fabrics that do not fray need not have edge turned and stitched; simply turn hem, baste to position and catch-stitch. Trim away surplus at bottom corners, as at **D1**. Turn in ends of lining hem as at **D2**.

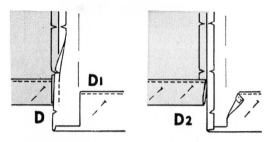

Make ½″ turn along top of lining. Pin to position over edge of top hem, mitering corner as at **E**. Press. Finish corners as shown and slip-stitch lining to drapery heading.

Slip-stitch drapery and lining hems to position, as at **E1**. Miter and finish bottom corners of drapery as at **E2**.

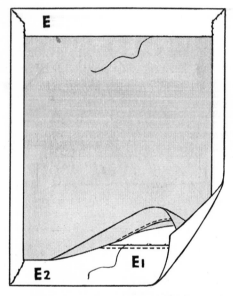

Putting Weights in Draperies. Cut a square of fabric three times the diameter of the weight. Fold in half, lay weight inside fold and turn corners over, as in **F**. Stitch along raw edges to enclose weight. Slip inside hem of drapery at corners and stitch in position. The "pin-on" weight, as in **G**, is convenient to use and can be removed when cleaning or laundering.

For lightweight draperies, use yardage weights in the bottom hem. Lay weighted tape along creased edge on hem allowance so tacking stitches

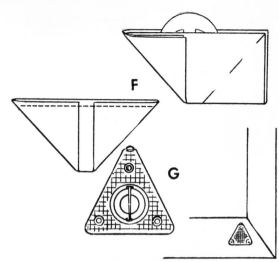

will not show on right side of draperies. Use a long diagonal-basting-stitch to hold in place.

Interlined Draperies. Work on a large, flat surface, the floor if necessary. Once the drapery fabric is smoothed out, it need not be moved until it is completely finished and ready for pressing.

The length of interlining should be shorter than the drapery length. At the top it comes just to the hem turn of the drapery. At the bottom, the edge of the interlining hem can come just to the top of the drapery hem as shown at **J**, or to the turn of the hem. The interlining should be narrower than drapery fabric by the width of the two side hem turns. Cut buckram strip for top stiffening. Stitch to top edge of interlining, as in **H**. Finish bottom

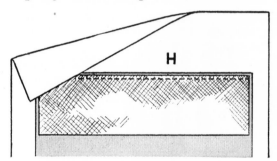

edge of interlining with a ¼″ to ½″ hem. Lay interlining on wrong side of drapery fabric, buckram side up, as shown. Turn top hem down to cover buckram. Smooth out carefully and pin. Diagonal-baste drapery edge to interlining, as in **I**, using long stitches.

Turn bottom hem of drapery and catch-stitch in position, as at **J**, opposite page. Trim surplus from corners, as at **K**. Notch side hems ¼″ at top of bottom hem as at **L**. Turn side hems, smoothing fabric over interlining and pin. Turn top corners in, forming a miter, as in **M**. Whip in position.

Courtesy of Crawford Furniture

Two Ways with Prints

The two bedrooms here show how one decorating scheme can create quite different effects. Both use a restful wall tone contrasted with a white-background print with related colors. Yet the room below has a monotone, sophisticated, modern feeling; the one above, greater contrast and a more traditional atmosphere. The chief difference is in the style of the fabric furnishings. Below, plain pleated draperies, slip-covered headboard and bed flounce make use of the print, while the wall color is matched in the straight, heavy-corded overspread. Above, the print is trimmed with plain fabric. The bolster roll and valance board match one wall color and are trimmed with the plaid.

Courtesy of Better Homes and Gardens

American Informal Furniture by Tomlinson

Bedrooms with an Air

Fabric-covered headboards lend their own decorative quality to the two rooms shown here, the one above combining chintz and velveteen in a distinctive way, the one at the right, softly padded and meticulously fitted, adding its touch of clear color and roundness to the modern geometrical effect of the room. The whole fitted spread and pillow covering above is rich velveteen, over a full flounced skirt. Below, the white cover, quilted in color and squares, offers a subtle echo of the wall pattern behind.

Courtesy of Living for Young Homemakers

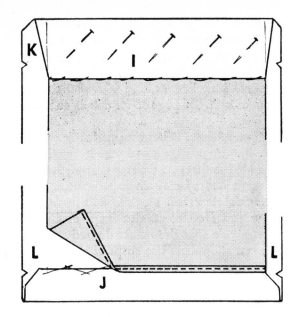

From notches on both sides at top of bottom hem, turn raw edge under and whip down where it overlaps drapery hem, as at **N**. Slip-stitch side hem edges to interlining, using long stitches.

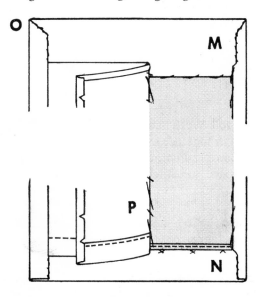

Remove selvages from lining fabric. Measure length of lining and put in bottom hem. Finished hem should just cover catch-stitching holding edge of drapery hem. Clip side edges of lining about every 10″. Make narrow hem turn on side edge of lining and stitch. Right side in, fold lining in half lengthwise and crease. Lay lining over interling, centering crease on drapery. Turn center edge under, pin and slip-stitch lining to drapery along hem edge, as at **O** (above). Tack lining to interlining along crease with long stitches, as at **P**. Take short stitches in lining and interlining, as at **Q**, and long stitches between the two. Turn

raw edge of lining under along top, pin, and whip in place. Slip-stitch side edge in place. Press.

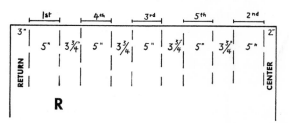

Top Finishes. Finish curtain or drapery completely. Press. Then use any of finishes illustrated below to add interest to top of your window.

Pinch Pleats. Pleats should be made in groups of uneven numbers—three, five or seven, depending on the depth of pleats desired and the width of the fabric. Usually when 36″ fabric is used, three or five pleats are sufficient, but 50″ fabric may require five or possibly seven pleats on each side.

To measure for pleats, determine how much space on the rod the drapery is to cover. In draw draperies, the two sides of the drapery come together at center of rod. Generally draperies are pushed back to cover an even space on each end.

For example follow the simple steps below:

Finished drapery	45″ wide
Rod space to be covered 17″ plus	
3″ return	−20″
(Return is from turn of rod	
to wall. See page 175.)	25″ surplus

Divide the 25″ surplus into 5 pleats.

First pleat placed at curve of rod—measuring 3″ from the outside edge. Second pleat placed on opposite side—2″ in from center edge.

Measure exact center between first and second pleats for third pleat. Get the exact center between the first and third and second and third for position of fourth and fifth pleats.

Mark exact position and width of pleats as shown in **R**, using pins or light pencil line.

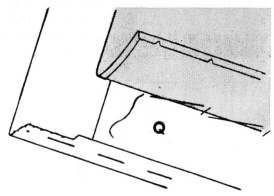

Bring two marks together to form pleats. Pin and stitch from the top edge to the depth of the hem, as at **S**. Then divide the pleat into a cluster of three even pleats. Pin together and stitch twice across cluster, as at **T**. Continue in same manner to make pleats, until all are finished, as in **U**.

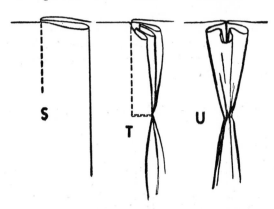

A variation on the pinch pleat can be made as in **V**. When pleats are creased, simply stitch down

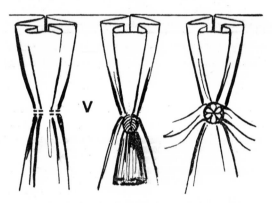

from edge to hem line and back. Divide pleat into four smaller ones, two to each side of stitched line, and flatten against curtain. Tack in position at hem line by hand. This type of pleating is practical if you want to add any decoration at point where pleats are caught—tassels, balls, buttons and loops, etc., as shown.

Cartridge Pleats. Divide and mark top edge into equal spaces for pleats. A 3″ pleat is good for short

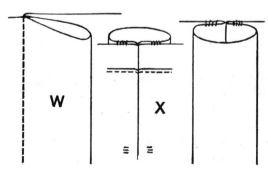

drapes, a 4″ for long ones. Join and stitch creased lines to form pleats, as in **W**. Skip a space and make another pleat. Continue until all pleats are stitched. Open pleats and tack to drapery on each side of stitching line, as in **X**, both at the top and bottom of hem. See page 48 for details on making.

Pipe Organ Pleats. These are made like cartridge pleats, but are usually longer, closer together and are padded so that round shape is firmly held. Try out length and spacing on paper pattern before marking fabric. Then measure and mark. Make rolls to pad each pleat. Cut strips of chintz or crinoline wide enough to make desired size of roll plus seam allowance. Use strips of cotton batting

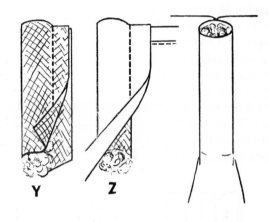

to pad roll. Wrap batting in crinoline strips, bringing edges together evenly, and stitch close to roll with Cording Foot, as at **Y**. Fold roll inside each pleat space and stitch with Cording Foot, as in **Z**.

Shirred Heading. Used in sheer curtains. Finish side and bottom hems. Make top hem of depth wanted for heading. Starting at bottom edge of hem, make three or five rows of shirring, as in **A**,

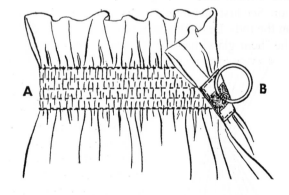

across top of curtain, with Singer Gathering Foot. Cut a piece of fabric for stay of the desired width and depth of rows of shirring plus seam allowance. Adjust fullness so that shirred part is same length as stay strip. Turn edges of strip under. Pin and baste to wrong side of shirred section. Hem along top and bottom of shirring and at both ends. Pin a piece of twilled tape lengthwise through center of strip on wrong side. Stitch in place from right side by stitching along two rows of shirring. Sew rings to tape, as in **B**, about 3″ apart. Rings should be large enough for curtain rods to slip through.

Corded Heading. First make narrow side hems with Foot Hemmer and finish bottom hems. Make top hem of depth desired for heading. Start cording at lower edge of top hem and make as many rows as you wish. See page 42 for instructions on Corded Shirring. Stitch across cords on front edge, as at **C**, and smooth fabric flat along cords for depth of front hem. Mark hem by placing a pin through each cord, as at **D**. Shirr fabric along cords to correct measurement. Allow for a flat back hem by placing a pin in each cord on this side, as at **E**. Stitch across cords at back edge of curtain or drapery. Turn side hems under and slip-stitch each cord to itself on wrong side. Pin hems full length. Then stitch or slip-stitch, as desired.

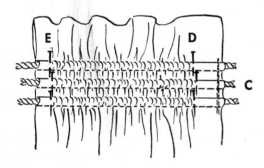

Hour-Glass Curtains. Make them straight at top and bottom and 1″ longer than a casement curtain. See first picture at the left on page 174. Place on the rods. Draw the curtain in at the point where the "hour-glass" band or cord is to come. If in the

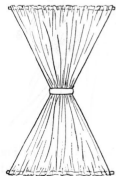

very center and there is slightly more length than needed, make a little tuck by hand underneath the band so the curtain will be as taut as possible throughout its length. Baste this tuck in, so it can be removed when curtain is laundered.

Ready-Made Pleating. Drapery and notion departments carry several kinds of ready-made pleating made in muslin or buckram. Get a circular of instructions with the type of pleating you buy so you will know exactly how best to apply it. With some you make the drapery, then stitch pleating to the back.

In the illustration shown here Pleatmaster Tape and hooks are used. These are perhaps the simplest of all and prove so satisfactory when drapes are washed or cleaned.

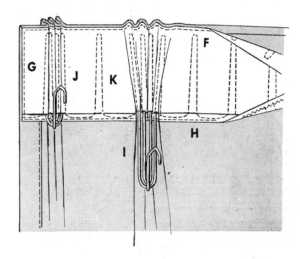

Measure drapery lengths, allowing for hems at bottom and a ½″ hem at top as shown. Tape is shown applied to an unlined drapery. First, finish the side and bottom hems. Turn top edge of drapery down ½″ as shown. Press. Stitch top of pleating along top edge, as at **F**. Turn raw end of tape under and stitch as at **G**. Turn under pinked bottom edge of tape and continue stitching as at **H**. Slip prongs of each hook (**I**) into four slots. When hook is in place it will appear as in **J**. You may put prongs in all the slots or skip one slot between every two hooks, as at **K**.

If you do not wish stitching to show on right side at the top, stitch the top of tape to the top of drapery, overlapping ⅜″. Press drapery on the ½″ line, then stitch bottom of the pleating through drapery.

French Café Drapes. These drapes can be made in three ways:

Straight Hemmed Edge. Hem the top edge of the drape, sew rings at intervals of from 4″ to 6″, and then put these rings on the hooks.

Bound Scalloped Edge. Cut scallops 4″ to 6″ wide and bind the edge with bias binding, snipping the corners between scallops so you do not have to miter, but continue the binding in the binder for the full length of the scalloped top.

Faced Scalloped Edge. (Preferred for very good work.) For facing, use a straight piece of fabric 2″ to 3″ deep and allow 4″ to 6″ for width of each scallop, depending upon the size of scallop desired. Pin facing to curtain, right sides together, edges even. Make a paper pattern for size of scallop, placing scallops so they come even in size and with a point at each side of drape. Mark scallops along top edge and stitch as at **L**. Trim ¼″ above

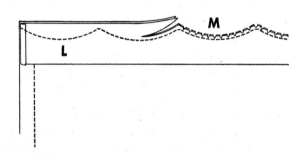

stitching line, then clip seam at intervals of ½″, as at **M**. Turn facing over to the wrong side and blind-stitch to position. Press. Sew the rings securely to the point of each scallop for hanging, as in **N**.

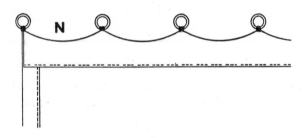

TIEBACKS

THE BANDS AND CORDS USED TO TIE CURTAINS AND draperies back from the window should match or harmonize with the curtains. They may be dainty, tailored, or formal and elegant, according to the style of the draperies and the room. A few possibilities for variety are shown here.

Shaped Band. Cut a paper pattern, shaped as in **A**. The curved piece should be about 4″ wide at the center fold, tapering to about 2½″ at the rounded end. Place pattern with straight end on straight fold of fabric and cut, adding seam allowance. Cut lining same size. Cut buckram same size as pattern without seam allowance. Center buckram on wrong side of lining and stitch close to

edge of buckram. Lay right sides of fabric and lining together and stitch around edge of buckram,

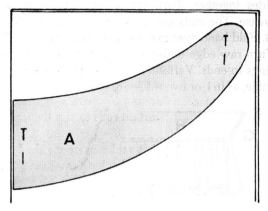

as at **B**. Leave a few inches open, as at **C**, so that tieback can be turned right side out. Turn and whip opening. Sew bias-cut loops, as at **D**, or bone

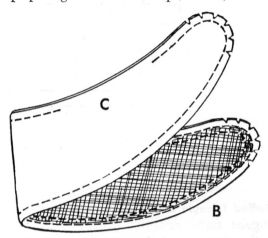

rings, as at **E**, to ends. These loop over hook at side of window and hold drape in place. Use same pattern to cut tieback without seam allowance that may be bound around the edges with ribbon, braid, or bias binding, as in **F**.

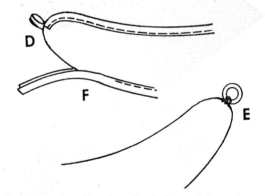

Ruffled Band. Cut band of desired length and twice the finished width plus seam allowance. Make a ruffle the same length as band and about as wide as ruffles on curtains and finished in the same way, hemmed, hemstitched or picoted. Stitch one edge of band to gathered edge of ruffle, right sides together. Turn raw ends in about ¼″ and crease. The ends can be straight or slanted, as at **G**. Fold band over to cover gathered edge of ruffle. Turn raw edge under and top-stitch, as in **H**. Sew rings to ends. Variations on this idea are a double ruffle, as in **I**, or two ruffles, as in **J**.

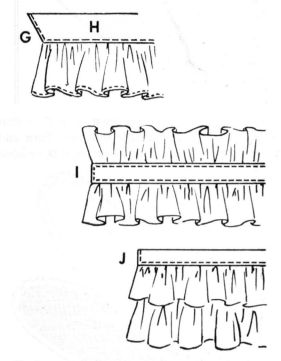

Ruffled Triangle Band. Make a pattern of a triangular shape, something like a Christmas tree with a stem, as in **K**. The triangle part is about 9″

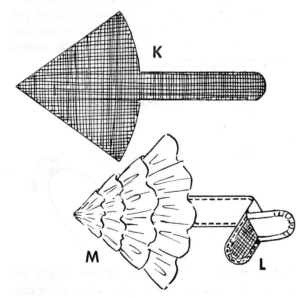

long and 7½″ wide at the base and the stem about 9″ long. Cut a piece of crinoline this size and two

pieces of fabric this shape with a ⅜″ seam allowance all around. Center crinoline on wrong side of one piece of fabric. Turn edges of fabric over crinoline to back and press. Stitch all around, close to edges, as at **L**. Make ruffles to cover front surface, as at **M**. Stitch them on in tiers as described on page 44, stitching right through crinoline. Face back with second piece of fabric by turning raw edges under and whipping in position. Attach loops or rings to both ends.

Flower-Covered Band. Make a narrow band about 1″ wide and 18″ long by covering a strip of crinoline with fabric and whipping it together on back, as in **N**. Sew rings at each end, as at **O**.

Cut 3 circles of fabric, 4″, 5″, 6″ in diameter. Run a row of stitching around each circle close to the edge. Draw up the threads and tie ends so as to form a flat, double circle, as in **P**. Cut six leaves, as

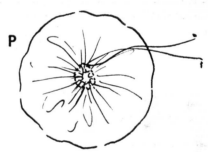

in **Q**. Lay two leaves together, right sides in, and stitch along two sides close to edge, as shown.

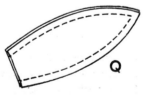

Turn leaves inside out and sew to band. Sew circles to bands, gathered center against band, using embroidery silk or cotton for centers of flowers, as in **R**.

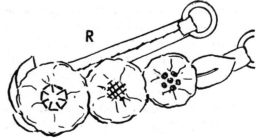

VALANCES

A VALANCE IS A TOP FINISH FOR WINDOWS WHICH serves to cover fixtures, shorten the apparent length of windows or give a unified effect to draperies. It can also serve to connect a group of two or more windows, thus forming a unit. It consists of a narrow length of fabric, matching or contrasting with the draperies, usually tacked to a board across the top of a window frame.

A *cornice* gives the same effect as a valance, but is usually made of wood or metal, often painted to match wall or woodwork. The wooden ones can be covered with fabric or wallpaper.

The depth of a valance depends on the size of the window and the height of the ceiling. Use valances with care or not at all in small rooms, especially if ceiling is low.

If the window is not to your liking, the arrangement of the valance can help to camouflage its proportions. See page 173 about changing window proportions.

Valance Board. A board attached horizontally at top of window frame to provide a means of hanging fabric valance. See **D** on page 173 for details of construction.

Plain Flat or Shaped Valance. Plan the shape of your valance and cut a paper or muslin pattern. Try against window before cutting into fabric. Allow 1″ for seams and make valance the length of the valance board plus the measurement of the two ends. Cut buckram exact shape and size finished valance is to be. Cut interlining ¾″ longer than buckram all around. Lay interlining over fabric on wrong side an even distance from edge on all sides. Pin and stitch together close to edge, as at **A**.

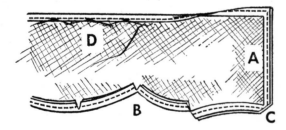

Center buckram on interlining and turn edges of fabric over and pin. Clip or notch edges on curves, as at **B**, and clip off corners, as at **C**. Baste or catch-stitch, as at **D**, using a long stitch.

Cut lining size of finished valance, leaving no seam allowance. Turn in edges of lining a scant

½″, clipping curved edges so lining will be smooth. Pin in position, as at **E**, and hem or slip-stitch, using rather long stitches. Sew strip of twill tape

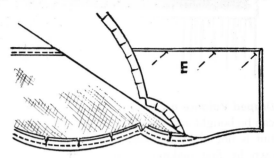

across top at back, whipping it on with strong thread, as at **F**. Use this to tack valance in place

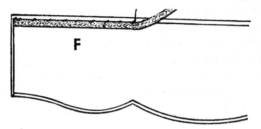

along board with thumb tacks, as in **G**. If preferred, valance can be attached with wood snappers. See page 66.

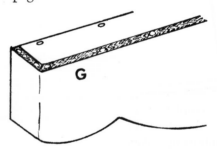

Valance with Bound Edge. For shaped edges, often binding is a more satisfactory finish than turned-in edge. Finish top and sides of valance, as above. At bottom, baste all sections together close to edge. Pin and baste binding in place along edge, then stitch. **H** shows an attractive edge.

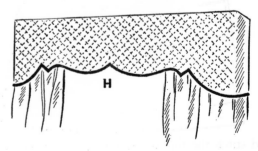

Box Valance. Make plain straight-edged valance as instructed above. Apply moss fringe along all four front edges, as shown at top of next page.

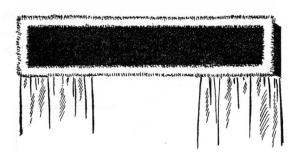

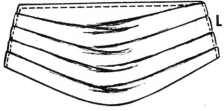

ning folds in place. The second pleat overlaps the first about one-half its depth, third overlaps the second, etc., until the entire piece is pleated. Baste or tack in permanent position; secure to valance board with thumb tacks.

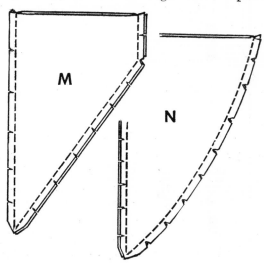

Draped Valance or Swag. A ready-made pattern can be bought and used to cut this type of valance, but is not really necessary. You can design your own by first making a muslin pattern, working with this until you obtain the amount of fullness and the type of drape suitable for your window. Cut the top on the crosswise grain of the fabric, making it the length of the valance board. The bottom edge should be slightly curved and wider than the top to allow for take-up in draping. Taper the sides, as at **I**. Draped valances are usually

Cascade. Make a muslin pattern before cutting fabric. Measure the length desired for your window. The average is about 30″. Make the width at the top about two-thirds of this measurement, or 20″. Then draw either a short straight line and then a diagonal one, as in **M**, or a gently curved line, as in **N**, for the third edge. Cut four pieces

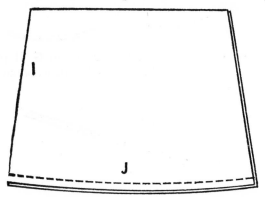

lined completely. If you are using a very heavy fabric, then face the lower edge with self fabric or contrasting color to the depth of 4″ or 5″ and use a lining fabric for the upper part. Lay the two pieces together, wrong side out, and seam only the bottom edge, as at **J**. Turn to right side

to this pattern. Seam the straight sides and the diagonal sides together, as shown. Clip seams. Turn right side out and press. Stitch top edges together. Mark width of side of valance board, then

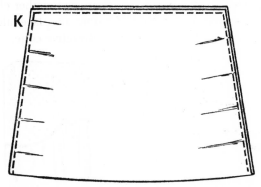

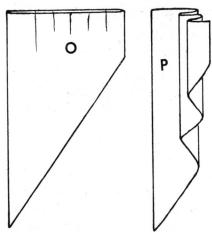

and stitch the top and side edges together, as in **K**. Divide the sides into even spaces about 4″ apart, by alternating marks, as shown. This helps the folds to break in the center. Then fold, as in **L**, pin-

divide the rest into five sections, as in **O**. Fold into pleats, as in **P**. Stitch. Tack in place along top of valance board, covering edges of swag. Swag may be hand-tacked to back of cascade.

Valances without stiffening are often used for the less formal windows. Three types are given here.

Circular Valance. Determine length required, including the measurement at each end of valance board, and then the depth of valance. Cut muslin pattern, as in **Q**. (See *Circular Flounce*, page 211.)

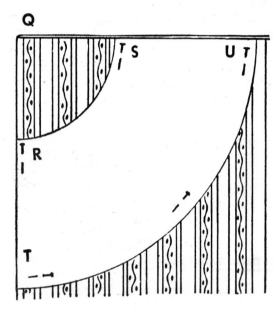

The curve from **R** to **S** equals one-half the length of the valance. To increase the top length, lengthen distance between **Q-R** and **Q-S**. This gives a longer curve. **R-T** and **S-U** are always equal to the depth of the flounce plus seam allowance.

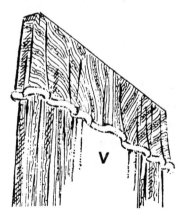

Either **S-U** or **R-T** can be laid on a fold to make center of valance, depending on the design effect you wish to obtain. Illustration **V** shows the stripes

running up and down at center of valance, so **R-T** of pattern was laid on fold.

When finishing bottom edge with fringe or cording, cut lining the same size and on the same grain as valance.

Smooth flounce out on a flat surface, right side up. Lay fringe along lower edge, as at **W**, so top

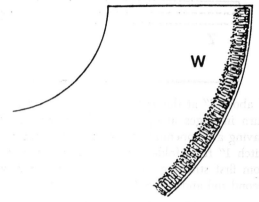

edge of fringe is along raw edge of fabric. Pin and baste. Lay lining over this, right side down. Baste. Stitch down one end, across the bottom, through the fringe, and up other side, as in **X**. Stitch twill

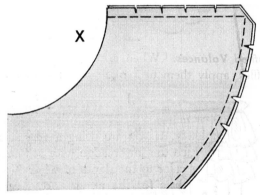

tape to top edge on right side. This will prevent stretching of bias edge and is used to attach to valance board. When using this type of valance, use valance board described in **E** on page 173.

When no edge finish is used, make a fitted facing about 2″ deep. (See *Fitted Facing* on page 78.) Cut lining fabric for upper part and stitch facing strip to this. Then lay valance and lining together, wrong side out. Stitch as described above.

Gathered Valance with Casing. Make valance about 2½ times the length required for window to give needed fullness. Double the depth needed and add seam allowance. Cut on crosswise grain of fabric. Remove selvages and seam lengths together. Press seams open. Fold strip in half lengthwise, right sides together. Seam raw edges together across top and one end, leaving an opening

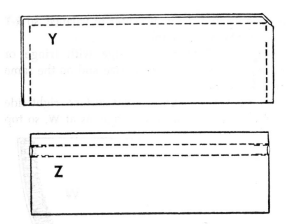

of about 2″ at this end, as at **Y**. Turn inside out. Turn in edges at open end and whip together, leaving a 2″ opening corresponding to other end. Stitch 1″ from folded edge for heading, then 1″ from first stitching for casing, as at **Z**. Put on a second rod and adjust fullness, as in **A**.

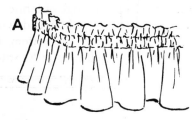

Ruffled Valances. When using groups of 3 or 5 ruffles, apply them to a plain foundation. Use a

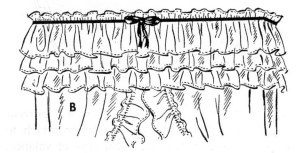

lining fabric and cut foundation to width of window plus ends and to depth desired. Make double, stitch and turn inside out, or make narrow hems on top and both ends, using Foot Hemmer, and a 1″ hem on bottom edge.

Cut and finish ruffles as desired. Gather with Ruffler and apply to lining in tiers. A bias fold or strip of ribbon stitched over shirring line and tied in a bow at center gives an attractive finish, as shown in **B**, in previous column.

Ruffled Shaped Valance. Make shaped foundation for valance shown in **C**. Top edge is on straight and bottom is an oval curve. Cut two pieces of size desired. Lay right sides together and stitch, leaving an opening for turning. Turn inside out and press. Mark with chalk or bastings the stitching line for ruffles. Finish ruffles and gather, then stitch in position. Turn ends of ruffles over top edge of foundation and sew in place.

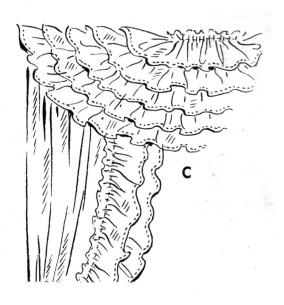

It is reported that from 1860 to 1900, more ruffles were used to decorate homes and wearing apparel than in all time previous. This was due, no doubt, to the convenience and time-saving work of the sewing machine.

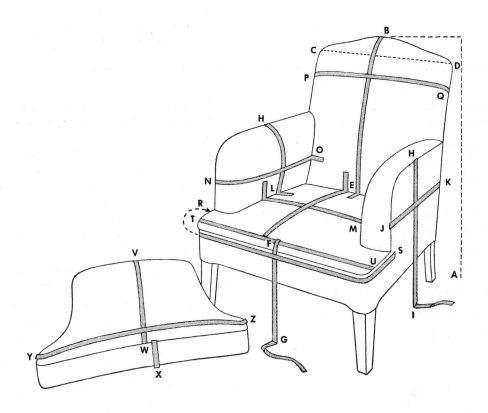

Slip-Cover Measurements Chart

〜〜

For

Yardage

BACK LENGTH—(*floor to top*)—**A** to **B** plus 2″ seam allowance.............*inches* ....*inches*

BACK WIDTH—**C** to **D** plus 2″ seam allowance.................................*inches*

FRONT BACK LENGTH—**B** to **E** plus 2″ seam allowance, plus 3″ tuck-in.........*inches* ....*inches*

FRONT BACK WIDTH—**P** to **Q** plus 2″ seam allowance............................*inches*

SEAT LENGTH—**E** to **F** plus 2″ seam allowance, plus 3″ tuck-in................*inches* ....*inches*

SEAT WIDTH—across—**L** to **M** plus 2″ seam allowance, plus 3″ tuck-in........*inches*

SEAT WIDTH—across—**T** to **U** plus 2″ seam allowance...........................*inches*

FRONT LENGTH—**F** to floor at **G** plus 2″ seam allowance........................*inches* ....*inches*

FRONT—across—**R** (on side) to **S** (on side).................................*inches*

SIDE LENGTH—(*arm to floor*)—**H** to **I** plus 2″ seam allowance...............*inches* x 2 =...........*inches*

SIDE—(*front to back*)—**J** to **K** plus 2″ seam allowance.......................*inches*

ARM LENGTH—(*inside*)—**H** to **L** plus 2″ seam allowance, plus 3″ tuck-in.....*inches* x 2 =...........*inches*

ARM—(*inside*) front to back—**N** to **O** plus 2″ seam allowance, plus 3″ tuck-in..........*inches*

CUSHION:—LENGTH—**V** to **W** plus 2″ seam allowance.........................*inches* x 2 =...........*inches*

　　　　　WIDTH—**Y** to **Z** plus 2″ seam allowance.............................*inches*

　　　　　DEPTH OF BOX—**W** to **X** plus 2″ seam allowance.....................*inches* ....*inches*

*To estimate yardage add up **lengthwise** measurements of pieces and divide by 36″.*

SLIP-COVERS WILL BE EASIER TO MAKE IF YOU FOL-
low this simple step-by-step procedure:

Take the measurements of the chair allowing, as
shown, 1″ for seams. This amount is desirable,
since it makes certain that you will have enough
fabric.

Estimate, then buy, yardage required. Estimate
and buy any trimmings to be used.

Make a muslin pattern (old, tender sheets are
ideal for this).

Pin-fit this carefully to your chair or couch.

Mark on muslin location of design motif.

Cut fabric (making certain that all pieces are cut
with design running the same way—usually *up*).

Pin-fit.

Determine trimming for seam finish.

Make trimming.

Join sections.

Apply flounce—if design calls for it.

Apply slide fasteners to opening.

Cover cushion or cushions.

Press slip-cover.

Put it on chair.

Taking measurements is one of the most important
steps in making a slip-cover. This is necessary in
order to estimate the amount of material required.

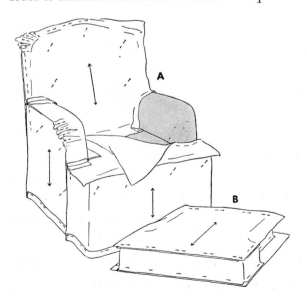

If chair is reasonably small, placing it on a table
or bench will make it easier to take measurements
and do the necessary fitting.

The width of the material chosen must be considered in determining the yardage required.
Most slip-cover materials come in either 36″
or 50″ widths. Generally, figure the total of all
lengths of all sections plus 1½ yards for flounce
and welting. When buying 36″ material with large
floral design, add a yard for matching. However,
with 50″ materials, some of the small sections may
be cut from the sides, particularly if material is
plain or of a small design. Side pieces may also
be used for box-pleated flounce, as piecing is possible under the pleats. See page 170 for approximate yardage estimates. Follow the order given
opposite when measuring. Measurements are taken
from the floor. When making a permanent upholstered cover coming only to bottom of chair, or
a slip-cover without a flounce, deduct an even
amount from the measurement of the back, sides
and apron sections. Be sure, however, to leave a
generous amount for hem, or for joining of flounce.

Trimming. Measure all seams to be finished with
welting or other trimming. An average-sized chair
with cushion requires from 10 to 12 yards of trimming. An arm or wing chair takes from 12 to 14
yards. A sofa with three cushions takes approximately 25 yards. If you plan to make trimmings,
see *Seams and Finishes,* page 195.

Making a Muslin Pattern. It is often a safeguard,
if you are not experienced at making slip-covers,
to make a fabric pattern of muslin or old sheet.
Also, if you have several chairs alike, the muslin
pattern may save you time in cutting and fitting
by providing one guide for all. Use the muslin to
cut fabric by and in placing design motifs, and
save it to use whenever new slip-covers are made.

First block your material to correspond to the
measurements for each section of the chair. For
example, if the back measures 39 inches high and
26 inches across, including a generous 1″ seam allowance, cut a piece of muslin this size. Be sure
the 39″ is on the true lengthwise grain of the
material by marking the center of each piece with
a lengthwise chalk line or arrow. Cut each section
just as carefully, then pin it in its place on the
chair and cushion, as in **A** and **B**.

Some chairs, such as the wing chair, take more sections, but the same procedure is followed in all cases. The "tuck-in" allowance between the wing and the back should taper from regular seam allowance at the top to a three-inch allowance at the seat.

Determine the exact center of each section of the chair, placing a pin lengthwise at both top and bottom. Place the lengthwise center of each section of fabric over lengthwise pins, as in **C**. As you pin-fit pieces on chair, place seam lines accurately to conform to original lines of chair.

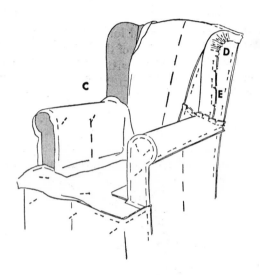

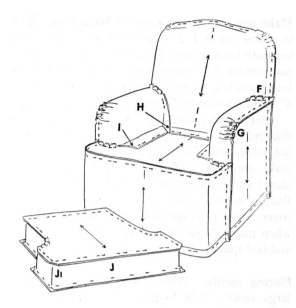

When the pin-fitting is complete, go over entire chair again, examining it critically, taking up any unnecessary fullness, straightening pin lines, and perfecting location of fullness. Mark with chalk at any points that will aid you later.

Then with a colored pencil, draw a line over the lengthwise pins on both sides of the seams. Using a sharp shears, trim all seams evenly to one inch. Notch seams at center points and where fullness in one section is to be controlled when joining to corresponding sections.

Block pieces for cushions as for chair sections.

Start with back and front sections, working from top center. Smooth out material above arms of chair, both front and back, keeping material straight with the grain. Draw material to fit snugly. Place pins along seamline. Work toward outer edge to where fullness begins in front sections.

Next pin side seams between top and arm. Then ease in fullness over rounded part by placing pins crosswise, taking up a little fullness between each pin, as at **D**. Pin both sections together across gathers, and make notches in seam allowance on either side of gathers. Clip seam allowance on all curves for smooth fitting, as at **E**.

Next pin front and inside arm sections. Seam must be snug over rounded part of arm and to the back, as at **F**, but taper to the full "tuck-in" allowance at the seat. Clip seam as shown, so it will be flat when stitched.

Join side arm sections to inside arm and back sections, easing material over the rounded part of the arm, **G**, as at the top. Then join the front section to arm sections and the seat. Be sure that the "tuck-in" allowance is accounted for at the back and sides, **H** and **I**.

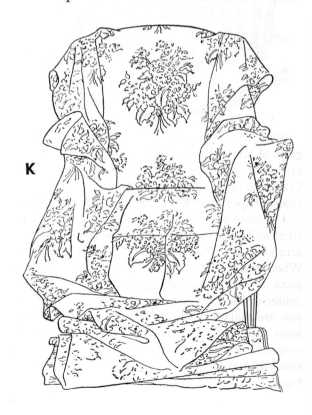

Make one continuous strip for boxing and pin-fit to pillow, as at **J**. If cushion cover is made with separate back section, as in **H** on page 198, follow instructions for cutting given there. Mark seamline, rounding slightly all square corners. Trim to ½″ seam allowance. Clip off all corners as at **J1**.

After making one slip-cover, you may decide that making muslin patterns for other chairs is not necessary. You found the slip-cover easy to make and feel confident that you can go right ahead and cut into the material for the next one. But *do* make a muslin pattern for your first slip-cover. Even professionals work with muslin first, when making new designs in curtains, slip-covers and bed spreads.

Placing motifs. When using fabrics with very large motifs, it is helpful to lay material over chair, as in **K** on opposite page.

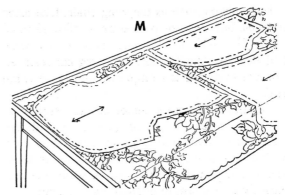

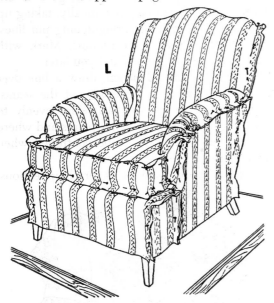

Work with right side of fabric out. Lengthwise grain of fabric should run up—up the back, up the arm sides, and from front to back on the cushion. Crosswise grain should run across each section of chair. Stripes must be matched at seam edges, as in **L**. Locate a stripe at exact center of chairback, front and cushion. Locate stripe at given point of arm and side pieces and match for opposite side. When laying out pattern, place center of each piece of muslin or paper pattern on lengthwise center of the motif or stripe in fabric, as in **M**. If you are making more than one slip-cover of the same fabric, place designs alike in all chairs. If economy of fabric is important, select plain or small-figured fabric, which cuts to better advantage.

Fitting. After all sections have been cut from pattern, fit fabric to chair right side out, as a double check. Check fabric grains, seamlines and notches.

Most fullness is eased in by a row of gathers between notches, as in **N**. Use two rows of gathers, if necessary, to make sure fullness is even and well controlled.

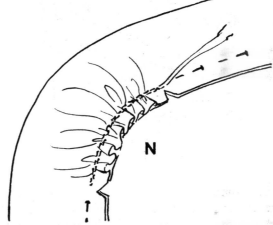

Darts can be used in place of gathers if a better fit can be obtained with them. Pin to conform to curve or corner, as in **O**. Mark with pencil or tailors' tacks. Avoid darts when they break a continuous line, as in a striped fabric. If very shallow darts are used they can be basted but not stitched.

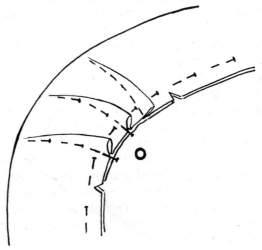

After seams of slip-cover are stitched, remove bastings in darts.

Construction details. After gathers or darts are put in where fullness is to be controlled, put slip-cover on chair, right-side out and check these points again. Make adjustments if necessary. Remove slip-cover. If cording is used, unpin seams of the outside arm, back section and lower front and stitch all connecting seams. Join the inside arm sections to front back section, as at **P**. These seams must fit snugly over the arm, but taper to the regular "tuck-in" allowance at seat.

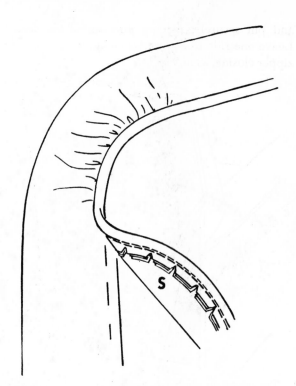

be stitched unevenly. Do one thing at a time. Join opposite side arm sections in the same way.

Apply seam finish to continuous line along sides and across top back section. Join back section to sides and front back, matching center-line notches,

Next, join seat section to inside arm sections on both sides and back, as at **Q**, making due allowance at the back and sides for "tuck-in," as shown.

If there is a seamline across front of chair, as at **R**, stitch this seam, inserting welting or fringe. Use the Singer Cording Foot with right toe for this stitching. Stitch trimming to top and front edges of outside arm and along side and top edges of back section. Place stitching line of welting directly over marked line. Notch seam allowance of welting on curves to eliminate excess fabric at these points, as at **S**.

The next step is to join arm sections. Apply side arm sections, placing corded seamline right side down over seamline, matching notches, as in **T**. Pin at regular intervals to hold sections in place, placing pins crosswise as at **U**, for easy removal in stitching. Never attempt to join shaped sections and insert welting, piping or fringe in one operation. Only on straight seams should this ever be done, and then by an expert. With so much thickness, one edge is likely to stretch, or the seam may

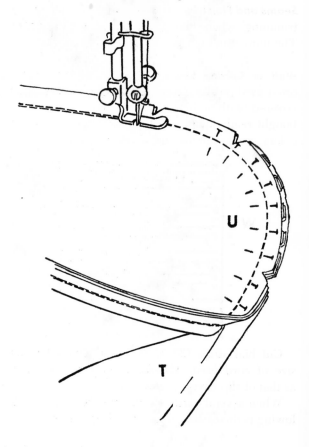

and pin securely, placing pins across the seam. Leave one side free 18 or 20 inches for placket or zipper closing, as in **V**.

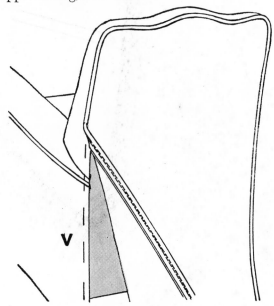

Try cover on chair for final inspection. Pin closing together at side back. Make any adjustments necessary to perfect the fit. Hem bottom edge. Finish closing with snaps, buttons or slide fastener. See pages 196 and 197.

Seams and Finishes. You estimated the amount of trimming when taking measurements of chair. The most usual finishes for slip-covers follow.

Welt or Corded Seam. This is the finish most often used on slip-covers. Welting is a cotton cord covered with a bias strip of fabric. It can be bought ready-made in a large assortment of plain colors, or you can make it yourself.

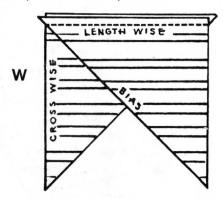

Cut bias strips 1½″ to 1¾″ wide, depending on size of cord used. The fabric may be the same as that of slip-cover, or a contrast.

When several yards of bias are needed, the following is the easiest procedure: First, cut a square

of material. Fold in half on the bias and cut on fold. Stitch lengthwise edges together, as in **W**. Next, bring crosswise edges together, slipping seam edges so that 1½″ or width of bias strip extends at each end of the seam. Stitch seam, thus forming a tube. Press seam open. Use the Singer Bias Cutting Gauge to cut even strips around and around the tube. Slip extended edge of fabric under Gauge guide, as in **X**. One yard of material 36″ wide will make 24 yards of 1½″ bias strips.

Place cord in center of bias strip on wrong side. Fold strip over cord, bringing edges together. Stitch close to cord with Cording Foot, as in **Y**.

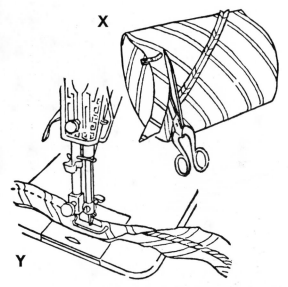

Fringe Seam. Fringe can be made of pearl cotton, wool yarn, silk floss, bouclé yarn, or silk or cotton or novelty braids. The texture of the fringe should be in keeping with the fabric; for example, cotton fringe on cotton fabrics, silk bouclé fringe on satins and taffeta, moiré silk floss on silk damask, brocades, satins, etc. By using the Singercraft Guide, you can easily make yards and yards of fringe. See *Moss Fringe*, page 135.

Bound Seam. Use only in lightweight materials and simple covers. Stitch and press seams together. Trim to a scant ¼″ and bind with the Binder Attachment. See *Bound Seam* on page 54.

Upholsterer's Welt Seam. Though not as effective as cording or fringe, this seam can be used on simply styled slip-covers.

Overcast Edges. All inside seams should be trimmed to a scant ½″ in depth. Overcast seams in materials which fray easily, using long even stitches.

195

Flounces. Mark line for joining skirt. Measure up from the floor the depth decided on for skirt plus 1½″ all around chair. Place pins or chalk marks at frequent intervals, as in **Z**. The average depth of flounces is 7″ or 8″ and they should clear the floor by about 1½″.

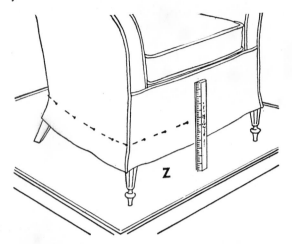

Strips for skirt are cut on the crosswise grain of the material. Add 2″ for seam allowance and hem. If finished skirt is to be 8″, cut strips 10″ wide.

Spaced Box Pleating. This type of pleating takes up twice its length. For one yard of pleating, allow a 2-yard length of material. If the slip-cover measures 3 yards around, cut 6 yards plus 6″ to 8″ for good measure. For full box pleats, allow 3 times the length. See page 47.

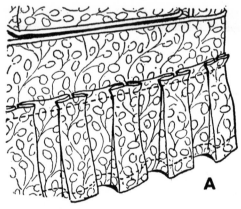

To apply skirt with heading, as in **A**, stitch bottom hem, turn in top hem and press. Lay in pleats, pin and baste. Pin top of flounce along bottom edge of slip-cover. Stitch, keeping an even distance from top edge to form heading as shown.

Group Pleats. See **B**. Decide number of pleats to a group—3, 5 or 7—and the number of groups. Multiply the number of inches taken up in each by

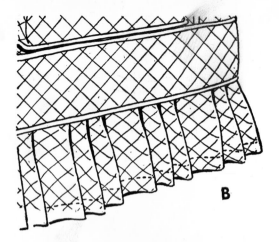

the number of pleats used and add length around chair. For example, if one pleat takes 3″ and 15 are necessary, you will need 45″ extra length.

Gathered Flounce. Allow at least one and a half times the measurement around the chair for fullness, as in **C**. This skirt is usually used in informal rooms and Early American types. If fabric is light in weight, allow twice around so gathers will not look skimpy.

Facing. A skirt may be finished with a facing instead of a hem, particularly if more color accent is needed. The color used for welting can be repeated in the facing. For the average length skirt a facing 1½″ wide is correct. Cut strips 2″ wide. See **H**, page 78.

Corded Slide Fastener Closing in Slip-Cover. The average chair needs only one closing and this is usually in the seamline of either of the back corners of chair. Use an 18″ or 20″ open-end slide fastener. Turn raw edge under along seamline and baste. Lay closed fastener right side up under this edge, as in **D**. Have the open end of fastener about 2″ below top of flounce as shown here, or have end

Courtesy of *McCall's Magazine*

Heavy Textures Seldom Need Trimming

When fabric is interesting in itself for its texture, weave, weight or design, little or no trimming is necessary. Simple lines, coordinated subtle colors, allow the fabric to speak for itself of restfulness and comfort. The room shown here seems quiet in color, at first glance, but it makes use of five colors —white, gray, green, yellow, and rose—all keyed to the print fabric of the slip-covers. Heavy cording, simple pinch pleats, a straight tailored flounce—these are the only construction details of the fabric decorations, offering the minimum of distraction from the interest of the material. The whole effect is serene.

Traditional Furniture Blooms with Appropriate Fabric Furnishings

Taffeta, flowered and plain, in rose and blue tones, brings out the warm tone of mahogany in the four-poster. The flowered fabric of the dust ruffle matches the draperies. The blue in the bedspread is repeated in the rugs and wallpaper. The more formal effect of the room below relates the dignity of fine furniture to beautiful fabric. The shaped valances at the windows, the canopy of the same design, and the matching flounce under an heir-loom all-white quilt are all appropriate to the period.

of fastener start just above top of flounce. Pin and baste. Lap the corded edge over slide fastener and baste along edge of cording. From right side, start

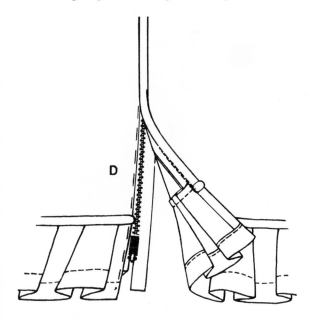

at top of closing and stitch close to cording with Cording Foot or Zipper Foot, as in **D1**. Open fastener, stitch across top end of opening and down other side, in line with basting, as in **D**.

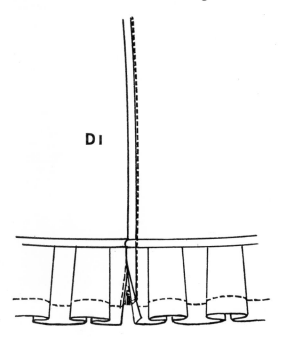

Trim seam even with tape and overcast edges together.

If a narrow flounce is used, the tape ends of slide fastener can be caught in top of hem. If the flounce is deep, turn ends of fastener tape under and whip securely in place.

Plain Slide Fastener Closing in Slip-Cover. A simplified closing can be made in a plain seam of slip-cover, as for instance, up the center back. Baste edges of opening together. Press seam open. Lay slide fastener along seamline, right side down, with open end of fastener toward bottom of slip-cover. Pin and baste to position as in **E**. Stitch as in **E1**, using Zipper Foot. Tape ends can be caught in bottom hem as shown, or turned under and whipped in place.

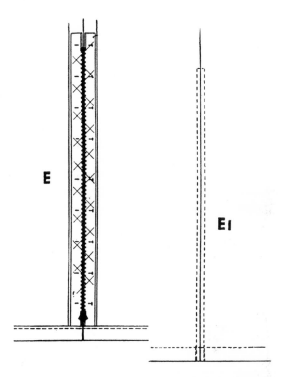

Finishing Cushion Cover. After pin-fitting, check to see that all lines are correct and sharp corners rounded, as in **F**. Stitch welting or fringe to top

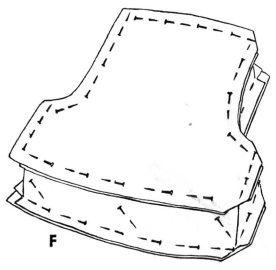

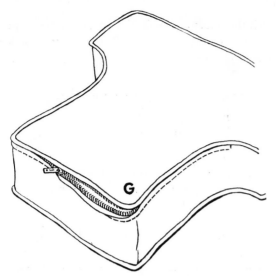

G

and bottom sections, following line marked for seam allowance. Join seam in boxing strip. In a T cushion, leave seam open on one side and across back, as in **G**. Clip or notch seam allowance on curves. Insert slide fastener at closing, following same procedure as for slip-cover. Overcast edge of fabric and tape of slide fastener together.

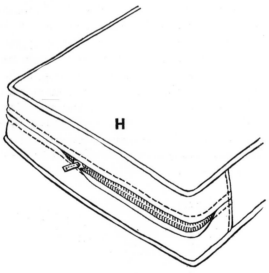

H

Another way of inserting the slide fastener is to make a separate back section, as in **H**. Make strip same length as slide fastener plus ½″ on each end for seams and 1½″ wider than boxing strip. Cut strip through center. Baste center edges together, on wrong side, to make a ¾″ seam. Press seam

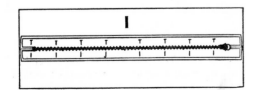

I

open. Pin fastener along seamline on wrong side, as in **I**, and baste. Stitch around fastener, as in **J**. Remove bastings. Join ends of section to boxing. Stitch boxing to top and bottom sections of the cushion.

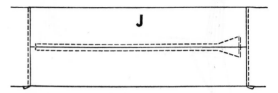

J

Underneath Finish. Allow for a 3″ turn-back on all four sides of chair. Mark seamline for finish around chair legs even with turn-back. Shape cover as in **K**, slashing material to ½″ of seamline and trim off between slashes. Finish around opening with welting or 1½″ bias strip, as in **L**. Clip seam and turn to underneath side.

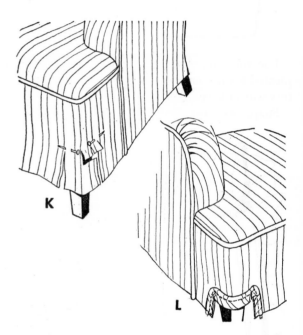

K

L

Cut a piece of heavy unbleached muslin or any other closely woven plain fabric to fit inside of turn-backs, as at **M**, allowing ½″ all around for seams. Stitch this section to front and one side of slip-cover, closing around one front leg, as at **N**. Press seam edges back and stitch again on the right side. Insert slide fasteners at side and back, as at **O**, using fasteners that open at both ends.

To put cover on chair, slip the front closed opening up over leg, smooth cover up over arm, then draw cover over back of chair. Smooth down all around and close back opening. Turn bottom of chair up and close slide fasteners at side and back.

This type of finish holds the cover neatly in place at all times and facilitates its removal.

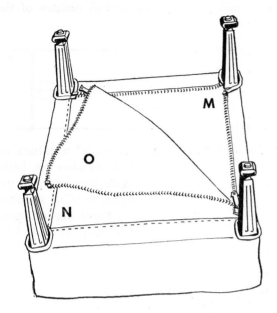

Use this same closing for chairs finished with pleated flounce or fringe, as in **P**, as it is a satisfactory way of keeping cover in place.

Snaps are also used as a closing and can be

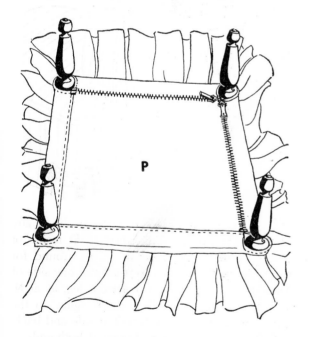

bought on a tape by the yard. A large hook and eye should be used at points where there is to be much strain. Whatever type of closing or fastener you use, be sure it is rustproof.

Covering a Sofa. To slip-cover a sofa or love seat, follow the same procedure as for a chair.

Fit the muslin as in **Q**. Follow as closely as possible the construction of sofa or the lines of the present upholstery.

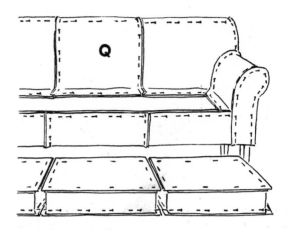

Work from top center to sides of sofa and down.

First, join three sections of the front and back. Press seams and keep fabric smooth. Then join the front and back sections across top. Join inside arm sections to back. Try cover on the sofa, placing center line of center section at center of sofa. Pin side backs to back and front sections, as at **R**. Pin side arms to inside arm section. When applying cording to curved pieces, front arm or side back sections, clip seam allowance of cording, as in **S**. Remove cover and stitch. Join seat section, allowing for the "tuck-in" across back and arms. Next, join front arm pieces to side arm sections. Seam apron sections together and join to seat and side arm sections. Slide fasteners are inserted for closing on either side, as at **T**.

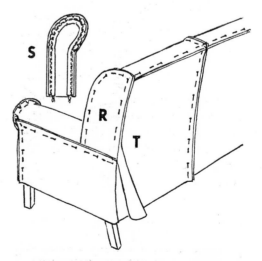

Follow same instructions for covering cushion and joining flounce as given on pages 196 and 197.

A plain box finish, as in **U**, is effective for a mod-

ern sofa or chair or for a very large sofa or chair. The edge may be finished with a plain hem, as in

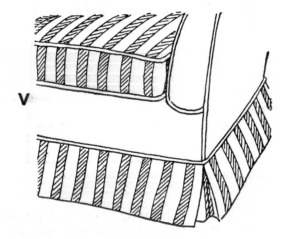

V, or it may be scalloped, as in **W**, and finished with cording or contrasting facing.

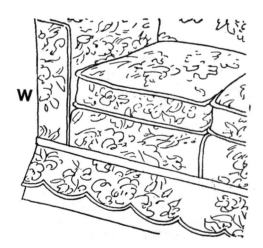

Miscellaneous Chairs. It isn't always the upholstered chair that needs a new dress. In almost every room there is a chair that at some time could

be covered to add a new note, a spot of color or a bit of freshness to the room. These other chairs usually require very little material, and are easy to cover.

Seam Finish. Decide what seam and edge finish you will use. Corded (page 57) or Moss Fringe (page 135), Welt or French (page 55), Piped (page 57) or Bound (page 54).

Straight Chair. Most often used in dining, breakfast or game room. Four cover sections are shown in Diagram **X**. Fit a paper pattern to your chair. Cut your cover with care, fitting it wrong side up or out on the chair. Mark the seam edges with pins or, if they are opened for cording or other trimming, with chalk.

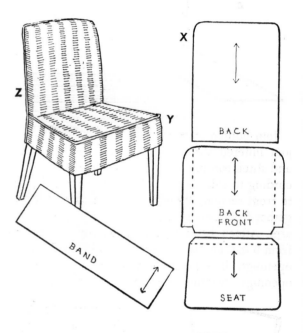

Join the seat and front back sections first. If cording is used as a finish, have it ready, pin or baste it in place, then stitch it around seat section, as at **Y**. Notch front corners, then pin and stitch band around seat section. Keep band smooth at corners so that there is no puckering. Darts may be taken on top corners of back front section and stitched or just folded in to make corner. Stitch cording up side, across top and down other side of back edge, as at **Z**.

Stitch back section in position. No opening is needed in this type of cover unless the back of chair is narrower at the base than at the top. If so, leave one side open and stitch zipper or snap tape, or hook and eye tape in placket. Hem or trim lower edge.

Arm Chair. Chairs of this type may vary, but the principle of cutting and fitting a cover is the same. Diagram **A** shows pattern pieces. It is recommended that a pattern of muslin be made and fitted first.

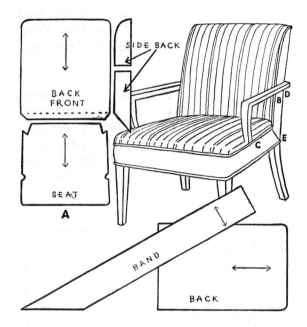

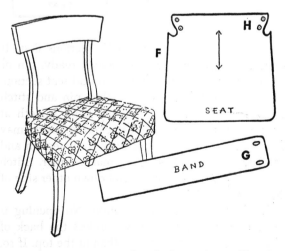

Join bottom of front back to seat section. Next join mitered corners of banding and side back, and stitch cording along both sides of band. Stitch cording to side sections above the arm and stitch to front section. Stitch front and back sections together from arm up, across top and down to other arm. Attach band to cover, leaving an opening from **B** to **C** and **D** to **E**. Snaps may be used to close openings. If a permanent cover is desired, pin openings together and finish with overhand stitches, using a curved upholsterer's needle.

A ruffle can be used to finish the lower edge on either of these covers.

Upholstered Seat. This type of cover can be made in two ways. For a removable cover, see Diagram **F**. The seat section and back edge are cut in one piece. A single strip is used for the sides and front. Make the band long enough so that it laps over the back section on both sides. Make buttonholes in ends, as at **G**, and sew buttons on both sides of the back, as at **H**. (Illustration at bottom of previous column.) Cover can easily be removed and laundered.

For a permanent cover, cut in one piece, as in **I**. Face openings at back, as at **J**. Clip seams on curve. Lay cover on chair, fold in front corners, and slip-stitch along folded edge. Overlap edges

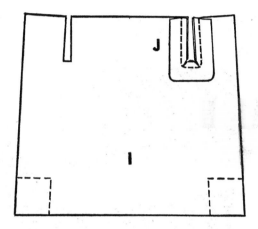

at back corners, turn top edge under and tack, as at **K**. Turn edges to underside of chair and tack. Cut a piece of muslin size of chair bottom. Turn edge all around and tack over raw edges of cover.

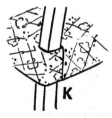

Tie-on Cushions. Thin cushions are easy to make and are appropriate for many types of chairs. Cut pattern of chair seat and cut two pieces of fabric the same size, plus seam allowance. Use cotton padding or several layers of old bath towels for padding, cut same size as seat, but without seam allowance. Place padding between the top and

201

bottom of the cushion; stitch the raw edges all the way around, ⅛″ from the raw edges. Trim the raw

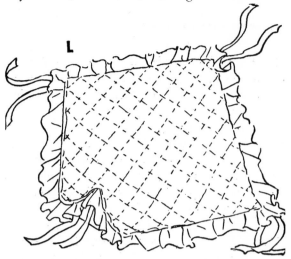

edge with bias binding.

For ruffled edge, as in **L**: Cut ruffle strip. Stitch ends of strip together to make one continuous strip. Hem lower edge with machine Foot Hemmer; gather top edge with Gathering Foot. Lay gathered edge of ruffle around one seat piece on right side, as at **M**. Full ruffle at corners (see page 45 for details); then stitch. Lay second seat piece right side down over ruffle. Stitch along edge, leaving an opening on back edge, as at **N**. Turn cover inside out. Insert padding, smoothing it flat. Whip back opening together. Quilt, using Quilting Foot (see *Block Quilting*, page 132). Sew tie strings to corners underneath ruffle. Hold cushion in place with ties around each leg.

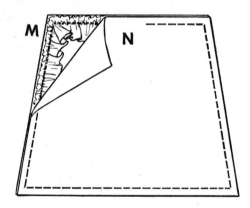

A flat cushion of this type is sometimes used as padding for both the seat and the back of Early American chairs, especially armless rockers. The ruffle can be omitted. For the back, loops should be substituted for ties on the two top corners. These loops slip over the posts or spindles of the back. Tie strings hold the lower corners in place at the side back.

Outdoor Cushions and Covers

Buy for such covers, fast-color fabrics such as cotton sailcloth or Duran, a plastic fabric, or any of the absolutely guaranteed synthetics. Orlon is increasingly important for outdoor covers. None of the fabrics mentioned are overly expensive. Buy them in high, bright color and pipe or bind the edges with an appropriate contrast or white. What you need for your covers is colorful, desirable fabric plus good fit and good stitching, to have a really smart job.

Measure cushions for amount of material needed the same as for indoor furniture. See page 190. Allow ample for seams—¾″ to 1″—also enough fabric for straightening. When pinning heavy fabrics, use a thimble to push in pins.

If you wish to use covered buttons as tufting trim, have these covered at your Singer Sewing Center. Usually when you work with a double thread you need to go through and back just three times in sewing these on. See page 217 for detailed instructions.

French-Seam-Finished Cushion. When covering old cushions that are soiled or faded, clean as best you can, then place new fabric over piece to be covered right side down. Fit to cushion, pin along edge, then cut, allowing a ¾″ seam. If a boxing strip is to be used, stitch it to top of new cover all way around, making a ¼″ seam. Stitch bottom of cover to boxing strip on three sides, making a ¼″ seam and stitching 1″ past each corner of the open end. Press the seams open, clip across each corner. Turn cover right side out and stitch around top of cover a generous ¼″ from the seamline, thus making a French seam. Stitch around bottom of cover except for open end. Insert cushion. Turn raw edges in and slip-stitch together. Finish French seam by stitching across end, using Cording Foot.

Twilled Tape Binding. Twilled tape makes a good, sturdy binding for outdoor covers and cushions. Make seam of cover on right side and stitch one edge of the tape on as you stitch material together. Turn tape over and stitch free edge down. Pin this every few inches so it will be straight.

The tape or binding should completely conceal the seam. Miter the tape on square corners top and bottom. Allow ease enough so outside corners cannot draw. Use thread of a color to match the binding so stitching will not show.

Dressing Up Your Bed

BEDS SHOULD BE DRESSED WITH AS MUCH CARE AND thought as you give to your windows, since both draperies and bed coverings last several years. Study these pages, clip magazine pictures of decorated rooms, assemble ideas, plan your room so that it is right for the windows and for the floor and wall coverings.

Consideration should be given to cleaning and to whether or not there is time for pressing and keeping in good condition. The new synthetics are easy to care for and give an effect that is completely desirable. For example, ruffled spreads and curtains are completely satisfactory in synthetics and represent a fraction of the upkeep that organdie requires.

Businessmen always weigh the pros and cons of every problem. Some make lists of the points for and against any proposition being considered. Women would do well to use the same system in planning their rooms, so that they put their efforts into a channel of safety as regards upkeep, yet indulge their tastes and preferences for beauty. Practical things need not be drab or unattractive. When right, they should be both attractive and practical.

Bed Linens. It is generally considered more practical and economical to buy sheets and pillow cases ready-made, but since fabric has become so important in decoration, beds and bedrooms offer the home decorator a splendid opportunity to display her skills in really lovely fabric furnishings. Drabness can be replaced with charm, color and cheer with a few yards of rightly chosen fabric and some well-applied ingenuity.

Blanket Covers and Cuffs. To protect light-colored blankets or comfortables against soiling, many use washable slip-covers. For a comfortable cover, make your slip-cover like a large bag, as in **A**. Since comfortables are usually 70″ wide, 36″ fabric is practical to use for the cover. Cut two lengths, measuring twice the length of the comfortable plus 2″ for hems. Seam the two strips together the full length. Press seam open. Hem both ends, insert ribbon or tape ties under edges, as in **B**. The center tie ends will cover selvages of center seam. Fold across, leaving room for top to turn over about a foot, as in **C** at bottom of previous column. Join side edges with French seam or binding. Tack the comfortable to the cover at top and bottom so it will hold in position.

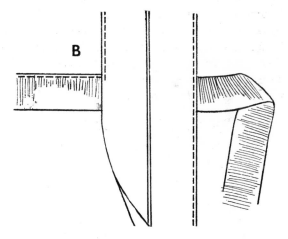

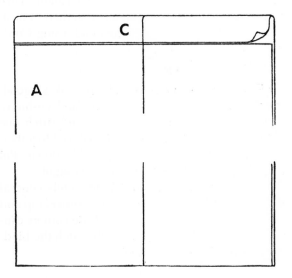

For blanket cover, make large straight cover like sheet, using any cotton, synthetic, or silk fabric that does not wrinkle easily. Challis and seersucker are suitable types. Finish edges with hems, lace edging, ribbon or binding. Use for protection when bed is undressed for sleeping, not as daytime spread.

To guard blanket bindings against soiling or wear, removable cuffs are widely used. These are especially good for invalids or people who read in bed. The 24″ cuff is a protection against newsprint from papers, also trays. Make depth desired, say from 12″ to 24″ deep and 1″ wider than blan-

203

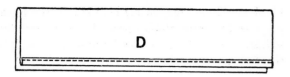

ket plus seam allowance at sides. Turn hems to wrong side, as at **D**, and stitch. Fold in half crosswise and French seam ends. Turn to right side and fit over end of the blanket at the top of bed. Hold in position by slip-stitching hem to blanket. This is the plainest type of cuff. Sheer fabric, lawn, voile, dimity, etc., are suitable. Lace insertion, ruffle along edge or any appropriate simple trim can be used for decoration.

COMFORTABLES AND THROWS

Tubular Comfortable or Puff. Measure bed from head to foot for length of comfortable. Add six inches for making. Measure the width you desire. Some like a puff the width of the bed. Others like an overhang of 2″ to 4″ on each side. Cut as many fabric strips as necessary to give the desired width and to cover both sides of the puff. For example, two widths of 40″, even 36″, are usually sufficient for a single bed and three widths of 40″ are enough for a double bed. Cut even lengths, stitch the edges together to form a tube, as in **E**, clipping the seams as shown, and press them open. Turn to the right side.

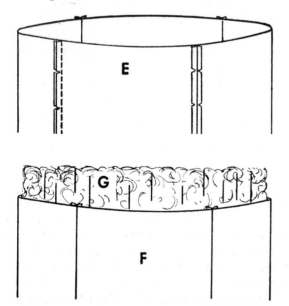

For the inner padding, take one or two lengths of open-weave cheesecloth. If two, lap the selvages of two edges and stitch together lap-seam fashion. Baste wool batting over this, using very long stitches.

For a full-size bed, place seams in tube of fabric so that upper section will have a center panel, as at **F**. Slip batting inside tube, as in **G**. Turn raw edges of ends in toward each other and stitch, as at **H**. To hold padding in place, tack or tie all layers together at regular intervals. Use a heavy cot-

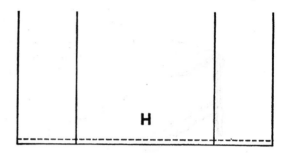

ton or wool in a large darning needle to tie-tack a puff or comfortable. Insert needle straight from right side, then bring up thread from underside, leaving a ¼″ to ⅜″ space between. Cut off thread, leaving ends long enough to tie, as in **I**, and then make a bow, as in **J**.

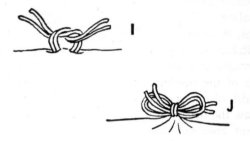

Square or Oblong Comfortables. Decide size comfortable is to be, or make it 72″ square, which is the average. Use a layer of lamb's wool about 2″ thick (not packed) for the filling. Place wool between layers of muslin or cheesecloth. If these have to be pieced for the correct size, use a lapped seam. See page 55. Hold filling and lining together by tacking at intervals.

When cutting the fabric for the covering, add ½″ on all edges for seams. To avoid a seam down the center, split one length through the center and stitch to sides of center panel. Press seams open in top and bottom sections.

Spread bottom covering out flat, right side down. On this lay the filling, then the top covering, right side up. Bring edges together all around and pin at intervals.

Baste along lines where quilting is to be. These quilting lines are usually about 3″ apart. See next page for some quilting suggestions. Finish with cording by stitching it to the right side of top covering. Turn in edges of bottom covering and slip-stitch to cording or welting.

If you are monogramming the comfortable, as in **K**, apply initials to top covering before making comfortable. See *Appliquéd Monogram* on page 228.

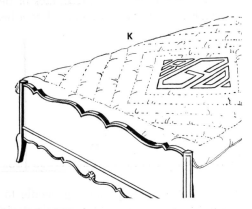

Shaped-Edge Comfortables and Puffs. Often bound scalloped or other patterned edges are used. Measure your length and width. Make a paper pattern of edge design, keeping it simple, because binding can then be used most effectively. Shallow scallop and point design, **L**, reverse scallops, **M**, or broad shallow plain scallops, **N**, are all suitable. An easy way to duplicate designs exactly throughout length of edge is to cut a strip of paper of the needed length, pleat it into folds the width of one scallop or one motif of your design, draw the design exactly as you want it on the top pleat, then cut through all layers at once. When strip is unfolded, each fold bears exactly the same design. Place this on edge to be cut. Be sure to plan and place design so corners are symmetrical.

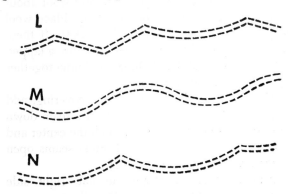

Arrange layers of comfortable as described opposite, quilt as desired. Make binding of bias strips of the fabric. See page 120 for making bias tube. If lightweight padding is used, edges can be bound by using the machine Binder. When comfortable has heavy padding, pin and baste binding along edge before stitching. See page 123 for binding scallops.

Throws. Throws may be made in exactly the same ways as the comfortables here. They are usually smaller in size. A throw may be used as a decorative feature of a bed or chaise longue.

Quilting. See page 132 for instructions for the various methods of quilting. Unless the padding is thick or the quilting design elaborate, the machine Quilter serves well for quilting comfortables, throws, patchwork and appliqué quilts. There are a number of ways of doing the quilting. One is simple block quilting—parallel lines evenly spaced and crossing each other at right angles. Another way is to go around and around, keeping stitching a determined distance apart, say 6 inches, until the middle is reached, as in **O**. Another way

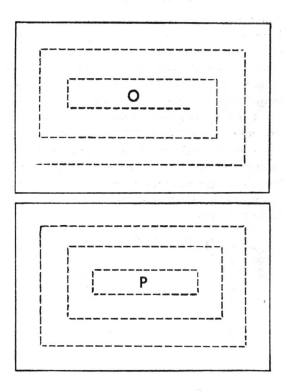

is to make a series of blocks, one inside another, gradually becoming smaller as you work toward center. See **P**. Still another way, if you are using a fabric with individual motifs, spaced evenly, is to outline the motif with the quilting stitching. See **V** on page 235 showing this type of coverlet. Also available are many designs that may be stamped or drawn on the fabric and followed in quilting.

Elaborate or very heavy quilting is done by hand, with a running-stitch. The whole quilt is placed in a quilting frame, so that it is kept straight for working and can be rolled up as it is quilted.

Patch quilts and appliquéd quilts usually are quilted in line with the seams of the piecing or the appliqué design. If there are plain blocks in the piece quilts, these are sometimes quilted in fan, feather or scroll motifs.

Crazy Quilts. These are patchwork quilts made of pieces of random size and shape. Usually they are made of wool or silk and velvet pieces attached to a fabric lining piece. The joining lines of the pieces are feather-stitched with bright-colored threads. These quilts are usually thinly padded and lined with plain fabric on the wrong side. The padding can be quilted to the wrong side of the lining so no stitching will mar the top of the quilt. The top is then tacked to the padding and all edges bound together, often with ribbon or velvet.

Patchwork. This is an old and respected American craft, formerly done entirely by hand, but now often adapted to the sewing machine. Three patterns with effective designs easily put together by machine are shown here as examples. *Nine Patches* is the simplest pattern to do, the second, the *Eight Point Star,* requires precise cutting to be attractive.

Instructions for making the *Maple Leaf* block are given opposite. Many Early American quilt blocks were made in complete squares of 12″ sides, joined together, either with plain fabric or another pattern of quilt block. Modern blocks may vary in size from about 8″ to 15″.

To make your pattern, cut such a square, mark all dividing lines and cut apart, marking what the color is on each piece. Then make a pattern of stiff paper or cardboard for each size. Cut all pieces by pattern, allowing ¼″ for seams all around. Use your presser foot as a guide in stitching all seams to be sure of uniformity of width. Cut many pieces at once by pinning pattern to layers of fabric. Smooth out pieces. Sort colors separately and pin together in neat stacks. Then, when you sit at your machine to sew, start with pairs of pieces to be stitched together, and stitch continuously without breaking your thread, as in **Q**. Just carry it

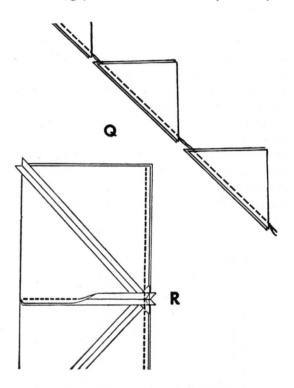

along for a few stitches to the next pair of pieces. Cut all apart when stitching is finished. In joining pieces, it is wise to work out from center when many pieces meet there. Otherwise plan your stitching so that as you join blocks, you make longer and longer continuous seams, as in **R**. Thus you save time, thread and trouble. The back of a paring knife can be used at your machine to press your seams open as you work. They must be pressed open to avoid overlapping at joinings.

The maple leaf design shown in **U** is excellent

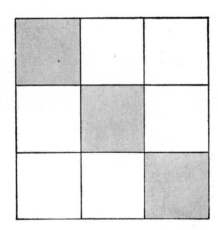

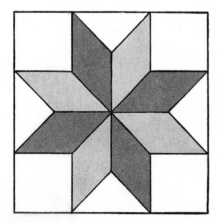

for doing on the machine. Each block is composed of nine 3″ squares, four of them pieced. Cut number of pieces as indicated in **S** and **T**. The pieces marked as white should be the same color in all blocks, as these form the background of quilt. The leaf in each block can be a different color, but the seven grey pieces for the individual blocks should be cut of one color. Choose leaf colors (green, brown, yellow, orange or red in various combinations) and make the ground pieces a harmonizing and unifying color. A border can be made of one color or of narrow strips of all colors used in the leaves.

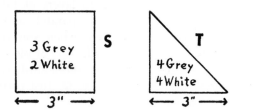

First, join the triangular pieces through the center, as in **Q** above. Make the stem piece by applying tape or binding diagonally across the block, as at **U**. Then join long seams to complete whole square, as in **V**. When all squares have been assembled for top, pad with sheet cotton, cover back with plain color, hem or bind edges. See quilting instructions, page 132. Some of the pattern companies put out quilt block patterns with full instructions. If you have had no experience with making quilts, perhaps these would help you to start.

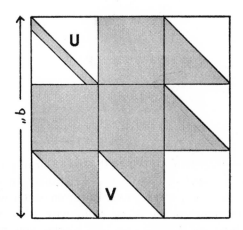

Appliqué Quilts. These may be made with all-over appliqué design applied to quilt blocks. When blocks are used, they are often put together with strips of plain color. See page 128 for instructions on appliqué. When top is completed, bind and finish as described on page 133.

A lightweight comfortable can be used to dress up your bed. Illustration **S** on page 235 shows a reversible comfortable used as a combined spread and pillow sham. Illustration **V** has a brocade covered comfortable which is finely quilted around the design motifs.

BEDSPREADS

Measuring for Bedspreads. (See chart on page 170.) Before you measure, bed should be fully made up with sheets and blankets as they are to be used. Start at headboard and measure full length of bed and down to floor at foot. Add to this the measurement around pillow, usually 36″. That is the total length for finished spread including sham. Get width by measuring from floor on one side, up and over bed and down to floor on other side. Add about 2″ to each side and each end for making.

Plain Spread. Usually two lengths of 50″ fabric will make such a spread. Place one length as a panel directly down center of bed. Split other piece lengthwise for the two sides. Thus no seam is placed in the middle of spread. Join selvage edges along panel seams. Pin and stitch. Clip selvage at intervals, as in **A**. Turn hem all around spread, mitering at corners. (See page 79.)

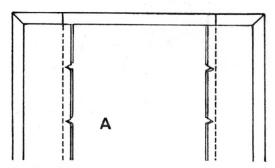

A plain spread can be varied by rounding the corners at the foot, as in **B**, by cording the panel seams and edges, by inserting lace or embroidered insertion along the panel seams, or by placing

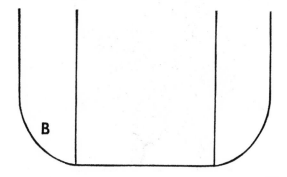

panel seam on the right side and covering seams with ribbon or braid. When corners are rounded, the spread may be made a little longer so that corners come to floor.

Tufted Spread. A plain spread can be decorated attractively with evenly spaced tufts, as in **C**, made with the Singercraft Guide.

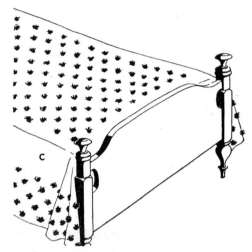

Unbleached muslin is usually used for the spread, with heavy crochet or pearl cotton thread for the tufts. Stamp or mark position on spread for each tuft. Average tufts are about the size of a nickel and are spaced 2″ apart.

Wind thread around Singercraft Guide, crowding the winding so tuft will be full, then stitch, using a medium-length stitch. Continue to stitch through slot of Guide to marking for next tuft, as at **D**. Wind thread again and stitch. Continue stitching and winding until design is completed. By stitching close to left hand side of slot in Guide, you make the length of thread loops about the same on both sides of stitching line. The point of your scissors can be used to even up the loops before cutting. Cut loops on both sides of stitching and shape into a ball with your fingers.

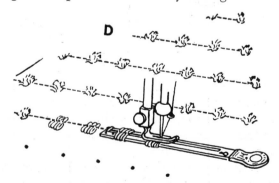

Straight Spread for Footboard Beds. For beds with footboards or corner posts, it is often desir-

able to cut away the spread corners at the foot and tailor them. Make your three sections and seam together. Place spread on bed, smoothed in place carefully, to get correct depth for corner. Pin corners, as at **E**. Remove spread. Cut off excess

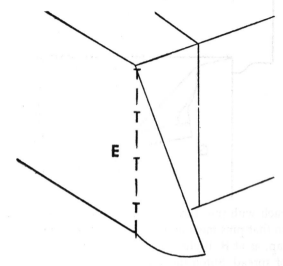

corners, leaving seam allowance, usually 1¼″. Clip corner to depth of hem, as at **F**. Fold back hem allowance to make square corners. Press. Tailor corners. (See page 79.) Hem spread, mitering other corners.

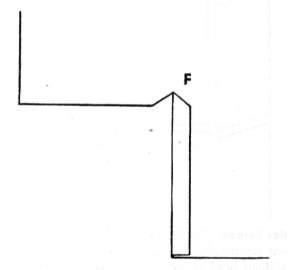

This type of spread may be made with the sham all in one (as in **P** on page 234), with a separate sham (see **Q** page 234), or with a sham cut separately and stitched on (see **H**, opposite). For this, cut pillow piece wide and deep enough to cover pillow amply and with allowance for hems and seams. Hem both sides and top edge of sham piece. Finish sides and bottom of spread. Make square corners on lower edge of sham and top edge of spread, as at **G**. Fold bottom edge of sham and top edge of spread in half, mark center of

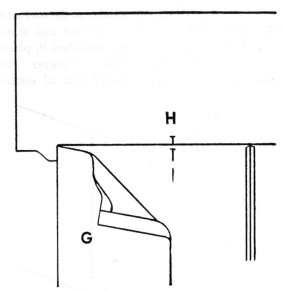

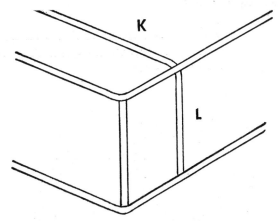

inserted in top section, as at **K**, then a matching corded seam should be made in overhang, as at **L**, so all seams are uniform.

each with pin. Lay sham and spread side by side so that pins meet and the edges to be joined overlap, as at **H**. Right side of sham is up; wrong side of spread. Stitch this lapped seam to within 2″ of the end on each side, as at **I**. Then turn under raw edges of seam on sham and stitch or hem by hand, as at **J**. Finish seam on spread in same way.

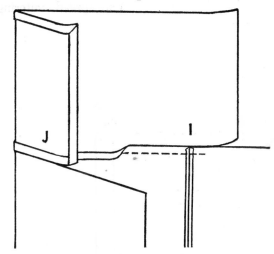

Seam top sections together and cord edges. Round corners slightly when applying cording to top of spread. See **F**, page 125. Make overhang and cord corners. Pin to top section and stitch together. Overcast raw edges of cording on underside, or, if desired, make lining for spread, cutting pieces as for outside and seaming them together. To put lining in, put spread on bed, wrong side up. Put lining on over it, right side out. Tack lining in place along seams of spread. Slip-stitch edge all around bottom.

If one end or one side of spread is against wall, that side need not be covered completely. In that case, cut pieces to go around the corners at sides, as at **M**. A narrow strip can be made to go across opening, as at **N**.

Box Spread. For beds with box springs and without footboards, for studio couches and for cots without head or foot, the tailored box spread is practical. Such spreads are often corded on all seams and may be either all in one piece, as in studio couches, etc., or made with a boxed part for the top and a separate flounce to be attached to the box spring. Pages 234 and 235 show a number of ways in which the box spread can be made attractively.

Measure length, width and depth of box part. Make enough cording for all seams at once. See *Cording*, page 124. If overall spread is to be made, bottom edge is usually corded also. If cording is

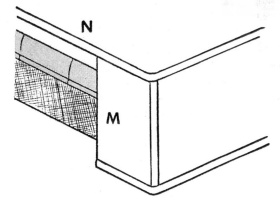

The overhang of a plain box spread can be decorated to suit any type of room. Hem bottom and ends of overhang. Then apply rows of ruffles, pleating or fringe. Illustration **A** on page 236 shows the use of fringe.

Ruffles may be uniform narrow ruffles covering whole surface, graduated tiers, or spaced rows. See page 43 for applying ruffles. Join overhang to top of spread with desired type of seam.

The overhang can also be given an attractive fullness by the insertion of godets at the corners and at regular intervals along sides and bottom of bed. Illustration **R**, page 234, shows flounce with godet inserts. See page 49 for cutting godets.

If spread is to have separately made flounce, finish box section with short overhang. Bottom edge should be 1" below top of box spring. Then use flounce for bottom sections.

Flounces. There are three main types of flounce —pleated, circular-cut and gathered. Each of these can be finished in a variety of ways suitable for your fabric and decorative scheme.

For a pleated flounce, cut fabric on the crosswise grain. Seam all sections together except for one seam, and hem bottom. Lay pleats. See page 47 for box pleats. Stitch across top of pleats to hold in place, as at **O**. Stitch twill tape along top edge,

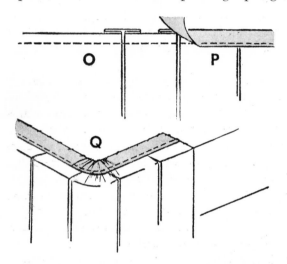

as at **P**. Finish ends with narrow hem. Mark center of pleated strip, place this at exact center of foot of bed. Then pin flounce in place along top of box spring, gathering tape in at corners, as at **Q**. Whip tape to ticking of box spring all along edge, using strong thread and a curved needle. The tape and sewing are covered when the mattress is in place.

Plain Tuck-in Spread. The pleated flounce described above may also be used with a plain tuck-in spread. Make such a spread according to directions for plain straight spread except that tuck-in allowance need not be as long as for overhang. Six inches allowance for tuck-in should be ample. Often an heirloom spread or quilt is used for the tuck-in spread and the flounce is made of material chosen to harmonize. A tuck-in spread is shown in the illustration **Z** on page 235.

210

Fitted Spread. This is the most widely used type of spread. Make a straight top for bed by seaming lengths together. Cut to fit just to edge of mattress, plus seam allowance. If top is to be quilted or decorated in any way, do this before applying flounce.

Cut type of flounce desired. Depth of flounce is from top of mattress to floor plus seam and hem allowance.

Gathered Flounce. You will need almost twice the measurement of the edges of the spread top for your gathered edge. The amount of fullness allowed depends on weight and texture of fabric used. Cut your lengths, seam them together, and gather, using Gathering Foot or Machine Ruffler. See page 41 for use of these attachments. If your

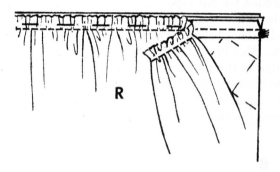

bed has a footboard or posts, make the flounce in three sections, one for each side and one for the foot. Finish ends of each section by binding or hemming to match finish on bottom of flounce. Pin and baste gathered edge of flounce along edge of top of spread and stitch, as in **R**. Cording inserted in seam, as in **S**, gives an attractive finish to top edge of a flounce. Bottom edge of gathered

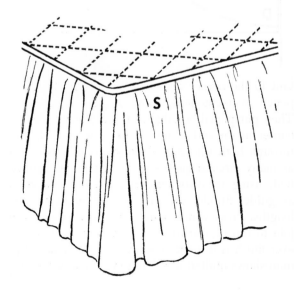

spread may be finished by a plain hem or binding, with scallops or with ruffles, as in **T**.

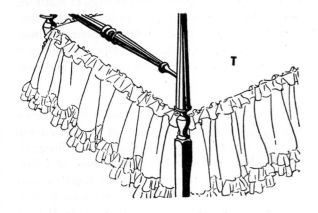

Circular Flounce. About 12 yds. of 50″ fabric are needed for this type of flounce. Lay fabric on table. When using a 50″ fabric, make a crosswise fold about half as deep as the width of the fabric. Pin. Measure up along the selvage from the raw edge of the folded piece to the desired depth of the flounce, plus 1″ for making. Mark this point **A**. Tie a string to your pencil. Hold the pencil point on the mark you made at **A**. Hold string

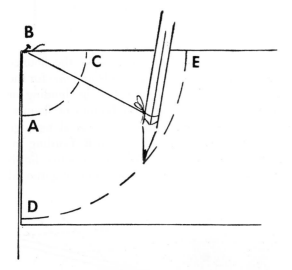

taut to the corner at the fold, as at **B**. Using the pencil as a compass, swing a curve to point **C**. Then put pencil on edge at **D**, hold string taut to corner again and swing curve to **E** at fold. Cut through both thicknesses along curved lines. Cut as many circular pieces as needed to go around bed, using measurement of curve from **A** to **C** as guide. Stitch selvage edges together to join lengths. Press seams open. Hem lower edge and join to top of spread with corded seam or whatever finish is desired. The illustration in next column shows quilted fabric cut in a circular flounce.

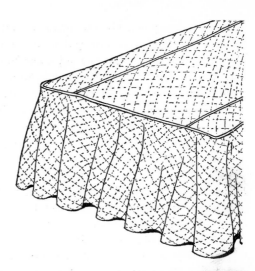

Sheer Spreads. For a dainty effect, a sheer overspread can be used as illustrated in **U** on page 235. A plain box spread is used to cover the bed. Use a sheer fabric such as organdie or net for the overspread. Cut-out motifs can be appliquéd in various ways. (See *Appliqué,* page 128.) A double ruffle gives an attractive finish to the edge of spread.

For Children's Beds and Cribs. Some prefer to make crib sheets and pillow cases for infants' and children's beds. Baby pillow cases are usually made of fine white linen or soft cotton fabric. They may be either slip cases made exactly like those for large pillows, with hemmed or hemstitched hem, or they may have ruffles or lace inserted in the seams all around the pillow. For such, make a placket closing with buttons, snaps or zippers 1″ to 2″ from one end on the underside. Dainty embroidery and fine appliqué work are also favored for such cases. Sheets are cut lengthwise of the grain, hemmed or hemstitched. Often full size sheets worn soft and thin are torn to make four sections, torn edges hemmed and these used for cribs and children's beds.

Crib spreads and carriage covers are made like a plain spread or comfortable, but of a size to fit crib or carriage.

PILLOW SHAMS AND BOLSTERS

PILLOW SHAMS AND BOLSTERS SHOULD USUALLY BE made of the material of the spread. However, when heirloom quilts, spreads or coverlets are too short, the bed requires ruffled, embroidered or tucked shams, or lace- or tuck-trimmed pillow cases.

Sometimes the spread is cut long enough to fold under and over and make a bolster-like cover for the pillows, as described on page 207, or an oblong piece of fabric, cut on the same fabric grain as that of the spread, may be used around the pillows. There are upright shams and flat shams, some tailored, some ruffled. A practical daytime sham may be made to cover the sleeping pillows, especially when a bed is used as a couch in the daytime. In any case, a bed seems incomplete without some means of covering its pillows.

Insert Sham. Perhaps the simplest sham of all to make. Measure off a piece of fabric twice the length of the pillow plus 2½″ for hems and 1″ for ease, cut so the grain is the same as that of the spread. Make this as wide as the width of the top of the pillow plus 1″ for ease. Turn ¼″ in at each end, then turn 1″ hems. Stitch these. Bring the hems together, as in **A**. Stitch from **B** to **C**, and

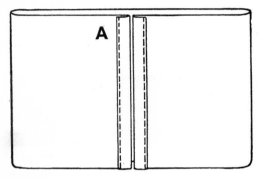

back across to **D**, thus reinforcing the opening. Stitch the opposite seam in the same way. Press the seams open, clip the corners. Turn right side out and insert the pillow. Tapes, if desired, may be used to tie the opening.

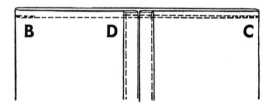

Ruffled Over-Sham. This sham can be made for a single pillow or made long enough to cover two pillows at top of bed. For a single pillow: Take a piece the size of the top of your pillow, plus 2″ on each side and each end. This should be on the same grain as the spread. Cut lining the same size. For a finished ruffle 5″ deep, cut a crosswise strip of fabric 11″ wide and double the measurement around the sham in length. For example, if your sham piece measures 22″ x 26″, you will need 96″ twice, or 5⅓ yards of ruffling for one sham. Seam all lengths of ruffle strip together to make a circle. Press seams open. Fold in half, right side out.

Gather top of ruffle ¼″ from the edge, catching both edges at once. Adjust gathers so that ruffle will fit around edges of sham.

Lay ruffle on right side of sham top. Pin gathered edge along edge of sham, fulling ruffle at corners, as at **E**. This is important to insure that corners of ruffle lie flat at outside edge. Stitch, using a ⅜″ seam so as to cover all gathering stitches. Lay sham lining, right side down, over ruffle. Pin and stitch, as in **F**. Leave an opening at one end through which sham can be turned. Clip off corners. Turn right side out. Slip-stitch opening together. Press the sham part from the wrong side. Simply lay this over your pillow to cover it completely.

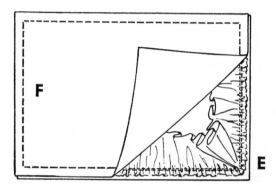

To Make a Square Bolster Form. Use corrugated paper board—a piece as long as the width of your bed and wide enough to measure four times the desired height of your bolster form. For an 8″ high form, you need 32″ of paper board. Measure with yardstick and mark off with pencil four straight lines 8″ apart on the width of the board. Score these with a razor blade, using the yardstick as a guide. Carefully crease on the scored lines. Square up the form with gentle pressure, bring the edges together, and fasten with gummed fabric or paper tape. Make a cover for this as described on next page.

To Make a Round Bolster Form. Take a piece of heavy buckram or lightweight linoleum wide enough to give you a roll of the height you want and as long as your bed is wide. Usually such linoleum strips can be bought at remnant prices at the linoleum department in your local store. If necessary, use your yardstick and razor blade to cut to the size desired. Then with an ice pick or nail, puncture holes in both long edges, about 10″ to 12″ apart. Slip lightweight wire through these holes, bring edges of roll together and secure the wires so they will hold. Cover your bolster form with muslin or drill, making a tube 8″ longer than

Photograph by the makers of Armstrong's linoleum

Use Related Colors in Adjoining Small Rooms

An illusion of spaciousness can be created for adjoining small rooms by the use of matched and related colors throughout, as in the illustration here. Notice how the golden yellow of the barrel-type slip-covers, the stripe of the sofa cover, and the lampshade are echoed in the far room by the curtains, the fringe on the bed-cover, and the tone of the chest. The bright accent of the elephant-ear pillows is picked up again in the next room by the picture-hanging device, and the soft gray of the floor covering, repeated in the striped fabric, is carried through to the rug in the next room. Harmonizing wall tints, floors, and fabric decorations all contribute to the effect of size and space. All the slip-covers—for chairs and couch—the bed-cover, the cushions, the curtains, are Singer sewing possibilities. Notice also that the accessories in the rooms are few and carefully related, to avoid the busy feeling that can make small rooms seem even smaller. The books and their shelves are used to lend color accents and interest to the connecting wall in an attractive and functional way.

Courtesy of Cavalier Corporat

New Color in Wood Tones

Scenic prints such as the one used above are always a challenge to use. They are beautiful, they drape or pleat nicely and harmonize perfectly with traditional or modern interiors. The wide scallops of the bedspread shown here are matched in the flouncing by wide box pleats. If design fabric is silk, use silk for the spreads; if cotton, then a corduroy will be attractive.

Bedrooms, living rooms, dining rooms—any one of the three—could happily effect a color scheme like that shown here. The fabric lends itself to the wood tones of the furniture in a way that is completely pleasing and easy to live with. Drapes, spreads, even flounces on the beds, should be lined to give weight in keeping with the furniture.

the form and just large enough in circumference to slip over the form. Draw the surplus at the ends in and tack so that they have a finished look. Make ornamental cover as desired.

A Soft Bolster Roll. Make a tube of drill or sailcloth as long as your bed is wide plus 8″ and about 32″ around for an 8″ high roll. Bring long edges together and stitch, as in **G**, thus forming a long

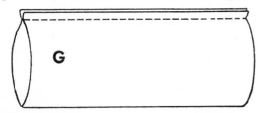

tube. Turn seam inside. Gather one end rosette-fashion, as in **H**. Fasten securely. Pack this tube evenly with kapok or other lightweight inexpensive packing. When packing has been put in smoothly, draw the open end together in same manner as first end. Then cover the roll.

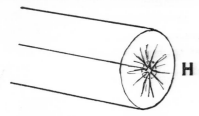

Covers for Bolster Forms or Rolls. Measure the roll to get correct length and circumference. Allow for seams. Join long edges of cover and stitch to make a tube, as in **G** above. Press the seam open. For square form, divide both ends of tube into quarters. Mark by clipping with points of scissors. Cut two square ends, allowing for seams. Pin and baste one end piece in place. Match clips to corners of end piece, as in **I**. Stitch as shown. Clip off all corners, as at **J**. Turn right side out. Slip square bolster form into tube. After cover is smoothed

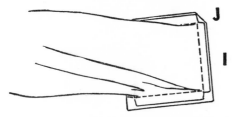

into place, crease seam edge on open end over form, turn under seam allowance all around other end piece and pin. Whip end in position, doing this carefully so that stitches do not show. This type of cover can be used on any type of bolster form. Only the end pieces change.

Twin Bolsters. If the bolster is to be used on a large bed or on the long side of a studio couch, it is usually best to make two forms, dividing the length in half. See **X**, page 235, and **Y**, page 236.

Bolster Cover with Gathered End. Cut cover to go around bolster, adding seam allowance. Allow enough length at each end to come to center of roll, plus 1″ for casing at each end. Make 1″ hem turn on end edges. Fold right side in and bring long edges together. Stitch from one end to the other, but not across casings. Turn right side out. Run a length of cord through casing at each end. Slip cover over bolster form. Draw up cord at center of each end piece, tie, and push ends through to wrong side. Cover the gathered end with ornamental button, tassel or rosette.

CUSHIONS AND PILLOW TOPS

RIBBON AND LACE CAN EASILY BE APPLIED WITH THE Edge-Stitcher to a plain foundation to make dainty and attractive cushion tops. Quilting can, when rightly used, give distinction to many types of sham, bolster or cushion. Braid and fringe can add smartness to tailored cushions or bolsters.

Box Pillow. This pillow can be made oblong or square and of a size and depth to suit your needs. Cut two pieces of fabric, making them as large as top of pillow plus depth of side, as in **K**, and a ½″

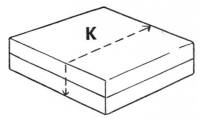

seam allowance all around. (Dotted line shows measurement needed.) Stitch back and front pieces together, wrong side out, leaving an opening for turning, as at **L**. Fold all corners diagonally,

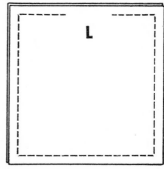

as at **M**, and pin so that corners will be square and of even depth when stitched. Stitch across each corner, as at **N**. Turn cover right side out and sew opening together.

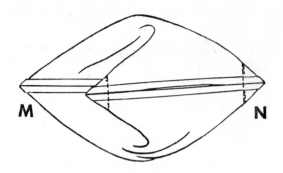

Flange-Hem Cover. Cut two pieces size of finished cushion plus hem allowance on all sides. Turn hems under all around, mitering corners, as at **O**. Stitch even distance from edge, as at **P**, leaving opening on one side to insert cushion. After cushion is enclosed, complete stitching line.

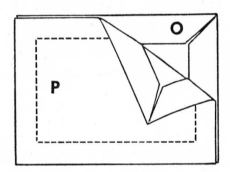

If felt is used for this type of cover, stitch together without hem turns, then pink edges, using your pinking attachment. Stitching line can be covered with decorative braid or cord.

Puffed Cushion. Cut two squares of size preferred. Use heavy cord to make enough cording for all edges (see page 124). Pin and baste cording along edge on right side, as at **Q**. Clip seam edge at corners and every two or three inches so that cording will lie flat. Stitch, using Cording Foot.

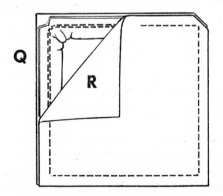

Pivot at corners (see page 125). Lay other cushion piece right side down, over cording, as at **R**. Pin and stitch, leaving an opening for turning to right side. Clip off all corners. After turning to right side, stitch a square in center, as at **S**. Use enough stuffing to make cushion puff attractively. Whip opening together.

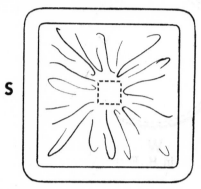

Pill-Box Cushion. Cut two fabric circles, say 8½" in diameter. Provide 52" of moss fringe (see page 135). Cut boxing strip of depth desired and 25" long. Cut length of fringe in half and lay one piece of fringe around edge of circle, on right side, as in **T**. Baste and stitch. Apply fringe to second circle in same way. Stitch ends of boxing strip together, making ½" seam. Baste boxing strip over fringe, as in **U**, clipping seam edge so it will lie flat. Stitch other side in position, leaving an opening so cover can be turned right side out. Stuff or insert cushion form. Slip-stitch opening together.

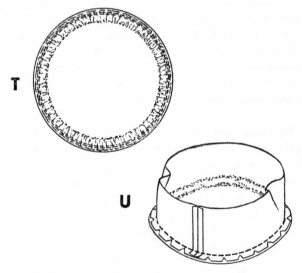

Round Flat Cushion. Cut two round pieces, possibly of two different colors, allowing a ⅞" seam all around. Lay right sides together and stitch around circle ¼" from edge, leaving opening about ⅛ of circumference of pillow, as at **V**. Clip seam edge all around, as at **W**. Press seam open, turn cover right side out and insert pillow. Turn in and slip-stitch raw edges of opening together, then with Cording Foot on your machine, stitch all around pillow ⅜″ from edge, as in **X.**

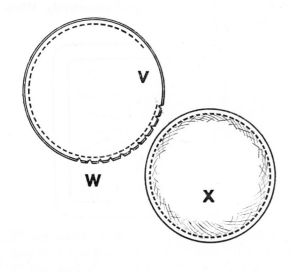

HEADBOARDS

THERE ARE THREE CHIEF WAYS OF USING FABRIC AS decoration for headboards that are used with Hollywood-type beds (box springs and mattresses without footboards). A framework of rough wood is made, padded with cotton, covered first with muslin, then with your decorative fabric. Sometimes the headboard of a regular bedstead is used and fabric applied. In such cases, a part of the woodwork may show above and around the fabric. We show here examples of all three methods, with suggestions for variation.

To Make and Pad a Headboard Frame. Make the framework for your headboard of lumber 4″ or 6″ wide and ½″ thick. Cut two upright pieces of the desired height and two crosswise pieces of the width of the bed. Sometimes one headboard is made for twin beds when they are to be treated as a unit. Nail boards together with sturdy nails, long enough to clinch on the underside, as in **A.**

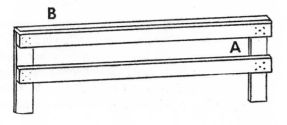

Cover top with thin strip of molding, as at **B.** Cut a piece of strong muslin or drill to cover back from side to side and over edges of crosspieces. Tack

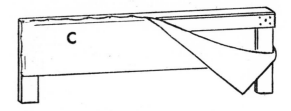

at intervals, as in **C.** Turn to front and stuff space between cross rails with crumpled newspaper, as at **D.** Cover whole front surface with cotton pad-

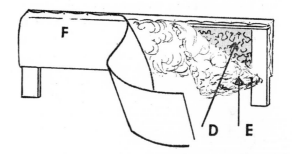

ding such as you buy for a comfortable, as at **E.** Have padding extend over all edges. Lay muslin over this, stretch evenly, using thumb tacks for holding during the stretching. Then tack in place along edges, as at **F.**

Prepare Fabric for the Cover. If headboard is too wide for the width of fabric you are using to cover it, place one length in center, split another length for the two sides, matching fabric motifs at joining. Cut the selvages off so seam cannot draw. Stitch these seams and press open.

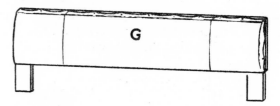

Place fabric over front, stretch, and thumb tack in place. Then tack in position all around, as in **G.**

The ends and top edges of the headboard may be covered in a number of ways:

Flat Band Finish. This simple finish is made of a 3″ strip, cut on the crosswise grain of the fabric, long enough to extend up one side, across the top and down the other side. Piece as needed for length; then fold it in half lengthwise and press. Fold raw edges back ½″ and press. Lay along headboard with creased line close to back edge, as in **H**. Then tack this band in place all along top and sides, as at **I**, so that fold can be brought over to cover all tacks as shown. Fasten with tacks at bottom of each side to hold fold in place.

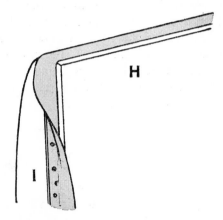

Corded Top Band. Another way is to cut a strip 1⅝″ wide to go along the top and both sides, cord both edges, taking seams of about ⅜″, as in **J**

(above) and lay strip wrong side up along headboard so that one cord lies along outside front

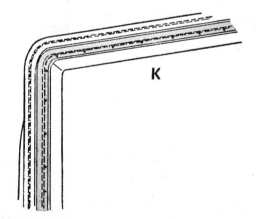

edge. Tack at intervals, as in **K**. Turn strip over, fold raw edges under along back edge and tack just inside cording, as in **L**, using invisible tacks.

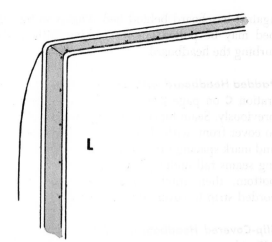

Ruffled Top Finish. The third finish is a stand-up ruffle all around. Make your ruffle of crosswise fabric 6″ wide and long enough for the top and side edges plus allowance for fullness. Fold it in half lengthwise, right sides out. Gather, using machine Gatherer, stitching about ⅜″ from raw edges. Cut a strip 2″ wide and as long as needed to cover edges of headboard. Stitch ruffle along one edge of strip about ½″ in, as at **M**. Make cording of the same length. Lay along stitching line of ruffle and stitch, as at **N**. With cording down, lay ruffle along

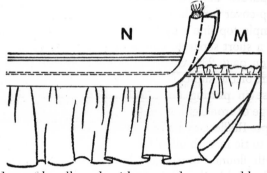

edges of headboard, with seam edges toward back, as at **O**. Tack close to stitching line. Turn straight strip back over tacks, fold raw edge under and tack with small headed, inconspicuous tacks, as shown at **P**.

When headboard is finished, screw it in place

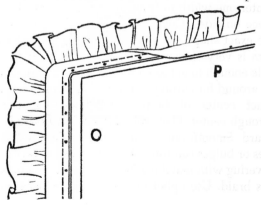

against baseboard behind bed. This is so that the bed may be pulled out for making without disturbing the headboard.

Padded Headboard with Unpressed Pleats. Illustration **C** on page 236. Make frame as described previously. Seam together enough widths of fabric to cover front, with allowance for pleats. Measure and mark spacing for pleats, planning so that piecing seams fall under pleats. Pin pleats at top and bottom, then stitch across. Use plain fold or corded strip to cover edges of board.

Slip-Covered Headboard. Illustration **S** on page 235. Almost any type of headboard can be fitted with a slip-cover to make it conform to the desired decoration of your room. Cut a muslin or paper pattern by fitting and pinning around the shape of the headboard. See method for chairs, page 191. If the headboard is wider at the top than at the lower part, a slide fastener may be inserted in the center-back to allow it to be put on easily. See page 196 for instructions. Finish seams with cording, moss fringe or add a ruffle to outside edge.

Separate Cuff for Top of Headboard. A plain slip-cover for a headboard with a straight or very simple top line may be enhanced by the addition of a short separate cuff with a ruffle, as shown in **U** on page 235. Cut your cuff exactly like the top part of the slip-cover, making it slightly larger for ease in putting on. Make ruffling for the lower edge of front, either single ruffle or center-stitched type. Ruffle may be of different fabric for contrast or to tie in with other fabric decoration of room or with flounce of spread. Finish bottom edges of sides and back with hem. Such a cuff may be taken off for laundering separately.

Upholstered Headboard. See illustrations **U** and **V**, page 235. For this type as well as others, if headboard is wider than fabric you are using, center one width in front, split another width and piece on sides. Cut a paper or muslin pattern of the exact shape of woodwork. If edge of wooden trim is very elaborate, muslin is best, as it is pliable enough to get exact fit. Pin pattern in position all around for cutting. Cut fabric to fit exactly. Get exact center of fabric by folding lengthwise through center. Place this at exact center of headboard. Smooth out toward sides so that no wrinkles or bulges can form. Tack all along wood edge, covering with matching or harmonizing upholster-er's braid. Use upholstery nails and, if necessary,

fabric glue under the braid for smooth, secure application. If fabric used for covering is to be quilted or decorated with machine stitching, do this before cutting from pattern.

Button Tufting. An attractive treatment of headboards is button tufting, as shown in **U** and **S** on page 235. For headboards, a single button tied underneath at desired intervals is used. For reversible articles, such as cushions or quilts, use two buttons, one on each side as shown. Use carpet thread doubled and a long darning needle. Fasten thread to first button by tying or sewing to shank. Insert needle, draw through cushion and through shank of second button. Then bring

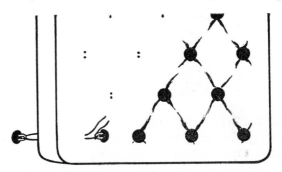

thread back through cushion under first button. Draw tightly together and tie securely. Cut off thread ends.

CANOPIES

DESIGNING AND MAKING A CANOPY SHOULD BE AP-proached with the same spirit as the creation of an oil painting. The new bed dress should last for many years. It should be correct in type for the style of bed and room furnishings. To realize the permanency of such a piece of construction, notice canopy beds in museums, in books, or interiors. Set out to do a really beautiful job all the way.

Delicate lightweight fabrics are usually favored for canopies, though many are made of hand-blocked linen, satin, even velvet. In bedrooms of Early American type, organdie, mull, eyelet embroidery, China-type silks and chintz are all appropriate. For Victorian and other periods, velveteen and other heavier fabrics are used sometimes to form a back-drape behind the bed, or to hang from a valance board construction above the head of the bed. The canopy should harmonize with the spread or the ruffle, both in fabric and trimming. The crocheted spread or heirloom quilt often serves as a spread. In such cases, the canopy and ruffle match.

Straight Ruffled Canopy. When bed has a straight framework at the top and the fabric of the spread matches that of the canopy, make ruffling slightly

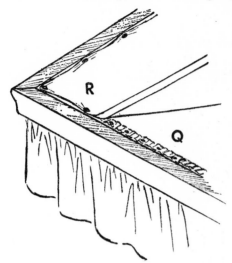

more than half the depth of the flounce used for the spread. Tack the ruffle inside the top molding, as at **Q**. Stretch a piece of fabric over the top of the canopy, covering tacks, as at **R**.

If framework is to be covered, finish and gather ruffle. Stitch twilled tape to shirring on wrong side. Use tape to tack or snap ruffle to molding. Stitching line, on right side, may be covered with a milliner's fold of fabric, ribbon, or braid. Narrow picoted ruffles, lace, beading with velvet ribbon, or ball fringe may be used as trimming.

Shaped Canopy. Some beds have a shaped canopy frame with curved top, as in **S**. For such a canopy, measure the top section from head to foot up over the rounded part, add to this the amount needed for shirring plus hem allowance for each end. Measure across the canopy from side to side and add to this enough for a heading on each side. Turn the heading on each side of top section and stitch with the machine Gatherer to required measurement. Finish ends with narrow hem. Seam together all flouncing pieces for each side, finish bottom edge as desired, using simply a hem, a ruffle, or ball fringe. A wide eyelet embroidery edging, as shown, is ideal for flouncing. Gather the top edge to fit the length of the canopy.

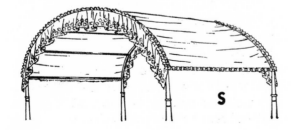

Lay heading of top section over gathered edge of flounces, pin and stitch. Attach finished canopy to framework with wood snaps or small tacks, or sew on tie tapes at intervals to tie to the framework.

Valance Canopy. (See **D** on page 236.) This type of canopy is attached along the edge of a piece of wood similar to a wide valance board. Attach board to the wall above the head of the bed with strong brackets underneath. (See *Valance Board*, page 173.) To give support, use one (centered) or two lengths (at the corners) of wire or fine chain fastened to the wall and extending to top of board, as in **T**. Wire is almost invisible when painted.

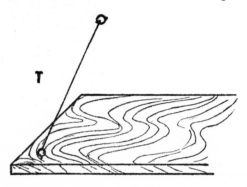

Either wires or chains may be covered with ribbon to harmonize with bed dressing. Make flounce or ruffle in any style suitable to the spread and attach as for valances. See **G**, page 186. A set of ribbons running from the back corners of the canopy to the bed corners helps to unify the bed and canopy.

Valance Canopy with Back Drape. Attach board to wall as described above. Hang the drapery beneath the board and against the wall. Make a tailored canopy to frame the head of the bed, just as you would an interlined valance. See page 186. Heavier fabrics may be used for this canopy if suitable for the bed covering.

Valance Canopy with Casing. A canopy effect can also be obtained by using a double curtain rod attached to the wall at the head of the bed. A curved or a square double rod can be used. See *Gathered Valance with Casing*, on page 188, for making valance ruffles. The under ruffle should be a few inches deeper than the outer one. The wall drape should be hung on a flat rod against the wall. This type of canopy is very shallow in depth and less permanent than the board described above, but is effective when the wall you must use for the bed has a door or window that you wish to eliminate in your decoration of your room.

Dressing Tables

DRESSING TABLES CAN BE AS VARIED IN THEIR DRESS as the women who sit before them. In fact, there is a dressing table for every type of bedroom, dressing room, or bathroom. You will see in the illustrations that follow that there are three main types. The basic principles for dressing all three are the same.

Measuring for Dressing-Table Skirt. After deciding what type of dressing-table skirt will best suit your needs, measure the length of the edges from which the skirt is to hang. Add to this the necessary allowance for pleating or shirring and for side hems. Measure the length of the skirt from top edge of table to floor. Add to this the allowance for hem at bottom and for hem or casing at top. Remember that where separate sections of the skirt meet, as at the center-front opening, the figure or pattern of the fabric, if any, should match.

Dressing-Table Top. Wherever possible, use glass or mirror for top of table, as it is easy to keep clean. Cut paper or fabric to fit table top to go under clear glass. Wallpaper to match the room paper is excellent for this. It is usually better to cover the top of the table before hanging the skirt.

Making Gathered Dressing-Table Skirt. For plain gathered skirt, hem or finish bottom edge as desired. Finish the side edges with a plain narrow hem or to match the bottom finish. Use Foot Hemmer to finish top edge. Then gather or pleat this edge with Machine Ruffler (see page 41). Stitch twilled tape to wrong side of shirring. Attach skirt to edge of table or board by tacking through the tape. An alternate way to attach skirt to table edge is to use wood snappers (see page 66).

The top edge need not be hemmed if it is to be covered, but edge should be stitched to twilled tape and tacks or wood snappers used on the tape.

A simple and practical way to finish the top of a gathered skirt is to make a narrow casing, as you would for a curtain, and run a cord through this to gather the fullness. Make knots in each end of cord, as at **A**. Put large-headed tack through knot and back edge of casing, as in **B**, and tack to dressing table, as at **C**. Tacks at center front and, if necessary, on corners will hold skirt in place. The cord may thus be removed so that skirt can be washed and ironed flat.

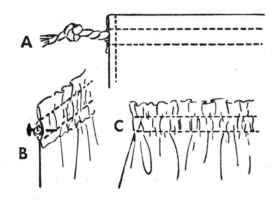

Straight Table. This type of dressing table may be treated in any one of several different ways. If it is to stand with its back against a wall, the front and two sides are covered by the skirt. If it stands in a corner, the front and one side may be all you need to cover. The styles shown suggest the variety that can be achieved with a few simple construction principles.

Usually the skirt is divided at the center front for convenience in sitting before the table. If a knee hole opening is preferred, as in **D**, the inside walls of the knee hole should be finished attrac-

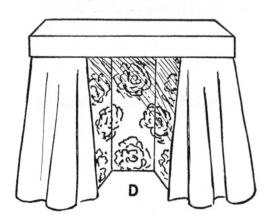

tively, since they can be seen. They may be painted or covered with wallpaper or fabric. If the table used has a drawer, make a separate skirt section to attach to the drawer, as in **E**. Then it can be opened and closed without disarranging the whole skirt.

The straight table shown in **F** is a small, unpainted kitchen table, the legs cut to a height right

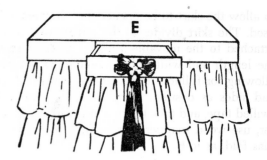

for the individual to sit at, and the top covered first with a fabric like the swag used around the edges, then covered with a glass. Make a plain skirt of taffeta or dimity with a lapped opening at the center front, the full overskirt of nylon marquisette or net. Gather the top of the net. Then stitch to twilled tape and tack in place, or use wood snappers as described on page 66. Cut a strip of bias taffeta 15″ wide and long enough to go around table. Hem both edges. Divide strip into sections. Form into swags, tack securely and cover top edge with bias fabric strips or flowers.

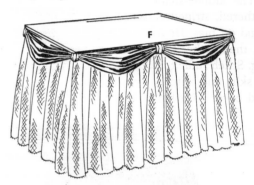

For other effects, use box-pleats or gathers all around or make a plain circular flounce, bound or faced at the bottom. Suitable fabrics would be cottons, chintzes, plain taffetas, etc. For fluffier types, sheer fabrics such as net, organdie, eyelet embroidery, etc., with an underskirt of matching color or other color under white are generally used. These may be decorated with ribbons, ruffles, flowers, tiered or draped lace—whatever appeals to you and fits in with your style of room.

Kidney-Shaped Table. Tables of this shape usually have swinging arms at each side of the front

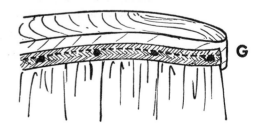

to allow the skirt to be opened and drawers to be used. The skirt divides at the center front and is attached to the movable arms, as in **G**. Measure the length and width of required skirt material, allowing for fullness and for hems. Finish bottom and sides as desired. Finish top edge, stitch to twilled tape, and tack to edge of table. If you prefer, use wood snappers (page 66). Cover with a bias fold, as in **H**.

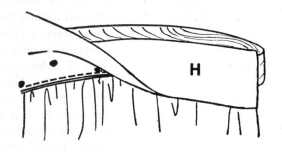

The kidney-shaped table in **I** is dressed in a gathered, striped cotton skirt. Cut ruffle and top band on bias. Hem top and bottom edges of ruffle, then gather top with Ruffler, making ½″ heading. Stitch ruffle to bottom of skirt, then gather top of skirt and stitch to twilled tape. Tack to table and cover with band finish.

Dressing-Table Shelf. Often where a mirror covers a wall or where a room is small, a shelf is made and held in position with brackets under a mirror. The shelf edge and ends may be covered by a dressing-table skirt. The method of making is the same as for a straight table. Usually fabric matching the skirt is stretched over the shelf as a top cover before the skirt is added, or a mirror top may be made to fit the shelf.

When space is at a premium, one or more shelves built into a corner can make an attractive dressing table. The front edge of the table may be either curved or straight. The skirt is measured, cut, pleated or gathered, and finished just as for any other type of dressing table. Apply skirt to edge so that there is no opening between the wall and the fabric.

Felt makes an attractive dress for the corner table. In the one shown in **J**, the skirt is circular, with pinked, scalloped border stitched to lower edge. For cutting, see *Circular Flounce*, page 211. Follow directions for making scallops at **N**, page 205. Then cut the bands of scallops with pinking shears. For the effect on the band, cut through the center of a row of scallops. Lay the straight edges along the edge of the finishing band and topstitch.

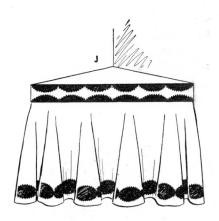

Change your colors with your moods. Put gayety where drabness dwells now with a bright, crisp, frivolous dressing table. Use embroidery, lace, ribbons, organdie, voile, ninon, taffeta, satin, plastic or quilted fabric—any lovely material that is colorful, that pleases you, and that will make for beauty in the prettiest, cheeriest spot in your room. You supply the inspiration and the plan. You do the assembling and the sewing machine will do the work.

Dressing Up Your Closets

PROTECT YOUR CLOTHES WITH CLOSET ACCESSORIES. Make such articles from new or used material or a combination of both.

Shoulder Protectors. Covers for shoulders of garments are simple to make. Cut two pieces 6″ to 10″ deep and as wide as dress hanger plus 2″. Shape top by sloping slightly and rounding off corners, as in **A**. An opening of 2½″ should be left at top for hanger to go through. Apply a 3″ strip of binding to center of one piece, as at **B**. Bind bottom edges of both pieces, as at **C**. Lay wrong sides of pieces together and stitch, leaving the 2½″ opening at center of top. Then apply binding on both sides and across top, binding only the single edge of center opening.

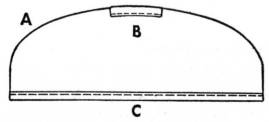

Garment Protector Bags. Separate bags are desired for some dresses. These bags are made in same way as the protectors above, usually cut as long as garment to be covered. With some evening dresses, it is practical to hang them on the hanger at the waistline. Then the protector needs to be cut the length of the skirt part. The bottom edge of the protector is bound and the bag slipped over garment, or bottom may be closed and one side left open and bound. Snap tape or slide fastener is used to close the opening.

Garment bags for storing six or more garments can be made any length desired. Buy a hanger frame of size wanted in notion department. Cut top section to fit frame, allowing ¼″ seam. The four side sections are cut to correspond to the depth and width of top. A long slide fastener opening should be made in end of bag facing closet door. Follow general instructions as given in **I** and **J** on page 198.

Dress Hangers. Decide the color and effect desired for hangers. Usually they are made in sets of 3, 6 or 12 to match other closet accessories. Cover plain inexpensive hangers by cutting two strips, one for each side of hanger, making them long enough and of a shape to fit around hanger. Cut cotton sheet padding the same size. Place this on the wrong side of the fabric; fold right side of fabric together. Stitch, making two tubes, as in **D**. Trim seams and turn right side out. Make bias tube for hook, as in **E**, and turn right side out. Slip three tubes on hanger, whip together in center, as in **F**, and cover joining with a bow, a rosette, or small flower.

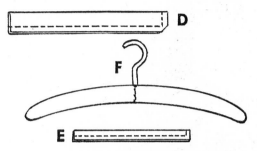

Fabric Shoe Supports (Trees).   Cut two pieces shaped as in **G**. Measurements shown, 5½″ x 6″, are for shoe of average size. Stitch seams, leaving opening in curve as at **H**. Trim, turn right side out and stuff very full with cotton, shredded tissue or crepe paper. When sewing up opening, sew in a loop of tape, ribbon or self-material.

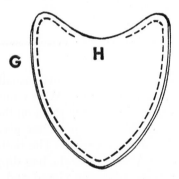

Shoe Bag.   The pocket shoe bag for wall or inside closet door may be made of any firm, durable material or of lighter-weight fabric quilted over a sturdier one. To make a holder of average size to hold four pairs of ladies' shoes, use the following measurements:

Cut back piece, as in **I**, 36″ long by 18″ wide. Cut three crosswise strips, 40″ wide and 10″ deep, and bind top edges, using machine Binder (see page 120). Measure each strip into four even sec-

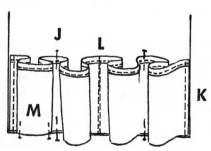

tions and mark with pins. Measure back piece into four sections lengthwise, mark with chalk. Lay one strip along bottom of back section. Match pins to chalk lines and pin, as in **J**. Stitch edges together, as at **K**, on both sides. Then stitch up and back on each dividing line, as at **L**. At lower edge, fold in a pleat on each side to take up fullness, as at **M**. After all pleats are in, stitch across bottom, as at **N**. Apply the other strips in same way, as in **O**. Cover raw edges along bottom of two upper rows of pockets with bias binding.

Finish by binding all around, as at **P**.

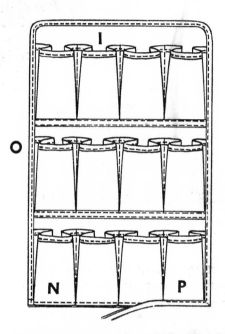

Individual Shoe Bags.   Cut a 15″ square of fabric. Bind one edge, as at **Q**. Fold bound edge in half and round off opposite corners, as at **R**. Make a 1″ loop at one end of a 25″ piece of binding. With loop at top end of bag, bind edges of cover together, as at **S**.

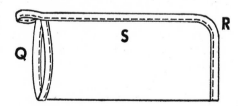

Fabric-Covered Hat Boxes.   Hat boxes can be covered to match other closet decorations. Choose a firm box of the size right for your type of hats. If box is broken in any place, repair with gummed or scotch tape. Cut fabric according to box dimensions. Measure around the box and add 1″ on length for seam. Add 2″ to depth so 1″ can be turned inside box at top and 1″ turned under at bottom. Lay ends of strip together, wrong side out, and stitch ½″ seam. Press seam open, turn right side out and slip over box. Smooth top edge down over box and glue or paste edge in place. A few paper clips or snap clothespins over edge of box will hold edges secure until it dries. See that covering is smooth before finishing bottom. Turn box bottom up. Clip edge about ¾″ deep so it will not pucker when being pasted down. Cut a piece of paper ¼″ smaller all around than bottom of box. Paste or glue this to bottom so that raw edges of fabric are covered. Set box on flat surface, put some type of weight inside and let dry for a few hours.

To cover lid, cut a section for the top with ¼″ seam allowance all around. Cut a bias strip for side, adding 1″ seam allowance on length and making it 1″ wider than depth. Seam ends together, making ½″ seam. Join top piece to bias edge with ¼″ seam. Notch seam and press toward center of top. Turn seams inside, smooth over lid turn edge to inside of box and paste in place.

A square box can be covered in a different way. Remove one side, as in **T**. Cut fabric to fit three sides, plus 1″ on all sides for turnover, as at **U**. Fasten fabric in place, using rubber cement or vegetable glue. Miter the corners, as shown, to eliminate bulk. Join side to box with a gummed cloth hinge, as at **V**, so that front side may be dropped forward to make it easier to use. Cover

this side of box, turning edges over on three sides, as at **W**. Glue the lower edge to bottom of box. If desired, line box with either plain or wallpaper, as at **X** and **Y**. The lid is covered in same way as instructed above.

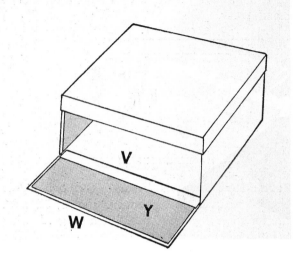

Cover a large firm suit box in a similar way for party dress or accessories.

Covered boxes can be trimmed with ruffles, braid, pleating or binding. This trimming should be stitched to covering before it is seamed and glued to box.

Shelf Edges. Decorative edgings are easily made when Singer attachments are used. For ruffles, use narrow Hemmer to finish edges, then pleat or gather with the Ruffler. (See *Ruffles*, page 43.) Use Pinker to cut narrow band trim of felt or any firm fabric. Use Binder to finish scallops for an effective trim. (See *Binding*, page 120.) Use the Edge-Stitcher for applying lace or ribbon, the Zigzagger for appliqué.

Attach edging to shelves with tacks or double-gummed tape.

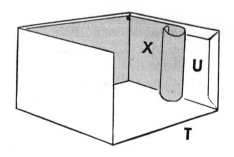

Much more consideration is given to the decoration of closets and to closet accessories nowadays than ever before. Some women have made a specialty of closet decoration, re-doing a closet completely to match room colors. Many women make beautiful boxes of fabric or paper, in sets, to use as shower gifts, bridal gifts, or for Christmas packages. Ingenuity, good workmanship and the will to succeed are the essentials for work such as this.

Dressing Your Table

Table Linens. Table cloths, mats and napkins may be made of almost any washable fabric that will lie smooth on the table. All "table linens" should be cut with the grain of the fabric so that hems and corners are true. The variety of styles and finishes is almost endless.

Sizes. Sizes of cloths and mats vary somewhat according to the width of fabric you are using. Plan to cut them so that you get the most out of your fabric. Conventional sizes are approximately as follows:

Luncheon cloths—54″ square or 54″ x 72″
Dinner cloths—60″ x 80″, 70″ x 108″, or longer
Banquet cloths
      all-over lace   72″ x 126″ or longer
      damask   72″ x 126″ or longer
      (linen and cotton damask by the yard
         available in both 60″ and 72″ width)
Bridge cloths—42″ x 42″ or 45″ x 45″ or 54″ x 54″
Breakfast cloths—range from tray or card table
         size to luncheon sizes
Mats—approximately 12″ x 18″. In rare instances
         for large tables, they are made 14″ x 20″

Napkins—range from cocktail size 5″ x 7″ to dinner size approximately 20″, 24″ or 28″ square
         Luncheon 12″ to 18″ square
         Tea sizes 11″ to 14″ square

Mats. These may be oblong, oval, round, square, or of irregular shape. Round and square mats are less practical to use than are the oblongs. Recently many attractive mats have been shown in shapes that conform to the shape of the table. For instance, a round table may be set with mats that are curved at the outer edge and tapered on the sides to a narrower straight edge toward the center of the table. If you have a table that is unusually shaped, accent it by making mats to fit.

Petticoat doilies as illustrated above, are gay and practical. In this case embroidery by the yard is gathered and French seamed to the ends of a plain piece of bleached muslin. The sides are finished with a narrow hem. On top of this ruffled mat is a plain linen mat, the edges of which can be hemmed or fringed. The top mats can go to the laundry after each using. The petticoat doilies,

225

being protected, need washing only occasionally.

The surface decoration of mats may be appliqué, hemstitching, cross-tucking—almost anything, according to the degree of formality and your own taste. The edge may be finished with a simple narrow hem, a hemstitched hem turn, fringe, lace, ruffles, contrasting facing or border. Refer to the instructions for each kind of work for details.

Illustrated below: (1) A mat shaped to fit a round table, with appliquéd print motif. (2) A place mat and napkin for a square or round table, decorated with a Fashion Stitch monogram and Singercraft fringe. (3) Crosswise bands applied to a striped fabric. Use subtle color combinations and apply with plain stitching or use the Blind-Stitch attachment.

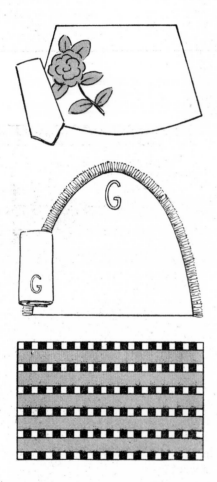

Table Cloths. Table cloths may be round, square or oblong. Round ones are attractive on a round table, but remember that they are more difficult to launder. They must be rolled around paper or cardboard rolls to prevent creasing after they are ironed. Like mats, table cloths can be made of many kinds of fabric. Formal cloths are of white linen damask or all-over lace and cover the whole table with an overhang on all sides of about 12″ to 28″. Other types of cloths for formal use may be of certain synthetic fabrics, linen and lace, or sheer fabric such as organdie with satin in appliquéd patterns and are sometimes in pastels. The damask are always hemmed, either plain or with the napery hem, formal cloths always by hand. Others are finished with deep lace border, with appliquéd shadow hem, etc.

Informal cloths—for luncheon, bridge, breakfast, supper—are made of cotton, colored linens, synthetics, in white or plain colors, stripes, prints and plaids. They vary in size considerably and have less overhang than formal cloths. They may have appliquéd motifs, surface embroidery, rick rack or braid borders, lace or eyelet trimming. Edges may be fringed, hemmed, hemstitched, faced or bordered with contrasting fabric. The Zigzagger is ideal for finishing and decorating table linens.

Napkins. Napkins, except the cocktail size, are conventionally square. Cocktail or finger napkins are usually 5″ by 7″ and are made of all types of fabrics, most often lightweight linen. Table napkins are of the same fabric as the table cloth, though not decorated to the same extent. When sheer fabric is used for the cloth, or with printed, vari-colored cloths, plain napkins are generally used. Formal damask napkins are hemmed plain or with the napery hem. Sometimes a monogram is embroidered at one end or in a corner.

Towels. It is not practical to make towels for general use. However, dainty little guest towels and tea towels can be made quite easily. Guest towels are made from lightweight linen and cotton materials, either white or in colors. They may be hemmed or hemstitched. They may be decorated with small embroidered motifs, monograms or small appliqué designs which fall on the outer fold as the towel hangs.

Yardage for tea towels can be bought in narrow widths with finished selvage on both edges. These require a narrow hem top and bottom and occasionally a loop of twilled tape is inserted in each hem for hanging. Elaborate decoration of tea towels, unless purely for ornament and not use, is not practical. Towels do not launder well if much decorated. For color, printed or bordered fabric may give the decorative effect you want.

At left. See how a monogram is worked on place mat and napkin. Use a transfer design or trace the letter you wish to use, then fill it in by machine, using the easy-to-do Bouclé Stitch.

Below. Here a wheat design, in gold and tan, on linen cloth and napkin is embroidered with the Etching Stitch, a Fashion Stitch almost as easy to do by machine as is plain stitching. Transfer or outline your design as you wish it to appear, then thread your machine and embroider with ease and speed.

Monograms

MONOGRAMS GIVE LINENS AND PERSONAL ARTICLES an individuality that can add to their value and interest. For gifts, they denote an individual attention that is flattering to the person who receives and about the one who gives. Your machine offers many possibilities for decorating and marking with initials and signatures.

In addition to the monograms shown below, attractive monograms can be made with the Fashion Stitches. See pages 113–118.

Monograms for Apparel. Fashion controls the use of such decoration completely. If you know how to use your machine well, you should be able to make many types of monograms, utilizing the Fashion Stitches without attachments, or by using the Zigzagger, Braiding Foot or Singercraft Guide.

Placing Monograms. On luncheon and breakfast cloths, place monogram about 3″ above lower hem edge and in center. On runner cloths, center monogram about 14″ to 18″ above an end hem. On damask and other formal types, be guided by fashion's dictation of location of the monogram. Sometimes it is placed where the serving platter is placed, in front of the host. Again, two monograms are used, one at each end or each side. Check with the best shops and determine what the practice is when formal cloths are to be monogrammed.

On napkins, monograms are usually smaller than on table cloths but made to match. They may be centered diagonally in the corner or centered square with the fabric grain in the right-hand corner, or centered above hem on lower edge. Fold must be planned so that monogram is up. On oblong place mats, center monogram just below upper hem. Center towel monograms ½″ to 2″ above lower hem, letters up, so that they are correctly placed when towel hangs on rack. On pillow cases and sheets, center monogram above hem—1″ to 4″ on pillow case, 2″ to 6″ on sheet.

Satin-Stitch Monogram. Good for table linens, towels, bed linen, garments. Stamp or transfer design to desired position on fabric. Place work in embroidery hoops. Remove presser foot and lower feed or cover with feed cover plate as if to darn. Use fine needle and thread. Insert hoops under presser bar, draw up bobbin thread and stitch around monogram outline. Then stitch with irregular stitches to pad surface inside outline by moving hoops back and forth under needle. Over this padding, stitch in regular rows crosswise from side to side all over monogram. Move hoops regularly and evenly for neat effect. This work takes practice, but is very effective if carefully done. You can also use the Darning and Embroidery attachment for doing the Satin Stitch.

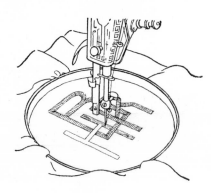

Appliquéd Monogram. Good for large initials on bedspreads, couch covers, cushions, etc. Cut initials from fabric, allowing ⅛″ on edges for turnunder. Turn this under and baste. Place initials in desired position and baste. Stitch around edges with Zigzagger, so that stitches catch alternately in initial edge and in fabric.

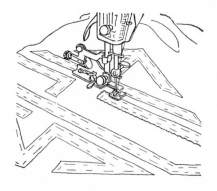

Darning-Stitch Monogram. Useful for many decorative effects in addition to monogramming. This stitch can be done without attachment, as illustration shows, or by using the Darning and Embroidery Foot. Prepare machine as for satin-stitch or for regular machine darning. Use thread suitable

Accent in Table Dress

Your dishes, your silver and location of table determine the type of linen. Gingham or denim can be used in striped effect as at right, for an informal cloth. If you eat on sun-porch or terrace, make this with napkin rolls as shown. Use 1″ cotton fringe to finish all edges of the cloth.

Runners for Convenience

Runners as shown below may be made of several types of material. Mesh, dotted swiss, dimity or nylon, banded with a plain color, fringed napkins to match banding, is ideal. Runners are especially good if your table is small and you need more places to a side than plate doilies allow for. Also decidedly practical to use for children.

Bands of Color

Use linen-like fabric as above and make inset bands of two tones of harmonizing or contrasting color. Machine-embroider the monogram on the napkins for a beautiful and individual table setting that you will use with pride.

Use Fringe, Ruffles, or Embroidery for Finish and a Flourish

The dainty femininity of the bedroom above is achieved by the use of yards and yards of snow-white ruffles on the curtains, around the pillows, and on the flounce of the bedspread. They give an air of real freshness to a room that is otherwise decorated, with its dark draperies and its sturdy tomato red slip-cover and cushions, in a practical and durable way.

Below are two ideas for transforming small tables that might otherwise lack interest. At the left, organdie panelled with embroidery and floor length gives the essence of daintiness to the tea table. At the right, dark green linen edged with deep white cotton fringe makes a striking table cover.

to weight of fabric—light for fine cottons, etc., heavy for coarser and thicker materials. Use needle suitable to weight of thread. Stamp or transfer design to fabric in desired position. Center monogram in embroidery hoops. Insert right side up under needle and presser bar; lower presser bar. Outline initial with long back-and-forth stitches on stamped line. First take long stitch backward, then a stitch forward, halfway the length of first stitch and to outside stamped line. Work back and forth to complete outline. Fill in space inside outline solidly with shorter stitches, making one row the length of the initial, the next row as close to the first as possible, and so on. Move hoops back and forward to form the stitches as the needle moves.

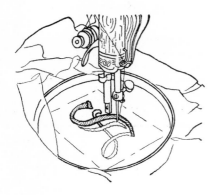

If using huck toweling, stamp monogram on sheer lawn and baste to towel. Then place stamped material taut in embroidery hoops. Proceed as instructed above.

Narrowest rickrack makes good initials and monograms. Mark the article with carbon, chalk or pencil. Stitch the narrow rickrack over the marked lines. Take care to tuck under any ends and to stitch back on them so they cannot fray.

Signature-Stitch Monogram. Makes corded outline effect appropriate for signature marking. Prepare machine as instructed on pages 113 and 114. Use No. 70 tatting cotton on top, finer thread in bobbin. Test for correctness of tension before be-

ginning work so that you get the corded effect you want. Transfer signature to fabric, place in embroidery hoops, so that it is taut, and insert under needle. Lower presser bar. Pick up bobbin thread with needle and draw it through to top. Following stamped outline, run machine at moderate speed and move hoops slowly, so that stitches pile one against another. A solid cord appears on top.

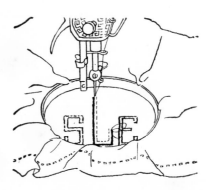

Singercraft Monogram. Good when raised or deep pile effect is wanted as on bath mat, candlewick spread, etc. Wind pearl cotton, crochet thread or carpet warp around Singercraft Guide. Stitch through slot of Guide, using short stitch. Remove Guide and, with heavy matching thread, stitch fringe to stamped line or monogram. Stitch again to make more secure. Cut loops on both sides. Trim and shape, rounding to top. If monogram is very large, fringe may be made and applied at same time.

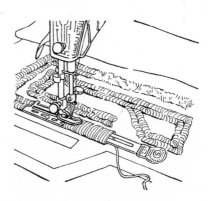

Work your linens with a monogram, or write the name or initials in the corner and then stitch over the written line, using the embroidery hoop, so that all your linens have an identifying mark. This is especially desirable for children's things, for handkerchiefs, for towels used at the beach or pool, and the like. Where there are several children, there will thus be no problem in identifying the possessions of each.

Singercraft Rugs

WOMEN WHO KNOW THE TIME-SAVING CONVENIENCE of the Singer Fashion Aids, realize how much more skill they can put into their sewing when they become expert in using these attachments. The Singercraft Guide is a very versatile tool, and in addition to making trimmings of many kinds, it serves admirably in making rugs, from the intricately patterned Oriental type to the Early American hooked and rag rugs. Only a few examples are shown here, but a skilled worker with the Guide can copy practically any rug design desired. It takes time and patience, but is enjoyable work and the results are indeed rewarding.

An instruction folder explaining the winding and placement of the Guide under the presser foot is provided with each Guide. Study it, practice with some odd lengths of knitting yarn, rug yarn and carpet rags until you are expert in winding and overlapping the rows. Then get a canvas with a design stamped on it, and begin work.

Winding Singercraft Guide. **A** shows the beginning—how to wind the colors, how to hold the Guide under the presser foot while stitching.

Modern Cotton String Rug. The original of **B** is a 36″ square of cut and uncut loops. It is made with the narrow extension, the rows placed ¼″ apart. It requires approximately six pounds of cotton string or four pounds of wool rug yarn.

Deep-Cut Pile Rug. This 44″ x 30″ rug, shown in **C**, is made of heavy rug yarn. Four pounds was required to complete it. The narrow extension on the Guide aided in placing the rows evenly ¼″ apart. The loops were cut as each row was made.

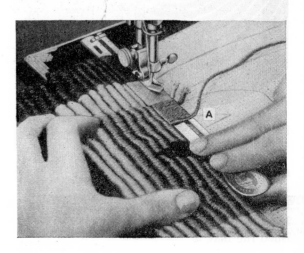

Rag Circle. This (**D**, next page), measures 35″ in diameter. The canvas or burlap should be at least 42″ square to begin the rug. Make of soft wool carpet rags of bright colors. Rags are cut or torn about ¾″ wide. They need no sewing. Simply fold the raw edges to the center and wind this under. Center is made first, then rows ¼″ apart of colors alternated around and around the circle. Measuring is important in this type of rug to keep the rows even. When the rug is finished, turn the sur-

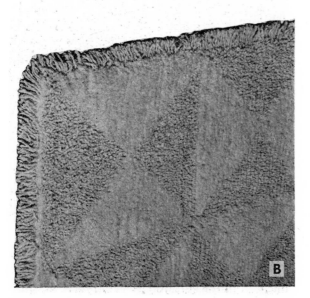

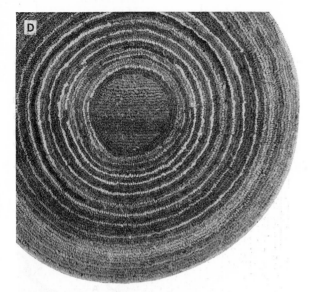

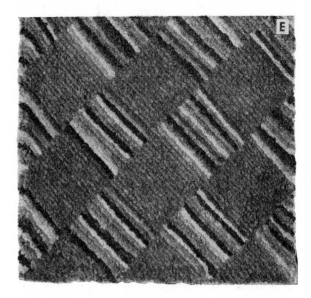

plus canvas to the wrong side, fold the fullness in at intervals, and whip the edge down.

Diagonal Multi-Stripe Rug. Make this, **E**, of wool yarn or of rags, using plain color for the monotone blocks and multi-colors for the alternate blocks. Begin at one corner. Make the rows ⅜″ apart. Finished rug may be square, oblong, or runner.

Fireplace Rug. Make **F** to measure 24″ x 34″ or 34″ x 44″. Block the design out on canvas with yardstick and pencil. First do the three blocks on each end, then work each side. If you have old draperies or upholstery fabric or old slip-covers

that you have discarded, cut these up, dye them to bright colors, if necessary, and use for making rugs; cut or tear the strips and sort into piles, so that you can reach a color quickly as you work.

Oriental Type Prayer Rug, shown in **G**, in a Singercraft rug made to duplicate, as closely as possible, in color, pile depth, and texture, a genuine Oriental. This is an ambitious undertaking, but thousands of women have enjoyed making such rugs. For detailed information regarding rug design 509 and where to get necessary yarns and designs, write to James Lees & Sons Company, 295 Fifth Avenue, New York, N. Y.

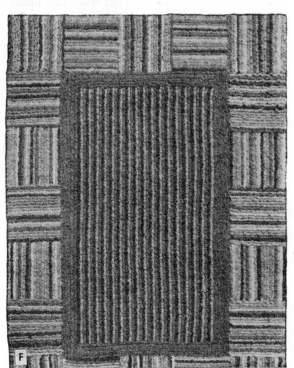

Decorators' Sketches

WINDOWS

THE GROUP OF SKETCHES THAT FOLLOWS SHOWS many types of window decoration, some suitable for formal rooms, some for period styles, some for cottage or country homes. In your selection for your own home, look for the ideas that fit your way of living, your kind of house. Remember that simplicity is always in good taste. Don't overdo the decorative effects, but strive to adapt the idea that appeals to you. No one sketch may be exactly right for your windows, but if you use your own ingenuity and taste, there should be some inspiration here that will give satisfaction. Just one variation from the usual, such as **F** or **H**, may give you a new feeling without being a radical departure from the type of curtain or drapery you prefer.

Cottage Curtains. Many like to buy ruffling by the yard, the kind that has been decorated with stitching, braid or embroidery, and stitch this in strips to a piece of plain lawn or sturdy cheesecloth to make an all-ruffled curtain, as in **A**. In doing

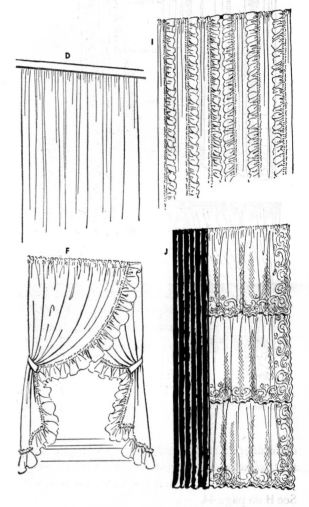

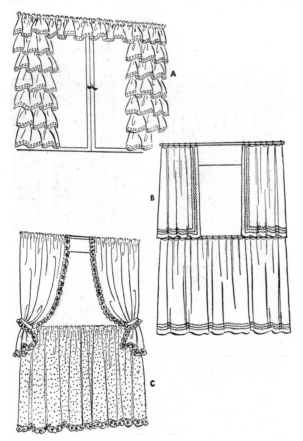

this, gauge the fullness by the ruffle itself. Overlap the ruffles just enough so that top edges of ruffles are covered. A strip of fabric can be stitched behind the gathers of the top ruffle to form a casing for the rod. See **K** on page 178. An effective variation of this idea is made with one ruffle of embroidery, one of checked gingham, then a ruffle of embroidery, another of checked gingham. See *Ruffles in Tiers* on page 44.

Marquisette or dotted swiss curtains can be trimmed along the edges with rick rack, bias binding or other braid, as in **B**, to emphasize or introduce a color in your decorative scheme. Such curtains are often finished without a casing or a heading and held in place with pin-pointed hooks.

Dotted swiss and plain organdie with embroidered ruffles, as in **C**, are favorites with many. The casing is made at the top of the curtains and the

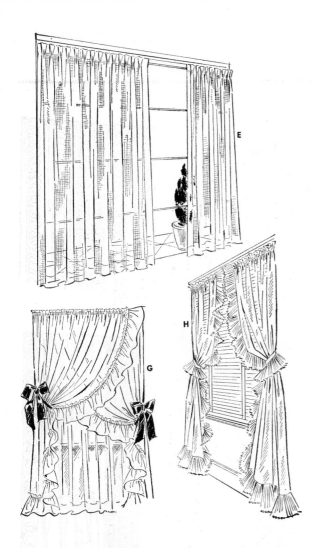

left for tiebacks to be inserted between the ruffle and the curtain. In **G**, the tiebacks are ribbon or fabric bows, matching bedspread or slip-cover. These curtains are tied back at uneven levels and have a straight sash curtain underneath to give more privacy.

Another variation on plain ruffled curtains is shown in **H**, where the ruffling is pleated. Pleated ruffles are less easy to launder than gathered ruffles, but are attractive. The tiebacks are bands edged on one side with the same pleated ruffling.

Lengthwise ruffles, as in **I**, can be used for an unusual effect. To make them, be sure to choose a fabric, such as organdie or dotted swiss, that has enough stiffness so that the ruffle will not drop down, but will stand out fairly straight. Make this ruffle by the yard; then apply it to your curtain, allowing enough width between the ruffles to get a soft draped effect.

Lace curtains are in favor at various times. In **J**, lace curtains are shown in tiers used with a drapery. Each tier is on a rod of its own and has a draw cord so that they can be pulled back separately. This is a desirable type for apartment houses, where privacy is essential. It could be used effectively on a small single window to give it more importance.

K shows how full-length windows or plain walls

embroidered ruffling added to the edges and to the tiebacks. Do not make such ruffles too full. Join them with a French seam for ease in ironing. See **H** on page 44.

An embroidered insertion can be gathered and stitched on as shown. See page 43.

Modern interiors often call for ceiling-to-floor curtains. Only a hem is necessary at the top if the curtains are hung on fixtures recessed in ceiling or covered by a narrow molding, as in **D**. Hems are made the same width at top and bottom so that, as the curtains are washed and used, they can be reversed on the poles, thus distributing the wear.

In **E**, ceiling-to-floor curtains are finished at top with pinch pleats. Hung on traverse rods, they can be opened or closed as desired.

Even simple ruffled curtains can have variations in handling that add interest to your windows.

For instance, the two curtains can be made wide enough to be draped across each other, as in **F** and **G**. The tiebacks can be arranged to give an additional touch of originality. In **F**, a finished slot is

diagonally and finished with a slip-stitched or rolled hem.

A valance effect can be obtained with strip draped on a separate rod or pole, as in **O**. The drape should be worked out in muslin before cutting into actual fabric. Each window has to be draped individually and drapery held in place with pins, tacks or stitches.

BEDS

THE VARIETY OF BED COVERINGS ILLUSTRATED HERE IS offered to show you that your own ingenuity and taste can be utilized to make interesting and suitable types for any style of room or house and any individual preference. When simplicity is the keynote or when you want a tailored effect for a masculine room, one of the styles such as **P**, **Q**, **W**, **X**, or **Y** would be a good choice. For a more feminine bedroom, **R**, **S**, **T**, **U**, **A** or **D** should provide a happy solution.

For instruction on making such a tufted design as is shown in **P**, see page 208.

In **Q**, a fitted spread is accented attractively with braiding, for which see page 131.

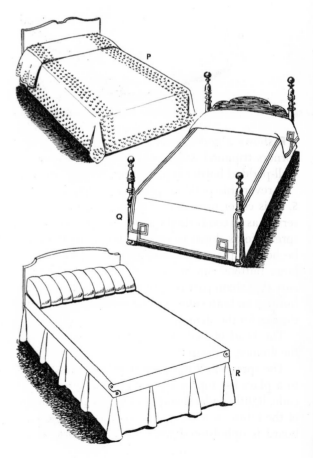

may be fabric-covered with sheer curtain material with a drapery fabric providing a finish at either end. Such curtains may begin flush with ceiling and extend from wall to wall.

Drapery only is used in **L** over Venetian blinds.

Draperies in modern houses follow the same construction principles as the curtains mentioned previously.

Your valance can be the point of interest in your windows if the style of curtains and draperies is not in itself too decorative.

Scallop the top edge of a quilted valance, as in **M**, keeping the bottom straight. Quilt the tiebacks to match the valance.

A draped effect, as in **N**, which might appear heavy for a single window, might be very effective where two windows are dressed to make a single unit. Make a plain interlined valance. See **A** on page 186. Mark placement of holes, spacing them according to length of valance. These can be faced, or bound with bias fold. Stitch facing or binding to right side of valance, turn to wrong side and whip securely. A straight or bias strip is drawn through the holes and draped. The ends of strip are cut

234

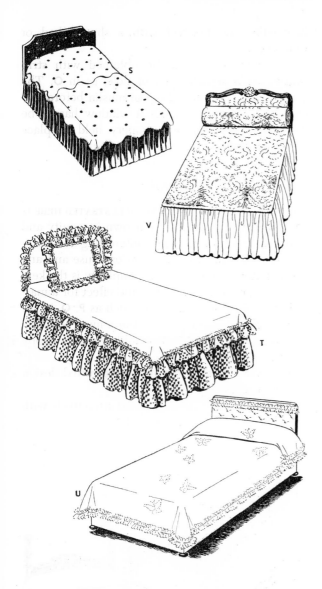

overspread and a matching bolster completes the picture.

A slip-cover edged with a ruffle covers the headboard in **T**. A full ruffle is attached to box spring, extending to the floor. The spread is flat with a ruffled edge. The pillow cover is made as in **A** on page 212 with a ruffle added around edge.

The dainty spread in **U** is made of a sheer fabric with applied motifs and a center-stitched ruffle on edge. Cut out printed motifs or make a paper pattern and cut from plain fabric. These motifs can be appliquéd to wrong or right side of cover, depending on effect desired. See 128 and 129 for appliqué details.

A plain-colored box spread has to be used under this type of cover to serve as lining for the sheer fabric. A cuff with matching ruffle can be made for top of headboard, as shown.

The change in living habits and need for conservation of space make day beds increasingly important. When a bed has to serve as a sofa or lounge, the boxed cover is practical. **W** is the sim-

R shows a godet flounce with a boxed top and corners trimmed with buttons and buttonholes. A well-padded bolster is made of matching fabric.

A reversible padded spread does double duty in **S**. This cover dresses the bed during the day and serves as a comfortable at night. The top of the spread folds down to cover pillows. Padding can be held in place by tying, as in **I** on page 204, or large buttons can be sewed or tied on. To make sure that sham part is right side up on the bed, use buttons on both sides for that method, and reverse the ties for the sham part.

The head of bed can be slip-covered to match the flounce, if desired.

The spread in **V** has a gathered flounce attached to a plain flat top. A separate over-spread of brocade, lightly padded and quilted around the motifs of the fabric, is used over the plain top. The headboard is upholstered with the same fabric as the

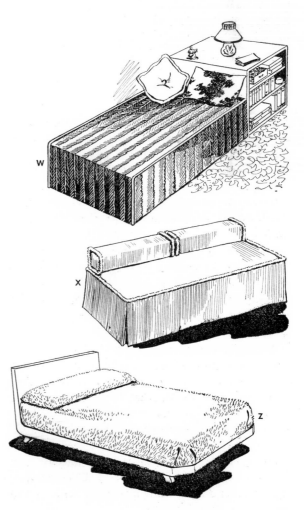

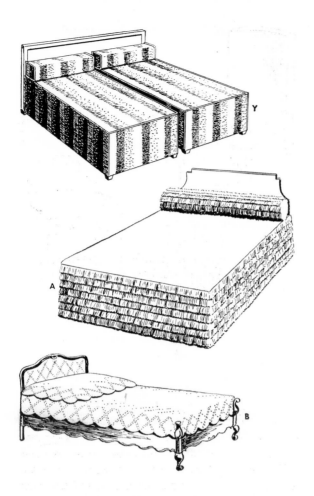

keeping each row of fringe in line. Allow the rows to overlap just enough to cover the stitching line. Stitch fringe to fabric of bolster before joining edges. Finish as shown on page 213.

A French Provincial type of bed, as in **B**, often has its headboard covered with quilted fabric to match the spread and pillow sham. If you have a favorite fabric that you wish to use, you can do this quilting by hand or machine. Use a piece of the quilting for the headboard and tack this in place with matching guimpe braid for a neat professional-looking job. See page 123 for scallops, and for block quilting, see page 132.

The softly pleated headboard shown in **C** has padding underneath. The fabric is pleated and seams concealed in the folds before being tacked in place. The edges are covered as in **H** on page 216. The spread has a plain top and a very full flounce which is made long enough to lie on the floor for 3 to 6 inches. This type of spread allows a rich fabric to show its full loveliness.

An Early American type of four poster is shown in **D**. To suit the period of the bed, a printed chintz

plest type, with cording along both sides. This arrangement is excellent for a room which is used as a sitting room as well as for sleeping. The back and one end need not be covered, because they are hidden.

In **X** an inverted pleat is used at each corner and moss fringe is used as trim around the top. Twin bolsters are covered to match and used alongside, when bed stands against a wall.

Twin beds can be attractively covered with identical box spreads. **Y** shows two covers with a single headboard. When the beds are placed together without space between, a single spread can cover both beds. For square bolsters of the type shown here, see page 212.

Z shows a plain straight spread tucked in at the corners on a modern bed. It gains interest from the texture of the fabric, which is long-napped to give a furry appearance.

For the fringed spread and bolster, shown in **A**, any plain-colored firm fabric 54″ or more wide is suitable. Make a crosswise band of muslin as a base for the fringed overhang, and stitch the rows of fringe in position, using a ruler to guide you in

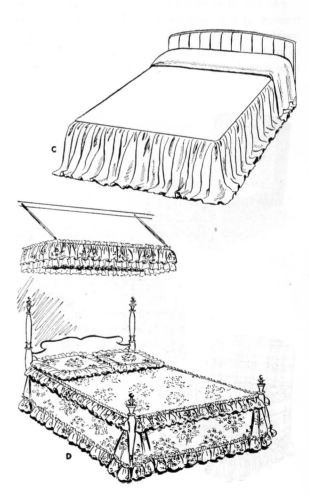

is used for the spread, with ruffles around the top and at the bottom of the overhang. Directions for making a ruffled sham such as the one shown are given on page 212. Note that the overhang, instead of being straight, has a circular godet added to the end of each section to fall in attractive fullness at each side of the bedposts. See page 218 for instructions on making the type of canopy illustrated. This has two ruffles, the under one plain white, the over one of the same printed fabric as the spread.

CHAIRS

NOWADAYS MORE AND MORE WOMEN ARE FINDING IT practical to make slip-covers for plain straight-back or side chairs, because of the ease of cleaning such slip-covers, because color combinations and fabric textures in a room can be so easily varied in this way and because of the protection afforded the original material.

The slip-cover in **E** is made exactly as instructed on page 200 with one exception: a boxing strip is used not only around the seat, but also on the sides and top of the back.

For the bow effect shown in **F**, make a 2″ extension at the back edge of the seat to make an overhang. Extend boxing strip at the back enough to make the bow as large as desired. When the bow is tied, the overhang is held in place.

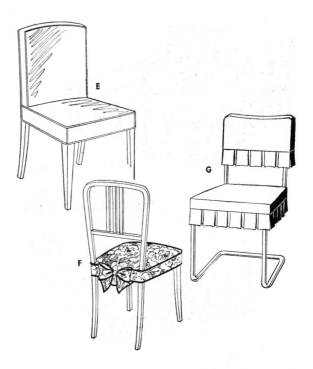

Even tubular metal chairs can be slip-covered, as in **G**. Make seat cover and cuff for back separately. Add the box-pleated flounce for interest.

The slipper chair in **H** is covered with brocade and, instead of having a flounce, is finished with deep fringe extending to the floor.

Plaid velvet or velveteen makes the slip-cover for the small armchair in **I**, with a plain-colored cushion and flounce of the same type of fabric. This cover gives a feminine feeling, suitable for a small chair.

In **J** a club chair is covered with a sturdy heavy tweed type of fabric to give a tailored, masculine effect. The plain flounce has inverted pleats at the corners for ease in slipping cover on chair.

The following chairs all offer special fitting problems and should be undertaken only after you have had some experience in making slip-covers and upholstering. In each case, follow seam-lines of the chair itself. Fit each section carefully.

K shows a small barrel-back chair with a button-tufted cushion, covered with a combination of plain and printed chintz. Cover the cushion as shown on page 213. Use self-covered buttons or regular upholsterer's buttons, heavy carpet thread and very long needle. Follow instructions as on page 217 for tufting. The inside back presents a problem in that ample fabric must be allowed for tuck-ins all the way across. Joining seams should be placed to fall inside a tuck-in. The outside back should have its joining in the center with a slide fastener to allow removing it. The flounce, of course, is applied in the usual way.

The round-backed wing chair in **L** is covered with brocade and finished at the bottom with ball fringe. Cover the cushion in the ordinary way. Leave an opening at center back for removing cover. The cover may be held in place by an underneath finish as described on page 198.

The striking print cover of the modern chair in **M** may also need to be tacked in place on the underside. The back may either have one side left open, then slip-stitched in place after being put on the chair, or if the curve of the back is not too shallow, a center-back opening will allow cover to be removed.

The one-armed modern chair in **N** is covered with a bold print and has corded seams. It is an ordinary slip-covering job with no variation except the omission of the one arm.

The arm chair in **O** may be either slip-covered or upholstered, as preferred. It is dressed here in a combination of plain and striped fabric, and edged with tassel fringe. If the cover is to be removable, leave an opening at one side back or center-back.

Fabric covering for chairs and couches becomes increasingly important as more houses are dressed in modern furniture or, as we see so often, when modern and traditional are used together. A woman who wants to be her own decorator should learn to slip-cover a chair or to upholster it with her husband's or neighbor's help, and do it with as much skill and pride as she would experience in making a becoming dress.

MENDING IS A TERM THAT COVERS ALL SORTS OF FAB-
ric repairs—replacing broken stitches, reinforcing
places that have worn thin, filling in holes, joining
tears, all the little jobs that prolong the life of
worn, but still valuable articles. Your machine can
save you much time and effort in mending; use it
to darn, patch, reinforce and restitch, and see how
it speeds the task and restores the fabric.

Threads and Needles. A fine needle is usually
best for fine mending. Thread should match the
fabric as nearly as possible in color and weight.
Two-toned fabrics, such as woolen tweed, may be
mended almost invisibly by using dominating
color in needle and secondary color in bobbin.
Warp threads of a fabric may often be used to
darn small holes by hand. For a fine stocking darn,
separate the strands of darning thread and use
only one or two strands in a crewel needle.

Machine Darning. Use the Singer Darning and
Embroidery attachment and cover the feed with
the special plate **A2**. After removing presser foot,
attach the Darning Attachment by fitting it into
place at the right of presser bar with lifting finger
A above needle clamp, fastening securely by tightening thumb screw **A1**, at the left. See the attachment instruction book for complete directions. Use
the Darner for stockings and the Flat Darner or
embroidery hoops for linens, towels, etc., so that
the place to be darned is held taut as you stitch.

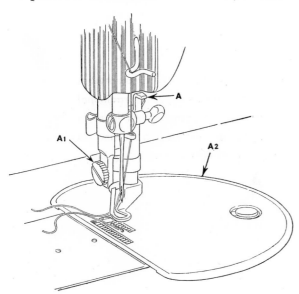

Flat Darning. Trim away frayed edges around
hole. Center hole in darner frame or in embroidery hoops, right side up, as in **B**, and place under
needle. Turn balance wheel slowly by hand, hold
upper thread and pull up under thread. Take several stitches until threads are securely locked; then
cut off loose ends. Hold frame with both hands
and move it in time to the needle. First stitch
three times around hole about ⅛" from edge. Then
stitch back and forth across the hole from one side
to the other, covering the whole opening with
stitches running to the outline stitching. Complete

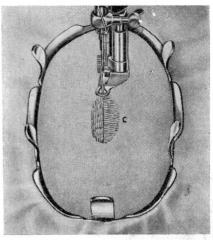

B

the stitching in one direction; then turn frame so
as to stitch across at right angles to first darning,
as at **C**. Cover hole from edge to edge within the
outline as before. Thread should be strong, but
not so heavy as to pull away from thin or weak-
ened fabric around hole; fine mercerized cotton is
usually satisfactory for linen darns. If fabric is
sheer, looser texture of darn can be made by moving hoop enough to make long stitch; for heavy,
closely woven fabric, move hoop less so as to make
short stitch. This type of darn is good for towels,

D

sheets, table linens. A cigarette burn is mended
almost invisibly on damask if fine thread is used,
as in **D**.

Darning Stockings by Machine. Put the stocking on the Darner in this way: Run your hand inside the stocking to the place where the darn is to be made. Grasp the frame of the darner with the hand inside the stocking, as in **E**, and turn the

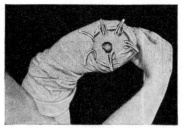

E

stocking inside out over your hand, rolling the excess length softly under the anchoring hooks. Turn over and apply the Darner spring, as in **F**. Bring

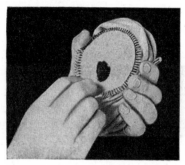

F

hooks to position, as in **G**. The right side of the stocking should be inside the Darner, with the hole to be darned in the direct center, as in **H**.

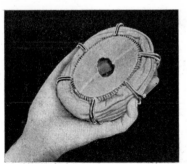

G

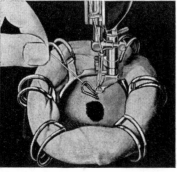

H

Ease edges of hole gently toward each other so that grain of stocking is straight up and down and across. Using darning cotton, run line of stitching around edge of hole. Trim edges away. Then, as for flat darning, stitch back and forth in one direction across hole inside outline, as in **I**. Try to make stitchings connect chain lines of stocking. Turn and stitch back and forth the other way across darn to complete, as in **J**.

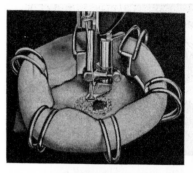

I

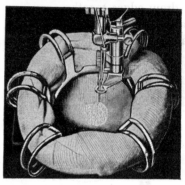

J

Darning by Hand. With small running-stitches, begin about ¼″ from edge of hole and work across to a few stitches beyond opposite side, laying thread over opening in parallel lines until hole is filled. Then turn and work across these threads, weaving alternately over and under in parallel

K

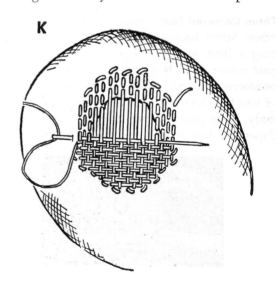

rows until fabric is replaced, as in **K**. For stockings, work over darning ball so that darning threads are not drawn so tight as to pucker edges of darn.

Straight Tear. Stitch back and forth across the tear, as in **L**, making about five stitches on either side and beyond each end. If tear is long or on

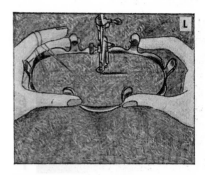

bias, draw edges together first by hand, as in **M**, or baste over paper to prevent slipping. Tear paper away when stitching is complete.

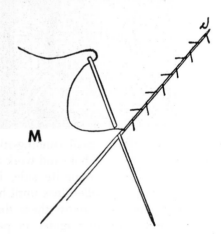

Three-Cornered Tear. Smooth edges toward each other. Stitch back and forth across edges, beginning a little outside one end and going slightly past corner, as in **N**. Cross stitchings at corner for reinforcement and continue stitching across edges of tear to a little beyond other end. If fabric lacks body, baste paper to wrong side before mending. Paper will tear away from under stitches.

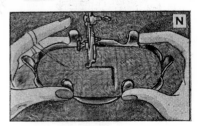

Stocking Runs. To mend by machine: Turn stocking inside out and fold along run. Pin edges along run, placing pins at right angles to the fold and spaced an inch or so apart. Make machine-stitch very short and use mercerized sewing thread of correct color. Begin stitching about 2″ above beginning of run, slanting the seam gradually in from edge to take in full depth of run. Stretch stocking slightly as you stitch to allow sufficient "give" in seam. Stitch down alongside run and taper seam off to edge about 2″ below end of run. Sometimes using paper under the seam helps to make a truer stitching line.

To mend by hand: From right side, whip edges together with small close stitches. Stretch lengthwise to prevent drawing seam.

Patching. When a hole is large, use a patch instead of trying to fill in with darning. Use fabric of the same piece if possible. Cut a patch piece from a facing, under a collar, or some place where it will not show. Patch this place with any similar fabric and use the piece for the part that shows. If there is no piece of the same fabric available, match the color, weight and texture as nearly as possible. Trim away ragged edges around the hole, cutting a square opening exactly along the fabric threads.

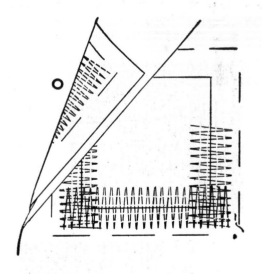

Darned Patch. Cut patch about 1″ larger than hole. Baste under hole, matching grain of patch to garment. Darn on right side, stitching back and forth across each edge of patch, running about five stitches beyond on each side, turning and crossing stitchings at corners, as at **O**. Remove bastings. Trim off edges of patch close to stitching on wrong side.

Inserted Patch. Good for heavy fabrics because it eliminates extra bulk. Cut patch to fit squared hole exactly and to match grain of fabric. Place patch in hole, as in **P**. Cut a square of old net, cheese-cloth, or curtain mesh about 1″ larger than the patch and baste under it on wrong side. Thread machine with thread matching color of fabric. Darn on right side as for darned patch. When stitching is finished, trim off edges of mesh and pull out threads of mesh under stitching if desired.

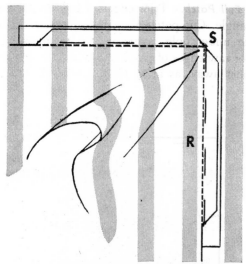

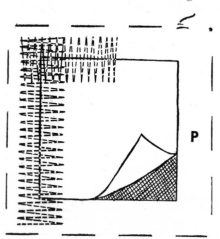

Tailored Patch. Prepare hole by clipping diagonally at each corner, as at **Q**, turning edges to wrong side and pressing. Cut patch about 1″

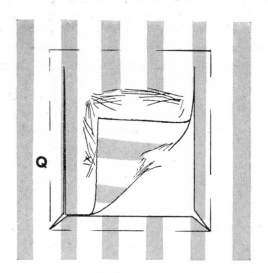

larger than hole, matching fabric grain to that of garment. Lay patch under hole and, from wrong side, baste it along pressed crease. Take a small back-stitch at each corner to hold in place while stitching. Then stitch along basted line on all four edges of hole, as in **R**. Make a few small overhanding stitches at each corner for security, as at **S**. Trim edges of patch to width of turned-back edges

of hole. In wool, catch-stitch down on wrong side, as in **T**, making sure stitches do not go all the way

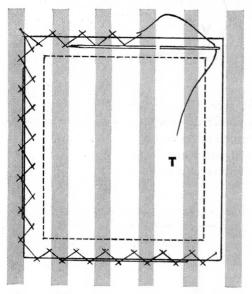

through to right side. In cotton, overcast edges. The right side of patch should appear as in **U**.

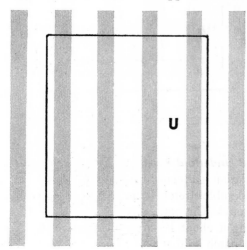

Flat Fell Patch. Trim edges of hole to square or rectangle. Cut patch about 1½″ larger than hole. Place under hole, matching fabric grains. Turn under raw edges of patch and baste flat, trimming corners away, as at **V**, to prevent bulk. Turn to

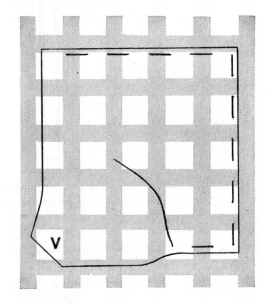

right side. Clip corners of hole diagonally and turn under raw edges, as in **W**. Baste. Stitch close to turned edges on both sides. If finished by hand, turned edges are hemmed on both sides. This is also known as a *hemmed patch*.

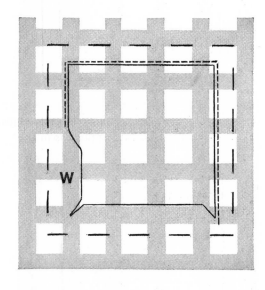

Round Underlaid Patch. Good for knit-wear and foundation garments made of material that has considerable stretch. Trim ragged edges of hole to form circle. Cut patch piece of same type of fabric, making it about 1″ larger in diameter than hole. Place patch so that knit ribs match those in gar-

ment. Baste in place, as in **X**. Catch-stitch edge of hole to patch, using strong thread and small stitches. Turn to wrong side and catch-stitch around edge of patch, as in **Y**.

Decorative Patches. Sometimes patches can be made to seem a decorative feature of a garment rather than a mend. On a blouse, for instance, use an appliqué motif or series of motifs to cover holes, placing with care so as to give impression that design was planned purposely. Finish with decorative stitches, if desired, to carry out design. On tailored garments, sometimes applied bands may be used to hide holes or tears. Plan and apply these also so that they carry out a decorative line. Even if only one is needed, say on one half of a skirt front, apply a matching one opposite to give the planned appearance. Hobo patches, panels, borders—all may be used to do the work of patches without betraying that they are really mends.

Reinforcing. Fabrics that have not torn or broken through but simply worn thin can be reinforced by backing with another piece of fabric. For elbow reinforcement, use a fabric with some "give" for reinforcing piece, so that elbow movement will not be restricted. Chiffon, net or sheer stocking piece will serve well for wool dress. Nylon stockings no longer wearable make excellent reinforcement pieces, especially under the knees of trousers or elbows that have worn thin. Heavier fabric may be needed for heavy garments. Place piece over all of thin spot on wrong side and pin. Make a

243

small running-stitch around edge of patch, as in **Z**. Start with a few back-stitches, then take tiny stitches through both fabrics so that those on right side barely show, while those on wrong side are ⅛″ to ¼″ long. Keep stitches in rows lengthwise on fabric, spacing rows about ¼″ apart, until reinforcing piece is securely fastened under whole thin area, as at **A**. If necessary, make a few rows of stitches in opposite direction for extra body. Press.

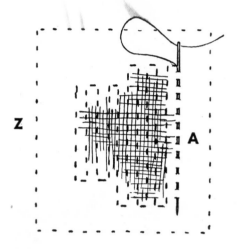

Terry Darn. Torn edges of towels, wash cloths, etc., can be repaired by placing a piece of paper

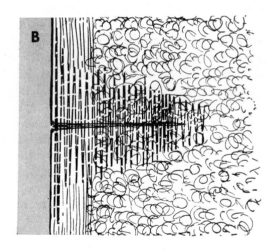

under the tear, drawing edges together and stitching back and forth across them and through paper, as in **B**. Pull paper away when edges have been securely joined all along tear. If edge is frayed, turn back once and stitch with heavy thread.

Scallop Darn. Embroidered scallops on linens, garments and other articles often tear at the join-

ings of scallops, as in **C**. To mend, hold edges of tear together and stitch across, back and forth,

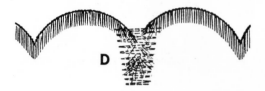

until edges are securely joined from edge to end, as in **D**. Turn and stitch back and forth at right angles to first stitchings, as in **E**.

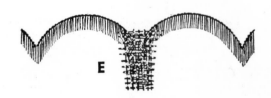

Mending Hemstitched Bed Linen. Sheets and pillow cases with hemstitched hems often break along hemstitched line. The simplest way to make them strong again is to tear off hem, lap it a little over edge, pinning at intervals crosswise of the joining, and stitch in position.

Never were there more apt words assembled in a sentence than "A stitch in time saves nine." Do take stitches where needed in a slit in a garment, a break in a seam, or a torn place in a piece of linen. Mend promptly and with skill, and be proud of the mend. Your mending will not only save you money but will protect good merchandise—rightfully a responsibility of every homemaker everywhere.

Pink and Gray Go Modern

This is another room that shows a modern feeling without starkness. The paint of walls and woodwork is perfectly matched in the fabric. The dusty pink spreads, dressing-table skirt and stools are made of a soft spongy fabric which looks velvety and luxurious, but is appropriate for any season or climate. A similar fabric in gray is used for the tufted side and head of the bed and the under flounce with its inverted pleats. The decoration is ideal for a guest room.

Courtesy of *The American Home*

Courtesy Bigelow-Sanford Carpet Company

Victorian-Inspired Bedroom

This room sets off bright-colored fabrics against the sheer whiteness of ruffled curtains and the white tracery of the Victorian dresser stool and iron bedstead. Dark green makes the gathered flounce for the dresser, the straight, block-quilted overspread, the draped valance, and the padded stool seat. A bright plaid is used for the full gathered flounce of the bed dress and the tie-backs. The wall-to-wall carpet of red gives the warmth and cosiness characteristic of the period.

Courtesy Bigelow-Sanford Carpet Company

Organdie with Gingham

A girl's room can be made gay and dainty with a combination of organdie and plaid gingham. The plaid peeps out like a petticoat from under the ruffled flounces of the bedspread and dressing-table skirt, gives a crisp accent to the edge of spread and bolster cover, and is as perky as an old-fashioned hair-ribbon where it serves as a tie-back. The green and red of the plaid are repeated again in the slip-cover and the flowered carpet.

When You Live in One Room

Many remodeled houses and even new apartments are being designed for economy of space with such arrangements as this with the bathroom and closet-dressing-room off one end. They require decoration which is appropriate for sleeping, working, eating or relaxing. Imagination can have full play in such quarters. Think what fun you can have in covering an old piano or organ stool for the dressing table, of redoing old, out-of-fashion chairs, to make them charmingly new. To dress up your bed so that it belongs in your living room, buy quilting by the yard and make a spread of the type shown here. Choose your colors to delight the eye and carry them over into any small cubbyholes apparent from the main room. Make a unified picture with fabric, paint, linoleum or rugs. Your sewing machine will help to simplify the job of making curtains, draperies, bed covering, pillow rolls and other fabric furnishings.

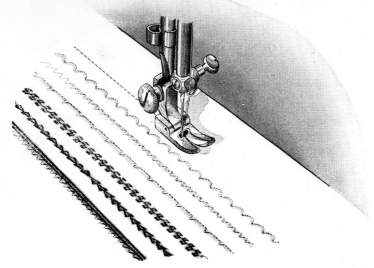

Zigzag Machine Stitching

THOSE WHO OWN A SINGER ZIGZAG MACHINE ARE IN great good fortune, because such a machine not only does plain stitching but it embroiders, monograms, decorates with motifs and borders, trims hems and edges, sews on buttons, makes buttonholes and eyelets, does applique, finishes both seams and hems, blind-stitches, darns and mends, and does a great number of exciting as well as practical kinds of sewing, perfectly and quickly.

The Singer Zigzag Machine is an example of modern engineering wizardry. With it you will have at your finger-tips the magic for the making of beautifully decorated apparel and articles of very real value for your home—and at the same time, without fuss or bother, you have a machine eminently excellent for all regular sewing work. These machines have almost unlimited possibilities in sewing, from beautiful straight stitches to magical embroidery. In addition, they provide the practical time-saving seam and hem finishing and mending that any home-maker has to do. Imagine having a machine than can do all your every-day, every-week sewing chores and yet give you, by the setting of a stitch or the placement of a simple

plastic disc, exquisite decorative design—and all in a fraction of the time handwork requires.

Two Needles. The "twin" needles provided with your machine allow you to do beautiful double stitching, using two different-color threads, if desired. Examples are shown at lower left.

Presser Foot Types. There are several different presser feet, as well as attachments, as you will see in your machine instruction book. Each of these is to aid you in doing good and varied work.

Automatic Stitch Patterns. Decorative designs as well as practical multiple-stitch zigzagging, blind-stitching and scalloping, can be done easily and without any special skill with the Singer "Automatic" Zigzag Machine.

Select the disc pattern and simply set the width and length of the stitch to obtain the desired effect. We show a variety of these stitch patterns here.

Decorative designs need not be limited to those done automatically, however, for the possibilities of creative design are endless.

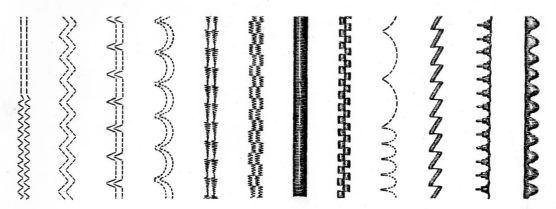

Zigzag Machine Seams and Finishes

IMAGE THE CONVENIENCE OF A MACHINE THAT does straight stitching in any amount you need to do, yet has the advantage of being able to finish edges—overcast them, if you please—even turning and overcasting, if you want. You can bind fabrics that fray easily, stitch and finish seams in any weight of fabric from coatings to gossamer nets and laces, all on your Zigzag Machine.

Seams in Jersey and Tricot. (**A**) Such fabrics are ever so simple to stitch and finish with the Zigzag Machine. One need not stretch such a seam when stitching it, as the stretch needed is provided by the zigzag stitch. The pliancy and elastic quality of the seam coincides with the same qualities in the fabric and assures against seams breaking.

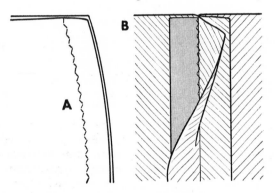

Stayed Seams in Jersey. (**B**) Often, bias seams are used in garments made of jersey. Stay such with seam binding placed along the seamline. Use a small zigzag stitch and catch one edge of binding into the seam as you stitch. Press seam open, or press seam to one side, binding to the other.

Chiffons, Georgettes, Sheers of All Kinds. (**C**) Sheers, especially the synthetics, are so easy to finish with zigzag. You simply straight-stitch on the fitted seamline, then put a row of small zigzag stitches just outside this line. Trim close.

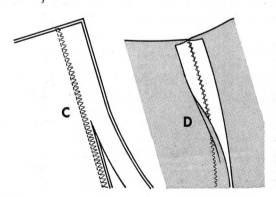

Stayed Curved Underarm Seams in Velvet or Jersey. (**D**) Nylon or rayon velvet that frays easily, as well as jersey, may have the body seams stitched, then the seam steamed or pressed open and a medium zigzag stitch applied over the first seaming. This gives a sturdy non-fray seam.

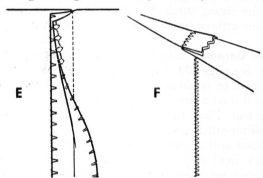

Seam Finishing. (**E**) A zigzag stitch makes an ideal finish for both raw edges of a pressed open seam or to hold two edges together. The blind-stitch can also be used to advantage as illustrated.

Lingerie Seam. (**F**) Generally used in satin, crepe or taffeta slips where a bias flat rip-proof seam is needed. From wrong side, straight-stitch seamline. Press both edges to one side. From right side, use fine zigzag stitch to top-stitch seam.

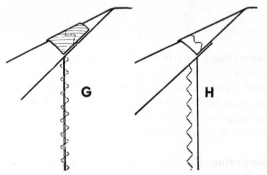

Interfacings and Interlinings. Darts and seams in interfacings can be lapped or butted over bias muslin and zigzagged together (**G**). The zigzag or multiple-stitch disc can be used when interfacing an undercollar, as shown on page 107. Interlining seams can simply be lapped, then held securely and pliantly with these stitches (**H**).

Lace Seams and Edges. Perhaps no other medium stitches and finishes laces as does the Zigzag Machine. See lace finishes, pages 129 to 131. Use your Zigzag Machine for seams and edges as shown there.

WHEN YOU MEND, MATCH YOUR THREAD COLOR TO the article to be mended. Fine thread works best and the multiple zigzag stitches provided by this machine give you the needed strength in the mend. The use of the multiple-stitch disc has the further advantage of giving additional elasticity to the zigzag stitch. Its capacity to stretch under strain without breaking is a real safeguard.

Hole Darning. Can be done with straight stitching. See page 239. For zigzag darning, take a piece of lawn or organdie to match in color if possible. Cut this on a true bias ½″ larger on all edges than the tear. Place this on the cloth, then using the multiple-stitch disc or a small zigzag stitch, darn around and around or back and forth across the patch until it is completely covered. This patch is good for holes in girdles. (See **A**.) The bias fabric makes a pliant stay that harmonizes with the zigzag stitching and prevents a tight, packed look.

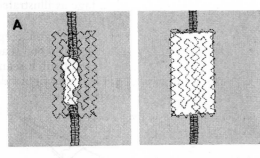

Camouflage Reinforcing. This is done in a way similar to *Hole Darning*, with or without the applied patch. Use zigzag or multiple zigzag stitching, in a size for the fabric, and work in line with the heaviest thread in your fabric warp or woof, so that the darn is as nearly invisible as possible.

Restitching Garters. (**B**) Often garters tear off girdles and foundations. To replace, use the zigzag stitch with width and length right for the texture of the garment. Restitch any broken seams or edges. Here again the elasticity in the stitch is

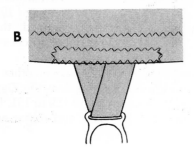

a protection against breaking and provides a good finish. The method of refastening garters is used also for shoulder straps on slips and bras.

Reinforcing Torn Pockets. (**C**) Many work aprons, smocks and blue jeans have large patch pockets, and frequently they catch and tear. Place a patch of fabric over or under the tear, allowing for seams. Bring edges together neatly. Stay edges with multiple zigzag stitching, bring the pocket back to position and restitch to place. Bar tack the corner.

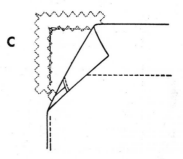

Sturdy Patches. Frequently patches, decorative or practical, are applied to elbows, knees and seats, especially of boys' corduroys and jeans. Such patches are made secure and edges well finished when zigzag stitches are used with one or two rows around the edges of the patch.

Bath Towels that Fray on the Outside Edges. Simply stitch along frayed edges, using a wide zigzag stitch. If there are tears in the towel, this will hold the torn edges together. Make secure by going over this with a smaller stitch, to darn the tear and make it strong.

Broken Hemstitching. Place the hemstitched line under the presser foot and use a medium stitch with the automatic blind-stitch disc and rejoin the edges. If edge of pillow cases and sheets are worn, secure them with zigzag stitching.

Buttonholes can be redone, ends made new. *Glove seams* can be resewn. *Runs in jersey or tricot* can be seamed with narrowest zigzag stitch and the run stopped. Zigzag is ideal for repairing torn inside pockets. As you do mending, experiment. Find a stitch combination just right for the fabric you need to mend, stay, or reinforce.

Pages 239 to 244 give instructions for mending. Practically all may be nicely done on the Zigzag Machine.

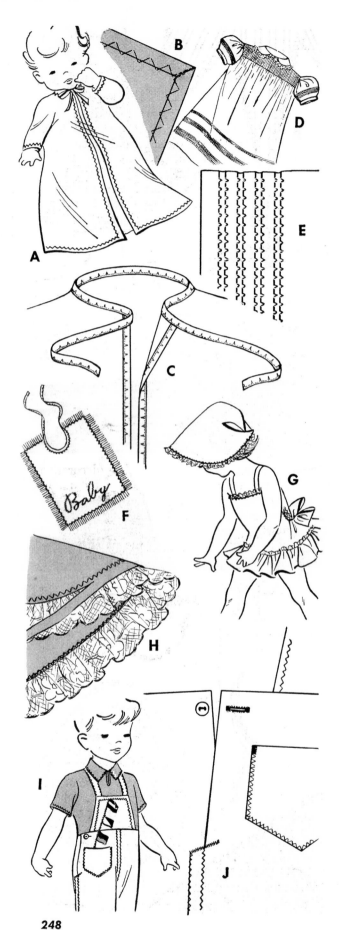

Zigzag Machine Stitching-

LITTLE TOTS' CLOTHING, WASHED SO FREQUENTLY, rinsed so completely, take a beating tub-wise. Just one reason why zigzag stitching is a boon for such garments. Every raw edge can be securely protected and strengthened, trimming stitched in like hand-embroidery rather than applied. All parts of a garment, from buttonholes and buttons to frilly edges, can be given endurance with this machine.

Baby Wrapper. (**A**) Make of lightweight wool or cotton flannel. All inside seams finished, outside edges either turned hem-fashion and held with zigzag or decorative stitching (**B**) or bound with washable ribbon (**C**)—every stitch, in fact, done on your Zigzag Machine.

Infant's Dress, Twin-Needle Stitching. The dress (**D**) is decorated with tucks formed with two-needle stitching (**E**). See pages 159–161 for ideas and details for infants' clothes.

Baby Bib. (**F**) This has the top of the fringed edges and neck binding held to place with small zigzag stitch, the word Baby in Script Stitch. All done easily yet with a sturdiness that the daintiness almost contradicts.

Play Suit and Bonnet. (**G**) Every stitch done with zigzag. These take tubbing just as readily as the sturdy jeans at lower left. See **H** for lace and ruffle application. Draw up the heavy thread at top of lace to gather it, then zigzag this to raw edge of the ruffle. Or lace can be used at top and bottom of ruffle, then gathered ½″ in on fabric to make a heading and stitched on the gathered line.

Overalls or Jeans. (**I**) Note the construction of the overalls. Zigzag stitched throughout, including all seams, edges, hems, buttons and buttonholes.

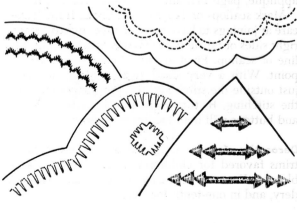

-Children's Clothes

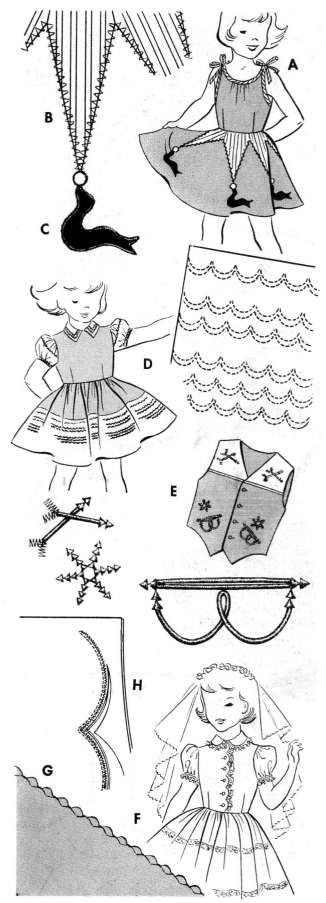

See detail **J**. The applique signal flags spell out the little wearer's name or initials.

Zigzag Applique Is Easy and Effective. The circus-design dress (**A**) has two types of applique. A red ball and playful black seal are stitched with matching threads. The point applique (**B**) is done in a bright red thread to contrast with the green fabric of the dress. No matter what type of motif you wish to use, you can applique it easily. Apply curved motifs first, with narrow satin-stitch (**C**), then with small sharp scissors trim close to the zigzag line. On points having straight-line edges, turn raw edges under and then stitch, making the zigzag decoratively large.

Decorated Dress, Twin-Needle, Two-Color Thread. (**D**) This dress, trimmed with twin-needle scalloping, is a good example of the effectiveness of such work. Quick, easy—gives opportunity for use of contrasting-color threads. Decorative, practical and economical, no matter what type of appropriate fabric you are using. Use your ingenuity in combining fabrics, in grouping stitches, in using colored threads. Trimming, subtle or gay, can add value to your garments.

Play Suits and Sports Apparel. (**E**) Many of these have embroidered designs, such as we illustrate. Pockets, buttonholes—all can become decorative features. Use bright-color threads and a combination of suitable stitch patterns.

Party or Confirmation Dresses. (**F**) Such dresses no longer pose a problem, no matter what appropriate fabric you choose—satin, taffeta, nylon sheer, organdie or even all-over embroidery. Use your Zigzag Machine to make, finish and decorate the dress, even finish the edge of the veil **G**. See ideas for decoration, pages 145 to 147, shadow applique, page 141, and lace, pages 129 to 131.

Mark scallops on lapping side of the front. Take care at joinings to have them connect rightly. Place right sides of fabric to the facing. Stitch on pattern line of scallop. Pivot at end of each to get a true point. With a very small zigzag stitch, go along just outside the stitching line. Trim edges close to the stitching, **H**, turn right side out. Buttonholes and buttons will hold facings to position.

Decorative Trims. Opposite are a few typical trims favored for children's dresses, smocks, and blouses. You can so easily imitate hand-embroidery, and in one-tenth the time.

Zigzag Trim for Lingerie and Blouses

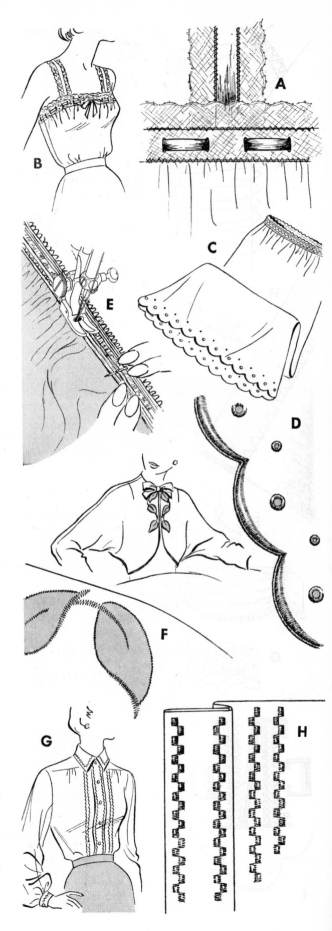

SHEER FABRICS HAVE TAKEN ON NEW IMPORTANCE, with cotton fashionable the year around and sheer synthetics gaining in interest. Sheer lingerie, negligees and blouses are all highly favored, and it behooves one to know how to make them up attractively and so they will stand the strain of wear and washing.

Camisoles. Increasingly in demand—and dainty they must be for wear under sheer blouses. The Zigzag Machine can unite lace, ribbon, embroidery and fabric so neatly and securely that they look as though woven that way (**A**). The camisole (**B**), of opaque nylon with lace, lace insertion and ribbon as trimming, is simple to make, and a joy to wear.

Petticoats, Slips, Nightdresses, Negligees. With the use of two-piece outfits, petticoats come into their own. The one shown (**C**) was of pure silk crepe, the scallops, the eyelet embroidery (**D**), even the elastic at the waistline done with the Zigzag Machine.

Nightgowns and slips can be elaborately or simply trimmed, to suit your purpose. Negligees glory in lace, applique and velvet trims—all easy to do when you have a Zigzag Machine.

Applying Elastic to Waistlines. (**E**) Buy a length of lacy-type elastic about 3″ less than your waistline, form a circle by joining ends with zigzag stitch, then mark it with pins in four even parts. Divide waistline of petticoat or panties in same way. Match the pins. Stretch the elastic over the seam edge of the garment, hold it taut, and stitch with medium zigzag. A second row of stitching will add strength to the joining and help in finishing the fabric edge.

Applique Motifs on Velvet, Silk or Wool. (**F**) Satin makes ideal applique. Baste motifs on your garment, straight-stitch around edges, carefully trim any surplus away, then zigzag over the stitching line, using a close stitch.

Blouses—Sheer or Otherwise. The front tailored pleat done with plain zigzag (**G**) or an automatic stitch pattern (**H**) with two rows along each side, decorates a shirtwaist, especially when you use the same stitch for collar and cuffs.

Imagine all the lovely trims you can design with your Zigzag Machine. Applique, embroidery or monograms make for a distinctive garment.

Choose one or a combination that is right for the fabric you are using. See pages 142–146, 151, 228 and 229 for ideas.

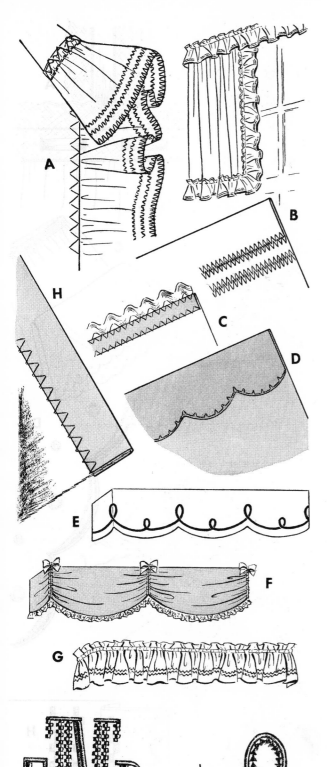

USE YOUR ZIGZAG MACHINE FOR MAKING ANY OF THE lovely things shown in the color pages in this book that appeal to you. See especially Home Furnishing pages 177 to 189 and 202 to 238. On this page we give just a few suggestions of how to achieve interesting results with a minimum of time and effort.

Quilting can be done, vanity skirts trimmed, bedspreads and closet accessories beautifully made, all with your Zigzag Machine.

The new sheer or crisp man-made fibers—nylon, Orlon, Dacron, and so on—are enticingly inexpensive and so easy to launder that it seems every bedroom, bathroom, kitchen and pantry window can be dressed attractively and kept so.

Ruffles. (**A**) Such as shown are no problem at all for the Zigzag Machine. You simply stitch one or more rows along the edge to do the dual job of finishing and decorating. You gather the top edge of the ruffle and zigzag it to place, rarely needing to make a French or flat-fell seam.

Decorative Trims. Just imagine how easy it is to hem ruffles or curtains, or dress up a bed, when you can zigzag hems and joinings. We show you here three types of hems, practical, yet easy to do.

Hem Finished with Multiple Cam Stitch. (**B**) Turn and baste. Use twin needles and the multiple stitch cam and set the stitch to obtain effect desired.

Hem with Wide Rickrack and #5 Binding. (**C**) Turn bottom edge ¼″ to right side. Apply rickrack and binding at the same time with a zigzag stitch.

Hem with Scallops. (**D**) Turn hem edge, use zigzag stitch or automatic blind-stitch and outline the scallops. Trim fabric close to the stitching.

Valances. A window valance can have a decorated hem to match its own sash curtain. Braid is applied in decorative loops, **E. F** shows a feminine lace trim. **G** is decorated with an automatic stitch pattern at the hemline. See pages 186 to 189.

Blanket Binding. (**H**) Fold ribbon over blanket edge and baste. Stitch, using the multiple-stitch or a wide zigzag stitch.

Monogramming. (**I** and **J**) Unusually attractive monograms can be easily made by combining decorative stitch patterns. An effective trim for table linens, bedspreads and pillows. See pages 226–228 for ideas and placement suggestions.

251

ONE WHO SEWS CAN OFTEN MAKE EFFECTIVE GIFTS for birthdays, Mother's Day, Father's Day, Christmas, Easter, Valentine's Day, shut-ins, showers, weddings, church bazaars and new babies. Some gifts may be very practical, others fluffy whiffs of remembrance or of sentiment, others substantial gifts of affection.

Study the magazines, visit gift departments, especially art needlework departments. See the attractive things that can be made with fabrics—a shirt case for a man who travels or who is contemplating his vacation, a scarf or piece of neckwear, a new blouse or slip for a business girl, lingerie for the bride, a nightdress or bed jacket for the expectant mother, a practical easy-to-iron apron for the mother or grandmother, a fluffy Sunday night supper apron for the young married woman, pajamas or cowboy shirts for little boys, pinafores or nighties for little girls, baby pillows, carriage robes, receiving blankets, kimonos for infants.

Choose your fabric with care as regards color, appropriateness to the design, and usefulness to the recipient.

Begin gift making early enough so that you will have time to enjoy the making. If Christmas gifts are in order, start immediately after Christmas to plan, buy and make for the next year.

Imagination, the ability to adapt, thoughtfulness of needs, the desire to delight a loved one—all these should go into the making of gifts. Money can be saved and earned by gift making and much pleasure can be given, especially when enthusiasm, a sense of the appropriate, good taste, and sewing skill enter into the making.

A few more suggestions are given here for possible gifts to make. Perhaps they will help you to look in the fashion books for patterns and to search for the ideal fabric in the perfect color.

For woman

place mats
umbrella case
handbags
slippers
hats
belts
closet accessories
sewing or jewel bags or envelopes
dickies
lingerie cases
blanket covers

For babies

bibs
stuffed toys
blocks
quilts
throws

For little boy

mittens
slippers
carpenter's apron
bean bags
scrapbook (paper muslin pages, oilcloth cover)

For man

pullman slippers in case
barbecue apron and cap
fringed scarf
shirt cases
book covers
robes

For little girl

aprons
handbags
doll bassinet
doll clothes
appliqué pictures
quilts

Gifts from plastic

tobacco pouch
aprons
cosmetic case
diaper bag
children's mats
beach bag
ice box bags
covers for equipment

SUGGESTIONS FOR GIFT-MAKING

See toys of fabric shown in pattern books, gift shops and department stores. See novelty apparel for children, aprons, play suits, pinafores, bonnets, slippers, bathrobes. If it is of fabric you can make it. A right pattern is always the first requisite, and colors and textures are highly important in creating any gift items, whether to give or to sell.

Boutiques, or specialty shops, in stores offer many suggestions. Try whenever possible to duplicate the fabrics used in the original you are copying, then the result will be completely satisfying.

Closet gifts, especially matching sets, are always acceptable and often can be made at a fraction of the price asked in closet accessory shops or notion departments in stores.

Kitchens today boast the prettiest possible ensembles—curtains, pot holders and aprons all made to match.

Items for infants—bassinets, crib blankets, swaddling robes, bootees, gertrudes, pillow slips with matching top sheets, carriage equipment—all need but the desire plus an idea and the right fabric and trimming for one to make ideal gifts.

Birthday and Christmas dresses, lace-trimmed slips and panties, especially of nylon—all such are welcomed by little and big girls.

Gifts need an air of just-rightness in materials and their combinations. And try not to over-sew them. A crisp daintiness or soft luxuriousness is ever to be sought. Work for beauty and suitability and your gifts will be used and appreciated.

259